FOR ALL: DEMOCRATIZING BIG IDEAS

BY HANS MANZKE

NEW DEGREE PRESS

FOR ALL: DEMOCRATIZING BIG IDEAS

ISBN 978-1-63676-558-7 *Paperback*
978-1-63676-138-1 *Kindle Ebook*
978-1-63676-139-8 *Ebook*

FOR ALL:
DEMOCRATIZING
BIG IDEAS

We don't see things as they are.
We see things as we are.

— ANAÏS NIN

He who has a 'why' can endure any 'how.'

— FRIEDRICH NIETZSCHE

Not knowing when the dawn will
come, I open every door.

— EMILY DICKINSON

For Trish, who finds me in the dark, always.
Wild horses couldn't drag me away.

For Skye, who showed me another world
exists, and who stands tall.

CONTENTS

ACKNOWLEDGMENTS

I am nothing if not the product of the heartbreakingly beautiful web of people who have walked a part of my path with me. Writing this book wasn't easy. It wouldn't have been possible in the first place without energy from a village's worth of people.

To my family: Mom, Dad, Brother, Grandma, aunts, uncles, cousins, and more. You are the foundation that gives me purpose and meaning in this world.

To my team at Georgetown and New Degree Press: You made something that felt impossible possible, and helped me achieve a childhood dream. Immense gratitude to Eric Koester, Alexander Pyles, Brian Bies, and Cynthia Tucker.

To my family at The Clearing: I've found meaning at work and in life through each of you. Thank you for inspiring me every day for the last six years.

To those of you who I had the good fortune to interview for this book: Your mindshare makes the world a better and wiser place. I hope I've done that justice here:

Matt Goodrich
Sharon Benjamin
Martha Johnson
Marty Lanahan
Mari Kuraishi
Admiral Frank Morley
Ken Haas
Jens Hansen

To Matteo Becchi—a huge thank-you for creating a beautiful, compelling illustration of the Ladder of Inference. To Benno Bos and Ulf Ehlert—gratitude for graciously granting permission to use your wonderful products in this work.

To my beta reader community: thank you for believing in me. For preordering this book to make publishing possible, helping to spread the word about *For All: Democratizing Big Ideas*, and helping me to produce something I'm proud of. I have a story with every single one of you. I hope we get to make new stories through the connection that is this book.

Adam and Melody Cook
Adam Barbina
Adithya Balaji
Alexandra Harris
Angelo Frigo
Anna-Ruth Beckman
Anthony Abate
Anthony Macri
Ashley E. DiAna Lucas
Ashley Mahan
Ben Kubany
Beth Pacifico
Brandon Lumm
Brigham Lumm

Buck Sleeper
Cara Valentino
Carla Fletcher
Celina Montoya and Luke Girdley
Chris McGoff
Christina Merideth
Christine Beinhacker
Claire Bukovac
Clifton Johnson
Courtney Disabato
Dale Bell
Daniel Scheeler
Daniel Stone
David Lindholm
David Landeck
Dayton Rutherford
Deborah Lee
Deborah Maher
Donna Anthony
Drew Saunders
Dylan Sundy
Earl Crane
Elizabeth Byrd Ahrens
Emily Reynolds
Eric Koester
Erin Sherman
Eduardo Maeyama
Evan Isaacs
Gabby Hernandez
George Lewis
Hal Manzke
Helen Jarrett
Jarah Meador
Jason Bricker
Jason Miller
Jay Huie
Jennifer Kim
Jesse Leifert
Jessica Howard Jackson
Jim Nichols
John Burchill
Jolene Davis
Jon Tolbert
Julia Smadja
Julisa Mandeville
Justin Herman
Kailin Delaney Toomer
Kathiana LeJeune
Katie Free
Kandace Robertson
Keenan Pallone
Keina Bowling
Kelly Olson
Kelly Pippin
Kelly Barlow
Ken Haas
Ken MacGarrigle
Kim Acquaviva
Lauren Strange
Lee Manzke
Lindsey Milligan
Liz Glodek
Magdy Mansour

Maria Manzke
Mark Hagen
Mary Lopez
Mary Jennifer Vanmeter
Maxwell Jones
Meena Aladdin
Meghan Rixey
Michael Lee
Matt Goodrich
Nicole Earle
Nicole Polk
Nicole Unger
Pablo Fernandez
Philipia Hillmam
Rachel Scott
Ravinder Bhatia
Rebecca Nathan
Rene Collin
Robyn Klem
Rose Spero
Sam Harper
Sara Hayes
Sarah Manzke
Sonya Patel
Steven Venturi
Suzanne Davis
Taylor Ferrell
Theresa West
Travis Johnson
Zach Baldwin

INTRODUCTION

What lies behind us and what lies before us are tiny matters compared to what lies within us.

—RALPH WALDO EMERSON

It was 104 degrees outside. Hot enough that it seemed to suck the moisture out of your body and place a palpable weight on arms, legs, and head alike. This not being my first 104-degree Texas day, even at the age of four, meant that I could both cope with and observe the environment around me. My four-year-old peripheral vision was keen enough to pick out a large group of blackbirds moving through the air in a fluid but inexplicably random manner, and it was there I snapped my full attention with all the speed I could muster in the heat. The proverbial gears began turning in my head, and I pulled in a lungful of pea soup air so I could blurt out a question. Simultaneously, the right edge of my mom's mouth curled upward in a knowing grin. I like to imagine her and my dad's own mental gears warming themselves up in response to field another Hans Manzke original in question form.

As a young child, I grew up confident in my parents' ability to calmly and satisfactorily answer my seemingly endless parade of "Why" questions. Here are some of my greatest hits:

- Why does the water go round and round to the left when I flush the toilet and not to the right?
- Why are some clouds puffy while others look like string or straight lines or a Teenage Mutant Ninja Turtle?
- Why does one dog year equal to seven human years?

Ideas have always had a gravitational pull for me. Their abilities to hook and hold our attention and to work their way into our brain's smallest crevices mean that some part of their DNA is left in us whether or not we consciously acknowledge it. I felt from a young age that getting to the bottom of things, using big ideas as tools, would make me happy. I didn't know it then, but I'd be lucky later in life to be exposed to a multitude of those big ideas relatively early on. Further, I'd endeavor to apply what I would learn about equity and inclusion to the big ideas I displayed a proclivity toward as a small child.

As I got older, my "Why" questions shifted in focus from observations of the world around me to more mature ruminations. I also found that the older I got, the more I kept those questions for myself, holding onto them as if they'd evaporate if others learned of their existence. Some that come to mind include:

- Why do the fifth graders act like they run the elementary school?

- Why is it so difficult to choose just one topic for a college essay?
- Why are immigrants and people who are different treated so poorly the world over?

Fundamentally different sorts of questions, but the constant is their source in me. I am, and always will be, a seeker of things: knowledge for its own sake, insight from experience, and context to serve as a ready cup to hold my observations. I began the deliberate peeling back of the many layers of ego and personality that make me *me* comparatively late despite a number of head starts in life. For whatever reason, my early independent days lacked the particular spark to turn my energy inward; what I know now to be called a self-awareness journey. For all my seeking—the constant asking of the question "Why?"—I realize now in hindsight that I would've made some different decisions along the way had I been equipped with the ideas laid out in this work. Perhaps I would've applied myself more in my first two years of my undergraduate days at Middlebury College, so I wouldn't have had to dig out of a deep academic hole during my last two years. Maybe I would've invested energy differently in my first jobs out of college in order to more actively seek out my own purpose at work. Or maybe each step occurred specifically as it should have, when it should have. I do believe in serendipity, and I'm grateful for my full journey and the mentors challenging me along the way to continue my own journey inward as well as invest my energy back out into the world around me.

I WROTE THIS BOOK FOR A REASON

I believe that big ideas have the power to begin eroding the layers of inequity and unfairness we've seen and experienced. They truly can level the playing fields of work and life. Furthermore, the big ideas collected in this work drove a personal transformation. I shifted from someone going through the motions to a more mature version of myself who is open to tough feedback the same way I am to praise, and who deliberately chooses tough challenges that will push my personal boundaries. I've had the good fortune to learn and deliver alongside business leaders, engineers, career government executives, artists, nonprofit founders, scientists, school administrators and professors, architects, lawyers, doctors and nurses, and dedicated, talented, and high-potential young people from all walks of life. I'm better for each of those diverse interactions, and I share many of their most meaningful epiphanies in this work for the good of all.

Another reason I felt compelled to embark on this work was that I'm at an inflection point in my career. I exist in the space between the upper-most echelons of leadership and junior staff. This gives me a rare opportunity to view big ideas from two very different perspectives. Both are rich, multifaceted, and critical for all to grasp. As a management consultant with a concentration in leadership development, executive coaching, and meeting design and facilitation, I am expected to deliver for clients and produce quality outcomes while also building capacity in my colleagues via mentoring and training. I help grow our business by creating and leveraging relationships with all sorts of people in order to create new, different, and exciting opportunities for others. I have the benefit of considerable hindsight, but I'm also retirement and thinking about my legacy. H both allows me to exist with a foot in each wor inhabiting and sharing insights from these two distinc spectives is a big part of why I feel this book is important.

In short, I wanted to write the book that twenty-one-year-old me needed—college degree in hand and not the foggiest idea of what could or should come next. Equally important, I also wanted to write the book that fifty-five-year-old me will need to tune back into the power and unclouded wisdom that young people offer the world each day.

THE WORLD TODAY

The intentionality that I strive to apply to my day-to-day life is something I believe is sorely lacking in today's professional world. Many of us go through the motions, resigned to what we deem as our professional fate, a word we choose for a particular reason. Fate implies that the reality of a sub-optimal job, work environment, or coworkers was preordained by some unseen force. This is a far simpler reality to swallow than the simple fact that no one else controls our professional destiny than us. Our true charge is to build intention into all we do, including leaving a job you can do with one hand behind your back and for a comfortable salary in order to search for something far more fulfilling. Building intention and seeking meaning in our work lives are two of the hardest and most complex things we'll ever do in the workplace.

Now, take the complexity we just discussed and multiply it by a factor of ten, and you'll begin to approach the intricacy introduced by the fact that America is getting both younger and more experientially diverse. For the first time in history, five different generations are actively representing the American workforce. Why does this matter? Simply put, five distinct groups, each with its own cultural touchstones, shared experiences, and values with regard to work and life, are attempting to coexist in the workplace. Communication styles, and the business outcomes that follow effective communication, differ for each. Negative stereotypes abound for all five groups. To focus on just two, we often think of Boomers as stubborn, backward-looking, and untrainable, while Millennials are entitled, tech-reliant, and overanxious. Like all stereotypes, these actively corrode our ability to get things done together. Each views the other with distrust for a series of perceived slights or assumptions, and few take the time to deeply engage with one another in order to build that all-important intentionality we discussed earlier.

In my career, I've encountered the idea from those who have 'paid their dues' that young people need to 'earn' the right to access and deploy the big ideas resident in that system. Earning that particular access varies from system to system. For some, it is level of seniority, while in others, it's completing certifications or externally demonstrating your expertise. The professional universe is one steeped in the concept of 'subject matter expertise.' That is to say, individuals with 'bona fides' excel in ecosystems who place the majority of their value currency in the achieving and maintaining of certifications, titles, or high levels of achievement. While this has some merit, it can reward those who excel at manipulating a system or who 'test well' as opposed to those with the biggest and brightest ideas regardless of experience or access. Even worse, it can actively deny access to a space that someone has earned. This harms not only the individual who's worked hard for something by unfairly denying what they've earned but also the organization that does the denying. They remain less diverse, less rewarding for their employees and customers, and ultimately, less competitive in the marketplace.

WHAT'S REALLY GOING ON

Each day, young or underprivileged people contribute their big, bold ideas into networks of their peers in the place of more traditional systems like companies, professional organizations, or alumni associations. This paradigm, sometimes referred to as 'subject matter networks,' are powerful frameworks that can help level the playing field and give organizations access to the best minds, regardless of their place of birth or their access to traditional professional entry points like business school or professional recruiters. Sometimes, they manifest within a work context, but not always, and often span across geographical boundaries as part of a diverse collection of like minds all interested in the same thing. At the heart of this emerging paradigm is the fact that "people contribute when and where they feel they belong;"[1] that sense of belonging doesn't always show up where or in the way we may expect. Subject matter networks change the landscape of how we apply big ideas, generate value, and build resilience for those who need it most. Even more importantly, they empower those who need it most.

---

1 "Jessie Ball duPont Fund," Jessie Ball duPont Fund, accessed October 14, 2020.

I'm most inspired by those who do great things with little to start. Their stories are proof positive that talent, dedication, perseverance, and vision know no boundaries. The best and brightest deserve and demand the same opportunities that those with privilege enjoy. Our nation's recent racial and public health crises are proof of that. I imagine and mourn for the brilliant minds, open hearts, and expansive ideas in whose beauty we could never marvel. Their owners' lives were cut short by a virus that disproportionally targets the poor and at risk, or by unjust violence perpetrated by law enforcement. The world is a less beautiful and poorer place for it.

WHERE WE'LL GO TOGETHER

We'll cover a lot of ground in this work. Generational demographics aren't the only thing shifting in the workplace. How organizations derive and assign value, or value currency for short, is also shifting. Open access to information from basic sources like the Internet and other networks to subscription sources like Masterclass and the Khan Academy means the continual lowering of systemic entry barriers continue to be lowered. That can only be a good thing for our collective future.

The quarter-life crisis is an inflection point where a first taste of the deep structures entrenched into work and social life and financial independence combine to create a sense of existential dread for many in their mid to late twenties.[2] Through this lens, the ideas I've collected and contextualized

---

2 Ran Zilka, "Why Your Late Twenties Is the Worst Time of Your Life." *Harvard Business Review,* March 7, 2016.

here can be considered quarter-life frameworks, tools for any person, regardless of age, to jump to their next personal S Curve.[3] That might manifest as making a jump to a new job or environment or just getting 'un-stuck' in one's own mind. These frameworks are possible principles for life, work, happiness, and success, depending on how you define that for yourself. Let's take a quick look ahead at some of these big ideas.

Okinawa's unique social structure, culture, and history combine to generate some of the longest-lived and fulfilled human beings in the world. Their encapsulated secrets incorporate into the ideas of *ikigai* and *moai*.

Some of the world's most admired people suffer from a pervasive sense that their hard-earned success is a result of a grand trick they've played on the world around them, and it will all come crashing down once their fraud is exposed. Impostor syndrome is pervasive across age, race, and other demographics, and an understanding of the concept and how it shows up for you as an individual can speed your self-acceptance.

The basics of brain chemistry, including the careful balance of serotonin, oxytocin, dopamine, and cortisol, as well as the environmental factors that trigger spikes in each, is a powerful tool for self-awareness and a seemingly magical ability to predict the behavior of those around you.

---

3 Chris McGoff, *The Primes: How Any Group Can Solve Any Problem* (Hoboken: John Wiley & Sons, Inc., 2012), 58-61.

These ideas and frameworks are important for your life regardless of your job title, passion, or age. They will push your thinking and crystalize your focus inward and externally.

LET'S GO

This book is for everyone; young people who feel disenfranchised, disillusioned, or otherwise marginalized within their systems. This book is for any person who is up to something big and needs a new way of looking at things to bound past their personal tipping point. This book is also for leaders and managers up in the rarified air. Your organizations' future depends on your deep engagement with future leaders both inside and outside your system.

Most importantly, this book is for all the seekers searching for something beyond themselves. You ask tough questions that cause others to reexamine the world around them. You've held onto the spark that Peter Matthiessen eloquently wrote about: "Soon the child's clear eye is clouded over by ideas and opinions, preconceptions, and abstractions. Simple free being becomes encrusted with the burdensome armor of the ego. Not until years later does an instinct come that a vital sense of mystery has been withdrawn. The sun glints through the pines and the heart is pierced in a moment of beauty and strange pain, like a memory of paradise. After that day, we become seekers."[4]

These concepts satisfy my innate seeking in a way that's immensely fulfilling, all while being powerful tools to institute

---

4 Peter Matthiessen , *Nine-Headed Dragon River: Zen Journals 1969-1982* (Boulder: Shambhala Publications, 1986).

personal and systemic change for myself and those around me. Take advantage of the outcomes of a lifetime's energy from my inner seeker by reading on, enjoying, and asking a few "Why" questions of your own.

PART 1:

MECHANICAL ADVANTAGE AND SIMPLE MACHINES

CHAPTER 1

THE POWER OF BIG IDEAS

The mind, once stretched by a new idea, never returns to its original dimensions.

—RALPH WALDO EMERSON

I grew up in a house near the center of downtown San Antonio, Texas. Built in 1937 and made of limestone quarried nearby, the house was small, but comfortable, and had a sprawling front and back yard. Wonderfully lived-in for the past forty years by my family, I've never known another home. My younger brother Marc and I would roam, explore, and occasionally upend parts of the yards and house, getting into trouble not infrequently. I didn't go into my parents' bedroom often, but much of the time I did spend there was near their closets in a small alcove with a high window and two full-length antique mirrors, both wall-mounted and facing each other. The resulting effect was such that I could gaze into one of the mirrors and see a seemingly unceasing procession of reproduced versions of the mirror space with me included, stretching into oblivion where my young eyes could no longer differentiate the nested reflections. I spent hours and hours over the course of my youth gazing into that stacked series of reflections, tinged ever so slightly green due to the chemical properties of the aged tempered glass. As a child, I could easily hold the tunnel of reflective images in my mind no matter where I was. As a seeker, a litany of my famous childhood questions usually accompanied that image: "How is this possible?" "Where do the reflections stop?" "Do they ever stop at all?"

Some ideas are sticky. They stay with us long after other, often more important experiences, memories, and concepts have long since come and gone. Sometimes, I struggle to recall specifics about the sensations I experienced during birthdays, important family milestones, even my high school and college graduations. However, I can recall the gentle tilt of the dozens of reflected images as they receded into infinity because of a slight warp in the old mirror glass. Big ideas are like that. They work their way into our subconscious, staying wedged into some older part of our long-term recall. Some big ideas return to us every now and then as a vivid memory, while others unconsciously shape our behavior or worldview toward a particular person, place, thing, or concept. Still, others are top of mind every day, making decisions for us whether we know it or not. Just as any particularly well-crafted, perfectly balanced tool can make a task feel simple, so, too, can a big idea make a previously insurmountable challenge feel accessible.

I found some thought-provoking and inspirational insights in my friend Travis Wright's recently published book *Making New Mistakes* that helped me crystalize why big ideas should matter to all of us. One that stood out to me grapples with the power of mental models and frameworks—prime examples of the big ideas I consider in this work. In his book, Travis outlines the perspective of Charlie Munger with regard to models as a form of big ideas: Munger serves as Vice-Chairman of Berkshire Hathaway and partner and advisor to Warren Buffet. On the topic of the necessity of mental models and their criticality for learning and growth, Munger stated: "Well, the first rule is that you can't really know anything if you just remember isolated facts and try to bang 'em back. If the facts don't hang together on a latticework of theory, you don't have them in a usable form. You've got to have models in your head. And you've got to array your experience, both vicarious and direct, on this latticework of models. You may have noticed students who just try to remember and pound back what is remembered. Well, they fail in school and life. You've got to hang experience on a latticework of models in your head."[5]

Munger's insights resonate with me. Models and frameworks, in particular, have the power to reify a structure seemingly out of thin air—Munger's 'latticework.' Instead of blank space or void where facts, insights, hunches, and hard work can seem to fall clattering to the ground, or worse yet vanish, a big idea can give us the foundation and framing we so desperately need to build our proverbial houses on. Big ideas exist everywhere. Even the famed Shaolin Temple, a locus of ancient and modern Buddhist wisdom, training, and monastic practice, has its own frameworks. The Five Hindrances,

---

5 Travis Wright, *Making New Mistakes: Leading Through Disruption With a Minimum of Chaos* (Potomac: New Degree Press, 2020), 89-90.

or obstacles on the path to achieving personal clarity, are a structure on which Shaolin monks balance their spiritual practice and self-awareness journeys.[6] Even the most enlightened, mindful, and contented people in the world, it would seem, need the guiding power of big ideas.

THE POWER OF PURPOSE

By age thirty-three, Leila Janah had founded two wildly successful companies, both with a powerful social impact mission at their core. SamaSource and LXMI, the former a data analysis and impact sourcing organization that employs and trains at-risk people around the world, and the latter a high-end skincare products brand that employs marginalized women in Northeastern Africa to gather and process natural materials, both pay their employees roughly three times the level of average local wages in their communities.[7] The daughter of Indian immigrants, Janah's personal 'why' shifted her course in life.

Big ideas don't always take the form of a well-researched, peer-reviewed effect or model replete with jargon and internal logic. For Janah, the big idea that drove her life's work and personal purpose was basic in nature, "by providing dignity through work, we can eliminate global poverty."[8] Janah deployed her big idea, wonderfully simple in nature, to shift the commonly accepted approach for addressing global poverty on its head. Her observation was that the traditional approach, a combination of targeted development projects,

6 TedX Talks, "Master Shi Heng Yi – 5 hindrances to self-mastery | Shi Heng YI | TEDxVitosha," February 13, 2020, video, 18:36.

7 "Leila Janah," Leila Janah, accessed July 24, 2020.

8 Ibid.

charity, and philanthropy, addressed symptoms and not the cause. More often than not, this provides a short-term solution only. Her alternative philosophy for eradicating poverty was to actively erode what is known as the informal economy, a structure wherein over one billion people work and still earn less than one dollar a day.[9] I was amazed to learn of the scope of the crisis. More than one-eighth of the world's population toils with jobs like collecting garbage for pennies from recyclers, all for less than one hundred pennies each day.

In service of reaching her goal to reclaim human beings from the informal economy, Janah attempted to address what she viewed as the root cause of poverty: a lack of access to well-paying jobs. Thus, her companies focused not only on hiring those mired in these terrible situations, but also training and continuously up-skilling them so they could grow while giving back to the next wave of incoming employees. Janah's two companies and other programs and organizations employ over fifty thousand people across the world, lifting them out of poverty in a virtuous cycle that still functions and grows to this day.

Leila Janah passed away from complications due to epithelioid sarcoma, a rare form of soft tissue cancer that tragically strikes mostly teenagers and young adults, at the age of thirty-seven. I happen to be thirty-seven years old as I write this book, and I marvel not only at the breadth and amplitude of Janah's accomplishments, but also her indomitable drive to make the world a better place by direct engagement with the

9 TedX Talks, "Reversing global poverty | Leila Janah | TEDxAmsterdamWomen," November 13, 2017, video, 11:03.

world's least fortunate. Her legacy extends beyond her family, her companies, even the tens of thousands of human beings whose lives were forever altered for the better because Janah existed in the world. Her legacy also includes her big idea, one whose power outlives its creator as all great big ideas do.

THE POWER OF PERSONAL DEVELOPMENT

It was late January 2020, and I had the good fortune to find myself in sunny, warm Ponte Vedra Beach, Florida. Those of you who have spent time in DC in the winter know that this is the right time of year to do the snowbird thing and flee south (at least that's this Texan's take on things). The Clearing, the management consulting firm where I work, had offered the opportunity to my colleagues and I to lead a portion of an executive retreat for the Jessie Ball duPont Fund (JBdF), a Jacksonville-based foundation whose "work in grantmaking, impact investing and strategic partnerships is governed by a focus on equitable access to opportunities and resources for members of society who have historically been excluded, and placemaking to build stronger communities where all voices are heard and valued." They asked us to facilitate the process of deploying and deeply understanding Gallup's CliftonStrengths talent assessment framework. I recently received my CliftonStrengths coaching certification, so needless to say, I was excited.

After getting a chance to meet JBdF staff and trustees participating in our two-day session, I grew more excited. The diversity of age, race, thought, and goals of the leaders in the room astonished me, and each person I met was gracious and engaged. I was able to quickly locate a big part of the source of that positive energy—JBdF's leader. The duPont

Fund's president, Mari Kuraishi, is a luminary in the worlds of international development, innovation, and more. She's also one of those people who manages to speak softly and with authority at the same time. The room gets quiet and awfully intent when she begins speaking. You'll read more about Mari later in this book.

The Chair for the JBdF's trustees, Marty Lanahan, shared many of Mari's powerful traits. She, too, has an air of authority and positive self-assurance that few can access. Marty is a self-professed CliftonStrengths aficionado, having deployed Gallup's framework in various places over the course of her career as a banking executive. We quickly bonded over our shared love for the depth and power we both felt CliftonStrengths could offer this group if framed, examined, and applied properly. I observed her genuine and profound interest in the well-being of those around her, as well as her desire to make sure that her Board colleagues and the JBdF staff could focus on the hard work at hand. Two things became apparent to me. First, Marty invests time and energy into her own personal development, and equally important, she cares just as much about investing in the development of those around her.

With this powerful foundation to build on, our two days of work together were a success. We made some profound discoveries and had conversations that pushed hard against the usual boundaries every group erects around itself. When thinking about whom I should speak to for this work, Marty immediately came to mind.

In speaking for this work, Marty shared that she had the good fortune to partner with management consulting guru and thought leader Peter Block on a week-long project with members of an American bank's C-Suite. After flying to Charlotte for some on-site work, and after having spent some time together, Block approached Marty to say, "You're not a banker. You must feel different all the time." Marty characterizes those words as having a profound impact on her. Block had picked up on a sentiment that Marty herself had long felt. Not only was Marty a woman, itself a rarity at the executive level in the banking industry at the time, but she often reflected on the feeling that she thought and approached problems differently from her colleagues. Block's words helped Marty commit to being true to herself instead of changing to conform to the system. As Marty relayed to me, "To know yourself authentically at thirty-five is the greatest gift."

I asked Marty what big idea she would gift to herself if she could go back in time, and her response relayed another important mental model that gets to the heart of gender inequity, especially in professional fields and especially at the upper echelons of organizations that Marty has been a part of for years. Marty won the City of Jacksonville Spirit of Rosie Award fairly early in her career. Inspired by Rosie the Riveter, the city gives out the award to one woman each year. Upon receiving the award and giving her acceptance speech, Marty focused on her belief at the time that a glass ceiling didn't exist for women in banking. She, after all, was living proof of it, standing on that stage as a woman banking executive. Looking back on the experience now, Marty wishes she could've shifted her message that day, "if you believe in a glass ceiling, it will exist," implying that not believing in one would make it not exist. When she did eventually experience that glass ceiling in her career, Marty wished she could've listened to the women who flagged their own reality for her benefit in a different way. The glass ceiling, itself a powerful big idea that can and must be systematically dismantled to ensure true equity and inclusion in all fields of endeavor, has held many deserving people back for no good reason and through no fault of their own. Today, Marty's day-to-day actions are fine-tuned to ensure women get equal and fair treatment in the professional spheres she operates in. Her career and investment in personal and professional development, manifesting that day as it did in our two-day seminar, is a testament to her dedication to and passion for equality of development.

Marty's success and insights powerfully illustrate the power of big ideas. Whether those models, frameworks, and concepts orientate at self-awareness, professional development, or interpersonal interaction and deep learning, they have the power to change the narrative of a life.

THE POWER OF FAILURE

Sorrow happens,
hardship happens,
the hell with it,
who never knew the price of happiness,
will not be happy.

—YEVGENY YEVTUSHENKO

August in DC is sultry at best and unbearable at worst. More than any other month, the humidity seems to settle into your very being, with not so much as a puff of breeze to stir the proverbial pea soup. Growing up in south Texas made me no stranger to sweat, so the sweltering environment didn't seem to flatten me so much as it did others. That said, in this particular August, 2006 to be precise, I felt a growing sense of internal inertia that seemed to complement the oppressive outdoors. While I was distinctly attuned to this sensation of weight and sluggishness and could sense it growing larger and deeper with each passing day, I struggled mightily to pinpoint its source.

I was in month eleven of my first professional job out of college as an editorial assistant at a DC book publisher, and like most other days, I felt as if I was running headlong into a brick wall at high speed. My responsibilities included creating and running reports on our clients and connections in the company's customer relationship management tool, organizing and executing letter-writing campaigns for writers, editors, and other contributors each time a new book was published, and a slew of other detail-oriented administrative tasks.

Not only was I terrible at this job, but I also disliked it. This wasn't true because my colleagues and bosses were unkind, the office environment was unwelcoming, or because I wasn't capable. I underperformed and never invested fully because the job required precisely all of the skills, mindsets, and approaches that siphoned energy from me. The result was that I left work each day empty, feeling as if I had little to give to friends, my roommates, or family. Creativity felt inaccessible.

I didn't know this about myself in 2006, but the free and regular interplay of ideas, personalities, and information, what most would call collaboration, unlocks the best in me.

The catch was that the set of responsibilities this particular job called for relied on no one else. It was utterly solitary. I distinctly remember riding my bike to the office each day; every revolution of the pedals brought on a mounting and ineffable sense of dread that grew with each mile covered. Knowing my work sucked was bad enough, but as a person who thrives on context and seeks to answer the 'why' question in any situation, not identifying the root cause of my discontent was truly maddening.

Ten o'clock at night is no time to find yourself alone in the office, and yet that's precisely where I ended up one Friday. The cleaning crews had long come and gone. Through the thick double-pane sixth-floor windows of our Dupont Circle office building, I could hear revelers marching from one bar to the next, crowing their joy to the skies. Holding an image of connection, laughter, and bad decisions in my mind, a crushing sense of solitude set in. I'd been trying, and failing, to construct and run a particularly complex report in a system I simply couldn't wrap my head around. After my seventh or eighth failed attempt, I pushed my chair back from my desk and waved the proverbial white flag.

I knew my boss was unhappy with my performance. We'd had two direct feedback conversations about lack of timeliness and inaccuracies in reports I'd run. I'd vowed to increase my vigilance and keep the tight timelines expected of me, but I was far outside of the realm of my intrinsic talents. Not only did I not have actionable strategies to remedy my shortcomings, but I lacked any sense of the deeper change I needed to instill in myself to approach my career differently. I knew I was lost but lacked a map or compass to reorient myself.

I'll never forget calling home in tears. It was the first time I'd ever done so. As my mom did her best to comfort me, I said plainly that I was afraid of losing my job, getting evicted from my house in a city that was not yet home, and not knowing what my next step would be. Thinking back on it now, I realize what I was truly afraid of was failing, especially in the eyes of those who'd invested so much in me.

I limped along at that job for another three weeks, never feeling settled, most certainly never feeling successful or vital to the organization or my colleagues. My boss terminated me one Friday afternoon. While hearing her words wasn't easy, I remember a glimmer of happiness even then. While I lacked any vocabulary to express or structure to hang my thoughts and feelings on, what I did know was that I'd discovered a job and profession that I should never enter into again, and that what I sought in a career lay elsewhere.

I'd go on to work at my local bike shop full time for a year. There, I rediscovered my love for working on a team as I tested my thinking and approaches by near-constant questioning and making frequent mistakes. For the first time, I felt what it's like to meld a passion (my love for cycling) with a job. Fourteen years later, I still volunteer at my friends' bike shop, whom I met during that time. Each shift I take at Arrow Bicycles feels like a mini-vacation because I'm stepping into an environment that generates energy and anchors me.

After a year at the bike shop, a close friend from school in Texas introduced me to a friend who worked at a growing management consulting firm. Despite not knowing how to spell 'business' and being perplexed by what 'consulting' was, I was fortunate enough to land a junior position because of my communication and interpersonal skills. I quickly deployed into a role directly supporting a federal client who was out to drive transformation in the government technology space. His passion drew me in, and I tasted professional success for the first time in the form of a pair of promotions.

When our team lead left for another job, I threw my hat in the ring to assume his role. I felt like I was ready. I lobbied, called in favors I'd accrued over the five intervening years that had passed since I started, and for the first time in my professional life, didn't back off of my request in the face of some pushback. I was dismayed to learn that another person would come in to fill the role for optics and staffing purposes. From my perspective, these reasons rang hollow to me, and I knew our company's decision did a disservice to the clients I'd come to care for greatly after almost five years of daily partnership.

I learned to adapt and accept this new working norm and was glad to hear that we'd bring on a new team member to backfill many of the administrative and labor-intensive responsibilities I was actively working on at the time—great news to be sure. What was challenging, however, was the negativity that our new team lead exuded. The negativity was so encompassing that I found myself taking much of that viewpoint on myself. I found excuses to avoid assignments and dodged opportunities that would bring in any more work than was necessary. In that way, our team often showed up as laissez-faire, and when our contract found itself on the chopping block, it caught us all by surprise. The fact that our play-it-safe approach had brought us to that brink never entered our minds at the time.

One morning, my teammate and I arrived at the office to discover our team lead visibly agitated. He hustled us to a private room and delivered the news that he'd heard rumors that gave him reason to believe that our contract renewal wouldn't happen when it came to an end in the coming weeks. He advised us to find other employment immediately. Though our contract did get renewed after all, my teammate found a new job two months later. Largely due to my comfort with our clients, I stayed on for another year before joining a rival consulting firm and never looking back.

In retrospect, I wonder if our collective indifference and dissatisfaction resulted from the latent realization that our skills could be better used elsewhere. I hold this experience closely because it taught me to be honest with myself and those around me when a job or opportunity has run its course and doesn't have anything left to offer me (and vice versa). I also learned the hard lesson of what leadership in hard times does *not* look like, just as important as what it *does* look like.

Mindsets and, by extension, big ideas can be the difference between fighting for yourself and those around you or waving the white flag. I'm not proud to admit I availed myself of that proverbial scrap of light-colored cloth more than once, but my failures broadened my spectrum of experience. I realized I was solely responsible for my growth and development. No one would advocate or do it for me. That insight was hard-fought, and I left some blood on the ground to gain it. We probably each have our own stories to tell in this vein, and yet taking our own future into our hands can feel impossible at times. Why is that?

CONCLUSIONS

Americans invest roughly 10 billion dollars a year in self-improvement, books, courses, and the like, with an annual growth rate of 6.1 percent. This area of practice also has a high rate of recidivism. The person most likely to buy a self-help book is a person who's already bought one or more self-help books in the past.[10] Everyone is after a quick fix. Wouldn't it be nice to have a handy guide to help us decipher why we think the way we do or decide the way we decide?

The simplicity and elegance of a silver bullet will continue to call out to humankind. However, the sum total of our human experience cannot be deciphered or decoded in a book or approach. It can, however, provide a latticework of logic and a bit of anchoring in a seemingly unmoored inner world for those of us dedicated to the years of hard work required to realize our own potential. As Malcolm Gladwell states in *Outliers,* "That does not mean everyone will be above average, as the old joke goes. It does mean that the average should rise, and everyone willing to put in the work be able more fully to realize his potential, if not necessarily his dreams."[11] We've investigated the power of purpose, personal development, and failure. These will help us dig into some of the building blocks of big ideas and how we can deploy them to make the world a better place.

---

10 Lindsay Myers, "The Self-Help Industry Helps Itself to Billions of Dollars," *Brain Blogger* (blog), May 23, 2014.

11 Malcolm Gladwell, *Outliers: The Story of Success* (New York: Little, Brown and Company, 2008).

Gladwell was right to suggest that there are no shortcuts in the game of self-awareness and the achievement of our inherent potential. We can, however, help ourselves by discovering, examining, and deploying the right big ideas to help our cause.

CHAPTER 2

FOUNDATIONS

As a single footstep will not make a path on the earth, so a single thought will not make a pathway in the mind. To make a deep physical path, we walk again and again. To make a deep mental path, we must think over and over the kind of thoughts we wish to dominate our lives.

—HENRY DAVID THOREAU

What are some of your earliest memories? What vivid experiences do you still recall and recount now, in a different season of life? If you had a particularly formative experience back again, might you do something differently, or is it the kind of recollection you'd keep hermetically sealed and preserved forever? How have those experiences affected your trajectory in life? How have they made you, you?

Were your parents set on you going to college after you com pleted high school, no matter what? Or was that decision left up to you? Did you have an intact nuclear family, or did you spend most of your time with one parent or any at all?

Was your youth stable? Unstable? Did you need to care for a sibling or family member at an age when most are worrying about grades and tests and young life?

We're all products of our upbringing, environment, and experiences. They are what collectively shape us as people. Human life spans a spectrum that reaches farther than our worldviews allow us to comprehend. Some of us grow wise early in life and some later; some not at all. No matter what, we all have ideas and experiences that stick with us as we mature. Our early memories reveal much about why we think the way we do, decide the way we decide, and form or destroy relationships with others.

Here's one of my early memories that shaped a bit of my worldview. It will also reveal some of the big ideas that still influence my life to this day.

MATH IS HARD

You need to be an optimist to fly a rocket ship.

—CHRIS HADFIELD, FIRST CANADIAN TO WALK IN SPACE

On a warm March Thursday in San Antonio, Texas, fourth-grade me experienced an ebullience that I've only matched a handful of times in my life since. To tell the story properly, I need to rewind to before I began fourth grade at Cambridge Elementary. My parents were both high school teachers when they met, and after starting a family, planned a series of career shifts to allow my younger brother and me to attend one of the best public schools in the state. They

accomplished this by virtue of my mom securing a position as a Spanish teacher at the high school in that system, not particularly close to where we lived. Education had always been paramount for my family, and they were determined to give us the best they could. That great gift wasn't without its drawbacks. We had a decent drive across town each morning and each afternoon to reach the school system, and I occasionally felt that geographical separation acutely.

My own family's humble life led me to frequently compare myself to others in what was a hyper-materialistic and sometimes superficial environment. Even at age eight, I was aware that distinct socioeconomic and racial strata existed within our school system and its surrounding communities. But on this balmy Thursday morning, I was focused entirely on the Math Olympics. Instead of spending time in our usual classes, the entire school would compete against one another in a series of exercises, activities, and classroom contests. Suffice it to say, we all looked forward to this day as a chance to pause the routine and compete against one another.

I distinctly remember bending every fiber of my being to the tasks presented to us, not because of choice, but because of necessity. Math had never been my strong suit. I excelled in Reading, History, and English, and I marshaled every faculty and resource available to my eight-year-old mind to have a shot at achieving the audacious goal I'd set for myself. Through this combination of determination and grit, I managed to feel good about my effort in the contests. After a couple of agonizing hours passed for our teachers to assess our efforts, we eagerly gathered to hear the results.

This being a fairly large public school, I lined up down a long corridor on the ground level along with a couple hundred fourth-grade classmates to learn who would be recognized.

Remembering my tentative confidence from the day's activities, I permitted myself to wonder what it would be like to receive the recognition and *adulation* of the entire school. Our principal stepped up to the microphone at the end of the corridor, with hundreds of students' necks craned in her direction. Third place went to a fifth grader who rushed down the corridor to claim their bronze medal. We all cheered raucously and then struggled to settle back down to hear the results for second and first place. Our principal called for quiet, glanced down at her notecard, and called my name for second place. A series of alien sensations washed over me, and I experienced a version of tunnel vision as I stepped down the corridor lined on both sides with cheering faces. I hardly felt the pats on my back and high fives as I made my way to the front, and don't clearly recall the silver medal being placed around my neck. If you offered me a million dollars today to recount who won the whole boondoggle, I'd be unable to. The wave of euphoria was too great for me to hear or process that information.

Looking back on that experience today, the intensity seems a bit trivial in the grander scheme of things. And almost thirty years after that day, it's one of my most vivid and visceral memories. In retrospect, and through the good fortune of my professional experience, I understand some of what was going on in my fourth-grade brain that day. I've often wondered what sense I would've made of a sneak peek into the inner workings of brain chemistry and if that knowledge would've led me to act or think differently. Would that self-awareness, applied out of context, have thrown me off and led to a less satisfactory outcome? Or would it have been the extra jolt I needed to take first place?

Moving through my life, I've been lucky to have access to tools, frameworks, learning, and people that help me unpack a series of questions and observations I've explored about myself in my own self-awareness journey. Often, I've felt beholden to my mind and body's reaction to certain situations and individuals. In my self-awareness journey, I've found investigating the 'why' question allows me to make better decisions. I also find that I want to partner with others who care to ask why, both about themselves and others. I've been fortunate enough to explore many of these topics in my work as a leadership coach, meeting facilitator, and management advisor. In turn, my work creates a virtuous circle wherein I get to walk similar paths with others. The learning and growth of those who I get to partner with mirrors and informs my own. In short, I love what I do and wouldn't change my profession for anything else I've experienced so far in life.

I believe that each of us must embark on and stick with our own self-awareness journey to become the best versions of ourselves. I posit that a juxtaposition set up by the increasingly connected nature of our work and lives, and the increasingly disconnected nature of our culture and society, emerges more fully each day. This environment requires that we know ourselves as deeply as possible in order to shape our desired realities while learning and growing from the tripping hazards we encounter along the way.

So, how can we understand ourselves better, given that it is so critical now and will only become more so in the future? One avenue that's had a great impact on me is a functional working knowledge of neurochemistry. I endeavor to make plain what happens inside our brains in certain situations: both when interacting with others and when we're sitting alone, quietly, with nothing but our thoughts. I also hope to name and shed light on the inequality that holds our organizations, systems, and people back every day, as well as some of the most prevalent and critical social dynamics at play any time two or more people convene or collaborate. I explore these topics here so we can spend less time asking ourselves why and more time driving a positive impact in a world that is crying out for it.

LENS ONE: TIME ON EARTH AS SOCIAL COMPLEXITY

Today's society is like no other we've experienced. We may never see another quite like it again. For the first time in history, five distinct generations exist in the workforce, each with unique formative experiences, needs from peers and leaders, fears, and dreams. This is complexity in its purest form. Two individuals born in the same period, with similar backgrounds and life experiences, pursuing the same professional goals will find themselves at odds sooner or later. Multiply those variables by an order of magnitude because one individual was born in 1952 and another in 1989, and you'll begin to approach the intricacies of what we each step into every day when we enter our workplaces or open our laptops.

FIVE-GENERATIONS—ONE WORKFORCE AND ONE SOCIETY

One of the most pervasive and deeply entrenched inhibitors to the prevalence and positive saturation of big ideas is my first lens: that of age. Seniority and age drive many facets of our society: household and family structure, clubs, leisure endeavors, and of course, work. Let's take a closer look at that last one.

Earlier, I mentioned that our workforce comprises five distinct generations for the first time in history. Here's how that breaks down in terms of the American workforce:

- Two percent are Traditionalists, or those born between 1925 and 1945
- Twenty-five percent are Baby Boomers, or those born between 1946 and 1964
- Thirty-three percent are Generation X, or those born between 1965 and 1980
- Thirty-five percent, officially the largest group in the American workforce, are Millennials, those born between 1981 and the year 2000
- Five percent are Generation Z, or those born in 2001 and later[12]

One fascinating environmental note to add some flavor to the broth is that while Boomers comprise a significant percentage of the workforce, their ranks are shrinking: about ten thousand Boomers retire each day.[13] Generation X and Millennials, each viewed as minorities in their turn, are now firmly ensconced as the heart of the workforce. Generation Z is just beginning to hit traditional working age, but it's safe to say the years to come will see their influence grow.

---

12 "Generational Differences in the Workplace [Infographic]," Purdue University Global, accessed September 11, 2020.

13 "Millennials Want Workplaces With Social Purpose. How Does Your Company Measure Up?," Talent Economy, accessed September 11, 2020.

The fundamental shifts occurring in the American workforce continue to become more complex as time goes on. People around the world are holding onto jobs longer as time goes on for a variety of reasons, effectively lengthening the envelope of generation. I joined the workforce in 2006, entering a population that featured four generations for the first time in history (all of the aforementioned generations aside from Generation Z, many of whom were still in elementary school at the time).

Interesting facts, but how can we put them to use? One critical application is helping us engage with one another in more respectful, productive, and meaningful ways in the supercharged environments where we work, play, and gather. How might we learn to recognize and encourage each group's and each individual's intrinsic strengths instead of focusing on the chasms that separate us? Genuine curiosity is as good a starting place as any, so let's focus on some of the characteristics that comprise each of the five generations themselves:

Key insights:

- Traditionalists
  - Shaped by the popularization of movies and radio; World War II
  - Communicate via methods that leverage a human touch (letter writing, etc.)

- Baby Boomers
  - Shaped by the Civil Rights Movement, Vietnam War

- Communicate via the most efficient means (don't text or e-mail when a phone call will suffice)

- Generation X
  - Shaped by the emergence of the Internet; the AIDS epidemic
  - Communicate much the same as Boomers; most efficient available means

- Millennials
  - 9/11; Shaped by emergence and popularization of social media
  - Communicate via instant messaging, texts, and especially for those born toward the beginning of this age group, e-mail

- Generation Z
  - Shaped by boom-to-bust economics; omnipresent technology
  - Communicate like digital natives; social media and almost exclusively digital[14]

As one might expect, a distinct sense of hierarchy can manifest, given that so many gradations are at play. This presents a major challenge even for organizations that are collaborative at their cores—for those built on a highly vertical or command and control structure, it can further reduce generative interaction across generational gaps and cut down on innovative thinking. It's no wonder that those newest to

14 "Generational Differences in the Workplace [Infographic]," Purdue University Global, accessed September 11, 2020.

the workforce often find themselves in organizational contexts that don't align with their personal beliefs, which was a bother for earlier generations but far from the showstopper it can be for Millennials and members of Generation Z.

The beauty of this novel new reality is that there's never been a better time to learn in a way that complements and elevates your own perspective. This isn't always easy. Each generation, and individual within each generation, has their own way of communicating, and preferred ways of working and decision-making. The road is often bumpy and sometimes downright hellacious given the significant switching costs required to jump from one context to another and back again in rapid succession. The rewards, however, can be profound.

SO WHAT?

I'll never forget my first coaching engagement for my firm, The Clearing. I'd just finished up two different leadership development certifications with the support of my company. Armed with my newly minted qualifications and riding one hell of an achievement high, I confidently accepted an offer to coach a senior executive from a private sector organization for whom we'd recently begun working. The day for our first meeting came, and I made sure to pack a decent suit and double-check that I hadn't forgotten anything important like a tie. I embarked on the fifteen-minute bike ride to our office in Dupont Circle, arrived safely, and prepared myself for a wholly new experience.

After setting up in our intimate corner conference room, I got a call from our front desk saying that my client had arrived and was ready for me. As I approached, I got a smile as well as a flash of something else I couldn't quite place. We walked back to the conference room, exchanged some pleasantries, and got into the first part of our conversation. This entailed sharing some things about ourselves that would allow the other party to quickly get to know us better, all with a goal of establishing a bit of the groundwork for a trust-based relationship. As I talked through some bits and pieces of my life and mentioned I had a college-age son, I glimpsed the same fleeting facial expression I'd noticed a few minutes prior. I took the risk to pause our conversation in order to ask if something was wrong. The response both surprised me and made sense in my own impostor syndrome-tinged mind. My client, themselves a mid-fifties to early sixties senior executive at the peak of their power in their particular system, shared that they'd expected someone older. The underlying implication I took away from that simple statement was that they were seasoned, accomplished, and had many decades of insight under their belt and that I looked like a twenty-something to their untrained eye. Now I had a choice to make.

I chose what I felt was the most direct route, and plainly stated my age, all of thirty-five at the time. A blinding shock of the obvious hit me as I realized I'd freshly shaven, likely making me look younger than I might otherwise. I gave an overview, perhaps unnecessarily, of my bona fides and years of experience in the field. I also openly acknowledged that this was my first formal coaching engagement. After a moment, the executive nodded and said he could benefit from a fresh perspective and was ready to get down to business together. We did just that and have an excellent relationship to this day where we offer each other perspective and mentorship when the situation calls for it.

This is one situation that I felt would reinforce the commonly held misconception that youth and authentic leadership are mutually exclusive. Perhaps you've bumped up against the idea that you're too young or inexperienced to know what you do to perform the job with excellence.

Or maybe you've been a part of an environment at work or inside of a pastime you care about, like a hobby, volunteering opportunity, or a passion project, where the system incentivizes hard-to-reach assets that only the most connected individuals can access. This can manifest in a variety of ways, such as the time, context, and proverbial keys to execute original research, create and field-test your own thought leadership, or gain the support of your organization to pursue training and certifications that will help you grow. These things are often held up as the paragon of personal learning and revealing our own "North Star" for the given pursuit, wherein we can uncover the meeting point of our personal passions and systemic success.

Finally, some believe that personal achievement is dependent on a series of external factors aligning. Nefarious dynamics like nepotism, corruption, and bias are alive and well in many of our society's systems. Many times, there's no substitute for being in the right place at the right time. In short, environmental factors, many outside our control, have a say in decisions that can determine our path in life. For those of us who sweat and bleed for the teams and organizations we're a part of, that's a grim prospect to consider.

The good news is that not all is lost. My experiences and the insights I've uncovered in this book-writing journey show that early-career individuals and those in the early stages of their own self-awareness journeys have much to teach even the most experienced and effective leaders in addition to the most self-aware, Buddha-like individuals. Humans have always learned by storytelling, and we all have powerful stories to relate to those around us.

Furthermore, I've found that a multidisciplinary perspective can generate and refine an accessible and vital collection of big ideas. I'm a proud product of a liberal arts education that taught me to encapsulate a problem, examine and consider it from multiple perspectives, and deploy the best thinking from many fields simultaneously when in solution mode. This approach is an order of magnitude more powerful when we broaden our aperture to include concepts and mindsets from different disciplines, fields, and cultures. When we walk this particular path, we efficiently allow not just ourselves, but those around us to rapidly explore diverse alternatives while staying true to what really matters, both personally and organizationally.

Finally, environmental factors do affect outcomes, even when we do our utmost to tightly control every factor within a project, personal milestone, or decision-making framework. And a deep sense of self-authorship, a seeking curiosity, and good old-fashioned persistence and determination combine to make external factors far less powerful. In essence, we get closer to being the masters of our own destiny when we inhabit the mindsets named above.

THE PROOF IS IN THE PUDDING

These aren't just my arbitrary observations. According to DDI's triennial Global Leadership Forecast, organizations that extend the development of high-potential talent below senior levels are 4.2 times more likely to financially outperform those that restrict their developmental resources to senior levels exclusively.[15] Investing in future leaders, whether that's in a professional sphere or a more personal one, makes sense for the bottom line and builds long-term resilience for all. One critical step on the path to true investment in those future leaders is to bust some myths.

Myth: Younger generations aren't willing to invest the time and energy it takes to grow and lead at work.

Reality: Regarding the stereotype that younger generations care less about developing themselves, it is well and truly time to debunk this one once and for all. According to *Forbes*, 84 percent of Boomers and 81 percent of Gen-X'ers surveyed committed to making self-improvements in a variety of contexts, while fully 94 percent of Millennials made the same commitment to focus their time, energy, and resources on actively creating a better version of themselves—a difference of over 10 percent.[16] Approaching the same concept from a purely financial perspective further debunks this myth. The same study revealed that Boomers were willing to invest an average of 152 dollars a month on self-improvement efforts, while Millennials stated that they'd spend almost twice that

---

15 "Global Leadership Forecast 2018," DDI, The Conference Board, EY, accessed September 11, 2020.

16 Caroline Beaton, "Never Good Enough: Why Millennials Are Obsessed With Self-Improvement," Forbes, February 25, 2016.

at 300 dollars a month. This figure is especially compelling when taking into consideration lower overall compensation levels for the younger cohort. In short, young people aren't just ready to aim their money, time, and talent to create the best versions of themselves in service of work, pastimes, and personal life; they're already doing it and wondering why those around them aren't doing the same.

Myth: Younger generations don't care as much about work as they do other parts of their lives.

Reality: Younger generations are pushing business and societal envelopes more each day by working from locations other than a primary physical office, which may be unusual for those more familiar with traditional office paradigms. It doesn't make them any less serious or dedicated. Far from the unearned lackadaisical stereotype, 24 percent of Millennials forfeited unused vacation days each year compared to 19 percent for Gen X'ers and just 17 percent of Boomers.[17] The data clearly tells a different story than the myth noted above. However, a workaholic generation that can often view themselves as "work martyrs" is no healthier than the myth itself—another ready opportunity for the right and timely application of big ideas.

Myth: Younger generations are always looking for the next best opportunity. Why else would so many leave for a new job every two years?

---

17 Sarah Green Carmichael, "Millennials Are Actually Workaholics, According to Research," *Harvard Business Review*, August 17, 2016.

Reality: Millennials and their younger Gen Z counterparts do indeed shift jobs more than their older counterparts. However, those frequent moves usually aren't to seek a higher salary or better perks, which is a common misconception. Purpose matters greatly to young workers, so much so that fully 75 percent of Millennials would take a pay cut to work for a socially responsible organization versus the national average of 55 percent.[18] On-the-job engagement and job fulfillment results for 88 percent of Millennials when they're provided opportunities to make positive social and environmental impacts at work.[19] With this data in mind, perhaps a more likely reason for the more frequent jumps that the American workforce sees from younger generations is because an employee that cares can't connect to their purpose. If that is indeed the case, the question that established leaders should be asking isn't "Why are my young colleagues always looking for the next best opportunity," but rather "*Why are we not providing our young people the purpose they need from their work to feel fulfilled*?"

This is not the only problem with the aforementioned artificial barriers. Like any partition, its purpose is to serve and further entrench those with power and to systematically strip away access, goods, and knowledge from those without power. Inequity is bad for systems and is toxic to our culture. Our world can afford no more of either.

---

18 2016 Cone Communications Millennial Employment Engagement Survey," Cone Communications, accessed September 11, 2020.

19 Ibid.

LENS TWO: ACCESS, PRIVILEGE, AND TRENDS

Talent is equally distributed. Opportunity is not.

—LEILA JANAH

Grit and determination led me to a second place showing in a school-wide math contest. Intrinsic talent or knowing the right person on the evaluation team did not. While that small slice of reality is heartening, life today isn't a series of elementary school math contests. Systemic inequality and privilege are rife within most systems that we interact with on a daily basis. Today's society is increasingly willing to name that reality for what it is and tackle it actively, largely due to the bravery of young people around the world. Due in no small part to their efforts, the diversity of our workplaces and social groups increases with each day that goes by.

The late Leila Janah sagely observed that the universe equally distributes talent, regardless of age, sex, race, or socioeconomic status. An equal cross-section of the brilliant, the deeply empathetic, and the most determined are present in poor Black, Latino, and other minority communities just like they are in affluent white communities. However, as Janah notes, opportunity and access to the tools, structures, and mindsets needed to capitalize on and amplify that intrinsic talent is not equally distributed. Organizations, individuals, and those with what they perceive as the most to lose guard that access and opportunity under a thousand different guises. Worse yet, only 55 percent of respondents to a series of Gallup surveys stated their companies have policies in place to promote diversity and inclusion, and 45 percent of Americans surveyed stated that they'd experienced some form of discrimination or harassment in the last year. Against this backdrop, what might be possible in our professions, families, and world if we could equalize talent and opportunity? None of us can truly rise while holding others down.

Again, the data tells a clear and compelling story. As of 2019, gender diverse companies are 25 percent more likely to outperform their peers, while ethnically diverse companies are 36 percent more likely to excel past their competition.[20] Organizations with more women on their Boards statistically outperform their male-dominated counterparts in the long run. Finally, teams that focus on inclusive practices, structures, and approaches outperform their less-inclusive counterparts by 80 percent in team-based assessments.[21] If those data points aren't compelling to you, consider those gargantuan sums of money and amounts of energy being invested every year into managing workplace attrition resulting from inequity. American businesses lose an estimated 64 billion dollars each year, replacing the two million employees who leave their jobs due to workplace discrimination.[22]

The young and aspirant often view their work and passions through a lens of self. Many future leaders look to be parts of organizations where they see people like themselves in positions of power because it makes success feel a bit more

---

20 Sundiata Dixon-Fyle, Kevin Dolan, Vivian Hunt, and Sara Prince, "Diversity Wins: How Inclusion Matters," accessed October 19, 2020.

21 "The Stats," Inclusive Outcomes LLC, accessed September 11, 2020.

22 "The Costly Business of Discrimination," Center for American Progress, accessed September 11, 2020.

accessible. These character traits are called 'inherent diversities,' traits that one is born with, such as ethnicity, gender, disability, or sexual orientation. Businesses whose leadership inhabits three or more inherent diversities, as well as three or more 'acquired diversities' (those gained from experience), eclipse their competition in terms of innovation and business performance. Furthermore, employees at these companies and members of organizations with leadership that exhibits both inherent and acquired diversity are 45 percent more likely to experience growing market share and up to 70 percent more likely to report that their company broke into a new market entirely.[23]

Furthermore, when at least one team member has traits in common with the end user, the entire team better understands that user. A team with a member who shares a client's ethnicity is 152 percent more likely than another team to understand that client.[24] In short, equality, access, diversity, and inclusion aren't just buzzwords. They're powerful drivers of business viability and the bottom line. They're also foundational building blocks for any system that wishes to be truly resilient.

DEMOCRATIZATION IN SYSTEMS

Knowing as much as we do about the importance of equity, diversity, and inclusion for all, our shared reality still includes many organizations that meter access to their most valuable assets and coveted opportunities using outdated, arbitrary, or opaque rationales. Or worse yet, some

---

23 Sylvia Ann Hewlett, Melinda Marshall, and Laura Sherbin. "How Diversity Can Drive Innovation," *Harvard Business Review*, December 2013.

24 Ibid.

organizations meter that access for no real reason at all aside from tired aphorisms. You might have heard things like "It's always been done this way" or "We all had to earn our stripes in this system." This mindset was unacceptable when first trotted out, and it's unacceptable now. It is our collective duty to name it for what it is out loud, for ourselves and with our colleagues, friends, or family. And we can't stop there. It's all for naught if we don't also dedicate energy and resources to actively combating it. Let's look at how big ideas can level the playing field and cut through the shabby rationale that can manifest in defense of the status quo. The time is now.

Truly democratic systems open up access to the things that matter to as many people as possible. Big ideas are no different. They are not assets to be held under lock and key, whose value can only be extracted by those with power. During my six years at The Clearing, I've been fortunate to get to know Swiss futurist Jens Ulrik Hansen in our day-to-day work and as a friend and mentor with whom I can tackle big ideas. During our conversation focusing on this work, Jens and I dove into the concepts of ownership and equity as powerful drivers of personal success and mastery. Through this lens, Jens tuned me in to Robinhood, "a company that leverages technology to encourage everyone to participate in our financial system,"[25] as a prime example of a tool that puts more economic power in the hands of more people. The impetus behind Robinhood's creation was its founders' realization that Wall Street firms pay effectively nothing to trade stocks while individual investors pay varying fees that can be as

---

25 "Careers," Robinhood, accessed September 19, 2020.

much as ten dollars per trade.[26] Jens called my attention to Robinhood as an important example of the democratization of equity and ownership, effectively lowering the barrier to entry for entrepreneurship and ownership. Jens made these abstract ideas concrete for me. "For many, this is a whole new way of existing. You're not relying solely on a salary anymore. You know *you* matter. You can make a difference in your own life directly and maybe even shape a different path for yourself because you're immersed in the idea of ownership instead of equating your personal value solely to your salary." I'd had some experience with Robinhood before our conversation, but Jens' insights cast it in a whole new light for me. This is but one of a whole new generation of apps and tools that open access to traditionally stratified and privileged systems.

In this work, I aim to democratize access to big ideas, both directly and indirectly. We'll accomplish the former by exploring a number of big ideas head-on, and the latter by focusing on capacity building and curiosity of mind so each of you can go out and continue to level the playing field using big ideas as tools for good long after you've set this book down.

---

26 Ibid.

CHAPTER 3

TRIPPING HAZARDS AND WHY WE FALL

Did they get you to trade
Your heroes for ghosts?
Hot ashes for trees?
Hot air for a cool breeze?
Cold comfort for change?
Did you exchange
A walk-on part in the war
For a lead role in a cage?

—PINK FLOYD – "WISH YOU WERE HERE"

As soon as we learn to walk as young children, we learn to fall back down. In fact, the fall is the intrinsic part of learning to walk, while the physical and mental act of placing one foot in front of the other while maintaining balance is the part that feels foreign and unnatural. Once we become cognizant that objects and environmental factors like an uneven walking surface or a foreign object can cause a fall, we realize that tripping hazards are everywhere. Our own navigation of society and environments, whether that be the working world, our interactions with family and friends, taking public transportation, or going grocery shopping, is no different from those first days learning to walk. Through time and experience, we learn to more readily identify and more deftly navigate around the tripping hazards that are always present. In some circles, that's called wisdom.

What might your life be like if someone had come along and forewarned you about a tripping hazard you'd experienced before it had the chance to cause an unforeseen tumble? What impact would that foresight have had on you? Would you decide or act differently? If so, what path would that small shift have set for you?

Whether you're a student making your way through high school or college as best you can, are a rising up-and-comer in your profession, are ready to forge a new path for yourself in life or at work, or are a star finding your way out of inequity, identifying and properly acknowledging those tripping hazards can increase your personal power and your ability to contribute to and grow within systems.

For some, one different choice or small change could alter their life's trajectory. Let's take a look at a few that show up for different types of people from different walks of life.

TRIPPING HAZARDS

FOR THE YOUNG AND AMBITIOUS

Overconfidence. Let's say you're a twenty-seven-year-old working your second job out of college. You put in the hard hours, learned a lot at your first job, did well, and made an intentional move to your second employer to maximize your growth. You're on an upward trajectory, and you'd like to be the CEO of a company one day.

You've never received negative feedback before in your career. In fact, your performance reviews each year are some version of a 'You're amazing' victory lap. That lack of negative feedback, or really any reason to need to tap the proverbial brakes, has a marked effect when taking on greater responsibility, entering into new and unfamiliar environments, and other generalized risks. In environments like that, it can be easy (maybe even natural) to extend yourself far beyond your limits. For those who find themselves in this situation, the realization of the overextension often doesn't come until it's too late, and consequences almost always follow. Furthermore, the experience can be jarring, especially when someone in this position considers themselves a top performer who's never truly failed in this context before.

Lack of Self-Awareness. If asked whether or not we believe ourselves to be self-aware, most would probably answer yes. After all, who knows us better than ourselves? It's important to name that the term 'self-awareness' can mean different things to different people. Definitions range from 'an awareness of one's own personality and individuality'[27] to 'the ability to see yourself clearly and objectively through reflection and introspection.'[28] Keep this fact in mind when discussing the topic of self-awareness with your colleagues, family members, and friends.

We each embark on our self-awareness journey at different times in life, some early, and some much later. Our ability to name and acknowledge that we want to know more about ourselves, for the sake of the exercise and the knowing as opposed to seeking that knowledge to accomplish a specific outcome, is a critical step on the path to true self-awareness. Finding meaning and purpose in the journey itself, what Mihaly Csikszentmihalyi calls an *autotelic pursuit*, can open up whole new worlds of understanding and possibility. The reality of the situation is rather grim. Though when asked directly, most people would characterize themselves as self-aware, only 10 to 15 percent of those who participated in a long-term study matched the criteria for self-awareness.[29]

How can a lack of true self-awareness hold us back? When approaching important milestones and decisions, we may make the wrong decision and not truly know why. We will feel more compelled to lie, cheat, or steal because we're less honest with ourselves about what we truly need from life to feel satisfied. Our relationships with loved ones and

---

27 *Merriam-Webster.com*, s.v. "self-awareness (*n.*)," accessed August 3, 2020

28 "What Is Self-Awareness and Why Is It Important? [+5 Ways to Increase It]," PositivePsychology.com, accessed September 15, 2020.

29 Tasha Eurich, "What Self-Awareness Really Is (and How to Cultivate It)," *Harvard Business Review*, January 4, 2018.

coworkers will be less strong and less resilient.[30] For all these reasons and more, a lack of self-awareness is one of the most critical tripping hazards to be aware of for all of us, but especially for the young and ambitious.

FOR THE BRILLIANT AND UNDER-PRIVILEGED

The playing field is not level. Let's state what we all should know to be true: the playing field is not level. The game that we call work, life, and simply moving from one day to the next is rigged in favor of those who already have power in any given system. The mere fact that some can even consider any of the aforementioned facets of life a game, as some do, reinforces the underlying premise. Any society with "haves" has "have nots," and by its very nature promotes inequity. Worse, far too few directly acknowledge this reality about our economy and culture, and either support it indirectly through rationalization or directly by ignoring or avoiding it entirely.

Some would quibble that it's difficult to quantify the positive impact that diversity, or the representation of minorities (often the "have-nots" we've already discussed), has on organizational success. Today, we know that the data supports that direct linkage. The Center for Talent Innovation performed a study that consisted of over eighteen hundred survey respondents, forty Fortune 500 company case studies, and interviews with over one hundred recognized innovators. Their results were staggering. According to that study, organizations without diverse leadership create environments where "women are 20 percent less likely than straight white

30 Ibid.

men to win endorsement for their ideas; people of color are 24 percent less likely, and LGBTQ+ individuals are 21 percent less likely. This costs their companies crucial market opportunities because inherently diverse contributors understand the unmet needs in under-leveraged markets. We've found when at least one team member has traits in common with the end-user, the entire team better understands that user. A team with a member who shares a client's ethnicity is 152 percent more likely than another team to understand that client."[31]

That same study uncovered six critical behaviors that unlock innovation regardless of the environment, be it a school, a for-profit business, a government agency, or a volunteer organization:

- Ensuring that everyone is heard;
- Making it safe to propose novel ideas;
- Giving team members decision-making authority;
- Sharing credit for success;
- Giving actionable feedback; and
- Implementing feedback from the team.[32]

A growing and compelling body of knowledge proves that a level playing field truly benefits us all. There is discrete action for each of us to take—no matter where and how we exist in a given system. For those of us who are part of a dominant social, economic, or cultural group, we must actively elevate

---

31 Sylvia Ann Hewlett, Melinda Marshall, & Laura Sherbin, "Looking for Innovation in All the Wrong Places," *Stanford Social Innovation Review*, September 12, 2013.

32 Ibid.

and prioritize the voices and experiences of our c classmates, and neighbors who are fighting their o uphill battle. We must also interrogate, confron mantle our own inherent bias, conscious or unconscious. We all have important work to do. A common aphorism states that 'a rising tide lifts all boats.' While its rooting in free-market economics has proven to be troublesome at best, a rising tide of inclusion and equity will lift us all to a higher level of success.

<u>Lack of resilience.</u> Overcompensation, overcommitting, and overachieving. These are all common tactics, often unconsciously applied, by those who are brilliant and under-privileged. When you feel like you're fighting an uphill battle against unfair odds, it can make sense to devote more time, more energy, and more focus. This tactic does lead to outcomes: more work product, more or better results, and more profitability if you work in an industry where you charge for your time. However, consider for a moment the long-term effects of such an approach. There comes a time where your energy investment becomes untenable. Your efforts begin to weigh on you. You feel less sharp, have a harder time focusing, are constantly worn out, and don't have energy for the things and people you know you love. In short, burnout. It's happened to many of us, and it's a particularly difficult experience for those who equate much of their identity with achievement because a burned-out individual can't achieve at their normal levels, if at all. Linking back to the self-awareness tripping hazard discussed above, tune into what you know you need to be well long-term. Whatever your endeavor—graduating with honors, moving to the top of your field, or marshaling the resources you need to jump

from one focus area to another—remember that it's a marathon, not a sprint. The sooner you develop healthy, sustainable long-term behaviors, the better you'll do in the long term.

Little or no backup. This tripping hazard is nuanced and related to the resilience topic we just covered. Imagine being on a basketball team. You think you're facing off against five other players from the opposing squad. You receive an inbound pass from your teammate, bring the ball up court, meet resistance from a press defense deployed by your opponents, stop your dribble, look for a teammate to pass to, and discover you're suddenly and inexplicably all alone. Reality is largely analogous for those of us who find ourselves overcompensating for a non-level playing field. We sprint out beyond a boundary hoping that our colleagues, classmates, leaders, and advisors are there with us all too often to find that we're effectively on our own. What does the data tell us about how this happens in the real world? "In 2018, only 14 percent of companies have a strong 'leadership bench,'" defined here as 'ready-now leaders who can step in to replace those who retire or move on.'[33] That's a grim reality for all of us, not just the brilliant and under-privileged.

FOR ESTABLISHED LEADERS

You think you know a lot. Maybe, but probably not so much. We'll discuss the Dunning-Kruger effect later in this work, but for now, let's leave it at this—if you believe yourself to be a wise, top-flight leader, you likely have some learning to do. That becomes even more true when applied to those

33 "Global Leadership Forecast 2018," DDI, The Conference Board, EY, accessed September 11, 2020.

around you when a generational or cultural gap applies. We all need different things. For instance, the lack of a reply to an e-mail or text might be considered disrespectful by some, while for others, it's simply a by-product of the pace at which they move or how they prioritize the time they spend communicating at all. You might consider a particular way of managing your to-do list as perfect, but others in your environment may have completely different ways of being productive. The chances are good that you could learn a lot from considering new ways of thinking, communicating, and acting, given the diversity of existence surrounding you. One thing is for sure—anything resembling an over-inflated ego will only do you harm in the long run.

Assumptions. These ideas often start small and may originate so long ago that we struggle to place their precise entry into our minds and ways of reckoning. In that way, assumptions can be some of the most insidious tripping hazards for any of us. Because established leaders likely have more experience and time in the leadership seat, their available boundary for assumptions to take root and grow is broader and can be more fertile than that of someone who is more of a clean slate. Once buried under layers of observations and confirmation bias, wherein the leader selects information that fits a particular hypothesis or assumption, it can be effectively impossible to return to the original presenting data instead of a 'conclusion' driven by those insidious assumptions. Now multiply the stakes by an order of magnitude given that the established leader must interact with a higher number of people than most individual contributors, and may even be directly responsible for the careers or even lives of others. Actions taken due to this process can lead to misunderstanding, hurt, and sometimes irreparable damage. We begin to see how holistically a tripping hazard can impact the lives of many and how much good can be done by finding ways to not trip over the hazard in the first place.

WHEN FACING TRIPPING HAZARDS—AVOID? JUMP OVER? PLOW THROUGH?

Knowing now just a few of the tripping hazards that face us regardless of our age, experience, or position in life, what can we do to better identify and not get caught up with the things that would bring us to the proverbial ground in a hurry? Specifically, with regard to the resilience and backup tripping hazards, recent data again illustrates the power of intentionally investing in the next generation of leaders: "Organizations that have a formal mentoring culture have 20 percent lower turnover, 46 percent higher leader quality, and can fill 23 percent more roles immediately."[34]

Developing the acuity of sight and peripheral vision to identify a tripping hazard, especially those you know you're particularly susceptible to, is half the battle. Many leaders who outwardly appear to have achieved immense levels of success still get caught up by the same thing over and over again because they haven't cultivated the will or ability to truly see those hazards for themselves. Their work and personal lives suffer as a result. Be courageous enough to be radically honest with yourself about what holds you back. Then try deploying that same level of vulnerability with others. They can be your accountability partners when it comes to naming and avoiding the hazards in the first place.

---

34 Ibid.

During my research for this work, I had the good fo to speak with Admiral Frank Morley, director of the International Programs Office. We'll learn more about the Admiral's leadership style and philosophy later in this work, but for now, I'd like to draw attention to a specific observation he offered as we discussed some of his biggest learnings from a career of service. Connecting to the inevitability of actually falling when encountering one of the tripping hazards we've explored so far, the Admiral's advice rang true with me. "If you are or will need to accept 51 percent of the responsibility for a job, task, colleague, or outcome, just accept 100 percent of the responsibility for that thing. In the end, the outcome is the same, but your mindset and the positive impact it will have on those around you will be immeasurable." While this can seem like common sense, the very human desire to abdicate responsibility when things go wrong is natural. True leaders take their responsibility in the bad times, not just the good times, as Admiral Morley eloquently states for us here.

Finally, for teams, I've done my best to surround myself with people who are good at things I'm not good at and whose life experiences diverge from my own. In this way, we form well-rounded teams, having given up on the myth of the truly well-rounded individual. Scholarship bears this approach out, as "leaders who give diverse voices equal airtime are nearly twice as likely as others to unleash value-driving insights." When we can label our own assumptions as such for ourselves and others, and empower every individual in a given system, we create an intentional, enacted, and powerful culture. "Employees in a "speak up" culture are three and a half times as likely to contribute their full innovative potential."[35] Consider for a moment what you might be able to create in an organization that is truly firing on all cylinders. Each individual can contribute their highest good, full intellect, and applied creativity. The possibility and outcomes in an environment like that can deliver paradigm-changing outcomes, and it's what every great team is chasing in today's hyper-competitive world.

In summary:

- See and name the tripping hazard for what it is—something that will slow you down at best and break a proverbial bone at worst
- Be brutally honest with yourself—you owe it to you
- Ask for help from others
- Deploy your self-awareness to brainstorm or discover tactics to avoid the tripping hazards
- Share your learnings with others

Lastly, and perhaps most importantly, find the value in the experience when you do get tripped up. It happens to the best and the brightest still, so be gentle with yourself when you notice you've been brought to the ground by a given hazard. Learn, share, and grow instead of beating yourself up. The world will be a better place for it.

---

35 Sylvia Ann Hewlett, Melinda Marshall, and Laura Sherbin. "How Diversity Can Drive Innovation," *Harvard Business Review*, December 2013.

PART 2:

BIG IDEAS

CHAPTER 4

BIG IDEAS FOR THE SELF

The Self wishes to create, to evolve. The Ego likes things just the way they are.

—STEVEN PRESSFIELD

The world's philosophical, religious, psychological, self-help, addiction recovery, and social science canons all share one thing. It is not a data point or set, common terminology, or achievement, but rather a common mindset. Each area in this wide-ranging list of disciplines emphasizes the criticality of diving deep into one's self. It's a journey that Aristotle held in mind when he stated "knowing yourself is the beginning of all wisdom." The world's most talented statistician can have the mind of a human-computer and be able to work multi-variable calculus in their head. If they lack interpersonal skills and even a modicum of self-awareness, the chances are that not only will they not be able to effectively advocate for themselves in systems like academia or the workplace, but they're also likely to alienate or keep others at arm's distance, blunting their own potential impact on their work and the world.

Self-discovery is not simple. Myriad environmental factors array against us. Lack of time, ever-shortening attention spans, competing cognitive strain, and ignorance of the journey's importance all conspire to keep us focused on other things. Sometimes we erect barriers for ourselves, unconsciously or knowingly, that inhibit our ability to peel back our own personal layers. Perhaps we're afraid of what we might uncover, like the creeping sensation one unfamiliar with the outdoors feels before flipping over a half-rotted log, anticipating otherworldly creatures below.

Though I feel I've only embarked on my own journey of self-discovery and internal awareness, a number of big ideas stand out for me that make me pause, think, and most importantly, act in a new way.

WHAT OKINAWA CAN TEACH THE WORLD

The Japanese island of Okinawa is a bit different than most of us imagine when we think of Japan. A subtropical climate and a distinct set of languages set it apart from mainland Japan. Fun fact—Okinawa is also the home of the fictional greatest swordsmith in the world—Hattori Hanzo (of Quentin Tarantino's *Kill Bill* fame). While you may not be able to procure razor-sharp Hanzo steel on Okinawa in real life, the island is the birthplace and spiritual home of ideas that cut just as deep into the Western professional and personal psyche. Many of these ideas continue to have an impact on me. Some of my favorites crystalized a fuzzy concept I'd had

in my head for years with regard to work, life, and personal purpose.

One fascinating fact that perhaps few know about the Okinawan Islands is they are one of the world's five Blue Zones: places where residents live considerably longer than average. Sixty-eight out of every one hundred thousand Okinawans are one hundred years of age or older, which is more than three times as many as in the United States proportionally.[36]

Some of the reasons behind Okinawan longevity are unsurprising—a healthy diet consisting of many raw fruits and vegetables, seafood, and little or no meat, as well as daily exercise and time outside—while others are less obvious.[37] Two Okinawan concepts rise from the island's shared experience that have much to teach the rest of the world, not just about long life, but a life full of fulfillment, meaning, and focused purpose. Often, insights are best examined through the lens of story. This is the story of two intertwined Okinawan ideas: *moai* and *ikigai.*

Moai is a simple concept. The word describes a social construct unique to Okinawan society, a formal, life-long bond between a small group of individuals, roughly five to be more or less precise.[38] *Moai* forms in Okinawan communities at childhood, and often survives for the duration of its members' lives. More than half of modern-day Okinawans are a part of

---

36 "A high-carb diet may explain why Okinawans live so long," BBC Future, January 17, 2019.

37 Ibid

38 "Moai—This Tradition is Why Okinawan People Live Longer, Better," Blue Zones, accessed September 21, 2020.

at least one *moai*, for which there are no hard and fast rules. They all share regular meetings (some weekly, some daily) for a common purpose, and a key function as a social safety net. These groups serve an important purpose in times of tragedy or hardship. They often pool financial resources when one of its members is in great need and spend an increased amount of time together when a spouse or close family member passes away. However, many Okinawans characterize their *moai* not as the net that arrests their fall in times of trouble, but rather as the people they can share anything with and who know them best. In short, *moai* actively strive against the loneliness and disconnection from the rest of the world contributing so greatly to many senior citizens' rapid health decline toward the end of their lives. Similar social constructs contribute to happiness in many other parts of the world.

Ikigai is another elegantly expansive Okinawan concept that roughly translates to 'reason to live' or 'life purpose.' Originating in the Heian period—794 AD–1185 AD—*ikigai* resides at the intersection of four critical concepts:

1. What you are good at doing
2. What you love doing
3. What the world needs
4. What you can be rewarded for[39]

---

39 "Ikigai: A Japanese concept to improve work and life," BBC Worklife, August 7, 2017.

Image 1: Ikigai[40]

Thus, *ikigai* is a pursuit or purpose which an individual is good at, loves doing, is needed by someone other than themselves, and for which that individual can be rewarded. Canadian jazz performer Tim Tamashiro describes *ikigai* as central to his life's trajectory, partially because Okinawa is his ancestral homeland, but also because he sensed something missing in his successful career as a radio personality, singer, and jazz musician. Tamashiro differentiates between a job, that being a recurring set of actions one performs to generate income, as distinct from work, that being a recurring activity designed to achieve a result or outcome that

40 "Diagram of Japanese ikigai concept," iStock by Getty Images, accessed October 20, 2020.

rs.[41] Perhaps unsurprisingly, *ikigai* is most readily le to those who have already embarked on their own self-awareness journey, having realized that self-actuation and self-knowing are central to long-term worth and happiness.

Indeed, after reflecting on the first phase of his profession and life in music after deciding at age twenty to enroll in a music school, Tamashiro stated, "I knew what I wanted to do, what I loved to do, and what I was good at, but I didn't understand why I was doing it and why the world needed that."[42] Effectively, while three factors were present in his current profession, one of *ikigai's* four cardinal points was missing, and thus, Tamashiro left a career he loved because he could not clearly understand what its greater purpose was for the world.

While Tamashiro's pivot may seem radical, his personal journey to discover his *ikigai* uncovered something even more radical. The nexus of *ikigai's* four cardinal points for Tamashiro did not produce a different job, a new field of pursuit, or a flurry of networking to build community and connections, but rather a mindset: 'to delight.' Rather than channeling his intention and life purpose through the lens of his job, his personal life, or some other facet of his identity, Tamashiro turned the paradigm on its head and used his personal *ikigai* to delight, to steer his decisions, actions, and pursuits. In this way, one is equally able to inhabit their *ikigai* whether at work, at home, or at play. Tamashiro aims to

41 TedX Talks, "How to Ikigai | Tim Tamashiro | TEDxYYC," September 8, 2018, video, 12:42.

42 Ibid.

delight others at all times because it is his *ikigai*, and from it, he derives not only joy, but deep purpose. In short, *leading* with your *ikigai* and shaping your life from it instead of vice versa can radically simplify and align much of what feels most complex in our day-to-day.

Ikigai isn't just an interesting concept. As it has for Tim Tamashiro, it can shift our life and perspective in ways that impact our happiness and satisfaction. This is something Americans need after marked declines in overall well-being over the last three years.[43] More of us sense a need to change something big in order to move beyond contentment and pursue meaning as time goes on. Case in point: Lori Santos teaches Yale University's most popular course. It isn't a political science or economics class, but rather, a course called The Science of Wellbeing. Therein, Santos posits most humans are profoundly bad at finding what makes them truly happy. Many Westerners would define happiness through a material lens—a high salary, a large and luxurious home, all the belongings their heart could desire. Santos defines it in a wholly different manner: via practices, specifically, acts of kindness, meditation or focused reflection, time affluence, and spending time with loved ones. While this all sounds ephemeral and difficult or impossible to attain for the average person, Tamashiro notes that "part-time *ikigai*" is a perfect stepping stone to the proverbial full monty. Over 50 percent of Millennials have 'side hustles,' activities outside of their full-time employment that Tamashiro posits help us closer to our *ikigai*. Santos adds the concept of a 'side helpful,' which

43 Dan Witters, "US Wellbeing Declines Halted in 2019," *Gallup*, September 25, 2019.

triggers our brain's altruism center.[44] *Ikigai* is available to us all. We should all create the time and space necessary to explore it with an open and curious mind.

The Okinawan way of life, a confluence of *moai* and *ikigai*, or life-long community and a sense of deep purpose, can act as a guidebook for our own self-awareness, growth, and fulfillment. The days of the ownership of material things defining happiness are waning. Seventy-six percent of Millennials would rather spend their money on experiences than material things.[45] That concept reminds me of someone who's had a big impact on my family's life. I met my friend Ken Haas through my wife Trish during their time as colleagues in the Navy. Ken has built partnerships in government and industry and has already accomplished more than most of us could in two full careers. Today, Ken is focusing on his contribution to systems and outcomes that benefit tomorrow, defining that broadly and being open to different ways it may show up in life. Sometimes that looks like providing value to the next generation via mentoring and teaching, as Ken did for Trish. That mentorship opened up a new world for her, including:

- Realizing she deserved a seat at the table, literally and figuratively, regardless of the context or who was in the room.
- Provided her first introduction to the senior-most flag officer level, where Trish now leads on a daily basis.

---

44 Eva Ritvo MD, "The Neuroscience of Giving," *Psychology Today*, April 24, 2014.

45 John Rampton, "What Millennials Can Teach You About Being Happy," Inc, July 31, 2017.

- Named it when Trish was experiencing impostor syndrome but couldn't pin the feeling down—more on this concept later.
- Empowered her to offer honest and direct feedback—one of life's most powerful and least utilized skills.

Trish relayed a story to me about Ken that helps paint the picture of this powerful mentorship. While attempting to finalize a year-long foreign military sales deal with one of our key naval allies, Ken and Trish traveled abroad for a series of high-stakes bi-lateral meetings where important hand would shake important hand. On the last day of meetings, which served as a crescendo to the days-long story arc, Trish made an important connection and jotted it down on a scrap of paper. She passed the scrap under the table to Ken, her senior and client, and Ken read the note. He immediately passed it back to Trish and mouthed, "Go ahead and say it." She did just that, and the outcome the US Navy needed was achieved, due in no small part to Ken's empowerment and deliberate ceding of some of his accrued personal power to Trish.

Ken and others like him, focused on their contribution, also invest their energy in the context of family (both those we're born into and those we choose). For Ken, that includes his amazing wife, Sharon, a consummate healthcare professional in an era when being that is more challenging than ever. Ken's focusing lens for continuing to deliver his important contribution to the world struck me. He crystalized the importance of not mentoring or coaching in a way that makes others conform to his own personal visions of success, but rather helping others connect to their own unique purpose. For me,

Ken's brand of contribution connects directly to the Okinawan big ideas we've just covered.

In this brave new world, we must deploy tools and ideas like *moai* and *ikigai* to question our assumptions, challenge old ways of thinking, and achieve new levels of fulfillment.

LIFE'S WORK

Everyone thinks of changing the world, but no one thinks of changing himself.

—LEO TOLSTOY

One afternoon, I found myself in a small but comfortably appointed room in a shared-use office building in downtown Washington, DC. The space offered all the hallmarks of being inhabited by a highly intelligent person for quite a while. Overloaded bookshelves sagged ever-so-perceptibly in the middle of their span under the weight of a wild mix of textbooks, psychological journals, compendiums of all flavors of art, and what drew my eye most: literature. As I scanned right to left, I picked out Nabokov, Vonnegut, Burroughs' *Naked Lunch,* and what I suspected was a first edition of *Gravity's Rainbow* by Thomas Pynchon. I remember my glance stopping on a well-loved copy of *The Death of Ivan Ilyich* by Leo Tolstoy. I made instant connections to my study of Russian history as an undergraduate and also to my later attempt at reading *Anna Karenina*. I'd never read this particular work from Tolstoy though I appreciate his full *oeuvre*, and in my inner universe, it centered the office's inhabitant as learned and as someone whose perspective I'd enjoy.

It was in this office that I learned the idea of mindfulness—not the overhyped, over-commercialized Western version, but the less boastful, stiller iteration embodied by those close to the concept's Buddhist roots. I left that office with a recommendation to explore Thich Nhat Hanh's work *You Are Here*. I picked up a copy soon after and set it aside until I felt I could devote the focus it required.

About a week after discovering mindfulness, I was flying to Denver with my son Skye, members of his Boy Scout troop, and other adult leaders. We were bound for the Philmont Scout Ranch, a sprawling mountain wilderness in northern New Mexico designed as a backcountry area where Scouts can embark on a two-week, unsupported backpacking journey. Despite a razor focus on pack weight, I'd brought my copy of *Be Here Now* to dive into outside of the realities of everyday life. Our backcountry guide, who accompanied us for the first few days of our trek, was a nineteen-year-old Oklahoma State University student named Nathan Moore. Nathan took an earnest and abiding interest in the book I'd brought with me, maybe because a book on a Philmont trek is a rare sighting. Or perhaps it was because of what I learned was genuine curiosity. I lent him the book, and he spent each minute of his limited downtime sitting alone under pine trees reading the words of a Vietnamese Buddhist monk. Nathan's focus and ritual inspired me, and as I later read the thin volume, a brief and dull ache in my temples told me that my mind was stretching in a new way. Separated from modern society's realities in the New Mexico high country, I observed each of our troop's boys demonstrating hallmarks of their own mindfulness: listening to each other more deeply and recalling information they'd only recently learned faster and with more fidelity as just two examples.

What appeals to me most about mindfulness as a way to focus mental energy is that it offers an unencumbered, readily available alternative to how most of us move through life each day. Whether our particular flavor is a laser focus on the future that manifests as planning and engineering, or a penchant to examine and reexamine the past, we can all tap into the wellspring of this concept. I tend to invest significant mental energy both in casting my mind back to past events in search of meaning as well as pondering what the future might hold. Mindfulness, meanwhile, tells us that something as universal and accessible as our own breathing can be the center of a different way. Author, naturalist, CIA officer, Zen teacher, and candidate for the person I'd most like to have a beer with Peter Matthiessen sums it up beautifully in his novel *The Snow Leopard*. I like to read this quote slowly, focusing on each word: "In this very breath that we take now lies the secret that all great teachers try to tell us."[46]

When I find myself deep inside my usual productive member of society mindset, I experience those words as overly didactic. But when I find my own centered, contemplative space, usually while riding my bike, a deeper meaning emerges. Especially in our modern world, it's common to yearn for simplicity and to feel overburdened by life's trappings—some chosen and some not. An intentional letting go, however brief, through a focus on the reality and availability of the

---

46 Peter Matthiessen, *The Snow Leopard* (New York: Viking Press, 1978).

current moment and nothing else gives us ready access to that simplicity and focus.

SELF-AUTHORSHIP

Like most lives, mine so far has been indelibly impacted by the human beings around me. I chose to study Russian history as a sophomore undergraduate because my Introduction to Russian History professor, James West, was the most enthralling storyteller I'd ever encountered. His ability to hook and hold my attention in the very first class of the semester turned into a degree focused on the topic. That degree sharpened my literary skills, which landed me my first job after school as an editorial assistant at CQ Press in Washington, DC. That job led indelibly to where and who I am today. As we hop from lily pad to lily pad in our lives, our leaps are often precipitated by human connection. Sometimes that dynamic manifests as a friend helping us land work in a new field. Other times, a family member jolts us from the stasis holding us somewhere or doing something that doesn't serve us. Relationships truly do shape the contours of our lives.

As important as social connection is to our childhood and adult development, it's no surprise that we often predicate our self-worth relationally, based on the feedback, emotions, or actions of those who matter to us. We truly do need one another. This can clash with the concept of personal self-determination that is common in some parts of the world. Scientist Matthew Lieberman offers an interesting perspective: "In the West, we like to think of ourselves as relatively immune to [the] sway of those around us while we each pursue our personal destiny. But I think this is a story we like to tell ourselves rather than what really happens."[47] No matter what our particular *zeitgeist* might lead us to believe, we are social, relational creatures. We need other people not just to feel like part of a pack but also to place our personal meaning in the context of something greater than ourselves.

To that end, it's worthwhile to explore developmental psychologist Robert Kegan's adaptation and interpretation of Jean Piaget's foundational work on cognitive development. Therein, Kegan overlaid a critical emotional dynamic that was absent from Piaget's earlier body of knowledge. Kegan dubbed his new construct the "Evolution of Consciousness," itself composed of five stages:

- **Order 0:** A phase that covers the first years of life, where infants exist in an "objectless" world until they begin to differentiate their surroundings.
- **Order 1:** A phase, usually beginning around two years of age, where a child grasps that they're in control of their own bodies.
- **Order 2:** Instrumental Mind. A young person begins organizing their thoughts and memories into groupings.
- **Order 3:** Socialized Mind. An individual grasps the basics of processing emotions and binds to the norms and beliefs constructed by their community.
- **Order 4:** Self-Authoring Mind. An individual seeks out relationships and environments that are beneficial for others instead of only for themselves; recognizes

47 Gareth Cook, "Why We Are Wired to Connect," *Scientific American*, October 22, 2013.

interpersonal relationships as a critical mechanism to further their own intentional personal evolution.

- **Order 5:** Self-Transforming Mind. An individual is capable of leading effectively in complex systems. They can hold multiple tensions and contradictions without erosion of their own problem-solving abilities.

Perhaps you are a self-authoring individual. Perhaps you 'can see knowledge as something fluid and changing' and 'are also able to differentiate more easily between [your] own values and societal or relational demands.'[48] For self-authors, the strong lines of demarcation that define a subject and an object shift to a model of interconnectedness and are highly permeable in nature. What comes from within is far more important than what is encountered without. There's an important distinction between a socialized mind and a self-authoring mind. Consider a soldier who acts in a just fashion because the Military Code of Conduct is important to them versus a soldier who acts in a just fashion because they've internalized and personally contextualized ideas like justice, truth, and mercy. Those soldiers might make the same decisions in a warzone, but their paths to that decision likely look quite different.

Self-authoring leaders have much to teach those around them and often spend portions of their lives doing just that. Some consensus picks for the world leader hall of fame, including names like Martin Luther King, Jr., Mahatma Gandhi, and Abraham Lincoln, are self-authoring individuals. Nelson

---

48 Sharon L. M. Stone, "Examining the development of self-authorship among student veterans" (PhD diss., William and Mary, 2014), 7.

Mandela, of course, is a part of that same rarified leadership air, and serves as a wonderful example of the concept we're exploring now. Theologian and human rights activist Desmond Tutu called Mandela a 'moral colossus' and 'the undisputed icon of forgiveness and reconciliation.'[49] Mandela credited his life's work to self-awareness and universal humanity as a foundation for action, rather than an externality like the apartheid system he worked to disempower and reconcile with: "If there was a silver lining to his years of imprisonment, Madiba said it was to look in the mirror and create within himself that which he most wanted for South Africa: peace, reconciliation, equality, harmony, and freedom. Perhaps his most profound impact and greatest legacy was to teach us, through vivid, living, personal example, to be human before anything else."[50] Mandela suffered and toiled so those around him, both in his native South Africa and the exploited around the world, could live a better life than he'd experienced himself. In this way, Mandela is an inspirational example of self-authorship.

THE SUCCESS EQUATION

In Chapter 1, we learned about the Jessie Ball duPont Fund and Marty Lanahan, Chair for the trustees for JBdF. Now it's time to learn about that wonderful organization's president, Mari Kuraishi. During our time collaborating in Florida, I marveled at Mari's quiet authority. She manages to be simultaneously kind and welcoming to her staff and guests while voicing her perspective with the kind of certitude and

---

49 "Nelson Mandela lived as a moral colossus," US Africa Online, December 9, 2013.

50 Kevin and Jackie Freiberg, "Madiba Leadership: 5 Lessons Nelson Mandela Taught The World About Change," Forbes, July 19, 2018.

grounding in facts that make those within earshot sit up a bit straighter. Mari counts the creation of the World Bank's Development Marketplace as well as the founding of the crowdfunding philanthropy platform Global Giving in her accomplishments, and I knew I needed a chance to pick her brain more.

Many of the insights Mari named during our conversation for this work stood out to me through the lens of big ideas for the self. When prompted what one big idea she would gift to her younger self, she responded that a recalibration on the factors that go into what she calls the success equation would have been an important epiphany for her. As a true achiever, Mari grew up believing that hard work, persistence, and raw effort were the sole determinants of success. However, her life experience showed that the concatenation of factors that she characterizes as 'initial start conditions' contributes to an individual's long-term success. Those conditions include things like socioeconomic status, race, health, personality and temperament, and other factors that impact a person's access to basic human requirements and higher order opportunity. Given our country's current reckoning with social justice, Mari's naming of initial start conditions resonated with me in a big way.

With the gift of this hindsight, Mari identified the value of teaching young people about the degree to which success is contingent on factors not in their control through a positive lens while still instilling in them the importance and value of hard work. I was struck by the criticality of being able to hold this distinction without feeling helpless to one's circumstances. Rather, we must be aware of the fact that none of us can control everything in our lives. There are absolutely times when an outcome will occur that we won't want irrespective of how much energy and effort we put into making a different outcome occur. This has important implications for how we can each judiciously invest our energy, and how we define what our own personal success looks like.

In retrospect, I feel privileged to have met Mari in Florida. As fate or luck would have it, JBdF staff and trustees were also finalizing their organizational values, using inputs from Global Giving as one of several touchstones. One of those values is 'Always Open,' something Mari characterizes as key "because good ideas can come from anyone, anywhere, any place, and we have to make sure that our preconceived expectations of who comes up with good ideas or where they come from don't get in the way of their actual discovery."[51] From my perspective, the idea of always being open perfectly encapsulates the concept of democratization, and it all starts with each of us.

OUR OWN PERSONAL WHY

'There seems to be plenty of it,' was all I would answer when the investigator asked me to say what I felt about time.

—ALDOUS HUXLEY, *THE DOORS OF PERCEPTION*

Each of us must find our own agency in our lives and circumstances. Our 'why' underpins the discovery that social con-

[51] TedX Talks, The Power of Us | Mari Kuraishi | TEDxTraverseCity." September 26, 2014. Video, 20:25.

structs, the opinions of others, and our environment need not rule how we move through the world. That intrinsic motivation looks different for each person based on our wants, needs, and what we value, and we must find it for ourselves in our own time.

Swiss-American psychiatrist Elisabeth Kübler-Ross states, "People are like stained-glass windows. They sparkle and shine when the sun is out, but when the darkness sets in their true beauty is revealed only if there is light from within." Your own inner light is out there waiting to be discovered. If you've already found yours, it's your responsibility to guide and teach others as they search for theirs.

Each day, we rely on technology, new business models, and modern mobility. The insights of others are more available to more people than ever before. There is no doubt that these things have substantively improved our lives, but perhaps they have also come to define us in a way. What's left of us when all of the wonders of modern technology melt away or must be left behind? What can something as simple as our breath and as deep as our unique personal drive teach us? Armed with the tools of mindfulness and the distinction of self-authorship, we can leave behind the noise and chatter that distract us from our true purpose to focus intently on the signal that can show us our way.

Perspective is everything. When considered by others, the particular 'why' that drives us as individuals can be difficult to fully grasp. However, for each of us, our own "why" should be immutable—concrete, tangible, and really real. Aldous Huxley was as great a philosopher and experimenter as he was an author, and his characterization of time as truly relative applies to big ideas as well. Now that we've considered some ideas that punch above their weight through the lens of self, let's begin to widen our aperture.

CHAPTER 5

SHIFTING FROM ONE TO MANY

All of humanity's problems stem from man's inability to sit quietly in a room alone.

—BLAISE PASCAL

On my most challenging days, few words speak more directly to my frustration, anger, or hurt more than these from Pascal. Ninety-nine times out of one hundred, that hurt stems from a botched interaction with another person, an errant word from another or to another, or something I observed between two or more other people. Humans are social creatures—every fiber of our being cries out for comrades and community. More often than not, the harsh realities of ourselves in relation to those around us can create distance. This sets up an internal tension that can often manifest externally.

Thankfully, many of the world's finest minds have tackled this precise issue, each from their own unique perspective. This is not to say that the work has been done for us, but rather to illustrate that a map and compass exist. We must choose not only to avail ourselves of them, but to properly orient our minds to and set out into the world with them. Before we embark on engaging with others, our loved ones, coworkers, or strangers on the street, it is vital to set our intention by tuning into what makes us uniquely us. Good, bad, and indifferent are all in play here and affect the world around us profoundly whether we realize it or not.

My best insight with regard to these highly interpersonal learnings is to try them on like a new coat, without attachment or too much hope for perfection. You'll know when you find something that fits.

THE ICEBERG: ACKNOWLEDGING AND DISMANTLING UNCONSCIOUS BIAS

Hello. My name is Hans. By sheer good luck, I was born into privilege. I came into the world, in no particular order:

- Caucasian
- Male
- American
- Intact nuclear family
- Food and home security
- Ready access to quality education
- No abuse at home or other institutions
- Not displaced by war, famine, or ethnic cleansing
- Not the direct target of racism

Though my mother and father were both born and raised in San Antonio, Texas, their family stories are very different. My father's family is predominantly German, having immigrated by ship from Europe, landing many years ago on the Texas gulf coast and working their way inland to the San Antonio area. Conversely, my mother's family is predominantly Mexican, making an overland journey from the south across the border into Texas, also several generations ago. The product of this strange-to-some-but-not-for-south-Texas union is a relatively fair-skinned, 'white-looking' person with one foot in each cultural world. As a result, I can inhabit my Hispanic roots, which I value and identify with deeply, when I feel I need to call on them. I choose when I want others to see me through the lens of 'other' here in the United States. That choosing is something that few have access to, and it is a privilege I recognize and am working to unpack and own more fully.

Despite the sea of head starts mentioned above, I stumbled upon the concept of unconscious bias relatively late in life, gaining exposure to it as I have so much in my adult life: at my firm, The Clearing. Throughout my journey, I've watched a common dynamic play out where value is shifted to the person with power and away from those without power. Consider, for example, a superior you may have worked for at one time who always seemed to give the choice assignments to your colleague with whom they shared many similar life experiences instead of someone with whom they shared little or nothing. Unconscious bias pervades everything around us, from our daily interactions with one another through the largest social constructs in the land, government, industry, law enforcement, social services, and many others.

To understand what unconscious bias is, we must first do three things. First, we must truly understand what it is. Next, we must wrap our heads around the fact that every human is biased—including ourselves. Finally, we must engage in frank conversations in diverse group settings about how we can broaden our perspective and empathize more fully with our fellow humans. All of these things combine to give us the latticework that we require to dismantle bias of all kinds, starting with ourselves. Each of these tasks is no small thing. Let's take them one at a time.

WHAT IS UNCONSCIOUS BIAS?

Sigmund Freud laid down the canonical distinction between the conscious and the unconscious mind, and their components and products:

Conscious = *Thoughts; Perceptions; Memories; Stored Knowledge*

Unconscious = *Fears; Irrational Wishes; Selfish Needs; Shameful & Traumatic Experiences; Instincts*

For the visual thinkers and processors out there, consider the distinction between conscious and unconscious thought thusly. Human thinking is like an iceberg. Roughly 10 percent is on display to us and others, above the waterline and visible to an observer. Fully 90 percent of our brain's activity, storage, and inner life is underwater and away from view both to us in our day-to-day life and to those around us. Similarly, only a small portion of our biases are known to us. Even when they are apparent to an independent observer, acknowledging our own bias is difficult and often painful or difficult. Some find it impossible to do or refuse to recognize their own inherent biases.

Freud believed that while the unconscious mind is largely inaccessible, its contents can sometimes bubble up unexpectedly. Dreams, Freudian slips, free association: these are all glimpses into a deep well of memories, connections, long-forgotten knowledge, and even trauma. Much of each of our biases are likewise unconscious in nature. Few of us actively choose to act, think, or feel in a biased fashion, and yet we are all biased. Researchers at the Vanderbilt School of Equity, Diversity, and Inclusion believe that unconscious bias most often occurs automatically as our minds pull on our own personal history, environment, and interactions to make split-second judgments about people and the world around us.[52] Through this lens, we can recognize that unconscious biases are biological in nature and even in origin. However, that doesn't explain away or render null the negative impact they can have.

Our 'reptile brain,' meaning our limbic system, and particularly our amygdala, play a large role in our biased observations and decision-making. One of the amygdala's primary jobs is to process inputs and equate them with a fear-based response, often out of scale and proportion with the input itself. Social scientist and author Daniel Goleman coined the phrase *amygdala hijack*, where our reptile brain overrides our conscious mind, itself in control of things like decorum and logic. In these situations, our decision-making can be overtaken by forces like unconscious bias, often for a

---

52 "Unconscious Bias," Vanderbilt University, accessed September 25, 2020.

biological reason. Our limbic brain, namely our amygdala, can process information several milliseconds faster than our prefrontal cortex. Literally, the part of our brain that triggers fear-based, fight-or-flight responses operates faster than our logical brain. Our logical brain not only can't keep up, but *can't catch up* on its own.[53]

Think of your brain as a massively complex filter, not unlike the water filter in your refrigerator. Part of its function is to let through the 'good' and catch the 'bad' by ingesting information from our surroundings and referencing it against past experiences and stored data. When pressured, stressed, or without ample time to process, we often revert to habits: ways of thinking formed long ago based on limited or biased information. When combined with the fact that our reptile brain, itself shaped and dominated by forces like our fear response and our biases, can function and dictate decisions faster than our brain's logic centers, it's no wonder that unconscious bias is so prevalent in society at large.

WE ARE ALL BIASED

Regardless of how well-traveled we are or how far along our self-awareness journey we fancy ourselves to be, the fact of the matter is that we are all biased. Biases are *deep structures* in our brains, patterns so well-worn that they become almost indistinguishable from our own personalities. Associating an emotional response such as joy, revulsion, arousal, or intense sadness with an object, place, or person is a perfect example of a *deep structure*. Thanks to Ivan Pavlov and his

---

53 Daniel Goleman, *Emotional Intelligence: Why It Can Matter More Than IQ* (New York: Bantam Books, 1995).

salivating dogs, we can now name that deep structure as a Pavlovian response (or classic conditioning for you purists out there).

We are all biased. There is no shame in acknowledging this reality to ourselves or others. The question is not whether or not we are biased, *but rather which biases are ours.*

Before we can take action, we must first carefully examine our own biases. In the case of unconscious bias, we may require candid observations and feedback from others, ideally in a safe environment where we can be as vulnerable and open as possible. In that careful self-examination and observation of those around us, we'll likely find some of those most common forms of unconscious bias. This is hard work. It also must be done if we want to be truly open to the power and potential innate in each of us.

In service of beginning this hard work, let's name and examine some of the most prevalent forms of unconscious bias. Have you ever experienced someone who shares much in common with you as more pleasant than someone who has little in common with you? If so, you're likely in the grips of one of the most subtle and widespread versions of unconscious bias: *affinity bias.* Ever heard a colleague or friend remark that a well-dressed individual 'cares more about themselves' than someone more casually dressed in the same environment? Or that someone who conforms to the traditional standards of attractiveness is more appealing than those who diverge from those same standards? That's *beauty bias* at work. Perhaps you've sometimes let the position or opinion of a group override your own, even when you're sure your position is right or valid. We've all been there—unconsciously in the thrall of *conformity bias*. Failure is always a complex experience, linked as it often is to the core of our identity. It's not uncommon to place blame where it doesn't belong in these situations—either on ourselves or on others. That's *attribution bias* wreaking havoc on our logic centers and making poor judgments on our behalf. Do you have a family member who only seems to engage with information or seek out interactions that reinforce their existing views on a particular issue, person, or facet of society? That particular echo chamber is built on *confirmation bias*. Anyone who considers certain tasks best suited for either a man or a woman, or more extremely, that men should exclusively do certain types of things and women others, is deep in the *gender bias* vortex.[54]

So, what's at stake if we don't acknowledge, deeply understand, and combat unconscious bias? That all depends on the context.

For individuals, unconscious bias can lead to:

- A lack of moral courage, or the willingness to stand up for an ideal in the face of apparent consequences [4] Rushworth Kidder, *Moral Courage* (New York: William Morrow Paperbacks, 2005).
- Ostracizing or alienating acts that are out of balance with more deeply held but abstract values, often in the context of social constructs like families and circles of friends

54 "12 Unconscious Bias Examples and How to Avoid Them in the Workplace," Built In, accessed September 25, 2020.

For groups and teams, unconscious bias can lead to:

- Excessive 'group think,' where outliers or dissenting opinions wither and die
- Reduced levels of creativity, as big thinkers tamp down or wholly extinguish their wildest and potentially most generative ideas
- Those same outliers tire of feeling alone within the group and leave to take their talents elsewhere

For businesses, unconscious bias can lead to:

- Being out of touch with their customer's needs, leading to irrelevancy as society evolves past or around them
- Alienated employees tire of a biased environment and leave for greener pastures, sometimes for a competitor
- A lack of felt safety blunts collective desire to invest the energy required to achieve organizational, financial, and strategic goals

Companies the world over are in an arms race for talent. And yet unconscious bias's prevalence is clear to see in a recent study examining the CEOs of Fortune 500 companies. Some of the data points are staggering. Fifty-eight percent are six feet or taller, while only 14.5 percent of American men are over six feet tall. Illogically, just over *6 percent are women*, while approximately *57 percent of the workforce* identifies as female. And finally, less than 1 percent of Fortune 500 CEOs are black, while zero are both black and identify as female.[55]

---

55 Michael Brainard, "The Impact Of Unconscious Bias On Leadership Decision Making," *Forbes*, September 13, 2017.

The question we must ask ourselves is this—are unusually tall white men better leaders than less tall women of color? Of course not. However, formal and informal systems build, incentivize, and perpetuate these out-of-proportion, irrational biases. Work, school, religious institutions, and governments are all examples of biased systems. Is unconscious bias at play at the highest levels of the world's most successful institutions? Assuredly yes.

ENGAGING UNCONSCIOUS BIAS HEAD-ON, AND GETTING TO WORK

Acknowledge and accept the fact that you, your neighbors, your family, and your colleagues are all biased. The sooner that happens, the sooner the shift can occur to doing something about it that will level the playing field for all. Remember, the question isn't whether or not we are biased, *but rather which biases are ours.*

Speaking openly and directly on the topic of unconscious bias can be frightening. It can shake some, especially those who believe themselves to be unbiased or particularly progressive at their core. Matters of identity are never easy to face head-on, but we each must. In order to most effectively and efficiently examine and then confront our unconscious biases, we should take a few tangible steps. First, create as safe a space as possible. Prioritize and ensure the comfort and empowerment of those on the short end of the power curve *first*, especially in team or group settings where not everyone has opted into an experience where unconscious bias will be explored. Each group defines 'safe space' differently. Set your group's intention by agreeing on the characteristics of the safe space together and record them in a way that can be referenced and reinforced whenever needed. Next, ask for some form of participation from all in a group or conversation. There can be no silent observers in a dialogue on unconscious bias. To abstain from digging into this and related topics is a prime example of how privilege comes into play for some and not others. Not everyone can decide to opt out of these dialogues because of factors beyond their control and choosing. If you are indeed capable of or are thinking about refraining from sharing with others on your own unconscious bias, make a *conscious* decision to become a more powerful ally by sharing and being vulnerable. Finally, make commitments and stick to them after the interaction or dialogue concludes. Actions speak louder than words, and rest assured that your family, friends, colleagues, and even strangers are watching to see if your actions align with your words and commitments.

THE BOTTOM LINE

Discrimination and bias are alive and well in American settings of all kinds. Our loved ones and valued colleagues suffer every day as a result of unconscious bias. Sometimes we're able to observe that suffering, but more often, it occurs below the proverbial water level. Each year, roughly two million Americans leave their jobs due to discrimination or unfairness, issues that can begin with a seed of bias. Examined through a purely financial lens, this mass exodus costs American companies about 64 billion dollars each year.[56] The mental, social, and emotional toll cannot be quantified.

---

56 "The Costly Business of Discrimination," Center for American Progress, accessed September 26, 2020.

One tangible step we can take to further acknowledge and manage or eradicate our own biases is to build our own checklists of 'small moves' that create *distance* in relation to those around you. These are small actions or words we deploy in relation to those around us. Sometimes we choose to do so, while other times, we fall into the words or behaviors like a reflex reaction due to our biases. Have you ever been having dinner with a group of friends and either failed to acknowledge or deliberately ignored another's idea? Maybe you've even moved on to champion the very same idea when it's put forth by another person or retold that person's story without crediting them. Perhaps you are consistently mispronouncing someone's name (we all know you're smarter than that). Maybe you look away or roll your eyes when a particular person contributes to a conversation. Each of these small moves creates a bit of distance between you and your fellow human. Those small spaces add up to big spaces over time and affect decision-making, mental health, and livelihoods.[57]

Equally important, build a similar list of small moves that create *inclusion and connection*. One example includes responding constructively and appreciatively when someone offers an opinion you disagree with, while another is to seek out someone whom you don't interact with often and solicit their opinion on a topic that you both have a stake in. Also, make sure you acknowledge the bravery required when someone shares a personal detail or story that you've never heard before. Set specific goals for yourself when it comes to eliminating unconscious bias from your own mind. Find

---

57 "Micro-Inequities: 40 Years Later," Psychology Today, accessed September 26, 2020.

an accountability partner who you know and trust, someone who won't let you off the hook in service of achieving your goal. Remember, unconscious bias not only hurts others, it doesn't serve you either. Eradicating unconscious bias removes the inhibitors that stop you from creating the best version of yourself.

My friend Martha Johnson served as my very first professional mentor, starting when she noticed a twenty-two-year-old bewildered employee desperately trying to find a groove as a new management consultant. Before we met at Touchstone Consulting Group, she served as an executive at many private sector companies, as well as a leader within the Clinton-Gore transition team. She'd go on to lead the General Services Administration under President Barack Obama, and in short, is one of the most gifted leaders and communicators I've had the good fortune to meet and know. When we got to talk through the lens of this book, Martha highlighted something I've long felt: the power of storytelling and its uniquely human gravity. I bring this up because I believe storytelling, especially Martha's brand of it, can be one of the most powerful tools we can all use to dismantle bias of any kind, but especially unconscious bias.

While actions speak louder than words, building precision and intentionality in our written and verbal communication can send a powerful, positive message. Words build part of the bridge we can use to shift from applying big ideas for ourselves to harnessing their power for good with others. Now that we're more aware of the unseen forces that act on us and have maybe even claimed some of our own biases, it's time to build intentionality into how we express ourselves.

WORDS AS TOOLS AND WORDS AS WEAPONS

Your beliefs become your thoughts
Your thoughts become your words
Your words become your actions
Your actions become your habits
Your habits become your values
Your values become your destiny

—MAHATMA GANDHI

The beginning of wisdom is to call things by their right name.

—CONFUCIUS

Words can shape our mindset, our emotions, and, most importantly, how we choose to act or not to act. For a practiced and skilled engineer of the written word, some careful consideration and a few minutes can make the difference between words that merely communicate and words that move humans. That engineer starts and ends their craft with an unwavering focus on the consumer of their words. What are their deepest desires? Where are their beliefs malleable? How can a carefully placed phrase shift their worldview just so in order to achieve a specific outcome? In short, how can the written word speak into the others' listening?

For a moment, consider how these two statements make you feel. First, read this statement out loud:

"My life feels hopeless. There is no one for me to confide in, let alone rely on. I have no hope that this will change anytime soon."

Then, read this statement out loud:

"This must be what hell feels like. There is no one to turn to. I am just a shadow of a shadow of a shadow—always trying to catch up with myself. My loved ones and sweetest friends have forgotten I ever existed. Life isn't worth living. I feel in my bones that no respite exists for me. In fact, I know my life will continue to disintegrate, though I cannot imagine a desolation deeper than what I feel now."[58]

In their essence, these two statements convey essentially the same information. Each is bleak. Each feels hopeless. However, perhaps you noticed yourself moving from word to word and sentence to sentence in the first statement without a creeping sensation of growing inertia. Perhaps it felt like a series of thoughts you have the power to navigate through, using and deploying well-worn coping mechanisms that we avail ourselves of in times of trouble. In short, the first statement is something you can probably read, experience, and move past without a massive investment of physical and emotional effort before going about your day.

The chances are that reading through the second statement felt more akin to a death march, one perhaps marked by a sinking feeling deep in your gut. You may have remembered a trauma from your childhood, or the too-soon passing of a loved one. For those fortunate enough to have a beloved wife, husband, or significant other, maybe you recalled a deep transgression that you've never had the courage to reveal. It

---

58 Adapted from Matthew Budd and Larry Rothstein, "You Are What You Say," *New Age* Vol 17:9 (2000) 1–6.

may call to mind despair, shame, desperation, anguish, or darkness. In short, the core of the second statement conveyed the same basic information as the first, but arrived there in a completely different way.

Chilean statesman Fernando Flores performed a series of similar exercises after learning about the power of words while in prison due to his associations with Salvador Allende. His time there cemented the linkage between words and action: specifically, the power of words to direct and influence action from others. Flores summed the difference between the first and second statements thusly: "Do you see that your speaking has changed your body, your mood, your physiology, and your possibilities for action? Language has generated a moment of life for you. The action of languaging changed you like a drug."[59] Flores rightly states that some words inhibit action while others energize it. For instance, in times of crisis, certain words and phrases elicit panic that may not in more 'normal' times, while other words that would not usually register on the emotional scale can be deeply comforting when an individual or group of people sense danger. Relatedly, those in the blush of new love, on the market for their first home, or newly pregnant are susceptible to different words, phrases, tonalities, and communication methods as compared to those not. Jewelry, wedding planning, and real estate companies know and exploit this to hook and maintain brand loyalty with their customers.

More universally, linguists and social scientists have long studied formulations of language for different purposes. For

---

59 Ibid.

instance, how can a manager most efficiently and clearly craft a message that features a request as its operative element? How can a leader in a non-hierarchical company formulate a command message without confusing or putting off their employees, or a two-star Navy Admiral persuade other officers and enlisted personnel to act or *not act* without a direct order?

Crafting a statement, request, or command that can go beyond merely conveying information is an art. Building intention into your verbal and written communication is one of the most high-value big ideas you can harness, regardless of your work, dreams, or current reality. Language and its crafting are equally accessible to us all. Thus they serve as a great equalizer. In order to most effectively harness this power for our own good, it is helpful to first understand a bit of the lineage and shift from linguistics as pure semantic exercise to crafted words designed to motivate and encourage action.

J. L. Austin coined the term *speech acts:* the choosing and use of words to achieve a specific, active outcome. This positioned the words we know as a powerful vehicle for social activity instead of simply conveying meaning. His best-known work is delightfully titled *How to Do Things with Words*, and would influence generations of linguists, philosophers, economists, and social scientists.

John Searle would pick up and run with Austin's concept of *speech acts* as a deliberate construction of words, grammar, syntax, diction, and emotional expression in his own work *Speech Acts*, and later, *Intentionality.* Searle draws clear lines between a series of statements that center on the same basic concept, but whose structure, direction, and punctuation make their recipients interpret them in completely different ways. For instance, consider:

1. Trish watched the baby bird fly.
2. Does Trish watch the baby bird fly?
3. Trish, watch the baby bird fly!
4. Would that Trish watch the baby bird fly!

Each focuses on the same basic premise (Trish watching the baby bird fly), but conveys different commands and inquisition with little more than small shifts in punctuation and sentence structure. Simple linguistic engineering opens up four possible intentions or suggested actions with basically the same words. Imagine what could be done when applying these same tactics to words of great consequence.

An example: consider the average Western workplace. A group of people, ostensibly convened to achieve a set of shared goals, comes together five days a week to invest their collective power. Communication flows constantly. Sometimes one person will make a statement and expect a response. In reality, their phrasing and choice of words requires no response (for instance *"I wish our company values were more up to date."*) Another kind of communication exists for individuals within the organization: a request (for instance *"Eliot, I'd like you to make our company values more up to date"*). There are two available responses to this communication: *yes* or *no*. Both are equally valid, given that the communication is structured and offered as a request. A third option also exists: a command. This type of communication makes us sit up a little straighter and focus, because it involves an expenditure of social capital (for instance *"Ivana and Evan, bring our company values up to date within five days*"). The only viable answer to a command is "yes," unless the receiver wants to challenge the authority of the command-giver. Though many of us hear the term "command" and immediately think of an order given from a superior to a subordinate, the reality is that anyone can deploy a command to anyone else given that the communication is conveyed in a structure built on trust.

I've been tuned in to the power of words since a young age, consuming poetry, literature, scholarship, and all things written (shout-out to my first-grade teacher Mrs. Brannen). Even then, my first exposure to our inherent ability to realize different outcomes by intentionally choosing our words and shaping speech and writing didn't come until I was exposed to The Primes at The Clearing. The Primes are series of forty-six universal patterns of high performance that show up consistently, regardless of what field you're in or what environmental factors affect you.

At The Clearing, we use The Primes on a daily basis—both with our clients and also with ourselves as colleagues and friends. I've used no other body of knowledge more consistently or to greater effect in my life and career. Let's take a look at a specific example through the lens of words as tools and words as weapons.

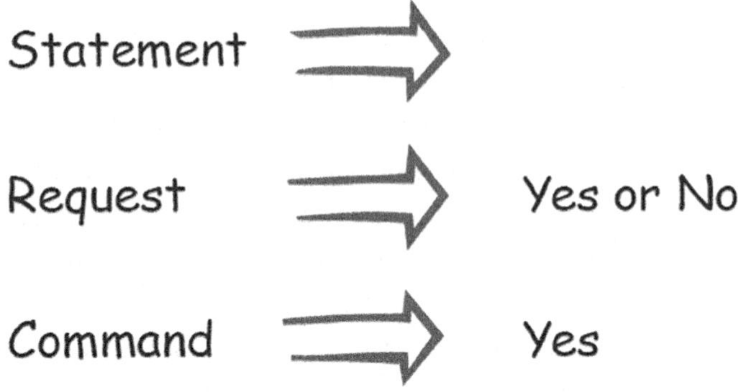

Image 2: Request Command Prime[60]

Powerful operators within systems, be it politics, a professional environment, a classroom, or a group of friends, carefully build intentionality into their external communication. Searle states that "to see a sentence as significant in general, we need to see that sentence as produced by an agent with certain intentions."[61] Powerful communicators consider the shape of the message they need to deliver, its urgency as well as the outcome they intend to achieve, for instance. They choose each word, punctuation mark, and verbal pause to achieve a reaction. This set of factors differentiates a casual statement aside from an urgent command.

Should the giver and the receiver of the communication come to an understanding about the terms of the communication itself, they enter into something called a *social contract.* Examples include an agreement to work together on a task or

60 Chris McGoff, *The Primes: How Any Group Can Solve Any Problem* (Hoboken: John Wiley & Sons, Inc., 2012), 128-131.

61 "Searle on Speech Acts," University of Idaho, accessed July 29, 2020.

for one person to deliver something to the other in a certain amount of time. Social contracts can be changed if needed, as long as both parties are earnest and are comfortable with direct engagement.

One of the most famous examples of a powerful and binding social contract was John F. Kennedy's declaration during his speech at Rice University on September 12, 1962. The Soviet Union had successfully launched Sputnik, the world's first artificial satellite, five years before Kennedy's speech. America was losing the space race, a point of national pride and perceived security. America felt the need to leap ahead of its geopolitical rival. At Rice, President Kennedy laid down a very public, carefully crafted piece of declarative leadership, imbued with the power of the Office of the President. "We choose to go to the moon. We choose to go to the moon in this decade and do the other things, not because they are easy, but because they are hard, because that goal will serve to organize and measure the best of our energies and skills, because that challenge is one that we are willing to accept, one we are unwilling to postpone, and one which we intend to win, and the others, too."[62] His words inspired an entire nation, helped convince Congress to dedicate an unprecedented amount of funding to the space race, and gave millions of involved people a tangible and motivational deadline. Neil Armstrong and Buzz Aldrin walked on the surface of the moon seven years later, a full five months before the president's deadline.

---

[62] John F. Kennedy, "Rice Stadium Moon Speech" (speech) September 12, 1962.

That social contract meant different things to different people. To the newly formed organization called NASA, it meant an unprecedented set of challenges and opportunities they would need to achieve in less than eight years' time. JFK tasked them with achieving the marker he'd laid down. To the American people, that social contract was a promise—an American to the moon and back, safely, before the end of the decade of the 1960s. Taking place during the heart of the Cold War, Kennedy promised Americans victory over an ideology, communism, that they felt threatened by at the time. It would be another great American triumph.

WORDS IN PRACTICE

Here again, I'm reminded of my time speaking with Admiral Frank Morley. In Chapter 3, we heard some wise words from the Admiral about taking ownership of and responsibility for your actions fully instead of passing the buck. As a senior leader in an organization as immense and distributed as his, Admiral Morley must choose his words carefully, persuading and convincing whenever possible, and reserving commands for when they're truly necessary. His considerable authority and span of control are powerful tools he can wield, but when we spoke, he focused much more on his successes and learnings from deploying words as tools to persuade, cajole, and convince. Like some of you reading this, Admiral Morley manages a diverse team that happens to be composed of both civilian employees and uniform Navy individuals. When I asked him what his most high-stress professional experience was, I was somewhat surprised to hear that it didn't come during his time as a Naval aviator. All Naval aviators are dynamic individuals, and Admiral Morley is no normal Naval aviator. In fact, he was the first to land the

Super Hornet jet fighter on a Navy aircraft carrier. And yet he stated that "flight is such a trained skillset that there actually aren't as many high-stress situations as you'd think. Focus is absolute; all distractions are engineered out or fall away." Rather, his most high-stress experiences came as the leader of a complex and diverse organization. While commands are still available to him, he must be judicious in how, when, and where he deploys that hard power. If he can solve an issue, remove a roadblock, or inspire a team to seize a responsibility with persuasion, a story, or some inspiration, that is far preferable. Admiral Morley reminded me of an important insight we can all take to heart: only call upon the hard power of a command when you have the necessary authority and when there is no other choice. Commands can come at a cost to you and others, but when time and efficiency are paramount, there are few things more powerful.

NOW WHAT?

Mastering your own words within your own context is one of the big ideas that's easiest for us all to harness. The precision required to intentionally use words as a mechanical advantage requires you to be much more precise about what you want, and how you plan to achieve it. More explicitly communicating what you want at work or with your loved ones increases your chances of getting what you want and need. People invest time, energy, and money in psychologists, coaches, and others who they think can help them achieve an outcome they feel incapable of achieving alone. In reality, using words as tools (and knowing how to avoid using words as weapons) could achieve many of the same goals.

One way to test out some of these ideas is to introduce the Statement / Request / Command structure into your written communication. Try using one of the three terms as the first word of the subject line of your next e-mail to ensure recipients know what sort of communication they're about to ingest. Then, go beyond tactics and frame your communication to fit. You'll find you get what you want and need more often.

Whether the concepts of intentional communication and speech acts are brand new to you, or you're a polished and experienced communicator, we all need to check back in with the concepts and tactics that make this one of the most important big ideas out there. The precision of language drives action, and actions make history. "Great leaders do not achieve great things by accident. They intend great things to happen, and in setting their intentions into a declaration, they give power to the ideas that motivate others to act."[63] How might you harness words as tools to build the reality you want to create?

---

63 Chris McGoff, *The Primes: How Any Group Can Solve Any Problem* (Hoboken: John Wiley & Sons, Inc., 2012), 58–61.

CHAPTER 6

BIG IDEAS FOR THE SELF + OTHERS

We've explored big ideas that can unlock introspection and drive change. We've also examined big ideas that bridge the gap between increasing self-awareness and how to amplify that growth and insight for more intentional interactions with others. This next chapter focuses on the next logical step: big ideas designed specifically to shift the dialogue, empower effective decision-making, and more intentionally coexist and interact with other people. As we've seen, self-growth is critical: growing in interpersonal situations is equally important.

GROUP DYNAMICS

It was the fall of 2014, and I was four days into a new job at The Clearing. Founded by Chris McGoff and John Miller, two established thought leaders in the field of group decision-making, The Clearing is differentiated from a veritable sea of competitors by its people-first approach to consulting rather than dogmatic adherence to any one approach or model. To add some context to the name, a clearing is a space where critical thought can flourish—a place where only the essential is allowed to enter in order to achieve an outcome that matters.

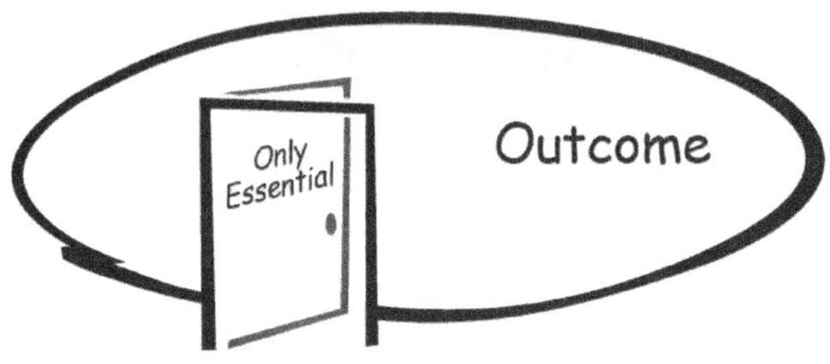

Image 3: A Clearing Prime[64]

We strive to create that metaphorical space for today's leaders who often find themselves bogged down by drudgery, routine, and minutiae. We strive to create an empty space where anyone can reconnect with their personal purpose and their most high-value outcomes. I'd had the good fortune to work at Chris and John's previous company: a management consulting firm that created many of the concepts and approaches perfected at The Clearing. It was also where I met a now dear colleague, Rasheedah.

It was the end of day four at The Clearing, and I was sitting just on the other side of the low divider from Rasheedah's

64 Chris McGoff, *The Primes: How Any Group Can Solve Any Problem* (Hoboken: John Wiley & Sons, Inc., 2012), 128–131.

workspace in our open bullpen. The day drew nearer to 5:00 p.m., and I resolved to press on through the seas of materials on specific projects I'd be supporting, The Clearing's methodologies, HR paperwork, and more. Suddenly, Rasheedah stood upright with a troubled look on her face. My eyes snapped up to scan her facial expression to see if I could readily discern anything. Lacking the context on which to hang my observations, this being a new office environment with different dynamics, I cut to the chase and asked what was wrong. Rasheedah said something that shifted the trajectory of my career. It turns out that one of our founders, Chris McGoff, was scheduled to lead a half-day Primes training session at a research-oriented federal agency in the DC area the next day, and the consultant slated to support Chris had a last-second personal emergency. In short, she needed to find a substitute within the next fifteen minutes before the potential replacements she'd need to tap began heading home.

As she explained the situation to me, I could sense that this was important. I told Rasheedah that I'd be happy to step in to deliver the session with Chris early the next morning, and as I saw the relief wash over my friend's face, I knew I'd made the right choice.

After a 5:00 a.m. wakeup and a before dawn metro ride out to Bethesda, Maryland, I met Chris near the main entrance to the agency where we'd deliver our insights to an intact leadership team of twenty. They represented the most senior leaders in the agency's Human Resources organization. I like to think I did a good job of hiding the fact that I felt a bit anxious and unmoored, and had only a functional knowledge of The Primes: our firm's group dynamics frameworks that Chris developed in concert with experts from numerous fields. I sat down and opened my laptop, ready to take notes, an echo of the behavior I'd learned from my previous job. Imagine my surprise when Chris told me, already knee-deep into delivery with our clients, to close my laptop, stand up, and 'get in the game.' At that moment, I felt my heart skip at least one beat as my mind raced to land on the proper response. Thankfully, I snapped into my response quickly, pushing my chair back to stand and striding to the front of the room with precisely no idea of what I'd do. In retrospect, I've never been more delighted to have been put on the spot and to have stepped into personal discomfort as I was to do so on that day.

Chris effortlessly held the group's attention, laying out the day's work and ensuring that each individual's voice made its way front and center with no delay. An enrolling function I didn't have a name for then but now recognize as a powerful tool arrayed against the collective inertia that silence in front of peers can engender. We moved from Prime to Prime: Consensus, Levels of Perspective, and Perimeter.[65] Each took center stage and gave our audience a name for things they'd sensed before but had never consciously acknowledged. Then, as he often does, Chris used the spoken and unspoken communication he received from the twenty humans in the room to call an audible that deviated from our session design for the day. He asked the group to stand, move to a different part of the large and open conference room, and form a circle. Then he asked an individual, we'll call her Anna, to come to

65 Chris McGoff, *The Primes: How Any Group Can Solve Any Problem* (Hoboken: John Wiley & Sons, Inc., 2012).

the middle of the circle. Chris asked each individual to think of a time when their most critical business outcomes relied in some way on Anna. Each individual shared a distinct experience, some more than one, and it became apparent even to me as a complete outsider that Anna was both wildly overworked and hopelessly overwhelmed. I remember focusing on her face as each of the twenty senior leaders shared their anecdotes and stories. Somewhere around anecdote number thirteen, Anna's facial expression began a curious deconstruction, which I had trouble placing at first. By the end of the exercise, she was in tears. Chris didn't even need to name the fact that there was a real-life tragedy of the commons issue at hand. On instinct, the leadership team rallied around Anna, both literally and figuratively, and their ways of working shifted in that moment. I truly learned to riff and improvise from Chris that day. Sometimes it's more important to trust your instincts and follow the energy that a group gives you in the moment than it is to execute a well-reasoned and agreed upon session design or overall plan.

That day with Chris marked the formal beginning of my professional journey down the path of observing and shaping behavior, both with individuals and especially in groups put together for specific reasons. In my work and life, I've seen human beings do and say things that have made me recoil and question our collective humanity. I've also personally experienced heartbreaking acts of self-sacrifice and bravery that fly in the face of logic. Most days aren't that interesting, but over the course of our lives, each of us has the opportunity to take in broad swaths of the spectrum of humanity should we choose to tune into it. We shape our own personalities and paths in life in large part based on our environments and the people who surround us. We are all products of our environments. Few things shape us more than collections of people: teams, companies, circles of friends, family, and many others.

Groupthink, herd mentality, the collective unconscious, esprit de corps, these are but a few of the dynamics that George Orwell, Gustave Le Bon, Carl Jung, and others raised from the unconscious to the collective consciousness and into each generation's *zeitgeist*. They name complex effects that defy our rational, polite minds and tap into something more primitive and primal. Within the human mind, and how one mind interacts with another, lies the cosmos' infinite depths and reaches. There is no more complex thing in the world.

With any complex system, certain things are in play when two or more people convene. Spoken and unspoken dynamics govern interpersonal actions, decision-making, and the distribution of resources. We're rarely as in tune with group dynamics as we are during the year-end holiday period. Think about the mental energy we invest in carefully recounting who has an issue with whom and how the awkward period of small talk during mealtime will go. That consideration veers between actual observation and experience and perception. Regardless, and whether or not we realize it, those dynamics govern our reality.

You can choose to understand group dynamics, and in so doing tap into some of their innate power to achieve outcomes either for yourself or in service of others. Consider the institutions we choose for ourselves. In a work context, we see leaders invest considerable energy into visioning, strategy development, and change and transformation efforts aimed at various future states precisely because those artifacts can serve as guides for the capacity generated by groups. A vision is just a conduit, built with intention, to channel the energy of groups of humans.

The frameworks mentioned above, The Primes, are universal patterns of group dynamics honed by years of experience and iterative improvement. Each Prime takes a pattern of group behavior and boils it down to its quintessence, all represented with a 'back of the napkin' style sketch imbued with a bit of color theory to boot. Why so simple? The philosophy that underpins this particular body of knowledge is that any person should be able to explain any Prime with little to no guidance or artistic skill, provided that they understand the content and have a connection to it from experience. In that regard, The Primes are a perfect example of effectively democratized frameworks. These patterns have unlocked a passion for group dynamics in me.

Another body of knowledge that excels at sourcing the wisdom of the crowd is Liberating Structures. One of my great mentors, Sharon Benjamin, reified the link between my knack for families of dynamics like The Primes and Liberating Structures, amongst others. This collection of approaches to effective group engagement fills the space between the overly structured and the too loosely structured. "Conventional structures are either too inhibiting (presentations, status reports, and managed discussions) or too loose and disorganized (open discussions and brainstorms) to creatively engage people in shaping their own future. They frequently generate feelings of frustration and/or exclusion and fail to provide space for good ideas to emerge and germinate."[66] I like to think of Liberating Structures as defined practices to ensure that every voice in a group is not only heard, but that every individual's best thinking is drawn out and applied to whatever goal the group is tackling.

Once you begin to observe group dynamics at work in the various systems that you're a part of, it can be difficult to not see them in play. Though I never studied economics in school and was, in fact, more comfortable amidst literature and history than statistics and science, there is a pleasing symmetry in the application of economic theory to human systems through my work today. One example that springs to mind is a key component of behavioral economics, namely Amos Tversky and Daniel Kahneman's *prospect theory.* Therein, we learn that a person or group's willingness to take a risk in order to avoid a loss (monetary or otherwise) usually outweighs the pleasure derived from receiving a guaranteed reward.[67] Group dynamics and other applied social sciences help us understand that the behavior not just of individuals, but of groups large and small is vital to understanding and attempting to predict how people and groups will make decisions and assign value. The social and economic implications of this field of study cannot be overstated; they hold value for each of us that we can and should tap into.

I feel it's important to name that my innate seeking nature is perhaps responsible for the abundance of energy I have for

---

66 "Introduction," Liberating Structures: Including and Unleashing Everyone, accessed September 23, 2020.

67 "An Introduction to Behavioral Economics," BehavioralEconomics.com, accessed September 23, 2020.

this topic. I acknowledge the same may not be the case for each of you. However, I strongly believe those who acknowledge the focus and intention that the right application of group dynamics can bring to a team or organization can build and offer more refined insights, products, and outcomes. Furthermore, you need not be group dynamics experts yourselves in every situation. In fact, an external, independent observer and guide can offer insight that may go unnoticed or unnamed by a group itself. Furthermore, we are fortunate to live in an age of near-ubiquitous knowledge resources. Anyone with the will can find a way to build their own expertise.

Great forces and dynamics shape our world, whether we acknowledge them or not. When we bend our will toward the uncovering of those patterns, we tap into the structures and energy that makes our societies function or fall apart. A working knowledge of some of the most prevalent, timely interpersonal and group dynamics can serve as a unifying force for good in a time when the world needs us to band together and remain intact more than ever.

LEARNING WITH MATT

My friend Matt Goodrich probably should've made an appearance earlier in this work. I feel I could write another entire book on our shared triumphs and the times we fell flat on our faces together: such is the volume of our shared experience. We met in our mid-20s, working on technology programs together, Matt as a federal employee and me as a management consultant. Along with our colleague Zach Baldwin, whom I connected with immediately and still call a confidant today, I always felt I had friends and allies at work.

In talking to Matt for this book, I remembered one of the reasons our relationship endures job changes, moves, and more: we both know and feel the value of engaging the whole human at work. Our personal work philosophy is a lot like our personal life philosophy: expand what's possible and have a hell of a lot more fun by offering access to each part of yourself to your colleagues. Of course, we also must make it clear we're interested in receiving the same back from them.

This said, boundaries are important, and I need to frequently remind myself that not everyone wants or needs to share as much of themselves as I do. Some prefer to compartmentalize their psyches by engaging in a professional context at work and a personal fashion at home. Matt and I, however, love the challenge of building trust outside of the traditional confines of the work sphere. We both think the most interesting things in life happen on the edges—around the boundaries between one thing and another. I've consistently been astonished by how powerfully my colleagues at The Clearing, as well as many of our clients and partners, choose to show up when you extend an invitation to connect on a more meaningful and personal level.

As good friends do, Matt reminded me of a simple idea that I've found punches well above its weight (especially in American business culture): *busy is not a badge of honor.* Both of us learned early on that being occupied signaled that you were valuable and important, so we found ways to take on far more than our true capacity could allow. Breaches of integrity can follow in those situations. Matt shared that he's had to deprogram himself from the idea of busy being a badge of honor and instead focuses now on delivering value in as efficient a manner as possible. Creativity and innovation emerge when you combine trust, the whole human, and some positive constraint.

Matt, here's to continuing our shared journey.

LADDER OF INFERENCE

Have you ever been a part of an action or occurrence that solicited a reaction, either from yourself or from another, that was so out of proportion to the original experience that it made your head spin? Perhaps one of your family members has a tendency to check their phone during meals or in shared settings, ostensibly 'family time.' That observable behavior can get combined with memories, past experiences, and the context of the setting or environment you're in to result in that out-of-proportion reaction. Perhaps in this example, a family member snatches the cell phone from their loved one's hands or demands that they ignore their phone for the remainder of the night. Maybe they even ban the use of the phone for some period of time. From the eyes of an independent observer, any of those reactions would be deemed overly harsh. The observer would also have difficulty connecting the observable behavior (family member checking cell phone at dinner) with the ultimate reaction (snatched phone or phone ban). A big idea that I use almost every day reveals what happens in between those two data points, and since I learned it, I'm unable to *not* see it at play all around me.

I first discovered the Ladder of Inference, a concept created by organizational and business theorist Chris Argyris, while reading Peter Senge's *The Fifth Discipline*. I was new to my job at The Clearing when the firm introduced the work as an important influence on our consulting approach. Recognizing that the text was fairly dense in places, a group of us decided to tackle the work in a book group in order to hold one another accountable. While our book group was wading into the Senge text, my wife Trish and I were about to embark on some air travel. I'm a relaxed flyer 99.9 percent of the time, but the search for the lost Malaysian Airlines Flight MH370 was ongoing, with no leads or demonstrable progress to show. In thinking about our upcoming flight, my internal monologue sounded something like this: "*No trace of that flight has been discovered after months of searching. Planes are disappearing into thin air for no apparent reason. Flying is unsafe right now. We need to reconsider our travel plans and should probably cancel our flights.*" Days later, my book group encountered Argyris' Ladder of Inference in *The Fifth Discipline.*

Image 3: Cortisol at Work[68]

68 "Create a Circle of Safety: EDSO in Action," Benno Bos, accessed September 29, 2020.

Image 4: The Gears Turn[69]

I distinctly remember this particular mental model hitting me like a bolt of lightning out of a clear blue sky. One of those moments when something you've sensed for a long time is finally revealed to be not just something you cooked up, but *a real thing with a name.* I immediately recognized not only that I was cycling through my own ladder when thinking about our travel plans, but saw the ladder at work in other parts of my life and work as well.

There are seven rungs in the Ladder of Inference:

- Observable data and experiences (as a video camera would record it)
- I select 'data' from what I observe
- I add meanings (cultural and personal)
- I make assumptions based on the meanings I added
- I draw conclusions
- I adopt beliefs about the world
- I take actions based on my beliefs

69 Ibid.

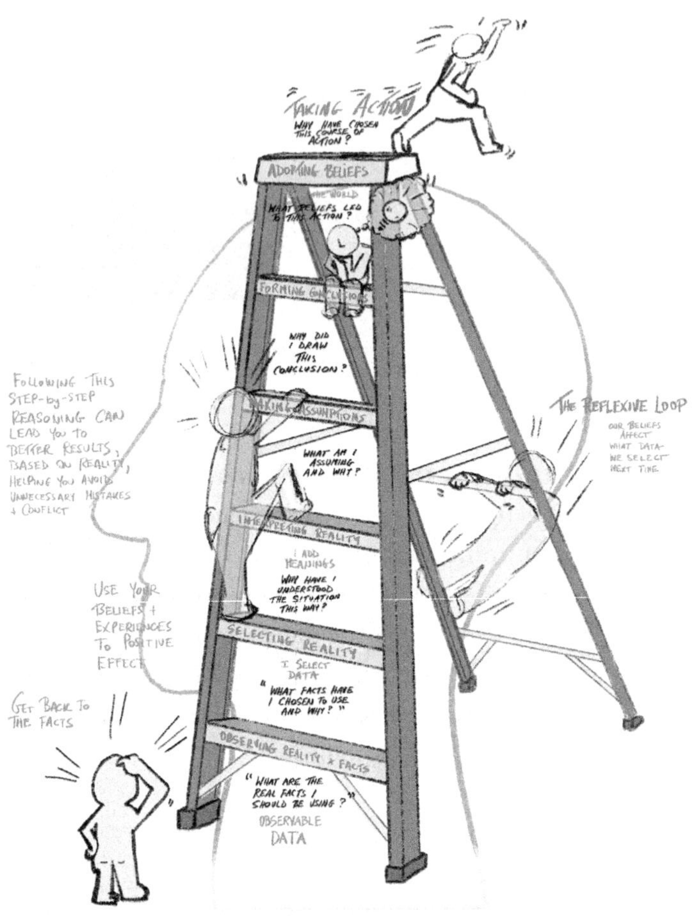

Image 5: The Ladder of Inference[70]

Only the observable action or data and the action you take (the bottommost and topmost rungs) happen externally. The rest occurs internally, meaning that the outside world misses out on the numerous in-between steps. In this context, the

70 Illustration commissioned with The Clearing, October 2020. All rights reserved.

linkage others create between observable behavior and your action means they show up as cause and effect. Maybe that cause and effect appears logical. Perhaps it does not. How others perceive the rationality or validity of our actions taken in response relies on them being able to make correct assumptions and logic leaps of their own: a tall task. One other critical thing to note about the Ladder is that we cycle through its rungs at lightning speed, a matter of seconds usually. This process is often largely unconscious. If an independent observer asked us to explain each of the steps we cycled through leading to our reaction, we'd probably be unable to do so.

Another critical characteristic of the Ladder of Inference exists: the *reflexive loop*. The beliefs we build when racing up the Ladder have a profound influence on the data we choose to select from future observable experiences. These beliefs self-reinforce over time, moving from *idea* to *hunch* to *belief we know is true*. This loop reinforces norms, stereotypes, and biases, both implicit and unconscious, about other people, society, and systems like companies and political groups. The calcified nature of our own loops causes commensurate loops in others around us, eroding deserved goodwill or gifting unearned goodwill.

Interrupting your own movement up the Ladder of Inference takes care and effort. As Senge astutely observes, "We live in a world of self-generating beliefs that remain largely untested."[71] In an upcoming chapter, we'll explore how we can apply the

---

71 Peter Senge, *The Fifth Discipline Fieldbook: Strategies and Tools for Building a Learning Organization* (New York: Doubleday, 1994).

Ladder of Inference to better ourselves, more intentionally process what goes on around us, and more effectively interact with the people who matter most to us. The key is to actively test our beliefs, with those around us, against data from a variety of diverse sources, and for the good of ourselves and for all.

DESIGNING TIME

Many of us appreciate quality design. We admire products that put intentional design first. Apple built an empire of focusing on *form and function* instead of just the latter. We pay extra to stay at hotels and visit places whose designs inspire us. Time is no different. Some of us would call time our most valuable resource. Why then do we call meetings, asking for hours of our colleagues' valuable time, and often forgo including so much as an agenda? Some believe their work is done once the meeting is calendared. This results in a lack of clarity on who should do what, when, and precisely how they should go about it. These meetings lead to wasted time and wasted money. Roughly eleven million meetings take place in America each day, and one-third of them aren't worth it. That equates to thirty-seven billion dollars lost each year in unproductive meetings.[72]

This is what's at stake when we don't design our time. If it's our most valuable resource, we should care even more about its structure and efficacy than we do about the sleekness of our devices or a well-crafted piece of furniture. At The Clearing, we believe deeply in well-designed time. As a matter of fact, we named our firm after it. Remember, a clearing is a place where

---

72 "$37 billion are lost every year on these 12 meeting mistakes," Business Insider, last modified June 6, 2019.

"we remove all facts, thoughts, technology, people, meetings, distractions, interruptions, biases, and legacies...a clearing is a place where the fewest people using the least resources can solve problems, drive change, and cause transformation in the least amount of time."[73] This is where I learned the difference between meeting for meeting's sake and building intention into our time in order to achieve outcomes.

The basics of our approach aren't rocket science. Anyone can do it given the energy and will to do so. At its heart, I love author Priya Parker's characterization of well-designed time: "creating a temporary alternative world."[74] Our guideline for a session where we'll convene a number of people is *2:1*—for a four-hour session, we invest a minimum of eight hours in preparation. That preparation includes the creation of a purpose statement (the why), outcomes (what everyone can plan to leave with once the gathering adjourns), a detailed agenda (how we'll get to the outcomes), and a meeting design (tactics, speaking notes, details on transitions, references to tools, and other cues). We'll dig into the finer points of the intentional designing of time later in this work.

SO WHAT?

Jean-Paul Sartre's play *No Exit* features a bleak apotheosis, "hell is other people."[75] When we're not self-aware enough and improperly equipped to interact in a positive or powerful

---

73 Chris McGoff, *The Primes: How Any Group Can Solve Any Problem* (Hoboken: John Wiley & Sons, Inc., 2012)

74 Priya Parker, *The Art of Gathering: How we Meet and Why it Matters* (New York: Riverhead Books, 2018).

75 "No Exit and Three Other Plays by Jean Paul Sartre," Vanderbilt University, accessed October 12, 2020.

way with our fellow humans, that can certainly feel like the case. Take the insights you've gained so far on our journey and make your own meaning of them. Place them into context for yourself by examining your own personal purpose and weighing the incentives within your professional and personal environments. The quality of your interactions and partnerships will skyrocket as a result.

CHAPTER 7

INNER CHEMISTRY

We are what we think. All that we are arises with our thoughts. With our thoughts, we make our world.

—BUDDHA

PEEKING INSIDE OUR BRAINS

The human mind is an endless sea. Your brain features roughly one hundred billion nerve cells or neurons, right around as many stars as there are in our Milky Way Galaxy.[76] Those hundred billion neurons are latticed together in such a way that they make about a million new neural connections every second of our lives.[77] You might dedicate every waking and productive moment of your life to a study of the brain and only fathom a small portion of it. This mind-boggling complexity means that no matter your

76 "15 Fascinating Facts you Didn't Know About Your Brain," *Safe Launch* (blog), April 2, 2013, accessed July 27, 2020.

77 "Introduction: The Human Brain," New Scientist, last modified September 4, 2006.

life pursuit or personal interests, it is vital to build and grow a functional understanding of brain science as applied in a variety of situations. That functional knowledge can give us schematics to predict emotional responses, fine-tune the intake, processing, and judgment of information we ingest, and much more. In short, knowing how and why our brains do what they do can make us better people.

THERE'S A BRAIN CHEMICAL FOR THAT

Earlier in this work, I mentioned that I consider myself to be a 'seeker,' an asker of "why" questions. As someone compelled to know the true nature of things, my greatest revelations so far on my path have all begun inside of myself. At various times in my life, I've felt guilt, bewilderment, and awe as I reflected on my past actions or current ways of thinking about my surroundings or the people around me. That can be a heavy burden to bear when coupled with a frustrating inability to answer those "why" questions. As such, I believe we should all wield a functional working knowledge of the basics of brain science, and the neurochemical processes that underpin some of our most frequent human reactions.

INDEPENDENT BRAIN CHEMICALS: WHEN WE'RE FLYING SOLO

Some brain chemicals require no interaction with others for their release. Two prime examples are dopamine and endorphins, neurochemicals that drive some of our deepest motivations for specific actions and reactions regardless of environmental setting.

Figure 6: EDSO[78]

Dopamine

Our body's dopamine stems from some of the most sociologically fascinating and complex situations we encounter in life. Most people familiar with the basics of brain science will tell you that dopamine is a goal-oriented drug, and they would be right. The sensation that accompanies achieving a major life milestone like finally landing your dream job or safely and successfully completing an athletic goal like running your first marathon, or holding yourself accountable to working out three times a week, are all predicated on dopamine flooding your body's various systems. For those of you who live and die by checklists, you get the same feeling

78 Bos, Benno. "Create a Circle of Safety: EDSO in Action." Accessed September 29, 2020.

when you check off a task, or even more pleasurably, check off that last task on a long to-do list. In short, dopamine is released by our brains as a reward response. All students of humanity know rewards are intrinsically motivating, regardless of upbringing, age, race, or other demographic. We're hardwired to covet prizes and recognition for our effort, a dynamic as timeless and pervasive as dirt.

As I write this, we are in the throes of the global pandemic. As of mid-May 2020, America's unemployment rate stood at roughly 15 percent, the highest percentage since the Great Depression in the early 1930s. Those of us fortunate enough to work from home full time with no impact to our pay or benefits are faced with a different, though not unfamiliar, set of challenges. Our days blend into one another, and more often than perhaps is healthy, we find our surroundings and devices activating our reward responses via dopamine. What triggers a splash of dopamine throughout our body? Eating, drinking alcohol, nicotine use, gambling, and the seemingly endless ping of notifications from our various devices. Often, these triggers combine, manifesting as a proactive and socially corrosive compulsion to check our phones and other devices too often. The facts are grim and prove dopamine's addictive nature. We tap, swipe, and click our phones roughly 2,617 times a day, unlock our smartphones 150 times a day, and spend over ten hours a day in front of a screen. What's more, 25 percent of adults actually wake from their sleep to check their phones. The impact on sleep cycles and the ability to focus that result is significant.[79]

---

79 John Brandon, "These Updated Stats About How Often You Use Your Phone Will Humble You," *Inc.* November 19, 2019.

The news on dopamine isn't all bad. Our mind's ability to equate an interim milestone within a larger goal is mostly a result of that brain chemical's effect. In a way, we can equate much of humanity's great achievements with our natural dopamine response.

Endorphins

Endorphins are a complicated brain chemical. A part of the opioid family, endorphins are front and center in the American zeitgeist without most of us knowing about it as a result of the heartrending tragedy of the opioid crisis. Through that lens, many of us are familiar with the drug's primary usage and purpose, *to dull or eliminate pain.* When we consider it in a more primal setting, a rush of endorphins allows us to surpass our own perceptions of our physical limitations in service of achieving a goal. Here enters many of our most memorable interactions with this particular neurochemical: a 'runner's high' (insert your choice of athletic endeavor here). As a competitive endurance athlete, I'm intimately familiar with the effects of endorphins on the body. From a purely biological perspective, the 'runner's high' effect produced by endorphins is not dissimilar from the physical state of being caused by psychoactive and recreational drugs like cocaine and heroin.

From a more positive perspective, our brains also release endorphins as a result of laughter. If you can remember the full-body sensation from the last time you laughed until you cried, you can bring to mind the feeling produced by a dearth of endorphins in your bloodstream.

RELATIONAL BRAIN CHEMICALS: WHEN WE'RE WITH OTHERS

Other brain chemicals are more interpersonal in nature and are released mostly in relation to our interactions with those around us. Whereas the release of dopamine and endorphins is predicated simply on external factors like a presenting threat or physical exertion, the following two neurochemicals rely on interactions with other humans for their release into our bodies. Thus, they are relational in nature.

Oxytocin

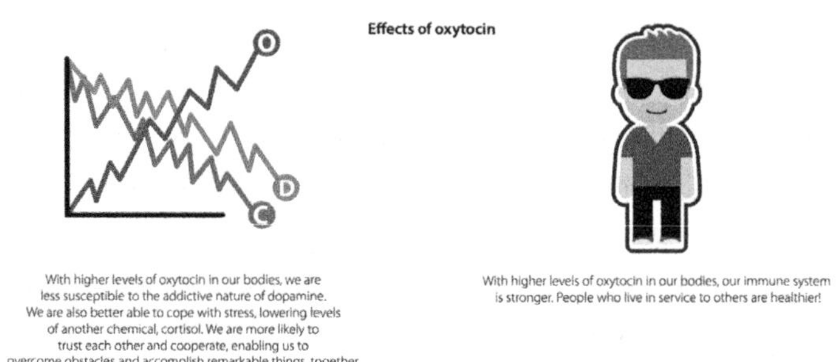

Figure 7: Effects of Oxytocin[80]

In our increasingly self-interested world, oxytocin can seem to be a holdover from an earlier, simpler time. This brain chemical boosts our willingness to trust and bond with one another, either in pairs or in larger groups. I recall a situation where I walked home after running a quick errand in our Northwest DC neighborhood. A young couple walked toward me on the sidewalk, doing their best to control their

80 Bos, Benno. "Create a Circle of Safety: EDSO in Action." Accessed September 29, 2020.

new puppy. Suddenly, the rambunctious pit bull moved in an unexpected way, as puppies are wont to do, and the couple lost their grasp on her leash. Intrinsically, I moved to help by whatever means necessary—coaxing, corralling, and offering imaginary treats. Once the well-intentioned pup was back safely in its owners' hands, they thanked me profusely, and a healthy dose of oxytocin flooded my body (I like to imagine the same was true for them). What's more, had passersby observed the interaction, they'd also have gotten a boost of oxytocin. All involved felt better than they did before the incident. Many of us recognize oxytocin at play as the 'helper's high' or 'selfish altruism' to paraphrase Anthony de Mello and the Dalai Lama.[81]

Another of oxytocin's particular effects is the incentivization of pair-bonding. This is something as simple as a quick embrace with a friend, coworker, or loved one, or longer-term relationships of a teaching or romantic nature. Some small moves are at play here as well. Our brains release oxytocin and its happy effects into our bloodstreams when we choose to write a hand-written thank-you note for a service we benefitted from instead of an e-mail or text message (the recipient experiences the same effect). Curiously, the presence of oxytocin can counteract the deleterious effects of cortisol and dopamine in our systems, making us more resilient and happier human beings. For instance, a situation that a child experiences as threatening can be instantly defused and made less frightening by the physical embrace of a parent, loved one, or friend. The sense of safety and relief that child

81 James Baraz and Shonshana Alexander, "The Helper's High," *Great Good Magazine*, February 1, 2010.

feels has a lot to do with the release of oxytocin, and the interruption of a potentially traumatic situation is invaluable.[82]

Serotonin

In terms of our work environments and identities, serotonin is one of the most critical neurochemicals for us to grasp, particularly for leaders, managers, or anyone who needs to inspire others to pursue an abstract goal or outcome or help shape organizational culture. Serotonin reinforces our bonds to others. Oftentimes, this manifests during the shared pursuit of some common goal. At work, this could be a team's collective revenue target, or when you deliver a product that is well-received by your colleagues or customers. Serotonin really kicks in if your manager acknowledges your hard work in a public setting, making you feel successful and appreciated. In our personal lives, an influx of serotonin might show up as watching a young man or woman you've helped lead achieve Eagle Scout or the Gold Award in Boy or Girl Scouts, especially when that young leader recognizes their peers as well as the adult leaders who helped make the achievement possible.

Serotonin's effects move at the speed of chemistry: too fast for our logical minds to process. It's simpler instead to focus on some of the concepts we can associate with serotonin. Social constructs like self-confidence and pride, as well as highly interpersonal dynamics like respect and status within a system all have much to do with the release or absence of

82 Bos, Benno. "Create a Circle of Safety: EDSO in Action." Accessed September 29, 2020.

serotonin. This neurochemical is often at play in two-person constructs between coach and athlete, boss and direct report, and parent and child.[83]

One of our brain's primary responses to our surroundings exists somewhat outside of the independent and relational chemicals we've discussed already. It can show up in both contexts: when we are by ourselves, and when we are around and interacting with others. That chemical process is a cocktail heavy on cortisol, something rooted even deeper than the four neurochemicals we've examined so far.

Cortisol

Whether or not we've engaged with the concept formally, we all know what our body's inherent fight-or-flight response feels like. At some point in our lives, we've all found ourselves in a situation we perceive as threatening. Therein, we intrinsically and unconsciously shift to one of two postures, preparing to do battle or readying ourselves to flee the presenting threat. Fight-or-flight is as equally at play at our jobs as it is with our families as it is moving from place to place in familiar and exotic locales. That response is fueled in large part by a potent mixture of chemicals composed primarily of cortisol and epinephrine, colloquially known as adrenaline. To illustrate how basic and primal these neurochemicals are to our essential biology, scientists have even discovered them in some single-cell organisms.[84]

---

83 Ibid.

84 Knut Schmidt-Nielsen, *Animal Physiology: Adaptation and Environment.* (Cambridge: Cambridge University Press, 1997), 510.

For me, one of our fight-or-flight response's most fascinating phenomena is that an abundance of cortisol and adrenaline in our bloodstream makes our bodies do things it usually wouldn't. One example is redirecting available energy away from what would otherwise be considered essential processes like the proper functioning of our immune systems. Others include physical growth and our body's ability to repair itself. It is plain to see then how the regular release of cortisol can damage our body's natural defenses, immunities, and healing mechanisms.[85]

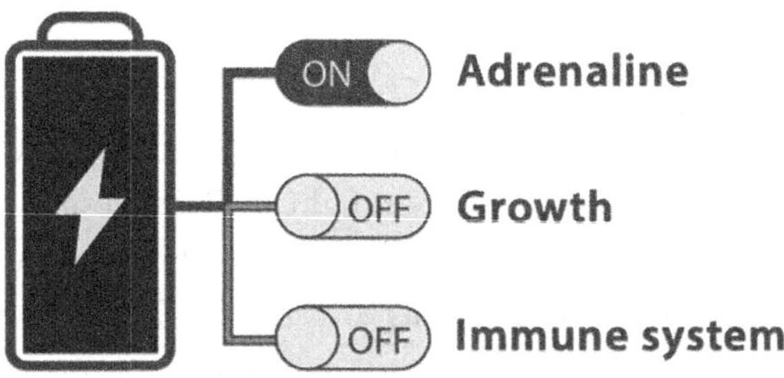

When cortisol is released, your body prioritizes where energy should be spent. Things that aren't necessary in that moment are shut down.

Figure 8: Effects of Cortisol[86]

When the threat of bodily harm or immediate damage to our well-being is present, the tap that dispenses a cocktail

85 Bos, Benno. "Create a Circle of Safety: EDSO in Action." Accessed September 29, 2020.

86 Ibid.

of cortisol and adrenaline opens before our conscious minds can perceive the danger. As soon as we perceive the threat as no longer present, the tap closes again, and we return to our more relaxed, 'normal' state of being. However, what happens when we live with a pervasive sense of imminent danger? Those fleeing persecution, injustice, and war know it well. We get a small taste of it when we live in constant uncertainty at work, revolving-door leadership, or frequent shifts in benefits like healthcare due to cost cutting or downsizing. Emerging science shows a linkage between high levels of stress (often driven by cortisol and adrenaline) and our long-term ability to be resilient.[87]

How can we consider dopamine, endorphins, oxytocin, and serotonin as a whole? Why does brain chemistry matter in the first place? Most critically, our biological reactions to the introduction of any one of these chemicals into our bloodstream drive any number of specific behaviors, ranging from arraying our defense mechanisms to going against an instinct to open some part of ourselves up to another. To understand the basics of brain chemistry is to have an array of ready tools at our disposal in any social situation, as well as when we're most alone and in need of self-understanding. Our social cognition might lead us to attribute the elevated heart rate and beads of sweat on the back of our necks caused by threatening situations to our own perceived ineptitude or lack of courage. In reality, those sensations are triggered purely by cortisol, and aren't an indictment of us as people, but are rather a fight-or-flight response we inherited from

87 Dr. Sanil Rege, "Neurobiology of Stress and Resilience," last updated April 28, 2020.

our ancestors. Grasping that oxytocin is contagious and that it can help us manage the harmful effects of dopamine and cortisol might lead us to volunteer more often, or to write the thank-you letter we've meant to focus on for weeks. These are small things that add up to be big things. While potentially trivial to us, they might be of tremendous importance to someone we care for or a stranger in need of a small taste of positive felicity.

When we are in a Circle of Safety, we gain our desired balance of EDSO.

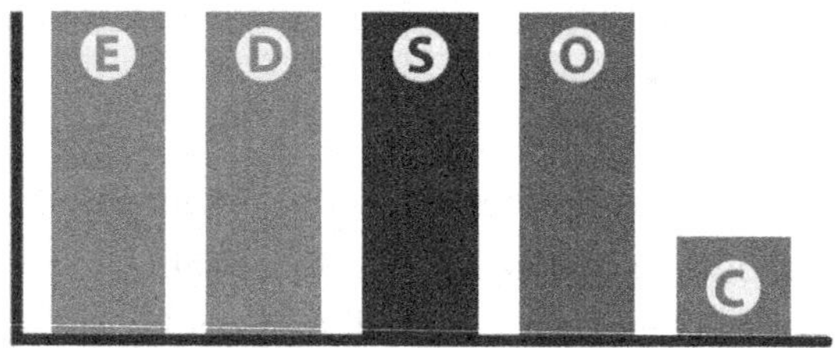

When EDSO is in BALANCE, our levels of cortisol decrease.

High E - exercise & laughter
High D - accomplishments toward clearly defined vision
High S - status, adoration, positive feedback, growth
High O - culture of service and helpfulness

Figure 9: EDSO in balance[88]

More often than not, the root cause of my seeking leads me back to a basic and near-universal chemical response occurring within my body, and largely independent of my logical brain. All of our minds, regardless of age, race, nationality,

88 Bos, Benno. "Create a Circle of Safety: EDSO in Action." Accessed September 29, 2020.

or whatever other distinctions separate us, function in these same fundamental ways. For me, this provides immense comfort. It also helps me understand myself and every other human in a new way. That's a big idea indeed.

EXPLORING A PARADOX: IMPOSTOR SYNDROME AND THE DUNNING-KRUGER EFFECT

Worry does not empty tomorrow of its sorrow. It empties today of its strength.

—CORRIE TEN BOOM

I'm a creep
I'm a weirdo
What the hell am I doing here?
I don't belong here

—THOM YORKE, RADIOHEAD, "CREEP"

Socrates was confused.

The Oracle at Delphi had just proclaimed him the wisest person in the known world. Funny thing: Socrates didn't agree with the high priestess of the Temple of Apollo. To test and contextualize his own wisdom, Socrates approached and questioned Athenian luminaries universally acknowledged as wise. These including statesmen, well-traveled merchants, and accomplished artisans. He found that none could match him in a test of wit, either by cleverness or experience. Being a learned and thinking person, Socrates couldn't wrap his head around this seeming conundrum. Each leading figure he'd questioned deemed themselves wise, some even with the conceit of near-omniscience, yet they lacked much in Socrates' estimation. A paradox emerged. Socrates wondered if the Oracle at Delphi was right? Was he indeed the wisest person in the world precisely because he had the awareness to appreciate the depth and breadth of his own ignorance and experience, unlike those with whom he'd interacted?

A well-known anecdote states that Socrates was illiterate. While this is not true in our modern conception of the word (he was indeed well-educated), it is accurate that Socrates wrote almost nothing. Instead, the works we attribute to him were recorded by his students Plato and Xenophon. The story of the Socratic inquisition that followed the Oracle at Delphi's proclamation of his wisdom, taken together with his unwillingness or inability to record his clearly profound thinking, tells us a lot about how the modern, successful mind works. Let's explore how.

Some of the world's most accomplished people go through life wondering when the perceived deception at the heart of their success will be discovered by a judging world. This sensation is known as impostor syndrome. It is pervasive and doesn't discriminate. The dictionary definition of the term characterizes impostor syndrome as "the persistent inability to believe that one's success is deserved or has been legitimately achieved as a result of one's own efforts or skills."[89] Through this lens, accomplishments are attributed to some great ruse or collective hallucination, no matter how profound or significant. The value and impact that those

89 Petula Alicia Fraser, "The 13 Best Ways for Stopping Imposter Syndrome to Elevate Your Confidence," last modified January 13, 2020.

achievements create can feel hollow, and those whose time, energy, effort, and will go into making them a reality often wait for the other shoe to drop and for those around them to uncover them as something other than who they are.

People young and old experience this saturating sensation frequently, often when they need self-confidence most. Impostor syndrome affects people from all walks of life and in all fields, professional and creative. Roughly 70 percent of us will experience some kind of impostor syndrome ourselves at some point in our lives. While the definition of the phenomenon serves as a useful basis for exploring, I find peering into the brains of some of the world's best who have experienced impostor syndrome to be even more valuable. Below is a sampling of their words. Pay special attention to the patterns that emerge in their independently delivered insights.

Poet and Presidential Medal of Freedom recipient Maya Angelou described her impostor syndrome thusly. "I have written eleven books, but each time I think, 'Uh oh, they're going to find out now. I've run a game on everybody, and they're going to find me out.'"[90]

Billionaire Atlassian CEO Mike Cannon-Brookes characterizes the sensation of being in the grips of impostor syndrome similarly. "For me, impostor syndrome is a feeling of being well, well out of your depth, yet already entrenched in the situation. Internally, you know you're not experienced, qualified, or skilled enough to justify being there, yet you are there.

90 Ibid.

It's not a fear of failure, and it's not a fear of being unable to do it. It's more a sensation of getting away with something. A fear of being discovered, that at any time someone's going to figure this out."[91] Most striking to me is Brookes' sense of being *stuck* within the situation inducing the impostor. It feels as if no alternatives exist regardless of how much someone may want to find an exit, much like Angelou's characterization above.

Facebook Chief Operating Officer Sheryl Sandberg described her experiences with the phenomena in her book *Lean In*, focusing on her time at Harvard. "Every time I took a test, I was sure that it had gone badly. And every time I didn't embarrass myself, or even excelled, I believed that I had fooled everyone yet again. One day soon, the jig would be up."[92] Here again the idea of 'fooling' or 'tricking' a perceived crowd emerges, and perhaps a trace of an underlying acceptance that this precise outcome will occur sooner or later.

Renowned author and artist Neil Gaiman describes his dealings with the phenomena and again focuses on a faceless 'they,' now with the power to make him change his life. "The first problem of any kind of even limited success is the unshakeable conviction that you're getting away with something, and that any moment now, they'll discover you. In my case, I was convinced there would be a knock on the door, and a man with a clipboard (I don't know why he had a

---

91 Ted, "How you can use impostor syndrome to your benefit | Mike Cannon-Brookes" December 21, 2019, video, 13:42.

92 "12 Leaders, Entrepreneurs and Celebrities Who Have Struggled With Imposter Syndrome: Sheryl Sandberg," Entrepreneur, accessed September 29, 2020.

clipboard, but in my head, he always had a clipboard), would be there to tell me it was all over. They'd caught up with me, and now I would have to go and get a real job."[93] The anonymity of the "they" in this case is brilliantly made personal in the personage of Gaiman's *man with a clipboard*, a perfect personification of impostor syndrome if ever I heard one. Leave it to one of this generation's best creative minds to make it so.

Knowing a bit about what impostor syndrome is and how to identify it is only the first step into a vast and deep world. There are critical dynamics to acknowledge outside of the essential sensations of impostor syndrome, important though those may be. In addition to its more obvious psychological and personal effects, the phenomena can also have a profound effect on interpersonal dynamics and one's relation to the communities of which they're a part. In that vein, I had the good fortune to attend a small liberal arts institution called Middlebury College for my undergraduate studies. I remember feeling out of my depth in my first year and a half there, and at a loss to identify what I wanted to focus on academically.

While there, I met many lifelong friends, but one classmate whom I fell out of touch with and have only recently connected with again is Dena Simmons. Since we graduated from school together, Dena has shaped a profound and meaningful life's work, and is now the assistant director at the Yale Center for Emotional Intelligence. Dena is easily one of

93 Neil Gaiman, "Commencement Speech, University of the Arts," video, 19:54.

the most accomplished people I know. Her education, experience, and a veritable avalanche of recognition, including a Fulbright Fellowship, a Truman Scholarship, a Soros Fellowship, a Doctorate from Columbia University, and many other bona fides are incontrovertible proof of her success and impact. And yet Dena openly acknowledges her struggles with impostor syndrome through the lens of community and race. "I have eternal impostor syndrome. Either I've been invited because I'm a token, which really isn't about me, but rather about a box someone needed to check off. Or I am exceptional, which means I've had to leave the people I've loved behind. It's the price that I and so many others pay for learning while black."[94] Dena's insight on how impostor syndrome can drive feelings of separation from community and loved ones is an important lesson we should all take to heart. Its connection to the process of learning and the environments in which we ask our young people of color to learn is an insight we need to square up to as a society. Dena, thank you for your bravery and integrity in a world short on both.

I have my own experience with impostor syndrome. For a long time, I didn't have the words to name the thing I felt. I would often place my own opinion, perspective, and wishes on the back burner in favor of those of others without any real reason or specific motivation to do so. Even when I knew that my thinking was accurate or important, I'd defer to others, only to hear the very ideas bouncing around in my head voiced by my classmates, colleagues, or peers. The tricky part for me is that this usually doesn't show up in profound

94 Ted, "How students of color confront impostor syndrome | Dena Simmons" January 17, 2017, video, 10:20.

or obvious ways, but rather in a hundred small ways over the course of a month or year, or in a certain ongoing interaction with a person or place. I find this to be more insidious and more difficult too. Discovering the vocabulary, mindsets, and tools that let me name and organize my unique strengths helped immensely. Now I can array the things I know I'm objectively good at and put into context the areas where I need help. The direct and unvarnished feedback of colleagues and loved ones, delivered with compassion and without rounded edges, has helped me square up to this reality about myself and how my mind works.

There is great power in knowing you are not alone. By seeing that some of the world's most successful people not only experience impostor syndrome, but openly and publicly acknowledge their struggles with it, we can lift some of its weight from our shoulders. Deepened self-awareness can assist us in actively managing and minimizing impostor syndrome, but more often than not, it is something that will probably never go away entirely. And that's okay.

Impostor syndrome lies on a spectrum of *cognitive bias.* A deep-seated and irregular view of self or others that deviates from the 'norm.' Think of cognitive bias as a spectrum. If impostor syndrome is near the hypothetical left end of this particular line where one not just doubts themselves, but *knows* that they don't deserve their own success, the *Dunning-Kruger effect* is near the opposite end. On this end of our hypothetical spectrum, an individual with a marked lack of experience with and knowledge of a thing illogically considers themselves to be an expert on that same thing. Their self-confidence is paradoxically mighty and completely unfounded. Thus a neophyte in any area of work, study, or experience would consider themselves not just experienced, but *wise*. Conversely, someone with a career's worth of operating in an industry or creative pursuit at a high-level grasps much of the breadth and depth of what they don't know. This leads them to conclude that they are ignorant when this is, in fact, far from the truth, and is colloquially referred to as the 'valley of despair' within the Dunning-Kruger effect.

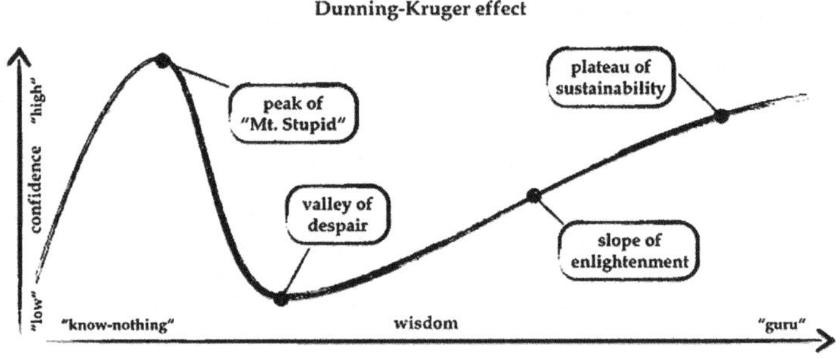

Figure 10: The Dunning-Kruger Effect[95]

Aside from its ready application to politics, business, family, and other social constructs, one thing that fascinates me about the Dunning-Kruger effect is the *actual source* of the irregularity in our own perception of ourselves. Social psychologists David Dunning and Justin Kruger discovered and lent their names to this particular bias. In their seminal study "Unskilled and Unaware of It: How Difficulties in Recognizing One's Own Incompetence Lead to Inflated Self-Assessments," they state that "the miscalibration of the incompetent stems

95 Ulf Ehlert, "The Dunning-Kruger Effect in Innovation, *Understanding Innovation* (blog), July 3, 2015.

from an error about the self, whereas the miscalibration of the highly competent stems from an error about others."[96] In other words, the inexperienced and incompetent person's deviation is *internally* generated, while the experienced and competent person's deviation is predicated *externally*. For me, this further reinforces the laughable tragedy inherent in this big idea: the irrationally confident need no one but themselves to be assured of their own genius, while the objectively experienced and wise correlate their self-worth against the perspectives of others when they need not.

While this big idea isn't particularly well-known outside of academic and select professional circles, its manifestations are legion. Each day, we see references to individuals whom we could objectively deem wise and imminently experienced openly doubting their own insight or value. We, of course, also see the opposite, where small people use bombast to masquerade as authoritative or even omniscient. Even more regularly, we see Dunning-Kruger show up in unexpected places, like President John F. Kennedy's famous 'moonshot' speech. "We meet at a college noted for knowledge, in a city noted for progress, in a State noted for strength, and we stand in need of all three, for we meet in an hour of change and challenge, in a decade of hope and fear, in an age of both knowledge and ignorance. The greater our knowledge increases, the greater our ignorance unfolds."[97] For me, the Dunning-Kruger effect shows up everywhere, and not just

---

96 David Dunning and Justin Kruger, "Unskilled and unaware of it: how difficulties in recognizing one's own incompetence lead to inflated self-assessments," PubMed.gov, accessed July 19, 2020.

97 John F. Kennedy, "Rice Stadium Moon Speech" (speech) September 12, 1962.

because of my own confirmation bias, which I acknowledge and know like an old friend. Our new shared understanding of this powerful big idea not only allows us to see it at play in the world but gives us the power to give ourselves grace as we embark on our own personal journeys of self-discovery. That journey is one where we *intentionally uncover the vastness of what we don't know.*

When I reflect on my life to date, I realize I have a couple of things going for me. First, through the wisdom and vulnerability of those around and before me, I learned about impostor syndrome and the Dunning-Kruger effect early in life. Navigating socially and technically complex problems for a living, surrounded by some of the world's brightest in Washington, DC, casts into stark relief the vastness of *what I don't know.* Even so, my colleagues at The Clearing see me for who I can be, challenge me to push myself, hold me accountable to my own personal vision, and support me throughout the journey. I feel strangely at ease, knowing I have comrades navigating the same uncharted territories of self-awareness and learning. Second, I have a wife, son, brother, mom, dad, and family who, at worst, chuckle at my self-doubt, and assure me I'm *usually* not *entirely* barking up the wrong tree. For both, I'm grateful.

In closing, some words from the objectively wise Neil Gaiman. "The problems of failure are hard. The problems of success can be harder because no one warns you about them."[98] When you feel out of your league, or like you're making it up as you go along, pause to realize that the sensation is common and

---

98 Neil Gaiman, *"Commencement Speech, University of the Arts," video, 19:54.*

is a sign of blossoming self-awareness. This is a good thing. Socrates' student, Plato, attributed the now-famous (though likely paraphrased) words to his teacher that we now know as the Socratic Paradox. "I know that I know nothing." The next time you feel the creeping self-doubt of impostor syndrome, or sense that you are in the Dunning-Kruger effect's valley of despair, remember that you have the world's best for company, and that you're treading a path toward an ineffable quality, wisdom.

CHAPTER 8

THE OPTIMIZED MIND OR: HOW I LEARNED TO STOP WORRYING AND LOVE MY BRAIN

Between stimulus and response, there is a space. In that space is our power to choose our response. In our response lies our growth and freedom.

—VIKTOR FRANKL

With regard to the human mind, the question of potential is a fascinating one. A popular myth states that the average person uses only 10 percent of their brain's capacity and potential performance. Its allure is easy to understand. If true, we might unlock the vast majority of our brain's ability, with untold mental acuity, capability, and insight as the prize. What might suddenly be in play if we could multiply our brain's effectiveness by a factor of ten? Fame? Fortune?

Wisdom the likes of which today's best thinkers could only dream of? A longer life?

As attractive as this idea is, it's almost assuredly false. As simple and elegant as things would be if we could somehow unlock the lion's share of our mental capacity, the reality is less reductive and not so simple. We use most parts of our brain almost constantly, though it is nearly impossible to hazard a reasonably accurate guess as to the percentage of mental capacity we use at any one point in time.[99] What we can say with relative assurance is that if we operate from a foundation of considered self-knowledge, we can fine-tune our patterns of thinking, behaviors, and choices to push the limits of our perceived abilities. The big ideas to follow all build on the concepts we learned about together in the last chapter. Connecting them will set you on a path to the most optimized version of your own brain. From there, the outcomes are truly limitless.

FLOW: ODYSSEY OF THE MIND

Remember back to a time when you focused on a particular task so wholly that time melted away. Upon the wildly successful completion of said task, you snapped back to yourself only to realize that the sun had set, your belly was clamoring for cheese fries, and you had seventy-one unread messages in the group text. At that moment, you experienced a concept called 'flow.'

'Flow' is a mental state where a person channels an energized and radical sense of focus and enjoyment into a task or

---

99 Robynne Boyd, "Do People Only Use 10 Percent of Their Brains?" *February 7, 2008.*

activity, or the "holistic sensation that people feel when they act with total involvement."[100] Experiences that trigger a state of flow are equal amounts challenging and demanding of our highest skill level, not too much or too little of either. In essence, flow is characterized by complete absorption in what one does, and a resulting transformation in one's sense of time and self. One can experience this mental state while doing just about anything. Yes, some of us may find it in activities that might spring to mind readily, like yoga, skiing, surfing, snowboarding, drawing, or painting. However, the activity need not be athletic or creative. Some can enter a flow state when gardening, organizing a new bookshelf, or working on a home renovation project. These experiences create a sense of excitement around what's possible. As a result of entering a flow state, individuals fully immerse in a feeling of energized focus, full involvement, and enjoyment in the process of the activity.

To properly explore the concept of flow, we need to tell the story of flow's father.

Mihaly Csikszentmihalyi was born in Hungary during a turbulent time in world history, 1934 to be exact. The ravages of the Great Depression still wreaked havoc on everyday life and geopolitics the world over. Hitler declared himself Germany's ruler, Stalin's brutal rise to power in Russia began apace, and World War II broke out just five years later. Csikszentmihalyi experienced all of this before even entering grade school. While Csikszentmihalyi's experience during World

---

[100] Mihaly Csikszentmihalyi, *Beyond Boredom and Anxiety: Experiencing Flow in Work and Play* (San Francisco: Jossey Bass, 2000.

War II wasn't common (his father's diplomatic status allowed his family three times the normal rations), no one escaped the worldwide conflagration untouched. Fortunate as his family was, they were displaced and forced to move several times as fighting spread. He lost both of his brothers to the horror of war. One died during the Siege of Budapest, and the other was sent to a Siberian labor camp.[101] Csikszentmihalyi's wartime experiences, combined with observations about his fellow Europeans coped in order to manage the shared trauma of World War II, forever shaped his life and calling.

Post-war life for Mihaly Csikszentmihalyi often felt rudderless and out of joint. At just fifteen years old, he decided that school wasn't for him. Tiring easily of rote learning and memorization, and feeling unchallenged and uninspired, Csikszentmihalyi observed adults around him struggling, and often failing, to cope with and heal from the deep wounds of World War II. Feeling as though he was seeking something, he left his home in Italy for a solitary trip to Switzerland. Due to an early spring thaw, skiing quickly became untenable. As he lacked the money necessary to access areas high enough into the Swiss Alps to find quality snowpack, he quickly found himself without diversion in the fairytale city of Zurich. While thumbing through the local newspaper, Mihaly's restless eyes landed on something strange—an advertisement for a free lecture on flying saucers. With nothing better to do and his interest piqued by the sheer strangeness of the premise, Csikszentmihalyi decided

101 Mihaly Csikszentmihalyi, "Kristine Marin Kawamura, PhD interviews Mihaly Csikszentmihalyi, PhD," interview by Kristine Kawamura, *Cross Cultural Management An International Journal.* no. 21 (2014), 476-492.

to attend. He had no idea what the evening would hold and had never heard of the lecturer but decided to attend to pass the time and learn about a novel topic.

Csikszentmihalyi entered the lecture hall and found a seat. Straight away, Csikszentmihalyi sensed that he'd entered a strange new landscape of ideas, one that pushed his thinking and worldview. The lecturer was a person completely unknown to him, who offered and examined a hypothesis regarding a strange phenomenon occurring across Europe. Since the end of World War II, people all over the continent had spotted strange discs suspended in the sky and moving through the air in seemingly impossible ways. While the war years saw a dizzying pace of technological advancement, scientists and observers alike were baffled and at a loss to explain the phenomena through a rational lens. The Swiss lecturer unfolded a tapestry of wholly alien ideas to his audience, including the rapt fifteen-year-old Csikszentmihalyi. That lecturer was none other than Carl Jung, by then a world-famous psychoanalyst who studied under Sigmund Freud and who had almost singlehandedly founded the still-nascent field of study of the human mind as it related to behavior.[102]

It was amazing that Csikszentmihalyi got an opportunity to hear Carl Jung speak, but what about those UFOs? At its core, Jung's hypothesis stated that the flying disc sightings were collective hallucinations, themselves a projection of a displaced yearning for connection and togetherness. The

102 Ted, "Mihaly Csikszentmihalyi: Flow, the secret to happiness," October 24, 2008, video, 18:55.

trauma of World War II led to the disintegration of huge swaths of European society and culture. Jung posited that it had, in fact, been decomposed into its constituent elements and flung apart in a chaotic fashion. He went on to label the flying discs and saucers 'mandalas,' a Hindi archetype for unified knowledge and values. Europeans were manifesting these sightings because they were yearning for reunification with their ideals, values, and a semblance of normality. The shattered psyche was crying out for a force to combat the intense fragmentation it had experienced. Csikszentmihalyi had never heard of any of these things before, but as strange and foreign as they were, they also fit together a number of disjointed mental puzzle pieces that he grappled with himself. He was bewildered and fascinated.

Csikszentmihalyi believed he'd found his life's calling. He would study to be a psychologist. However, this was the late 1940s. Psychology was a still-emerging field, not yet professionalized and completely separate from related areas of study like philosophy and applied medical science. Mihaly was hugely discouraged from learning one could take a course in psychology at university but could not specialize in the field. There was no depth of learning or practice available to him at home in Italy, or most other European countries for that matter. Human behavior was still largely a mystery, and luminaries like Jung, while well-regarded in Europe, were not taken seriously or were even derided in some other parts of the world.

Not one to let a roadblock stand in his way, Csikszentmihalyi discovered that the United States offered specialization in the field of psychology in his areas of interest, and so he left his home to become a student in America. He arrived in Chicago and worked nights to pay his rent while attending the University of Chicago full time. Csikszentmihalyi completely immersed himself in his work and learning but felt that something was still missing.

Upon reaching the final stages of his undergraduate studies in psychology, Mihaly felt a growing sense of discontent regarding the structure and content of the coursework his professors and department offered. As a field still struggling for mainstream legitimacy, psychologists of the day focused the vast majority of their time and energy on clinical trials and studies, usually on rats and other small mammals whose reactions and behavior could be easily observable. While logical, this did not sit well with Csikszentmihalyi. He'd traveled across the ocean to focus on psychology as a way of better and more fully comprehending the human mind and its stewardship of human behavior, not a rat's response to various inputs and stimuli. Csikszentmihalyi's observation of the shattered European psyche originally drove him to pursue this nascent field within psychology. I'm sure he felt he had important work to do with his fellow man. My hypothesis is that time likely didn't feel like his ally.

Csikszentmihalyi's perdition emerged not through a stroke of great luck or an escape from the realities of his new life in America, but by perseverance and grit in the face of his challenge. He endured the boredom and monotony of clinical studies as a young psychologist, the very reason he abandoned his studies as a teenager in Italy. He earned the freedom to refocus his efforts on human behavior after years of toil by sticking with the tactical application of concepts he longed to extend and explore for himself. After earning his bachelor's degree and a PhD from the University of Chicago, Csikszentmihalyi took a teaching position at Lake Forest College. He focused his research and teaching on the concept of 'play' with his students—activities or tasks that we all experience in everyday life that didn't feel like a chore to complete. Csikszentmihalyi was fascinated by the underlying mindsets and neurology involved with play, and his focus on this area would begin to evolve into a big idea called 'flow.'

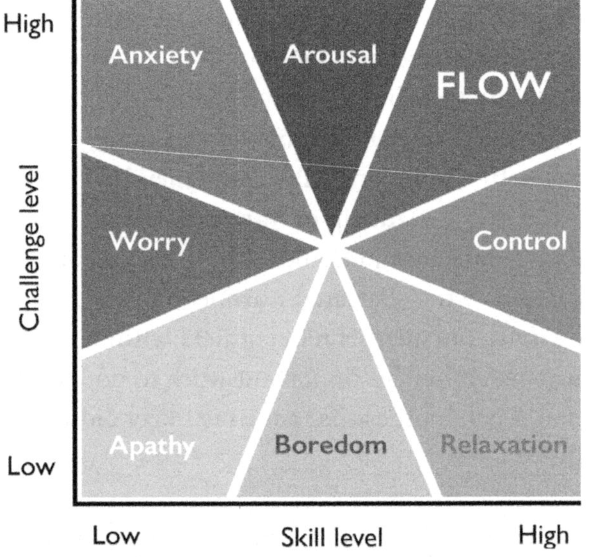

Figure 11: Flow[103]

[103] Hans Manzke, "Harnessing Flow to Drive Organizational Outcomes," *The Clearing*, (blog), September 1, 2020.

It's a catchy name that describes the sensations his human subjects experienced when engrossed in a task they chose for themselves and enjoyed immensely. It would shape modern psychology and reorient society's view of the field's potential for understanding human behavior.

How might groups, teams, and companies take the critical insights that flow uncovers and apply them at an organizational scale? Organizations—not just individuals—can embody flow.

FLOW IN ORGANIZATIONS: A CASE STUDY

Over seventy years ago, Masaru Ibuka founded the company we know today as Sony. One of his first actions as head of the new organization was to publish a series of statements he called 'Purpose of Incorporation,' a vision of the future organization Ibuka dreamed of creating. The very first Purpose of Incorporation statement reads as follows:

"To establish a place of work where engineers can feel the joy of technological innovation, be aware of their mission to society, and work to their heart's content." [5] "The Founding Prospectus," About Sony, Sony, accessed September 1, 2020.

Sony's de facto mission statement says nothing about transistors, radio receivers, or technology of any kind. It does not focus on products, services, profits, or growth. What it envisions delivering into the marketplace is nowhere to be found. Instead, carefully crafted words inspire, challenge, and give permission to its staff to seek contentment through their chosen profession—in essence, flow in practice in the work environment. Mihaly Csikszentmihaly refers to Ibuka's first Statement as "the perfect description of how flow functions in the workplace."[104] It still feels vital and gutsy over seventy years later.

THE HUMAN REBOOT

We close our laptops each afternoon or evening to call it a day and open that same laptop back up again the next morning. As the days become weeks, we notice our machines running slower and with perceptibly more effort. Perhaps we hear fans kicking on to cool overheated hardware. The strain is palpable. Maybe we even get far enough along in this slow march toward entropy that we find ourselves checking the machine's manufacture date, thinking it's older than it actually is, and wondering if it's time to start scraping our nickels together for a replacement.

In the realm of this increasingly common occurrence, our friendly neighborhood IT support people have a message not just for our struggling hardware, but also for their users. There's a reason that the most common helpdesk advice takes the form of the ubiquitous *"Have you tried turning it off and turning it back on again?"*

It turns out that fully powering down a laptop, tablet, phone, smart TV, pretty much any device that has hardware and software, performs almost the same function as getting a decent night's sleep, going on a particularly relaxing vacation, or journaling each day. Whether you fastidiously close each application and browser window, or you're more like me with

---

104 Mihaly Csikszentmihaly. *Good Business: Leadership, Flow, and the Making of Meaning* (New York: Viking, 2003.

a litany of programs and browser tabs going at once, there's a direct correlation between the period of time between full device shutdowns and that device's performance.

Humans are no different. Think of our laptop or phone's hard drive as our brain's limbic system, storing memories, sensations, and instinct. The CPU and motherboard link to our prefrontal cortex, our mind's logic center, responsible for more high-order thinking, morality, and much more. The device's operating system and the applications that we select and overlay on the machine's hardware are the learning packets our minds take in during school, jobs, hobbies, training, and task execution.

What happens when we don't occasionally power down our minds? Gone unchecked, memories, actions, old priorities, and other formerly important things continue to accrue, making our heads feel full and rendering recall, creative thinking, or improvisation effectively impossible. I liken the phenomena to cholesterol accumulation in an overworked artery. In time, your mind's capacity to function at its peak performance is steadily diminished. That manifests in any number of nefarious ways—lack of patience and anxiety, just to name two. The sensation feels like the human equivalent of running your car's engine 'in the red' consistently but crawling along at ten miles per hour. *Huge energy investment, very little return.*

With this new corollary in mind, *how can we most effectively mimic the hard reboot our devices so sorely need and reset our brains? Most particularly, how can we force reboot when things get truly dire?* For people, this is not so simple as reading and implementing a checklist they stumbled across in a blog like this one. Some most readily access their creativity and flow-like states when they're surrounded by inspiring things such as articles, books, quotes, videos, and art. This can lead to the very sprawl that slows and reduces the capacity of our devices and minds alike.

The key is balance. We almost always breathe a sigh of relief when we finally allow our machines to execute that software update and power down. When we hard boot our brains, we can begin anew with a clean slate and an opportunity to build and explore all over again.

Give yourself some space. One tactic is clearly demarcating physical space for your inspiration, especially if you're prone to sprawl. That space need not be expansive. In fact, Marissa Meyer taught us creativity loves constraint,[105] so challenge yourself to winnow your inspiration down to its essence by reconfiguring an unused corner or portion of a room. Better yet, build yourself a creativity kit that you can pack and unpack relatively easily. This makes your inspiration mobile and untethered to a specific area. To balance that engineered sprawl, have a similar space where you go exclusively to focus. If you're fortunate enough to have the purpose-driven tech for your work, more so, the better. A little positive compartmentalization goes a long way. The world can still be the fascinating place it is because of its infinite variety and complexity without all of the inertia that all of those things can create. In fact, you may find that lightening up a bit can unleash newfound ways of thinking and a refreshed ability to make connections.

---

105 eCorner, "Creativity Loves Constraint," May 17, 2006, video, 1:40.

A different approach to recall. Perhaps most importantly, small moves and practices can play an outsized role in effecting a human hard reboot in service of our short-term effectiveness and long-term resilience. Downloading outstanding tasks, random musings, and potential connections can work wonders for our mental bandwidth. Write out a list, create a visual, or simply journal. Whatever works best for you. This shifts what would otherwise be an act of mental recall to one of execution. Crossing things off of a list gives our brains a nice flush of dopamine. This helps us remain focused and continues the virtuous cycle of productivity. At an even more basic level, my mentor and The Clearing colleague Sharon Benjamin states, "Give yourself the gift of a recalibration of your own ability to work things, even when you don't know or can't see an answer." That is to say, instead of punching out of a challenge because it feels overwhelming or maybe even impossible, recalibrate how your brain engages with the situation. Sounds simple enough, but this brain work can be tough if you haven't rebooted your mind in a while.

Why does this matter? Modern life can drag us down. Without mental reboots, Everyday tasks feel harder than we know they should. The human nervous system can only process about one hundred ten bits of information per second. Listening to one person speak occupies over half of your mind's total bandwidth.[106] Now imagine how our brains must labor when all of the mental plaque that characterizes a mind that's gone too long without some quality downtime clogs up the works. We owe it to ourselves to clear our mental decks on a

---

106 Ted, "Mihaly Csikszentmihalyi: Flow, the secret to happiness," October 24, 2008, video, 18:55.

regular basis. This gives us the best chance possible to tackle the complex problems we each face each day—work, interpersonal, and societal. The positive outcomes that a regular human hard reboot can engender are available to us all, regardless of age, access, or our field of endeavor. Invest the effort in yourself and immediate results will follow.

Oh, and don't forget to power down that poor laptop of yours every once in a while.

PART 3:

YOUR TURN

CHAPTER 9

TIME TO MOVE OUT

To be hopeful in bad times is not just foolishly romantic. It is based on the fact that human history is a history not only of cruelty, but also of compassion, sacrifice, courage, kindness. What we choose to emphasize in this complex history will determine our lives. If we see only the worst, it destroys our capacity to do something. If we remember those times and places—and there are so many—where people have behaved magnificently, this gives us the energy to act, and at least the possibility of sending this spinning top of a world in a different direction. And if we do act, in however small a way, we don't have to wait for some grand utopian future. The future is an infinite succession of presents, and to live now as we think human beings should live, in defiance of all that is bad around us, is itself a marvelous victory.

—HOWARD ZINN, *YOU CAN'T BE NEUTRAL ON A MOVING TRAIN*

We've covered a lot of ground, and we're here because we care enough to do what's required to leave the world and ourselves better than we found them. Perhaps you're struggling to hold the totality of the big ideas we've explored in tension with one another. If so, fear not; this chapter serves as a quick field guide you can come back to you again and again as a refresher, or to reabsorb the information in a new or different way.

You know the aphorisms: '*we eat with our eyes*' and '*a picture is worth a thousand words.*' Both contain an essential truth, so where possible, I've included a visualization of the big idea we're covering to help bring the concept to life. Let's dig into some tactics you can use to take these big ideas from concept to application.

IKIGAI (COVERED IN CHAPTER 4)

Figure 12: Ikigai[107]

107 "Diagram of Japanese ikigai concept," iStock by Getty Images, accessed October 20, 2020.

Ikigai is a classic framework that you can take and use as an exercise in and of itself. Try the following steps to get clearer on what your personal *ikigai* might be:

- Print out or draw a large-format version of the *ikigai* framework pictured above—no need to be too fancy. Just get the basic shapes and words in there.
- Using sticky notes, pen or pencil right on the drawing or printout, or any other method that you prefer, brainstorm a list of responses to each of the four cardinal points within *ikigai*: What the world needs, what you can be paid for, what you're good at, and what you love.
- Explore overlaps between these four cardinal points and notice where centers of gravity emerge (i.e., where there's more than one idea listed).
- Based on your brainstorming and any centers of gravity you note, take a stab at brainstorming a statement that encapsulates your *ikigai* (remember, *ikigai* roughly translates to 'a reason for being').
- Road-test your *ikigai* by tuning into the sensations you feel when embarking on an activity you characterize as your *ikigai*. Does it bring you joy? Does the prospect excite you?

MOAI (COVERED IN CHAPTER 4)

Remember, *moai* describes a formal, life-long bond between a small group of individuals—on the island of Okinawa, these groups number roughly five. If you're interested in actively combating the social fragmentation we experience more and more each day, consider the following steps:

- Survey your social groups: would you characterize any of them as *moai*?
- If you answer yes, consider introducing the term and concept to that circle of friends. Remember, there's a tremendous amount of power in the correct naming of things. Calling your group a *moai* may reinforce its *moai-ness.*
- If you answer no, consider the environments and contexts you have available to you where you might cultivate a *moai.* Examples include work, athletic teams, volunteering organizations you participate in, religious institutions, or neighbors, just to name a few. Extend an invitation to a small group of individuals in one of these settings, and don't feel obligated to label it a *moai* initially if you're not comfortable doing so.
- Commit to meeting regularly, regardless of format. The more you can stick to a schedule, the more value you'll derive from your *moai.*

MINDFULNESS (COVERED IN CHAPTER 4)

Mindfulness is one of those words meaning many different things to many different people. Your specific definition may differ from mine, but here's a starter list to consider as you embark on your own mindfulness journey (in no particular order):

- Journal: Your thoughts, feelings, insights, epiphanies, failures, and other more mundane things like what memory a specific food spurred for you, etc.
- Meditate: In whatever way makes the most sense for you—some use mantras, some use white noise to get into the zone, while others use apps like Headspace.

- Breathe mindfully: Focus on each breath. Slow the pace of your breathing and inhale and exhale more deeply than you normally would. You'll feel a difference.
- Be radically present: Eliminate distractions and focus intently on the experience of the here and now. This one is especially tough in our day and age, so start small and dedicate yourself to being 100 percent present for a brief activity (five minutes or less). Turn off your cell phones and place devices far away from you if needed.
- Acknowledge, accept, and let pass your fear, worry, and judgment: These emotions are just as much a part of you as your joy, excitement, and other positive emotions. Rejecting or ignoring them will only amplify the power they have over you. Buddhist luminary Thich Nhat Hanh says, "Do not fight against pain; do not fight against irritation or jealousy. Embrace them with great tenderness, as though you were embracing a little baby. Your anger is yourself, and you should not be violent toward it. The same goes for all of your emotions."[108]
- Let your mind wander sometimes: Creativity is most active when we're freely associating our thoughts. Focus is also important, but you're more likely to find inspiration while daydreaming.

These are just a few tactics you can use to enter a more mindful space. Consider methods or ways of being that calm and center you that may not be obvious, and prioritize and cultivate them. Even when you're the busiest, make four to five minutes at any point throughout the day to deploy a mindfulness tactic. You'll be glad you did.

---

108 Thich Nhat Hanh, *You Are Here* (Boulder: Shambhala, 2010), 2–3.

SELF-AUTHORSHIP (COVERED IN CHAPTER 4)

Self-authorship is all about expanding your focus from doing, thinking, and feeling things that are worthwhile and good for others—not just for yourself. Self-authors know they cannot progress their own personal evolution without focusing intentionally on relationships with their fellow humans.

You'll recall in Chapter 4 that we dove into a model that includes self-authorship: Kegan's "Evolution of Consciousness." This shows us there really aren't any shortcuts or hacks for self-authorship, but rather a personal journey that we must each undertake on our own.

One tactic you can use to inch closer to self-authorship is to commit to focusing less on the judgments of others, and rather tune in to your own reason for acting or thinking in a particular way. That reason should be rooted in your personal purpose to whatever extent possible. This doesn't mean not to care about other people, but rather to invest less energy into the opinions and perspectives of others in relation to your actions. Do and achieve for yourself, not for others.

Martha Johnson, who we learned about in Chapter 5, introduced me to her distinction of ideas being *magnetically charged*. Essentially, the right idea at the right time will attract and align the right people to it, oftentimes independent of your direct influence or control. At The Clearing, we realize that to achieve a self-authoring declaration, one must trust a certain level of uncertainty to the universe. Martha's 'ideas as magnets' concept connects to self-authorship for me in a big way. If you're pursuing your own self-authoring outcome, broadcast that big idea of yours far and wide. While you're not guaranteed an earth-shattering response every time, you greatly increase your chances.

UNCONSCIOUS BIAS (COVERED IN CHAPTER 5)

Unconscious bias exists all around us, and most importantly, within us. Think of our conscious and unconscious minds, as well as our conscious and unconscious biases, like an iceberg. Only a small portion is 'above the waterline' or on display for ourselves and others to see. The vast majority of their mass resides below the waterline, hidden away from ourselves and others. To make the unconscious known, and to begin the difficult work of dismantling the unconscious biases that don't serve us and others, consider these steps:

- Remember, bias is a biological evolution to help us avoid danger and risky situations.
- Acknowledge that you are biased. Remember, the question is not whether or not we're biased, but rather *naming which biases are ours.*
- Make peace with your own bias and share your insights about your biases with trusted partners.
- Explore and unpack your own biases.
- Help others to do the same.
- Focus on being actively unbiased (for whatever version of unconscious bias lens you're focusing on) rather than telling yourself you can just 'let your biases go.'
- Consider small moves that create distance (things like yawning, rolling your eyes, or ignoring one person but paying attention to others) and commit to eradicating at least one of them.

- Consider small moves that create inclusion and connection (things like asking for clarification if you don't understand someone's request or point of view, or seeking out the advice of someone whom you usually disagree with). Commit to deploying at least one of them.

This is hard work. You'll need a safe space to achieve the best results, and accountability partners who can call you to task if you're not living up to your anti-bias commitments.

WORDS & SPEECH ACTS (COVERED IN CHAPTER 5)

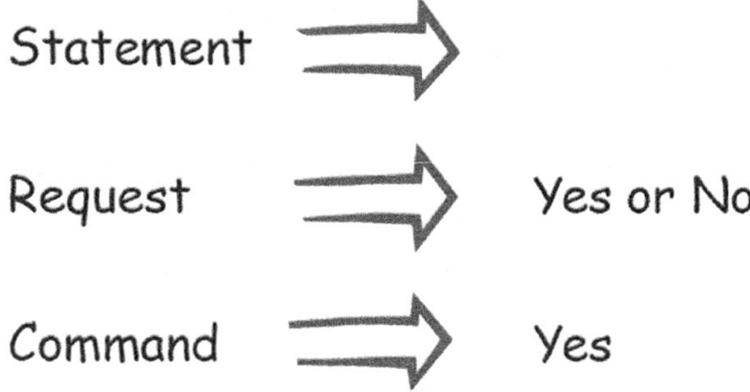

Image 13: Request Command Prime[109]

Words are power, so use yours with intention. Do so not just to get what you want, but also to keep your proverbial gunpowder dry for when you really need to call in a favor, have someone adhere to a command, or persuade another to do something that may not be in their own personal best

[109] Chris McGoff, *The Primes: How Any Group Can Solve Any Problem* (Hoboken: John Wiley & Sons, Inc., 2012), 129-131.

interest. The long-term good of the group will grow as a result. Here are some steps you can take to use your words with intention and to achieve the outcomes you're chasing for yourself and others:

- Distinguish between a statement (requires no response), a request (requires either 'yes' or 'no' in response), or a command (where 'yes' is the only viable answer).
- Ensure others know these distinctions as well and can discern between them in real-time.
- Practice framing your words to make it clear which path you're choosing, and request clarification from others if you're not clear whether you're receiving a statement, request, or command.
- Empower others, especially those who are your subordinates or juniors, to say 'no' to requests.
- When you say no to a request, articulate why you're doing so: "I'm going to say no to that request because I've already committed my time for the remainder of the week and don't want to fall short on my promises."
- Be clear on the repercussions of your 'yes' response to a command: "I'm happy to place running that report for you at the top of my to-do list, but it will mean that I miss deadlines for another action I have open with you as well as commitments with three other people. Are you okay with that?"

Also, consider the impact your words will have before delivering them, and examine whether you should sharpen or soften one or several words to either emphasize their importance or protect another person or idea.

GROUP DYNAMICS / THE PRIMES (COVERED IN CHAPTER 6)

Image 14: The Primes Book Cover[110]

Any time two or more people convene, certain dynamics are at play. Sometimes they're interpersonal in nature; other times, they're highly social at a meta-level. Still, other times, those dynamics are turned inward and cause us to do and think things based on how we feel others perceive us.

---

110 McGoff, Chris. *The Primes: How Any Group Can Solve Any Problem.* Hoboken: John Wiley & Sons, Inc., 2012.

My recommendation on tactics for group dynamics is simple—deeply explore The Primes. This body of knowledge, developed by The Clearing's founder Chris McGoff and many thought partners, is based on hundreds of collective years of experience with leaders and organizations around the world. The Primes are universal patterns of group behavior that explore areas like leading in uncertain times, patterns of powerful alliances, outstanding group performance, and group failure, as well as thriving in ambiguity. In these times of change and upheaval, our ability to tune into these dynamics and reveal the big ideas resident in them for the good of all is paramount.

Get to know The Primes and another wonderfully helpful set of frameworks—Liberating Structures—and try them out with whoever happens to be close at hand. Your family, your friends, your coworkers, or even allies of convenience and necessity can all benefit equally.

LADDER OF INFERENCE (COVERED IN CHAPTER 6)

Once you see and get to know the Ladder of Inference, it's hard not to see it at play with yourself and with others. This is one big idea that, at least for me, has just been *sticky* in that I see it again and again through the years. While many may assume a negative orientation to the Ladder itself (thinking that running up the Ladder leads to incorrect assumptions and unfounded or unnecessary action), it is just as readily applicable in a positive light. So, consider the following tactics when you sense or see this big idea in play:

- Stop, notice, and ask yourself, am I taking in this observable data as a video recorder would see it? Or am I seeing it through my own particular lens or bias?

- Question why you choose the facts you select from all available data. Be honest with yourself.
- Do your best to name for yourself when you're moving up the Ladder, and *ask yourself if that serves you and others at that moment.*
- Return to the full facts (all observable data) often. Don't just rely on a loose recollection of what that all-important first step was like, especially if it's in the distant past.
- Apply the overlays of your beliefs and experiences to positive instead of negative effect. *Be the chooser* in that regard and don't get hijacked.[111]
- Communicate. Always, always communicate. Irish playwright George Bernard Shaw famously said, "The single biggest problem with communication is the illusion that it has taken place." Never assume that your message made it through; rather, confirm and ensure out loud.
- When in doubt, try walking through your reasoning and rationale with a friend or colleague. Is it simple and straightforward to do so, and can that third party follow your logic? If so, you're probably on the right track. If not, it's likely time to return to first principles: the observable data.

The key is to build intention into each rung. Be in charge and aware of how and when you're moving up the Ladder whenever possible instead of doing so in an unconscious manner. The crux of this tool is to arrive at better conclusions, make better decisions, and make useful instead of faulty assumptions. When we're able to be honest and choose intentionality, we can deploy this big idea as a powerful force for good.

---

111 "The Ladder of Inference: How to Avoid Jumping to Conclusions," Mindtools, accessed October 7, 2020.

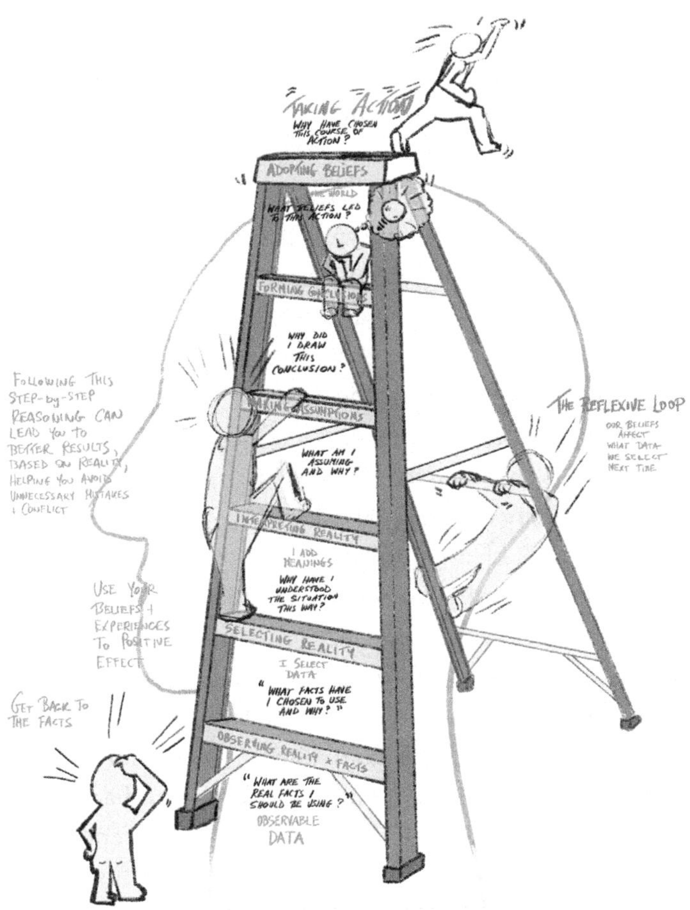

Image 15: The Ladder of Inference

INTENTIONAL DESIGN – TIME (COVERED IN CHAPTER 6)

The basics of designing time effectively, be it for a meeting, a social gathering, or something else, are malleable depending on the situation. However, some solid guidelines and tactics can serve you regardless of what outcome you're chasing:

- Whenever possible, budget at least twice as much time for planning and design as you will spend in the event itself. Thus, if you're convening and will lead a two-hour meeting, plan ahead so you can devote at least four hours to getting clear on what really matters and how you'll achieve it.
- The basics for most investments of time (especially in a professional setting) should have, at a minimum, a purpose statement (why you're asking for their time), outcomes (what they can expect to leave with), and an agenda (the group's path during the time that will empower them to achieve the outcomes). All attendees should have a chance to consume, and ideally comment on, these three things *before* the meeting occurs.
- If you can't clearly articulate any of these basics, you probably shouldn't ask for anyone's time in the first place.

True leaders realize time is our most valuable shared resource: when they ask for and receive time from someone (especially a group), they understand they've entered into a social contract. Honoring that contract as you would any other contract is not only required; your reputation depends on it. Thus we can and should expect our time to be as well-designed as we expect our smartphones, furniture, and other assets to be. Perhaps even more so.

BRAIN SCIENCE (COVERED IN CHAPTER 7)

Understanding the basics of our brain's internal neurochemistry was one of my own biggest a-ha moments. Earlier, we learned our brains are home to more than one hundred billion neurons. We have more of these nerve cells than there are stars in the Milky Way Galaxy. In the face of that incomprehensible complexity, I felt the basics of brain science explained more about me and those around me than just about anything else. Behaviors, thought processes, and communication all became much clearer and simpler to understand once I had my head wrapped around some of the fundamental building blocks of how our minds function in different situations. Let's break some of these tactics and applications down by brain chemical.

Dopamine: Our mind's chemical reward response.

- If you're a list person, make sure to check off your accomplishments as you go. That little boost you get each time you do is a mini shot of dopamine.
- Break down big, audacious goals into more consumable, achievable interim milestones. Not only will you feel good when you achieve one of those milestones, but you'll be able to see yourself and others tangibly.

Endorphins: Our mind's way of dulling pain so we can achieve tough goals.

- Exercise can bring about an 'athlete's high,' which can help to access a flow state (more on that below).
- Laugh. Seriously. Our brains release endorphins when we laugh. Not only is it good for you, but this is one of the simplest ways to access the positive parts of this particular brain chemical.

Oxytocin: Our mind's chemical incentive to help others.

- Put simply, seek out situations where you can help others as frequently as possible—volunteering, pausing to lend a hand to someone who could clearly use it, or being generous with your time and money for those less fortunate than you.

- The presence of oxytocin in your brain and body can actively combat the negative effects of cortisol, so seek it out!

Serotonin: Our mind's way of incentivizing our connections to others.

- Give credit to others when possible and when it's due: both you and they will reap the rewards and feel better to boot.
- Seek out and incentivize the creation and realization of shared goals instead of individual goals (for instance, a *collective* revenue target versus an *individual* revenue target).

Cortisol: Our mind's chemical fight-or-flight trigger.

- Notice when your blood pressure rises unexpectedly and when you feel flushed, hot, or begin sweating even when you're not physically exerting yourself.
- Pause to ask yourself if you're actually in danger, real or perceived, or if an unconscious trigger could be causing your cortisol response.

Explore some of your own neurological responses to different situations with family, friends, and coworkers. Ask them what they observe about you in different settings: when leading up a big deadline, when interacting with your superiors, and other dynamics. Their insights might surprise you and will almost assuredly broaden your self-awareness.

IMPOSTOR SYNDROME (COVERED IN CHAPTER 7)

Impostor syndrome is as pervasive in our world as it is corrosive to our self-esteem and self-belief. Roughly 70 percent of us will experience this phenomenon in some way during our lifetimes. Here are some ready tactics you can use to begin unpacking your own impostor syndrome or help others see their own in a safe way:

- Don't conflate approval from others (especially perceived approval) with love or worthiness. Above all else, don't allow your self-worth to become contingent on your achievements. In fact, unpack those two separate ideas to decouple them whenever possible.[112]
- Return to first principles often. Remember that you got *that job*, are attending *that school*, or have *that opportunity* because of your experience, intelligence, and because you're the right person for it. Positive self-talk seems obvious to an outside observer but can feel almost inaccessible to the person suffering from impostor syndrome.
- Both impostor syndrome and the Dunning-Kruger effect "generate a loss of connection with reality that hinders and alters our decision-making and perception."[113] One way to mitigate this is to focus on self-determination. Mihaly Csikszentmihalyi drove this point home when he stated, "Repression is not the way to virtue. When people restrain themselves out of fear, their lives are by necessity

---

112 Kirsten Weir, "Feel like a fraud?" *American Psychological Association*, November 2013.

113 Ricardo Vargas, "Cognitive Bias: The Dunning Kruger Effect and Impostor Syndrome—Part 3 of 3," September 16, 2019, in 5 Minutes Podcast, podcast, MP3 audio, 6:53.

diminished. Only through freely chosen discipline can life be enjoyed and still kept within the bounds of reason."[114]

- For particularly pervasive impostor syndrome, seek out someone who can listen and help. Quality therapy can be a game changer if none of the above tactics seem to work for you.
- Know that you're not alone.

My The Clearing colleague and mentor, Sharon Benjamin, whom we met in the previous chapter, has always been a champion for those having a rough go of it. During a constitutional law course that really challenged her, Sharon decided to shift the course to pass / fail instead of traditionally graded. When she earned the highest 'A' grade the professor had given in three years, Sharon requested she be allowed to revert back to the graded approach, but was not allowed to do so. That ended up being the difference between graduating cum laude and not. Sharon's lesson that applies powerfully to those struggling with impostor syndrome: *don't bet against yourself.* She also sagely stated we should "have the bravery to see and name it for ourselves and others if we suspect we're a horse of a different color." Sometimes we're just not made for certain systems. Don't shy away from that reality.

Finally, and perhaps most importantly, have the courage to name impostor syndrome for what it is with those around you. This requires more than a modicum of trust, as it can be a tough thing to hear. When it comes from a place of caring, naming this big idea can make all the difference in the world.

---

[114] Mihaly Csikszentmihalyi, *Flow: The Psychology of Optimal Experience* (New York: Harper Collins Publishers, 2008.

DUNNING-KRUGER EFFECT (COVERED IN CHAPTER 7)

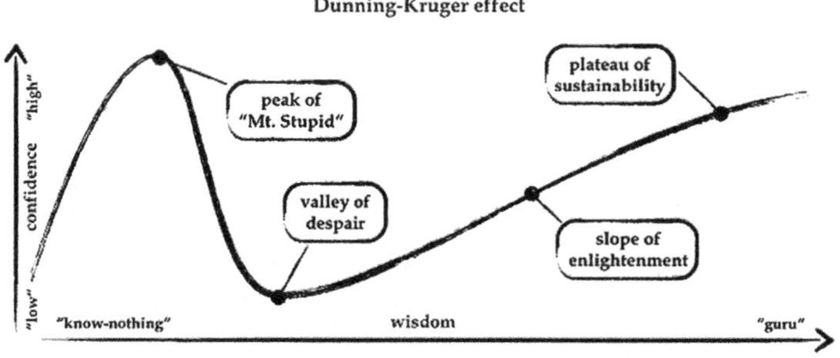

Image 16: The Dunning-Kruger Effect[115]

The Dunning-Kruger effect describes the strange reality where those who know the least view themselves as an expert on that same topic, whereas those who know much more:

- Stick with things and don't abandon them early. You'll notice a hook effect as your experience increases. Your confidence with any given topic will continue to rise over time as long as you don't push the eject button on your practice.
- Know you're not alone. Take comfort from that fact and use the positive energy to find and deploy your unique strengths.
- Leverage a strengths-based approach to your work when you sense the Dunning-Kruger effect in play. Tune in to your unique brand of talent, ability, and leadership, and channel the majority of your energy there instead of focusing on weak spots.

---

115 Ulf Ehlert, "The Dunning-Kruger Effect in Innovation, *Understanding Innovation* (blog), July 3, 2015.

Just as above, naming this big idea when you see it in those around you can and should be a practice you deploy whenever possible.

FLOW (COVERED IN CHAPTER 8)

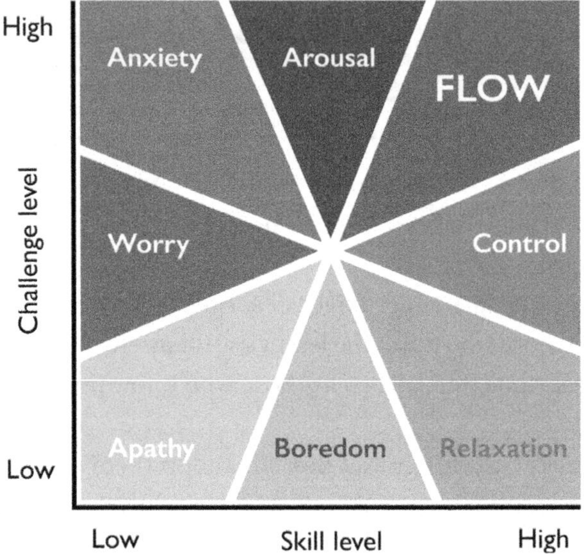

Figure 17: Flow[116]

You might know a flow state as being 'in the zone.' A state of being where the rest of the world temporarily melts away. We're capable of transcendent things when we can access a flow state. As such, it's worth investing some time into how we might increase the likelihood of accessing flow in everyday life:

---

[116] Hans Manzke, "Harnessing Flow to Drive Organizational Outcomes," *The Clearing*, (blog), September 1, 2020.

Stretch Your Limits—*but Not So Far Something Breaks*

If you find yourself performing tasks or focusing on areas that you can do in your sleep, chances are it's time to push your limits. Flow states are most accessible when a task requires you to lean out over a skill precipice, but not so far that you're likely to plunge over the edge.

Once you think you've identified the boundary of a particular skill or practice, notated here as '*n*,' focus on what '*n+1*' might look like. Then try on that step beyond what you consider your personal boundary to be. Critically, allow yourself the time and generosity of mind to remain in the discomfort and novelty of your intentional high-wire act. You may unconsciously deploy a personal defense mechanism or lapse into self-doubt. Do your best to maintain objectivity, and if possible, notate the sensations you experience. Those insights will be invaluable to you as you build your flow muscles.

Choose What Supercharges You and Ruthlessly Eliminate Distraction

Deeply understand the environment and factors you require in order to focus and tune into flow best and most often. To practice this, identify and stop doing tasks and activities that bore you: outsource, say 'no' to energy drains, and eliminate any unnecessary tasks that feel like chores. Simultaneously, try at least three new tasks, activities, or experiences each month. After each of these new experiences, ask yourself: "What specifically did I like about this task, activity, or exercise? What parts didn't I enjoy?" Record your findings in a way that makes sense to you. Treating these experiences as a lab for evaluating your focus and enjoyment will drastically increase your chances of accessing powerful flow states.

Recharge Your Personal Batteries Early and Often

No matter how packed your schedule is, the more in balance you are, the more likely you are to achieve flow. Prioritize a walk around the block, seek out and engage with a friend or colleague you wish you spent more time with, or just find a quiet space where you can set aside the day's rigors for a few minutes.

Seek Meaning in Your Work—Don't Stop 'til You Find It

No one can tell you what your values and personal meaning are or should be at work. Finding meaning takes searching, trial and error, and a willingness to fail, and that meaning can take different forms. Some discover meaning at work by contributing to a powerful mission like defending the environment or promoting social justice. Others derive their meaning from partnering with people they care about—colleagues and clients, for example. Still, others derive meaning from the opportunity to deploy a specific talent, gift, or skill—teaching or dancing, for example.

No matter which avenue provides the most meaning to you, it's critical to *feel* meaning in your work. Ask yourself: do you feel a sense of purpose and meaning from alignment with organizational mission, partnering with people, or getting to use one of your talents? It might be necessary to abandon comfort in search of an opportunity that more closely aligns with your values and give you the best chance to find meaning in your work. Feeling professionally challenged, fulfilled, happy, and positively defined at work is within our reach. Seek and you will find.

Seek Out Flow-Adjacent States—Alone at First, Then with Teams

Flow is just one of eight key mental states that Csikszentmihalyi identified in his decades of research. When arrayed on an x-axis of skill and y-axis of challenge level, the mental states of Arousal and Control appear on either side of Flow. As Flow is an optimal state and inherently more difficult to achieve, one system hack is to deliberately step into situations that slightly exceed your current skill level (Arousal) or situations where you don't need to use all available skills to meet a challenge (Control). For example, you can enter into an Arousal state by agreeing to lead the creation of a product that you know will present a true challenge, and which will require some quick up-skilling above what you currently possess. In this state, you feel almost over-alert, as you're deliberately testing the boundaries of what you can comfortably perform. A Control state could look like agreeing to lead the creation of a product that you have experience performing multiple times in the past. The overall challenge presented by this endeavor is lower, and you know your skill level is commensurate with what you're asking of yourself. As both of these mental states share a border with Flow, you can more readily access a Flow state by seeking out Arousal or Control states and fine-tuning the level of challenge and skill required.

This explains why we can't focus on and comprehend more than one person talking at once, and it also frames why many or all of our bodily sensations and external distractions melt away when we enter a flow state. When in flow, we are incapable of monitoring our hunger or fatigue, conflict with those we care for— even our self-consciousness and ego. Essentially, our brains turn off access to many cognitive functions in order to remain engrossed in one singular task.

THE HUMAN REBOOT (COVERED IN CHAPTER 8)

Our mind is the world's most complex computer. Every computer needs to be completely powered down from time to time to function at its peak performance. Here are some tips and tricks you can deploy to make your own human reboot more effective and feel more accessible:

- Clearly demarcate physical space for your inspiration, especially if you're prone to sprawl.
- Build yourself a creativity kit that you can pack and unpack relatively easily. This makes your inspiration mobile and untethered to a specific area.
- Have a similar space where you go exclusively to focus. Some positive compartmentalization goes a long way.
- Write out a list, create a visual, or simply journal—whatever works best for you. This shifts what would otherwise be an act of mental recall to one of execution.

THE BOTTOM LINE

Frankly, there isn't anyone you couldn't learn to love once you've heard their story.

—FRED ROGERS

I'll add one more tactic you can use with any of the big ideas we've explored in this book or any big idea that our wide world holds. Seek out a person whom you know and trust and just start talking. Don't worry about designing the conversation. Simply begin somewhere and see how the conversation evolves organically. Listen closely, actively, and with empathy. New eyes see things old eyes miss. A fresh mind can cut through a lot of the mental cholesterol you may have built up on a topic, so go out on a limb and be vulnerable.

Above all, keep your mind open, adaptable, and curious. Wonder at the world around you. Every now and then, your fellow humans will surely give you cause to drop your head in shame, anger, or disgust. More often than that, they will inspire and empower you. No matter what you do or how you choose to be in the world, do so with intention. Remember, unseen forces or other people don't steer your ship—you do.

CONCLUSION

Only a few achieve the colossal task of holding together, without being split asunder, the clarity of their vision alongside an ability to take their place in a materialistic world. They are the modern heroes...artists at least have a form within which they can hold their own conflicting opposites together. But there are some who have no recognized artistic form to serve this purpose: they are the artists of the living. To my mind, these last are the supreme heroes in our soulless society.

—IRENE CLAREMONT DE CASTILLEJO

Big ideas are levers—mechanical advantage to shift bigger, heavier things than we could move under our own power.

What are those weighty objects that we endeavor to move from one spot in our minds to another spot, or perhaps off the edge of a precipice altogether, never to be seen again? Memory and myths: about ourselves and others. Trauma: both individual and shared. The weight of expectations and the distance between what we want and what we have. More happily, those ponderous things are also our greatest successes: our wildest dreams, and the gifts we give to ourselves and those we love.

I've come to know myself well enough to realize that my seeking nature is innate. Uncovering the *why* that underpins a *what*, or that is associated with a *who*, holds a special kind of satisfaction for me. It hits all of my brain's pleasure centers. And I realize it is not so for all. I know my fellow seekers are out there, and for those of you who aren't wired quite the same way, I implore you: take the big ideas housed in this work and make them your own. As my friend and colleague, Sharon Benjamin taught me: break them apart, turn them inside out, ask hard questions of them, and bend them to your will. Then, do some seeking of your own. Find more and new big ideas. Perhaps make the leap and create some of your own.

Things feel harder, more divided, and less sure than ever before. And yet another world is possible. It starts with each of us; inside of each of us, to be specific. We all strive for meaning, purpose, beauty, and acceptance. Leadership, like time, is relative, and the world is crying out for it, and that same purpose and beauty, indeed love, are not to be wrapped up and shoved into a dark corner that we only access intermittently. Rather, they should be at our center. Step into your own brand of leadership and revel in the unique gifts you can offer the world. I take my stand for me, and so should you. Big ideas can help you do it—more meaningfully and with your full self.

My friend Ari Joseph, with whom I lived in the same hall as a freshman at Middlebury College, recently summed up the beauty of the human spirit more eloquently than I could hope to: "I think that this is the purpose of life; to be able to put aside the frailty of existence and live as though it were never imminent."

Set aside your frailty, step out into the turbulent air, make some noise, and move the world with your own lever. I'll meet you out in that green field that lies beyond.

Out beyond ideas of wrongdoing and rightdoing, there is a field. I'll meet you there.

—RUMI

APPENDIX

INTRODUCTION

Jessie Ball duPont Fund. "Jessie Ball duPont Fund." Accessed October 14, 2020.

Matthiessen, Peter. *Nine-Headed Dragon River: Zen Journals 1969–1982.* Boulder: Shambhala Publications, 1986.

McGoff, Chris. *The Primes: How Any Group Can Solve Any Problem.* Hoboken: John Wiley & Sons, Inc., 2012.

Zilka, Ran. "Why Your Late Twenties Is the Worst Time of Your Life." *Harvard Business Review,* March 7, 2016. https://hbr.org/2016/03/why-your-late-twenties-is-the-worst-time-of-your-life.

CHAPTER 1

Gladwell, Malcolm. *Outliers: The Story of Success.* New York: Little, Brown and Company, 2008.

Janah, Leila. Accessed July 24, 2020. https://www.leila-janah.com/.

Myers, Lindsay. "The Self-Help Industry Helps Itself to Billions of Dollars." *Brain Blogger* (blog). May 23, 2014. http://

www.brainblogger.com/2014/05/23/the-self-help-industry-helps-itself-to-billions-of-dollars/.

TedX Talks. “Master Shi Heng Yi–5 hindrances to self-mastery | Shi Heng YI | TEDxVitosha.” February 13, 2020. Video, 18:36. https://www.youtube.com/watch?v=4-079YIasck.

TedX Talks. “Reversing global poverty | Leila Janah | TEDxAmsterdamWomen.” November 13, 2017. Video, 11:03. https://www.youtube.com/watch?v=oQZJ4ot4ONQ.

Wright, Travis. *Making New Mistakes: Leading Through Disruption With a Minimum of Chaos.* Potomac: New Degree Press, 2020, 89–90.

CHAPTER 2

Beaton, Caroline. ”Never Good Enough: Why Millennials Are Obsessed With Self-Improvement.” *Forbes*, February 25, 2016. https://www.forbes.com/sites/carolinebeaton/2016/02/25/never-good-enough-why-millennials-are-obsessed-with-self-improvement/#7836f1877efa.

Carmichael, Sarah Green. “Millennials Are Actually Workaholics, According to Research.” *Harvard Business Review*, August 17, 2016. https://hbr.org/2016/08/millennials-are-actually-workaholics-according-to-research.

Center for American Progress. “The Costly Business of Discrimination.” Accessed September 11, 2020. https://www.americanprogress.org/issues/lgbtq-rights/reports/2012/03/22/11234/the-costly-business-of-discrimination/

Cone Communications. “2016 Cone Communications Millennial Employment Engagement Survey.” https://static1.squarespace.com/static/56b4a7472b8dde3df5b7013f/t/5819e8b303596e3016ca0d9c/1478092981243/2016+Cone+Communications+Millennial+Employee+Engagement+Study_Press+Release+and+Fact+Sheet.pdf.

DDI, The Conference Board, EY. "Global Leadership Forecast 2018." http://www.ddiworld.com/research/global-leadership-forecast-2018.

Dixon-Fyle, Sundiata; Dolan, Kevin; Hunt, Vivian; and Prince, Sara. "Diversity Wins: How Inclusion Matters." Accessed October 19, 2020. https://www.mckinsey.com/featured-insights/diversity-and-inclusion/diversity-wins-how-inclusion-matters

Hewlett, Sylvia Ann; Marshall, Melina; and Sherbin Laura. "How Diversity Can Drive Innovation." *Harvard Business Review*, December 2013. https://hbr.org/2013/12/how-diversity-can-drive-innovation

Inclusive Outcomes LLC. "The Stats." Accessed September 11, 2020. https://www.inclusiveoutcomes.com/the-stats/

Purdue University Global. "Generational Differences in the Workplace [Infographic]." Accessed September 11, 2020. https://www.purdueglobal.edu/education-partnerships/generational-workforce-differences-infographic/.

Robinhood. "Careers." Accessed September 19, 2020. https://careers.robinhood.com/

Talent Economy. "Millennials Want Workplaces With Social Purpose. How Does Your Company Measure Up?" Accessed September 11, 2020. https://www.chieflearningofficer.com/2018/02/20/millennials-want-workplaces-social-purpose-company-measure/.

CHAPTER 3

DDI, The Conference Board, EY. "Global Leadership Forecast 2018." http://www.ddiworld.com/research/global-leadership-forecast-2018.

Eurich, Tasha. "What Self-Awareness Really Is (and How to Cultivate It)." *Harvard Business Review*, January 4,

2018. https://hbr.org/2018/01/what-self-awareness-really-is-and-how-to-cultivate-it.

Hewlett, Sylvia Ann, Marshall, Melinda, & Sherbin, Laura. "Looking for Innovation in All the Wrong Places." *Stanford Social Innovation Review,* September 12, 2013. https://ssir.org/articles/entry/looking_for_innovation_in_all_the_wrong_places

Merriam-Webster.com Dictionary, s.v. "self-awareness," accessed September 14, 2020, https://www.merriam-webster.com/dictionary/self-awareness.

PositivePsychology.com. "What Is Self-Awareness and Why Is It Important? [+5 Ways to Increase It]." Accessed September 15, 2020. https://positivepsychology.com/self-awareness-matters-how-you-can-be-more-self-aware/.

CHAPTER 4

BBC Future. "A high-carb diet may explain why Okinawans live so long." January 17, 2019. https://www.bbc.com/future/article/20190116-a-high-carb-diet-may-explain-why-okinawans-live-so-long.

BBC Worklife. "Ikigai: A Japanese concept to improve work and life." August 7, 2017. https://www.bbc.com/worklife/article/20170807-ikigai-a-japanese-concept-to-improve-work-and-life.

Blue Zones. "Moai—This Tradition is Why Okinawan People Live Longer, Better." Accessed September 21, 2020. https://www.bluezones.com/2018/08/moai-this-tradition-is-why-okinawan-people-live-longer-better/.

Cook, Gareth. "Why We Are Wired to Connect." *Scientific American,* October 22, 2013. https://www.scientificamerican.com/article/why-we-are-wired-to-connect/.

Freiberg, Kevin and Jackie. "Madiba Leadership: 5 Lessons Nelson Mandela Taught The World About Change." *Forbes*, February 25, 2016. https://www.forbes.com/sites/kevinandjackiefreiberg/2018/07/19/madiba-leadership-5-lessons-nelson-mandela-taught-the-world-about-change/#6505229d41ba.

iStock by Getty Images. "Diagram of Japanese ikigai concept."Accessed October 20, 2020. https://www.istockphoto.com/vector/diagram-of-japanese-ikigai-concept-gm679938536-124665395

Matthiessen, Peter. *The Snow Leopard*. New York: Viking Press, 1978.

Rampton, John. "What Millennials Can Teach You About Being Happy." *Inc*, July 31, 2017. https://www.inc.com/john-rampton/what-millennials-can-teach-us-about-how-to-be-happ.html.

Ritvo, Eva. "The Neuroscience of Giving," *Psychology Today*, April 24, 2014. https://www.psychologytoday.com/us/blog/vitality/201404/the-neuroscience-giving.

Stone, Sharon L.M. "Examining the development of self-authorship among student veterans." PhD diss., William and Mary, 2014. https://scholarworks.wm.edu/cgi/viewcontent.cgi?article=6752&context=etd.

TedX Talks. "How to Ikigai | Tim Tamashiro | TEDxYYC." September 8, 2018. Video, 12:42.

TedX Talks. "The power of us | Mari Kuraishi | TEDxTraverseCity." September 26, 2014. Video, 20:25.

US Africa Online. "Nelson Mandela lived as a moral colossus." December 9, 2013. https://usafricaonline.com/2013/12/09/nelson-mandela-lived-as-a-moral-colossus-by-bishop-desmond-tutu/.

Witters, Dan. "US Wellbeing Declines Halted in 2019." *Gallup, September 25, 2019.* https://news.gallup.com/poll/266978/wellbeing-declines-halted-2019.aspx.

CHAPTER 5

Adapted from Budd, M. and Rothstein, L. "You Are What You Say" *New Age*, Vol 17:9. Watertown, MA: New Age Publishing (2000). 1–6

Brainard, Michael. "The Impact Of Unconscious Bias On Leadership Decision Making." *Forbes*, September 13, 2017. https://www.forbes.com/sites/carolinebeaton/2016/02/25/never-good-enough-why-millennials-are-obsessed-with-self-improvement/#7836f1877efa.

Built In. "12 Unconscious Bias Examples and How to Avoid Them in the Workplace." Accessed September 25, 2020. https://builtin.com/diversity-inclusion/unconscious-bias-examples

Center for American Progress. "The Costly Business of Discrimination." Accessed September 26, 2020. https://www.americanprogress.org/issues/lgbtq-rights/reports/2012/03/22/11234/the-costly-business-of-discrimination/

Goleman, Daniel. *Emotional Intelligence: Why It Can Matter More Than IQ.* New York: Bantam Books, 1995.

Kennedy, John F. "Rice Stadium Moon Speech," (speech). September 12, 1962. https://er.jsc.nasa.gov/seh/ricetalk.htm

Kidder, Rushworth. *Moral Courage.* New York: William Morrow Paperbacks, 2005.

McGoff, Chris. *The Primes: How Any Group Can Solve Any Problem.* Hoboken: John Wiley & Sons, Inc., 2012.

Psychology Today. "Micro-Inequities: 40 Years Later." Accessed September 26, 2020. https://www.psychologytoday.com/us/blog/the-superhuman-mind/201304/micro-inequities-40-years-later

University of Idaho. "Searle on Speech Acts." Accessed July 29, 2020. https://www.webpages.uidaho.edu/~mororurke/443-phil/06-Spring/Handouts/Philosophical/Searle.htm

Vanderbilt University. "Unconscious Bias." Accessed September 25, 2020. https://www.vanderbilt.edu/diversity/unconscious-bias/

CHAPTER 6

Baer, Drake and De Luce, Ivan. "$37 billion are lost every year on these 12 meeting mistakes." *Business Insider*, last modified June 6, 2019.

BehavioralEconomics.com. "An Introduction to Behavioral Economics." Accessed September 23, 2020. https://www.behavioraleconomics.com/resources/introduction-behavioral-economics/

Bos, Benno. "Create a Circle of Safety: EDSO in Action." Accessed September 29, 2020. www.bennobos.com

Liberating Structures: Including and Unleashing Everyone. "Introduction." Accessed September 23, 2020. http://www.liberatingstructures.com/

McGoff, Chris. *The Primes: How Any Group Can Solve Any Problem*. Hoboken: John Wiley & Sons, Inc., 2012.

Original work created by Matteo Becchi.

Parker, Priya. *The Art of Gathering: How We Meet and Why it Matters*. New York: Riverhead Books, 2018.

Senge, Peter. *The Fifth Discipline Fieldbook: Strategies and Tools for Building a Learning Organization*. New York: Doubleday, 1994.

Vanderbilt University. "No Exit and Three Other Plays by Jean Paul Sartre." Accessed October 12, 2020. https://www.vanderbilt.edu/olli/class-materials/Jean-Paul_Sartre.pdf

CHAPTER 7

Baraz, James and Alexander, Shoshana. "The Helper's High." *Great Good Magazine*, February 1, 2010. https://greatergood.berkeley.edu/article/item/the_helpers_high

Bos, Benno. "Create a Circle of Safety: EDSO in Action." Accessed September 29, 2020. www.bennobos.com

Brandon, John. "These Updated Stats About How Often You Use Your Phone Will Humble You." *Inc.* November 19, 2019. https://www.inc.com/john-brandon/these-updated-stats-about-how-often-we-use-our-phones-will-humble-you.html

Dunning, David and Kruger, Justin. "Unskilled and unaware of it: how difficulties in recognizing one's own incompetence lead to inflated self-assessments." PubMed.gov. Accessed July 19, 2020. https://pubmed.ncbi.nlm.nih.gov/10626367/

Ehlert, Ulf. "The Dunning-Kruger Effect in Innovation, *Understanding Innovation* (blog), July 3, 2015. https://understandinginnovation.blog/2015/07/03/the-dunning-kruger-effect-in-innovation/

Entrepreneur. "12 Leaders, Entrepreneurs and Celebrities Who Have Struggled With Imposter Syndrome: Sheryl Sandberg." Accessed September 29, 2020. https://www.entrepreneur.com/slideshow/304273#1

Fraser, Petula Alicia. "The 13 Best Ways for Stopping Imposter Syndrome to Elevate Your Confidence." Last modified January 13, 2020. https://thriveglobal.com/stories/the-13-best-ways-for-stopping-imposter-syndrome-to-elevate-your-confidence/

Gaiman, Neil. *"Commencement Speech, University of the Arts," video, 19:54. https://www.youtube.com/watch?v=ikAb-NYkseI*

Kennedy, John F. "Rice Stadium Moon Speech," (speech). September 12, 1962. https://er.jsc.nasa.gov/seh/ricetalk.htm

New Scientist. "Introduction: The Human Brain." Last Modified September 4, 2006. https://www.newscientist.com/article/dn9969-introduction-the-human-brain/#:~:-text=The%20brain%20is%20the%20most,billion%20nerve%20cells%2C%20or%20neurons.

Rege, Sanil. "Neurobiology of Stress and Resilience." Last updated April 28, 2020. https://psychscenehub.com/psychinsights/neurobiology-of-stress-and-resilience/

Schmidt-Nielsen, Knut. *Animal Physiology: Adaptation and Environment.* Cambridge: Cambridge University Press, 1997.

Safe Launch (blog). "15 Fascinating Facts you Didn't Know About Your Brain." April 2, 2013. Accessed July 27, 2020. https://www.safelaunch.org/15-fascinating-facts-you-didnt-know-about-your-brain/#:~:text=Your%20brain%20is%20estimated%20to,in%20the%20Milky%20Way%20galaxy.&-text=A%20piece%20of%20brain%20tissue,%E2%80%9C-talking%E2%80%9D%20to%20each%20other.

Ted. "How students of color confront impostor syndrome | Dena Simmons." January 17, 2017, video, 10:20. https://www.youtube.com/watch?v=8sQ2p89PoUs&t=135s

CHAPTER 8

Boyd, Robynne. "Do People Only Use 10 Percent of Their Brains?" Scientific American, *February 7, 2008. https://www.scientificamerican.com/article/do-people-only-use-10-percent-of-their-brains/*

Csikszentmihalyi, Mihaly. *Beyond Boredom and Anxiety: Experiencing Flow in Work and Play.* San Francisco: Jossey Bass, 2000.

Csikszentmihaly, Mihaly. *Good Business: Leadership, Flow, and the Making of Meaning.* New York: Viking, 2003.

eCorner. "Creativity Loves Constraint." May 17, 2006, video, 1:40. https://ecorner.stanford.edu/videos/creativity-loves-constraint/

Manzke, Hans. "Harnessing Flow to Drive Organizational Outcomes." *The Clearing,* (blog), September 1, 2020. https://theclearing.com/ideas-and-insights/harnessing-flow-drive-organizational-outcomes/

Mihaly Csikszentmihalyi. "Kristine Marin Kawamura, PhD interviews Mihaly Csikszentmihalyi, PhD." Interview by Kristine Kawamura. *Cross Cultural Management An International Journal.* no. 21 (2014), 476-492. https://www.researchgate.net/publication/279050513_Kristine_Marin_Kawamura_PhD_interviews_Mihaly_Csikszentmihalyi_PhD

Sony. "The Founding Prospectus." About Sony. Accessed September 1, 2020. https://www.sony.net/SonyInfo/CorporateInfo/History/prospectus.htm.

Ted. "Mihaly Csikszentmihalyi: Flow, the secret to happiness." October 24, 2008, video, 18:55. https://www.youtube.com/watch?v=fXIeFJCqsPs&t=53s

CHAPTER 9

Csikszentmihalyi, Mihaly. *Flow: The Psychology of Optimal Experience.* New York: Harper Collins Publishers, 2008.

Hanh, Thich Nhat. *You Are Here.* Boulder: Shambhala, 2010.

McGoff, Chris. *The Primes: How Any Group Can Solve Any Problem.* Hoboken: John Wiley & Sons, Inc., 2012.

Mindtools. "The Ladder of Inference: How to Avoid Jumping to Conclusions." Accessed October 7, 2020. https://www.mindtools.com/pages/article/newTMC_91.htm

Vargas, Ricardo. "Cognitive Bias: The Dunning Kruger Effect and Impostor Syndrome – Part 3 of 3." September 16, 2019. In 5 Minutes Podcast. Podcast, MP3 audio, 6:53. https://ricardo-vargas.com/podcasts/cognitive-bias-the-dunning-kruger-effect-and-impostor-syndrome-part-3-of-3/

Weir, Kirsten. "Feel like a fraud?" *American Psychological Association*, November 2013. https://www.apa.org/gradpsych/2013/11/fraud

Made in the USA
Middletown, DE
16 July 2022

69507752R00126

Empire Of Strings

The Space Between Souls

Jeffrey Lee

Empire Of Strings
Jeffrey Lee

ISBN: 978-1-956193-32-9
Book Design & Publishing done by:
Global Book Publishing
www.globalbookpublishing.com

Prologue: String The Stars

Fifteen Years Ago

Only artists ever walked the mountain path. It was said that the only thing worth seeing in the clearing where the river paused its climb up the mountain was the view of the city below. But so many paintings of that view hung in galleries all throughout Unity Falls—paintings Emilyn had seen a hundred times—that the view itself was both alluring and underwhelming.

Her father had said it was the spot where some of the city's most famous artists had begun their journeys. Sitting close to the edge of the mountainside, he seemed captivated by that very view. Emilyn did have to admit that the city looked a bit more alive at night from that high up, each light its own signifier of life. A family spending the evening together or one of the numerous galleries throughout the city trying to draw people toward its particular brand of art. Beyond that, however, to Emilyn, it was just the city from higher up. Nothing special about it. She felt no grand inspiration to paint the scene. She did enjoy the quiet, though. Things were peaceful up that high, with only the sound of the water gently flowing by or the occasional sparker buzzing around in the tree line. Things were so noisy in the city.

Jade seemed to enjoy it as well. The little carbuncle curled up in Emilyn's lap, her three ears gently folding down onto her little head as she relaxed, basking in the serenity of a quiet night. Emilyn ran her finger's across the ruby fur on Jade's back, caressing her friend, who loved nothing more than a little attention at the end of the day. Zarlyn glanced over at them and smiled.

"Someone's relaxed," he said, testing the statement by reaching over and just barely touching the top of Jade's head. To both their surprise, the carbuncle didn't shy away. Jade wasn't fond of Emilyn's father. They hadn't ever figured out why, but anytime Zarlyn ever tried to show her the attention they both knew she craved, she pulled away. "Really relaxed." He didn't push his luck, pulling his hand away after a moment and meeting Emilyn's eyes. "Ready?"

"Ready," she confirmed. She had been waiting all day, and despite the relaxing atmosphere suggesting sleep as a nice alternative, she wasn't about to let this pass her by. She wasn't going to let her incident in class get her down. She wasn't just required to get control over her light; she wanted to. It was exciting. Finally, she would get to be just like her father.

"All right, show me," he prompted, and she took a deep breath. She had been practicing hard to get this part right. Closing her eyes, she lifted a hand toward the stars in the night sky. She didn't need her eyes to find what she was looking for. It was there. It had always been there.

Extending a single finger, she let it drift a little across the stars until it settled on a pair just a little isolated from the others. But that was okay because they had each other. And they had all the tracers on Seranno like her and her father that felt drawn to them, or at least in their direction. It was like a candle always lit in the back of her soul. Most of the time it went about, its flame unnoticed, but in moments when the noise was quiet and the race of thoughts and memories calm, it was there. Calling to her. Tugging her toward that spot in the night sky like a tether.

"There," she pointed toward it, opening her eyes and watching her father's follow where she pointed. His eyes found the same point she had. He felt it too. Every tracer did. He gave an approving look, settling his gaze back on her as she lowered her hand.

"How do you know?" he asked.

"The look on your face," she retorted, and he smiled.

"And if you didn't have the look on my face to tell you?" he asked, letting the smile turn into a frown. "If you were alone?"

"I'm never alone," she said. "Because I can feel it." She let her eyes linger up toward those two stars. The candle let off a warmth that coated her—comforted her. She had felt it before, though she hadn't known what it was until after her incident. It was the first thing her father had explained to her.

"Where?"

"Everywhere ..." She paused, meeting his eyes again. "In my soul."

"Souls are tricky things," Zarlyn replied. "What comes from them isn't always clear to us. And yet ..." He hesitated, sighing. "We would be nothing without them."

"They told us in class that everything has a soul ..." She ran her fingers along Jade's back again, and the creature purred, unconcerned with the conversation. "And if everything has a soul"—she looked up again—"then so do stars, right? So, if we didn't have souls, we'd just be like the space between the stars." Zarlyn didn't say anything for a long moment, opting to let the silence scream in the air between them as he adopted a somber expression. "What's wrong?" asked Emilyn.

He shook his head.

"Nothing," he replied, managing a smile. "You're only eleven. I'm ... amazed and terrified at how wise you are. You're too young to start understanding what you just said."

"I am not," she pouted, folding her arms. "How can I be too young to understand it if I understand it? That just means I'm the exact right age!" she retorted, and Zarlyn chuckled.

"All right, well, let's put that to the test. What's the reason tracers associate that feeling with their souls?"

"Easy," Emilyn began. "Tracers can look inside their souls to create their illusions."

"Their own souls," Zarlyn said with a nod. "And others. Which is what I want you to do now. I've got an image I want you to create an illusion of. Think you can find and trace it?" Emilyn nodded. She had been practicing diving into her own soul, though she hadn't been able to project an illusion of her own yet. Her father said looking inward was simple because you were already there. But diving into someone else's soul was something else entirely. She hadn't admitted to him that it scared her a little. She wanted him to think she was confident. He was confident. And she wanted to be like him. He was a hero. "Tracing is all about focus, remember," he said, as if sensing the diverging paths her thoughts were taking. "Narrow your thoughts. Narrow the other person's thoughts. Find what you're looking for. Trace it. You can do this."

"You're forgetting the first part," Emilyn chimed in, and he narrowed his eyes at her.

"Hmm? Oh, right. Connect. Same idea. Focus yourself, find the bridge—"

"Walk across it," Emilyn finished, and he smiled at her. "I know." She didn't know. He had made it sound like something she needed to make happen, but the first time she did it, everything had just happened on its own. One second she was sketching over her classwork, and the next she was inside that boy's soul. She had no idea how she'd done it. But she supposed that was the point of all this. To figure that out.

"You can do this," he said, nodding to her. "My soul is wide open."

Emilyn could feel the bridge. It was a place she could reach just as the ground was a thing she could touch. But it wasn't a place she could see. And that made both finding it and crossing it a challenge. It wasn't in her soul like that spot in the sky seemed to be, but it was close. It was in the space between her and her father, but she couldn't quite find it. The most important step was the first one—that's what her father had said—but she couldn't take that step if she couldn't find the bridge. So, she let it slip away and sighed, shaking her head.

"Still can't find it," she said, her voice adopting a defeated tone. Her father extended a hand and placed it atop hers, passing her his understanding.

"Don't give up," he stated firmly and gently at the same time. "We promised we wouldn't."

"I know," Emilyn whined. "But I don't know what to do! You make it seem so easy. Why isn't it easy for me?"

He smiled. "Few things are easy the first time. It'll get better with practice. One step before the next, remember? Before you know it, you'll be where you want to be." She nodded, but she didn't believe him. And as the defeated expression lingered on her face, he gently lifted her chin with his finger, forcing her to meet his gaze. She managed a light smile. Satisfied, he pulled his hand away and looked up. "How about I tell you what I'm thinking instead?" That seemed counterproductive to her, searching his soul for it, but she didn't say that. Her father had rarely ever led her astray. He gestured to the two stars in the sky. "You're thinking something like ... they're alone, but they have each other, right?" he asked, settling back on her.

She tilted her head. "How did you know?" she asked, feeling like he had looked into her soul without her knowing. Something he had assured her was impossible.

"I know everything," he joked, and she pouted a little. "Look up at them," he instructed, and she did so. "Maybe it's not just companionship connecting them? Maybe there's something more? What do you think that would look like?" Emilyn gazed thoughtfully at the two stars and imagined some kind of cord linking them together. No, not a cord. A string. Tying them to one another. "Something that might change them from two stars into—"

"A single star," she finished, her voice an echo to her, something distant as something else took its place. The black of the night sky was washed over with a purple hue in an instant that came across as an eternity. A glow of the same color, though much brighter, resonated from below, and she gazed down to find purple liquid light streaming from her fingers and onto the grass below. Before she could even react, her father's hands were gripping her arms, a fierce but reassuring pride dripping from his eyes.

"It's okay!" he promised, holding her in place. "It's okay, I promise."

"The sky's purple!" Emilyn exclaimed, smiling wide. "It's purple!"

Zarlyn chuckled at her complete lack of panic, loosening his grip on her arms. "That happens when a tracer illusion is active," he replied, excited. "Though only tracers can see it," he clarified as she gazed at the bright light pooling in her palms.

"But you use the light all the time," she said, basking in the warm light he had been feeling all his life. It must've been so insignificant to him by that point. But to her, it was new and wonderful—like she had become what she was always meant to be. "I've never seen the sky turn purple."

"You weren't a tracer, then," he replied, gesturing toward the stars. "You are now."

She followed his gaze and found the two stars again. The string she had imagined lingered between them, allowing two stars to become one. She smiled, watching the illusion. The illusion she had created. "I didn't trace anything, though," she said, confused.

"You don't always have to," he replied and shook his head. "But we'll get into all that later. You did it!"

She had, and she was happy. Finally, she could be like him. She had a long way to go, but now she knew she could do it. And so much more. If she could string the stars, she could be anything she wanted.

Even Jade seemed impressed, slowly lifting her little head from her resting spot to peer up at the illusion. Or perhaps the glowing liquid light right next to her. It was hard to tell. She seemed drawn to it but not cautious of it as Emilyn would have expected. Instead, it seemed familiar to the little carbuncle as she became entranced. Emilyn wondered about that until she felt something else.

They weren't alone.

She wasn't certain how she had felt it or where from, but another soul had made itself known to hers. On instinct alone, she turned to the left and found a silhouetted figure farther down the clearing, having just emerged from the tree line. Zarlyn found the figure too and was quick to stand up. Recognition flooded his features.

"Dad?" she asked, and he looked down at her reassuringly.

"It's okay," he promised. "The illusion will fade in a minute. See if you can string those stars again, okay? I'll be right back." He walked away from her and toward the new presence, and Emilyn watched him. He seemed fearful but brave at the same time. She knew he could handle himself, though. He was a hero, after all. Trusting him, she refocused. The purple of the sky washed away back into its usual darkness, and the light seemed to retreat away from her hands, fading away. But where had it gone? How could she get it to come back? Jade had returned to resting, and she took a deep breath, willing her mind to focus as her father had instructed. She could do it again.

String the stars. There was no turning back. She was a tracer now.

A Crowd of Memories

Emilyn let the air linger in her lungs for a long moment before exhaling and fogging up the mirror, hoping her reflection might look different when it cleared. But those same dark blue eyes gazed back at her. She sighed, pleading with her nerves to find some semblance of tranquility. But the more her eyes settled over her chosen attire, the more impossible that seemed. She was decidedly not a fan of dressing up. It was a small miracle she had even let her hair down. But it was an important day, so she had begrudgingly accepted the sacrifice of temporary discomfort.

It was the opening of her very own gallery. All her artwork on display for the world to see. And critique. Coming to terms with that was challenging. On the one hand, she could handle judgment—file it away in some impenetrable box in the farthest corner of her soul. On the other hand, making art was what she knew she wanted to do. So what would she do if the gallery crashed and burned? Certainly not what her father had spent his life doing.

His reputation as the man who had saved the city from terrorists left him widely regarded as a good man. A hero. As his daughter, that reputation almost seemed expected of her as well. And while she wasn't unwilling to help someone if she could, it wasn't what she wanted to do. Her father understood that and never pushed her to be like him. But others hadn't understood. Almost every day, she was asked to do something he would do, and she was running out of ways to politely decline. She understood why people were asking her to do those things. They missed her father. She missed him, too. Though he wasn't gone, the likelihood of him performing the good deeds people had grown accustomed to was nonexistent.

She could help people, too. She was a tracer just like him, though she preferred tangible art to realistic illusions. Her father had encouraged her to pursue that as best he could. He was kind and good just as everyone said he was. But to her, he was just her father. A different kind of hero. She just wished he was there to see what she had created.

"Emilyn?" A perky voice brought her back from the wanderings of her mind, and she met her friend's eyes in the mirror. Kyshel looked stunning, a radiating exemplar of beauty and status. Her long blonde hair flowed naturally down her chest, blending flawlessly with the golden dress she has chosen. "You okay? I called your name four times."

Emilyn managed a weak smile at her friend. "Just thinking about Dad." She took another deep breath, comparing her own appearance to Kyshel's even though she knew that was the last thing she should be doing. Kyshel was religious in keeping up with the latest trends. She always had the perfect outfit for any occasion, and it always looked amazing on her. Emilyn was rarely seen outside of a dark shirt, leather jacket, long pants, and boots. Even rarer was her hair being stylized. Leaving it in a tail of some variety was typically the first thing she did when she woke up in the morning. It was auburn, naturally wavy, and while Kyshel often claimed she wished they could swap hair, Emilyn chose to view that as mere pity for her complete lack of style. For the occasion, she had traded her leather jacket with one more elegant. That, coupled with her hair falling loosely from her head, classified as dressing up for her. "I do not look like someone who is starting an art gallery."

"Relax," Kyshel stressed, putting her hands on either of Emilyn's arms and nudging her closer to the mirror. She smiled. "You look amazing."

"You look amazing," Emilyn retorted, gesturing to the dress that somehow managed to shine like the sun had been plucked out of the sky and draped over her. "I look like ... me, with a slightly nicer jacket than usual."

"Exactly. You look like you. That's the whole point. Today, you're putting yourself out there for everyone to see. Not looking like yourself while you do it would just make you another painting, and people would have to choose which is you—the girl whose story they're seeing in the art or the girl who looks uncomfortable in her own skin. This way, everything they see is definitively you. Trust me."

Emilyn knew she was right. She usually was. Given the fact that her best friend was an established and successful artist herself, Emilyn considered Kyshel's advice on all this law. More importantly than that, one typically trusted one's best friend. But this wasn't Kyshel's art. Kyshel wasn't the one splitting bits of herself into pictures for strangers to judge. Every picture out there was a part of her. How she presented herself was equally so.

"I know," Emilyn replied. "It's just nerves. A little bit of absolute terror, too. That's definitely there."

Kyshel smiled at her. "You have nothing to be afraid of," she said. "Your art is incredible. And so are you. They'll all see it." Kyshel pulled her into a hug, and it turned out that was exactly what she needed. Kyshel had been so good to her, supporting her through this process without doing it for her. She let Emilyn accomplish this on her own, only giving suggestions here and there.

Emilyn was grateful for that. Because she had accomplished this on her own. Only a single door remained between her and whatever came with that accomplishment. "Thanks," Emilyn said, managing a far stronger smile. "What would I have done if I hadn't met you?"

"The exact same thing, though you might've snuck into a few more galleries first," Kyshel said, chuckling. "Now, I did tell you I invited a few prospective buyers and studio heads, right?"

Emilyn's widened eyes nearly shattered the mirror. "You did not!" she exclaimed, feeling like her soul might tear itself free from her body. "I don't know how ... what do I even say to those people?"

"Relax," Kyshel stressed again. "You got this." She turned toward the door, grabbing the knob.

"That doesn't answer the question!" Emilyn said, grabbing the knob to prevent Kyshel from opening the door.

"You're the only one who can answer that question," she replied. "Like I said, just be you. That's all they want. Real. Authenticity. Heart and soul equal attention and profit. That's how these people tend to look at the world ..." She rolled her eyes. "Doesn't matter. Don't worry about impressing them. Just go out there and make sure people know who you are. Answer their questions. And I know you're perpetually against it, but for skies' sake don't forget to smile, Emi. You got this."

Emilyn cursed Kyshel for somehow both calming and further exasperating her. "I hate you."

"You love me," Kyshel corrected in a very matter-of-fact tone.

"I hate you right now," Emilyn amended, shooting her a brief glare. "Just ... maybe discuss inviting real artists with me next time?"

Kyshel let her shoulders fall and tilted her head, raising her eyebrows and putting her hands on her hips.

Emilyn sighed. "You're right. I never would have let you." She paused, settling on the door. "All right," she conceded, distantly feeling her hand shaking as she wrapped her fingers around the knob.

"Emilyn," Kyshel said, her voice taking on a more serious tone, and Emilyn stopped, looking into her friend's hazel eyes. "Your dad is here. In every painting out there and in every step you make and in every word you say, he's with you. And you are a real artist," she finished with a bright smile.

That was a nice speech, and as it turned out yet again, exactly what Emilyn needed. She nodded, silently thanking Kyshel. For the sheer miracle of being her friend. She may be her only one, but she was more than enough. Kyshel gently put her hand over Emilyn's on the knob. "Let's go make your dreams come true."

Together, they opened the door.

Guests had already begun filling in the spaces between paintings, more than Emilyn thought would have been there. Not a lot by the standards of the artistic center of Seranno, but it was something.

"I'm gonna start making rounds. You straighten your stance, smile, and talk to someone. Anyone." She stepped away but quickly turned back like her final words were an afterthought she had forgotten about. "Oh, and come find me if you start to split or something."

Words to live by. Kyshel wouldn't be far. Neither would be the loft upstairs if Emilyn decided to escape. She chided herself for thinking about escaping the room where her dreams may come true, even if it was normally an empty office space. Peering across the room and wondering what soul-crushing words might be infecting the air made that prospect incredibly alluring. At a glance, no one looked horrified. Many of them were gathered around the piece she had guessed would draw the most eyes. They Named Him A Hero. A depiction of the day her father had begun to earn his reputation by using tracer light to quell the mind of a particularly unstable tracer who had begun splitting. A crowd had formed to watch her father do the thing he did naturally, and they called him a hero. He always insisted he was simply at the right place at the right time. The ironic part was that the deed that had made his name known was the same thing that had left him with no choice but to abandon her.

Splitting was excruciating. Every tracer who had come out of a split in one piece had never been the same. Kyshel had described the numerous times she had split as her soul was trying to escape her body. Typically, this was the result of something overwhelming, like a tracer touching too many souls at once. There was only so much connection a single soul could handle. Kyshel had been one of the fortunate ones. Many were rendered comatose from a split, their soul in constant turmoil. Like her father. Many didn't survive at all. Splitting was an inevitability Emilyn didn't care to dwell on.

"Are you the artist?" someone asked, yanking her out of her thoughts. A male voice. She focused on him and managed a smile.

"That's me," she said, probably a bit too casually. "Uh, Emilyn," she was quick to add, offering her hand. The man took it and returned the friendly smile.

"Diselyn. With Sand Works Art and Illusions. An excellent depiction of your father's deeds," he said, gesturing to the painting. "I remember that day. He did a good thing. Probably saved that young man's life. Your depiction is curious. I suspect it came straight from the source," he whispered conspiratorially, then chuckled as Emilyn's face went redder than a carbuncle's fur. "Don't worry. I've worked with a lot of tracers. They see a lot they don't intend to and a lot they do." He shrugged. "There's no shame in using that, no matter what the Board says. I'm sure your father would be proud."

Emilyn breathed a sigh of relief. While it wasn't necessarily unethical of her to have used an image from her father's memory, it wasn't something she wanted to advertise. The Board had shut down aspiring artists for less.

"Thank you," was all Emilyn managed to say in response. He raised his glass to her and took a drink.

"Your work is solid, truly. I'd be happy to sponsor it at a venue of more stature in the future. Something more befitting of Zarlyn's daughter. If you like," he said, offering her a business card. There it was. Zarlyn's daughter. That was all she would be seen as by people in this city. That was what Diselyn wanted to sponsor, not her. Regardless, she gently snatched the business card and smiled. She wasn't going to voice her complaints. Not there. He was just one person. He raised his glass to her again and then rejoined the crowd.

Emilyn had seen a lot following her father around as a child, and just as much during her own futile attempts to follow in his footsteps. She didn't think it was wrong to use her experiences for her work, but not everyone would see it that way. These were her memories. These were the things that made her who she was. Walking through the gallery was like walking in a crowd of memories and not knowing which path to take back to the present.

That was okay. Her past remained her present. Paintings of Jade doing something mischievous or children playing in the streets or the water rising up the mountain comforted her—took her back to a time when things were better. These were all things she'd projected from her own memories to sketch and paint. There were advantages to being a tracer, and no one was expected to not take advantage of them, yet they were frowned upon. Every picture in the room could claim tracer light as its source. Because she found it easier to paint in isolation and away from the things she was actually painting. The city, animals, people ... she couldn't just paint them. Using tracer light focused her wandering mind—calmed the usual chaos that left her mind more scattered than the marketplace that bled into the twin rivers where supply boats arrived. Tracer light left her mind more akin to the city-center building, defined by the massive window of the governor's office overlooking the city. Definitely subtle. She had only ever painted one picture on the spot. Alone on the roof of their house after putting Jade to rest, she had sketched the view of the mountain at the city's edge as the water flowed upward. It had seemed to be struggling that day, and she had related. It was a simple picture, but it was hers and hers alone. Those feelings belonged to her, and that was what made it special. It was also the painting in the gallery that seemed to draw the least amount of attention, save for one soul who seemed fixated on it.

Making her way over to the painting, the gentleman examining it seemed fully unaware of her existence as he combed over every detail of the work. He also seemed fully unaware of a typical human being's level of cleanliness that lingered around mostly clean. Instead, he gave off a pristine image. Every hair on his head came across as perfectly positioned, resting above a startlingly clean-shaven face and almost eerily smooth skin. He wore an all-white suit, which was strange, to say the least, particularly in Unity Falls. But it was difficult for Emilyn to focus on any of that when hit with the aura radiating from this man. It was a discerning, almost uneven dissonance drooling off of him, off-putting and alluring at the same time. She could think of no other words to describe it, except perhaps with his name, which she intended to ask.

As she cleared her throat to get his attention, the man remained perplexed within the painting's borders. In some instances, that may be considered rude, but Emilyn supposed it may be a good thing on this occasion.

"Enjoying the painting?" she asked, her voice drawing the stranger back into his body. As if returned from somewhere else, he shifted his gaze to her. He had dark brown eyes to go with his darker brown hair, and they stood in contrast to his brighter attire. She smiled. "You seem pretty captivated."

"Hmm?" he asked, seeming to take a moment to register her question. "Oh, yes! It is rather exquisite, isn't it? This, uh ..." He paused, squinting at the name etched into the bottom of the painting's frame. "Emilyn should be quite pleased."

"She is," she said, extending her hand. "And you are?"

"Hmm? Oh, right, yes, introductions. I am Forest," he smiled as he took her hand, and while it wasn't odd by any means, it almost seemed like he struggled with exactly ... how to smile. "And you would be?"

Emilyn tilted her head. "Emilyn," she replied, and he managed a light chuckle as understanding dawned upon him.

"I do apologize," he said, though it was nothing to be sorry for. "I must have truly been lost."

"No problem at all. I'm glad you like it. Forest ..." She paused, lingering on his region name: Est. "Most of the people around here are Lyn, with a few Els. Never met an Est before," she stated, pondering where on Seranno that meant he was from. The majority of the population of Unity Falls were Lyns, like her and her father. Emi was her chosen name and Lyn her region name.

"Ah, yes, we're a rare breed from the southern continent," he replied with confidence. She had been born in Unity Falls and spent most of her life there, and as such had never been to the southern continent. "I'm on a pilgrimage of sorts."

That piqued Emilyn's interest. "What kind of pilgrimage?"

"I'm looking for an artist," he clarified, and Emilyn pursed her lips.

"Well, I'd say you came to the right place," she chuckled, but he remained unamused.

"Someone who is out of place," he continued, completely drawn into his words as if they were a whole other world, all their own. As if they made any kind of sense. "This is only my first stop. But I'm rather enjoying my time here."

"Good ... well, let me know if I can help you find who you're looking for," she said, silently cursing herself to an eternity of windless skies.

"That is very kind of you," he replied, a certain genuineness to his tone.

"What is it you like about this one?" she asked, shrugging. "It's one of my favorites, but it's not one I expected anyone to spend much time looking at. So, I'm kinda curious."

His eyes drifted from one corner of the canvas to the other and back again as he pondered an answer to the question. The silence that filled the space between them made that discerning aura that much more potent. "Well," he finally replied. "I am always happy to indulge curiosity. This painting is the most detailed depiction of the nearby mountain I have come across. The upward flowing water is fascinating," he said as if that were strange. Though Emilyn supposed it was possible. She had heard of places far away where the water fell from the top of mountains, crashing violently into the river below. That seemed loud and unappealing. The calm serenity of the water rising was one of the things she loved most about Unity Falls.

"Is it not like that on the southern continent?" Emilyn asked, and Forest again pondered the question for a great many breaths.

"Water flows the same direction everywhere, it seems," he paused. "So it stands to reason that—"

"Emilyn!" Kyshel interjected, manifesting from nowhere. Apparently, Emilyn had been just as captivated as Forest was, having failed to notice her friend, who looked like she had literally sprinted to her. In heels. "She's here," she said, breathless.

"She?" Emilyn asked, and then Kyshel seemed to notice Forest beside her. She looked the man from head to toe with no subtly and then pursed her lips together in ... praise?

"Bold choices," she said, approval lining her tone. "I like that. Not saying it works, at all, but good on you for trying."

"I'm uncertain as to what you're referring to, but your tone indicates praise. So, I thank you," Forest stated, and Kyshel gazed at him for a long moment. Emilyn wondered if she was feeling the same off-putting aura she was. After a moment, Kyshel seemed to shake herself out of it and look back to Emilyn.

"Crysalyn," she answered. "As in—"

"Curator of the United Illusions Gallery?" Emilyn finished. "That Crysalyn?" she asked, dumbfounded. What was the most well-known curator in Unity Falls doing in her gallery?

"That Crysalyn," Kyshel confirmed. "I may have invited her."

"You what?" Emilyn demanded.

"I didn't think she'd show! I invited everyone I know." She shrugged, defensive. "And that's ... well, that's a lot of people. Anyway, she's here. And she looks ... content. So c'mon! No one else here matters anymore." She took Emilyn's arm, dragging her away. She didn't hear a protest from Forest—not that she was expecting one.

Emilyn got a good look at Crysalyn as Kyshel narrowed her sights, ignoring people watching her drag Emilyn along, even though it was wholly unnecessary at that point. Emilyn was more than happy to talk to Crysalyn. She was the only one in the room that stood out more than Kyshel, dressed like it was a wedding but somehow making it look like it was her normal, casual apparel. It may very well be.

"Okay." Kyshel stopped as they neared the painting Crysalyn was investigating. Emilyn couldn't tell if she liked it or not. Her expression was blank. She was probably used to this sort of thing, perfectly able to control her expression and body language. Not like Emilyn herself, who felt, and likely looked, giddy at the prospect of speaking to her. Was this actually happening? "She's notoriously blunt, straight to the point. She doesn't like wasting time or people wasting her time. But she's more open when it comes to new talent. So, come off strong but not too strong. Obvious about who you are and what you want but not too obvious. Make sense?"

"No."

"Sorry. She's alone and you're up. Go!" Kyshel said, practically shoving her toward the woman. Emilyn pondered what she should say. Are you enjoying the art? Too indirect. Maybe mention the picture she was looking at? Work her way up to naturally introducing herself? That could work. Probably. Remembering she literally had nothing to lose, she took a deep breath alongside her first steps toward Crysalyn.

The scream came from behind her.

Purple Skies

Panic blanketed the room as if the ceiling had opened up and rained it down. It became something almost tangible, dancing in between every heart and soul throughout the chamber all the way to the man on the floor in the middle of Emilyn's gallery. His hands tore at the side of his own head as he let out a wail Emilyn could only describe as what it might actually sound like to hear the moment a heart broke. As Emilyn rushed to his side and a crowd formed around him, the focus her training as a tracer had instilled in her drowned out any and all other sounds, latching onto only the anguished scream.

Tucking her hair behind her ears as she knelt down to examine the man, she found his face a familiar one. Diselyn. She had met him just a few moments prior, and nothing had seemed to indicate anything out of the ordinary. But this ... this was something she recognized. And it truly was something that happened in a split second, like the snap of a finger. She recognized it from Kyshel and from her father and from so many people he had helped to avoid this fate. Diselyn was splitting. He hadn't mentioned being a former tracer. Her mind was quick to build a puzzle around why this happened just as she was about to have what might have been the most important conversation of her life, but she was just as quick to dismiss the thought. Diselyn was in anguish, and she could help him.

Kyshel emerged from the crowd, holding up her dress as she knelt on the other side of the man. “He’s splitting.” She met Emilyn’s eyes with ones that knew exactly what Diselyn was feeling—the terror that came with a soul trying to escape the body it called home. Those who had lived through the experience had an eerie way of knowing when it was happening to someone else. “You can help him, right? Like you’ve done before?” she whispered, likely hoping to avoid revealing her own condition to the crowd around them. Kyshel still had splits from time to time, and she had worked hard to hide that fact.

Emilyn nodded. “I can try,” she replied as she took off her jacket, spreading it out over Diselyn to help him stay warm. That always helped Kyshel during splits. “Get me some space,” Emilyn instructed, and Kyshel nodded, standing up.

“Everyone back,” she commanded, a natural authority weaving into her tone.

Her words and any reaction to them became distant to Emilyn as she opened up her own soul. Purple light danced out of her fingers, coalescing around them as her eyes glowed the same color. She became alive, the purest form of herself as her soul traversed every string of the purple light. Tracers weren’t uncommon, but several gasps found their way into the space surrounding her. She had little trouble tuning them out as she called on her father’s teachings. Her whole life she had been learning how to focus herself completely, and a single phrase could have this effect on her. A phrase that held more power over her than it had any right to.

String the stars.

She let the words dance through her soul and take her somewhere else, allowing the world to drip away around her. In its place came another, a void of sound and physicality that was the space between souls. An infinity of darkness and light, nothing and everything coalesced into a place so empty yet filled to the brim. The place she felt most alive, the closest she could ever be to herself. She stood at the precipice of the bridge that would take her to the soul she had linked her own with. It was manifested as little more than a slightly arched wooded bridge, rails that seemed unneeded jutting up from its sides. Stepping onto it and taking only a few steps to cross it, the other side was less familiar to her. A storm cloud filled the space of Diselyn's soul, silent and imposing yet inspiring as it fought for its own survival and wholeness. As Emilyn stepped into it, Diselyn's memories flooded over her, a swirl of color that gave way to where the purest spark of his being had either hidden itself to weather the storm or where the split had begun.

She was on a street she didn't recognize—in a city she had never been to. A little girl ran across the street, smiling as her father, a younger Diselyn, chased after her. He was smiling too. This seemed a happy memory, and maybe it began that way. But when it came to splits, Emilyn knew better.

The image shifted. The girl and Diselyn stood still as their eyes found a cloaked individual on a nearby rooftop. At the same time, the sky turned a tracer's shade of purple. Beyond the figure in the skies above him, the clouds parted, revealing a descending meteor dripping in tracer light. A larger illusion than any single tracer could ever generate. The girl screamed and ran. Diselyn stumbled over, slipping on the snow and hurting his leg. The cloaked man had vanished. So had Diselyn's daughter. She could feel the implication all around her as emotions flooded the memory. This was the last time he had seen his daughter. To this day, he didn't know if she was alive. All around her, the weight of grief and loss threatened to bury her, but she resisted, repeating her focus phrase in her thoughts. This split was making Diselyn relive his worst memory, but she knew what she had to do. She wasn't her father. She wasn't a hero. But in that moment, she was all Diselyn had.

She dug deeper, beyond this memory, searching for what lie beneath. Intertwined within the agony of losing his little girl were all the happy memories he had with her. Playing together, laughing together, reading to her, the joy of her taking her first steps. Emilyn felt it all. Every ounce of joy Diselyn had felt—all the love for his daughter filling the space around her. It was almost overwhelming and would have easily captivated someone less trained to deal with it. Though it did very nearly force many of her same emotions to the surface. Pushing them away, Emilyn picked one of Diselyn's memories and studied every detail, tracing the image with her eyes and capturing it within her own memory. She then closed her eyes, reaching back toward her soul's space in the space between. Letting her own soul embrace her once more, she was back in the gallery, opening her eyes to find a quiet terror surrounding her from the people who had come to see her art and now were witnessing a possible tragedy. Standing up, she nodded to Kyshel, who made certain again that the space was clear.

Using the image she'd traced from Diselyn's mind, that of the day his daughter was born, she projected the image in front of her, letting it flow from her soul to her hands and to the empty space above Diselyn like a river of memory, the light dripping from her fingertips and then flowing away to become the outline of the image. The illusion was born, the light swirling together to form every detail and illuminating the gallery in a purple hue. It was done in a moment. She sat down next to Diselyn and, gently, she held his head up.

"Look," she prompted as reassuringly as she could manage. "Open your eyes. Look," she prompted, but he shook his head.

"It hurts too much," he cried. "It hurts ..." he trailed off as the sound of his daughter's first cry found his ears, his eyes slowly opening. And he saw the memory play out. Reaching his hand forward, toward the memory, Emilyn saw tears finding his eyes. Maintaining her link with his mind, Emilyn could feel his soul stitching itself back together. The split was fading. Slowly, but fading. "Adalyn," he muttered, and Emilyn let herself sit back, breathing a sigh of relief. This was what her father had done all the time—what he had been doing in that painting she had made of him. Showing people their happiest memories in order to help them overcome their worst.

His cries filled the room, and every other soul was silent for a long few moments as he regained control of himself. Kyshel made her way over to Emilyn and sat down, linking their arms together, a silent reassurance that she was okay too. And an acknowledgment of the painful memories she knew the experience had brought up in Emilyn herself. Emilyn leaned into her, and together they waited in silence for the illusion to fade away.

As it did, Emilyn's eyes returned to their normal dark blue, and the light retreated inside her, warming her soul once more. In a startling unison, the lights of the gallery flickered out at the same time, leaving the room in near complete darkness save the distant lights of the nighttime city from the window. As if never gone, panic settled over the room once again. Emilyn and Kyshel stood up quickly, keeping their arms linked, and it was only a moment later that the light of the moon was replaced by a distant purple hue.

No one else seemed to notice it. No one else could. Only active tracers could see when the sky turned purple, an indication that tracer light was in use nearby. To everyone else, it was still pitch black. Several voices rang across the room, trying to calm everyone. Emilyn didn't recognize any of them, but one voice overpowered the others in an attempt to bind the chaos. Emilyn guessed that was Crysalyn's.

"Everyone remain calm," Crsyalyn urged. "Try to follow my voice. I think I'm close to the exit," she kept her tone neutral, careful not to be hopeful or afraid. That was good. But there would be a flight of stairs beyond those doors. Navigating down them in complete darkness would be unsafe. There were emergency lights in the office nearby. But before she headed that way, she turned to Kyshel.

"Purple skies," she whispered, and her friend turned toward her in the purple hue she couldn't see.

"You're sure?" she asked, and Emilyn nodded. She could see her friend swallow a bit of the same terror she had likely felt while Diselyn was splitting. Emilyn couldn't see her face, but she guessed she was putting up an expression braver than she was feeling. These were all the things Kyshel had wanted to leave in her past. Emilyn gripped her hand in reassurance.

"There are lights in the office we came from, to your left. Straight shot." Emilyn gestured their linked hands toward it. "Get them, and help lead everyone out of here," Emilyn instructed. Focus would help Kyshel more than anything else. Give her a task that would stop her mind from going to darker places.

"And you're going to be doing what, exactly?" she asked, and Emilyn looked toward the window the purple light flooded in from.

"A split, a power outage, and purple skies all at once? I don't think so." She shook her head. "Something's happening. I'm gonna go find out what."

Kyshel sighed. "You know you don't have to, right? Just because your father would have—"

"I do have to," she interjected. "You know why."

"Fine," Kyshel grumbled after a long moment. She knew exactly why, and she was the only one who knew. "But you better be right behind us. Take a look. See what you can find out, but nothing crazy. If something is happening, I want my best friend by my side."

"Me too." Emilyn smiled at her, gripping her hand tightly. "Right behind you, I promise." Kyshel nodded, let go of her hand, and headed toward the side office. Emilyn, with the light of the purple sky, began to make her way through the guests and toward the window. She felt ... something out there. Calling to her. This wasn't just an illusion happening somewhere in the city. It was several of them. Or one large one, like the meteor from Diselyn's memory. It was hard to tell. She needed a better look.

She focused on what she was feeling more than seeing. Several minds reaching out, connecting. But where was the source? Somewhere behind her, she heard Kyshel tell everyone she had lights and passed a few out before she led everyone to the exits. She helped Diselyn, who was still shaken. Emilyn could feel his fear and continual recovery through their link, which would sever as he got further away.

The guests dispersed quickly. So much for her gallery.

She felt that she was now alone, so she approached the window. The call she was feeling grew, and it attempted to penetrate her soul. She wouldn't let it.

"String the stars," she said out loud, a declaration to her would-be invaders. Looking out the window, she saw the purple sky. It had never frightened her, even as a child. She found it beautiful. It was what accompanied it that was worrying her. On a nearby higher rooftop a cloaked figure stood, solitary and immovable, a silhouette against a purple sky. She gazed at the figure for a long moment, debating what she should do. He was strong. It was all she could do to keep him out of her soul.

Suddenly, she felt his eyes on her, and the weight from them forced her to stumble backward, out of his direct sight. At the same time, she heard the door open behind her. Quickly returning to her feet and turning around, she saw another silhouette by the door—one that remained hidden in the dark beyond the window's light.

"I'm sorry if I startled you," the person was quick to say. His voice was weak, breathless, like he had been running up the stairs. He must have passed Kyshel and the guests, fleeing. Not the cloaked figure. She wasn't quite sure how she was certain of that. But she was. "I didn't mean to."

"Who are you?" Emilyn asked, cursing the fear hovering in the space between her words. She was not afraid. She was strong. She had to be. She began stepping closer to see the speaker, but he stepped farther back into the darkness. He didn't want her to see him. All the more reason she decided she needed to. From his silhouette, his head looked ... large. Deformed, maybe, but only on one side.

"I came to warn you," he said, quickly, panicked. "They're after you!"

Emilyn reached for his mind, expecting to find herself in the space between again, but she found she couldn't reach him. His mind wasn't blocked off from her. Instead, it was as if it wasn't there at all. No bridge to even try to cross. Not that she was going to let that stop her. She was too stubborn for that. She reached for a memory of her own—her memory of the mountain she had painted was the first that came to mind. Before he could run, purple light emerged from her hands and eyes, and she projected it to the space behind him, letting the purple glow illuminate him.

He stumbled back, but he didn't run away. She nearly did. His head wasn't deformed at all, nor did he look anything out of the ordinary aside from perhaps gaunt. But floating around his head, orbiting his head ... was a small moon.

The Boy & The Moon

Tracer illusions were made of dreams. Memories. Images. They could be incredible, sophisticated, detailed, and wonderful, but they were abstract. Projections. They were felt more than seen. You could pluck an image from your head and let the world see it, but it wouldn't be tangible. The moon orbiting the boy's head was real. Real in a way felt more than seen but real. It had a presence. It was tethered to the boy, moving with him. It was no illusion.

"Please don't be scared," he pleaded, desperation noticeable on his face even in the dim purple light. He was begging her not to be afraid of him as if the entire world depended on it. Maybe for his world, it did. "I've come to warn you, not hurt you."

"Warn me?" Emilyn stepped closer, and this time, he let her approach. She wasn't afraid. Alarmed, perhaps, and curious, certainly, but not afraid. There were things in the world that could scare her, but not a boy and not a moon.

"You don't look scared," he said, his tone shifting to something more akin to surprise as she examined the moon. Moons were things only displayed in artwork, based on stories from times long past where Seranno supposedly had one. "Most people run away as soon as they see it." His voice became more of a whisper as if uncertain any of this was even real.

"I'm not most people," she replied. Her father wouldn't have been scared of this boy. He would've wanted to help. He taught her to, at the very least, give everyone a chance. In a world of judgment, be an island of acceptance, he used to say. Emilyn met the boy's eyes, hoping to convey that. The color was so drained from them that only a faint and hollow grey remained, leaving the pupils and irises almost indistinguishable. He was scrawny, wearing torn and ragged clothes in layers, and his hair was an unclean and unkempt mess. "What are you trying to warn me about?"

"Right," he said and stepped back as if recovering from a stupor. "It's the architects. They're the ones doing this. And they're after you."

Official reports from the independent cities across Seranno described the architects as radical tracers that used illusions to instigate chaos and disorder. Emilyn only knew those reports to be accurate because the group had once been to Unity Falls when she was little. Her father had gained his reputation with his actions driving them from the city, breaking the illusion of a massive storm they had projected over the city. No single member of their ranks had ever been identified. Her father had spoken little about them, only that they were a force to be reckoned with. And now they were back in her home. Had they caught wind of Zarlyn's condition? Returned to finish what they started fifteen years ago?

"How do you know?" Emilyn asked.

"I saw them. They—"

"How do you know they're after me?" she clarified, and he sighed.

"I heard them," he said and paused, waiting for her to deny his claim. She did not. "I can hear—"

He was cut off by a flood of purple-pink light racing across the room. It covered every inch of the floor, crawled up the walls, and melded into an illusion more sophisticated than Emilyn had ever seen. A mountaintop formed around them, manifesting bit by bit from the light from the floor to the ceiling and leaving them standing on the edge of the mountain. Instinctively, they both stepped back.

"This is them!" he panicked. "We need to go." He stepped back toward the edge of the cliff, and Emilyn grabbed his arm.

"We'll have to wait for it to fade," she explained. "We can't see the door, and trying to go downstairs in an illusion like this would be a bad idea."

He peered past her, clearly debating something. "I can see through the illusion," he finally said, gesturing past the mountain's edge. "The door is right there."

"No one can see through tracer illusions," Emilyn said, becoming cautious. It was a trick or a trap or ... something. It had to be. Seeing through tracer illusions was impossible. Then again, so was a small moon orbiting someone's head. Still, it wasn't in her nature to trust easily. "Do you expect me to believe you can?"

"No," he shrugged. "But I can. And I can get you out of here, too. Do you believe what I said about them being after you?" She wouldn't have if not for the man she'd seen outside the window. Reluctantly, she nodded.

"But why are they after me? I'm no one." Not entirely true, but to anyone outside Unity Falls, her name would mean nothing.

"You're not no one. You're Emilyn."

"I never told you my name," she was quick to reply, and every instinct she had screamed at her not to trust this boy.

"I saw it," he replied, holding his hands up to try and ease her concern. He failed. "The same place I saw they were after you."

"I thought you said you heard they were after me?"

"I did. It's ... the same," he explained as if that were an explanation.

"It's really not," she replied. "Are you one of them?"

"No!" he said, frustrated but able to calm himself. "No. I can't explain it. I can ... form links with tracers. They don't realize it. I can hear their thoughts. It just happens when they're close. I can stop listening. But I can't stop the initial link."

"That's insane," Emilyn insisted. "Do you honestly expect me to believe that?"

"No," he let his arms fall in exasperation. "I don't believe it. But it's true."

"I'm a tracer," she said, bluntly. "What am I thinking?"

"You're thinking about your father upstairs," he said, with no hesitation. "And ... how he was involved with the architects when you were a kid," he went on, but that wasn't enough. Anyone could have found that out. "You're thinking ... string the stars. Whatever that means."

There was no way he could have known that. She had never said that to anyone besides her father and Kyshel. It was something sacred to her. What was she supposed to say to him knowing that?

"Say you'll come with me." He held out his hand. "They're after you, and I'm just trying to help. I promise."

Emilyn didn't take his hand. He could hear her thoughts, and she couldn't see into his soul. Fine. But that didn't mean she trusted him. If the architects were after her, she couldn't take the chance he was working with them.

"I've never done anything like this before," he confessed. "I hear tracers all the time. But not like ... them. They want chaos. And they want you. I don't know why. But for once in my life, I didn't want to just stay in the shadows. I want to help, and I think I can. I'm terrified! But I think I can. Please," he pleaded. He sounded so sincere.

She didn't know what to do. So, she closed her eyes and took a deep breath, focusing. "Okay," she said reluctantly, begrudgingly admitting to herself that she really didn't have another option, save waiting for the illusion to fade away. But one as powerful as this ... they may just put it right back up. "Say I believe you. The architects are after me. What is this, then?" she gestured around them. "This feels a lot more like a distraction than a trap. Meant to keep us where we are ..." she trailed off. Her father. What if the architects wanted revenge? She locked her eyes back on the boy. His motives no longer mattered to her. "You can see through illusions. Okay. Can you get me upstairs?"

"Does that mean you trust me?"

"It means I need you," she said, and this time she held out her hand. Whatever this boy was, if he was being sincere, he could be a huge help, and if he wasn't ... well, she never had handled betrayal very well.

He seemed content with this and took her hand. His skin was cold, and his grip was weak. She tightened her own. She wasn't going to take any chances until she could see what was real again.

He stepped out beyond the edge of the cliff first, and his feet found solid ground in the sky. He didn't urge her forward. He waited until she worked up the courage to do so on her own. That gave her pause, her thoughts from earlier rescinding, as this did scare her a little.

She closed her eyes. Tracer illusions were made of dreams. Memories. Images. They were abstract. Projections. More felt than seen. She repeated the words in her thoughts, and she found them coming from her father's voice.

Illusions only have power over you if you let them. She would not let this one.

She stepped forward, her feet finding solid ground. Opening her eyes, she stifled a panic and focused on the boy. He nodded to her, looking forward and stepping slowly, more for her benefit than his own. His grip became her lifeline, and she focused on it. His hand was less cold now, but just like his eyes, his hand had a hollow feeling to it. Couple that with his weak grip and gaunt form, and she wondered how he even had the energy to make it up the stairs.

She watched him push nothing open, yet heard the sound of the door creaking. Hundreds of feet in the sky. She had trained how to operate inside of full illusions before, but that didn't help ease the experience much. It was still disconcerting.

Illusions like this were what made tracers dangerous, and tracers like the architects were why Seranno's history was something tracers and non-tracers alike weren't proud of. An illusion of a bridge could be projected where there was none, or the single door in a windowless room hidden. Bodies and minds would treat these as real, as sight and sound were the dominant senses. It was why her father had trained her to close her eyes to focus. That way, one of the two senses instinctually relied upon far too often would be sealed away.

Sight is a distraction. By eliminating it, you leave yourself open to the world of dreams. And you know what dreams are? Dreams are just memories waiting to be born. That's what's so wonderful about tracers, Emi. You and I can bring dreams to life.

She was worried about him. The architects were after him. They had to be. She was just a misdirect. A distraction to keep the one person who might try to stop them away. He had never spoken much about what had happened between him and the architects. Whatever he had done to stop them ... it had changed him. He was a good man and a good father but he had become distant after the attack. What had he done? And why would the architects wait a decade after he split to come after him? Maybe to let him suffer. His soul was torn, and he was left in constant agony. But there was nothing that could be done for him. His body refused to die without a whole soul, and he would not awaken for the same reason. For a decade his soul waged a war with itself that would have no victor. All she could do was take care of him.

"Stairs." The boy's voice cut through her thoughts, returning her to reality even if reality wasn't what she was seeing around them. The illusion showed no signs of degradation. "Just go slow. Watch my feet. Follow my steps. Don't let go."

The worst that would happen if she did let go was falling down a few steps. It would hurt and slow them down. But with her father in jeopardy, she couldn't allow that. She did as instructed. One step at a time. It helped that she lived there. She went up and down those stairs every single day without thinking about it. She let those familiar instincts guide her. No different than any other day. They had several floors to go, so she decided it would be better to simply let her body do the work. Which meant she needed to distract her mind.

"So, what do you know?" Emilyn asked. "About what you can do, I mean." He was silent at first, but she felt ... something from him. She couldn't reach his mind, but she could feel fragments. Little echoes slipping through the cracks despite the door being locked. Fear. Pain. Loneliness.

"I don't remember my life before this." He gestured to the moon keeping pace beside his head. "But I remember having one. It's ... weird. I woke up one day and it was there like it had always been this way. I still knew everything I knew, but the actual memories were gone. I get pieces sometimes but that's all."

"That's horrible," Emilyn said, trying to take a less hostile approach with him. "Do you have family?"

"No idea," he said, and she knew it was true. "They're part of those missing years. I think I had one, maybe. But they weren't there when this appeared. I was alone. Everyone was scared of me ... but not as much as I was. No one would even speak to me. The first hospital I went to locked me up. I ran away the first chance I got. That was when I discovered I could hear tracer thoughts. One of the doctors. I learned the guard patterns from him—how the lock worked—and planned it all out. I couldn't stay there. They wanted to understand but not help." He paused. "I didn't know what else to do. I've been on my own since. Staying hidden."

"No indication at all who did this to you? Or why?" she asked, and he shook his head.

"I spent months going over every detail in my head. Nothing. The only explanation I have is that some cruel god decided to curse me. Maybe I wasn't a good person before."

Emilyn didn't believe in a higher power. Or maybe she did. She'd never really decided. She believed it all came down to experiences, and this led him to believe what he needed to believe, and who was she to say he was wrong? It must have been horrible, living alone and isolated like that. Not knowing who he was before or why this happened to him. Or why people like her didn't even bother asking him his name. She sighed to herself.

"Cidelyn," he said, then shot her an apologetic look for answering before she had asked. If he had heard anything else she was thinking, he didn't indicate as much.

"Cidelyn," she repeated. "So you're from Unity Falls?"

"I don't remember being anywhere else," he replied. She wanted to tell him she didn't think he was a bad person, but if she didn't know him, she supposed it depended on what happened at the end of this trek. That made her feel guilty.

"Is this your floor?" He stopped, helping her to ground herself between steps where supposedly a door waited for them. She still saw the sky above a cliff side, still standing on something but nothing. Based on how many flights they'd climbed from the gallery, she believed this was her floor. It was three floors up and they had changed direction six times. She nodded.

"Can't you tell?" she asked, trying to sound lighthearted. But it immediately felt like a bad idea.

"I'm trying not to," Cidelyn said. "I told you I can't stop the initial link with a tracer, but I can choose not to listen. Some thoughts are louder than others." He was trying to make her feel more comfortable, or respect her privacy. Or maybe he simply didn't want to. Her thoughts weren't likely to be of much use to him besides amplifying the things he was already feeling. Fear, confusion, worry. For her father. He didn't need that. She hoped her expression conveyed that she appreciated his efforts.

"Straight back. The door at the end of the hall." She pointed toward where she thought the door to her loft would be. It was a loft given to her out of the kindness of the father of the young man Zarlyn had saved from splitting, so long ago. Emilyn had insisted on paying for it, but the man had vehemently refused. She didn't like being indebted to anyone. But she didn't have much without her father. She was hoping her gallery would start to change that, but that particular dream had been drowned in the purple light she had tried so hard to not let her life revolve around—snuffed out by the illusions she had wanted so badly to create and now wished only that her father had never been a tracer. It was a selfish thing to wish. That young man Zarlyn had saved got to be reunited with his father. Emilyn feared she never would, and now all she had left of him was being ripped away from her.

Cidelyn got her attention, wrapping his fingers around what Emilyn perceived to be the door knob to her loft. It should have been locked, but she heard him turn it and push it open. Immediately, she felt a familiar weight bearing down on her, pushing at her very soul. The cloaked man she had seen outside the window when he had looked at her. He was there. She could feel his soul, though it was just as guarded as hers. With a focus so singular and pure that he could have weathered death itself with no fear. He was there. They had been correct.

He was after her father.

A Whisper of Solace

Purple light stole away the illusion of the sky and retreated, leaving the bland brown of the hallway beyond the door to accompany the unending gravity pushing against them. Cidelyn felt it as well. He was on his knees, and his hand slipped away from hers. Through that all, she could feel the presence more than see it. The cloaked figure. He stood in the open door to her balcony, purple skies silhouetting him as his cloak fluttered in the wind. In one of his arms was the limp and ever-unresponsive form of her father.

Emilyn couldn't see the man's eyes, but she could feel them on her, allowing the most minuscule of links to form between their minds so he could convey a single emotion: a challenge. Try and stop him from taking her father. What Emilyn could see of his face was a canvas blank of emotion. What she could feel of him was absolute nothingness. A complete lack of care. This wasn't personal to him. This wasn't anything to him. And yet he would be relentless in his task. A burning nothing that would never falter.

That should have terrified her. Instead, she met his challenge with one of her own: try and stop her.

The man stepped out onto the balcony beyond the door, Zarlyn under one arm. Emilyn darted after him as he vanished to the side out of sight. She reached the balcony, and the man was nowhere to be found. Reaching out toward his mind, she found the connection he had opened still present. There was no way that was a mistake. He was above her, and her eyes confirmed that, allowing a final glimpse of the man and her father climbing over the side of the roof. How had he gotten up there?

"Here ..." Cidelyn's voice manifested beside her, his hands grabbing at something she couldn't see. "Ladder." They must've shrouded it. Tracers could easily hide something by overlaying an illusion of whatever was behind something on it, making it blend in. Essentially invisible. Letting her hands find the ladder, Emilyn climbed despite that clearly being what the man wanted. But she didn't care. They had her father.

Climbing as quickly as she could, she pulled herself up over the side of the roof, finding the man standing on the next rooftop, too far away to have jumped. She suspected another concealed path across. He had stopped. He was staring at her, an aura of patience spilling from him. Like he had been waiting despite her being only seconds behind him. He held out his hand toward her.

Tracer light flowed calmly from his fingertips, seeping onto the roof beneath and flooding the area. An illusion began to rise from the light, consuming the entirety of both rooftops and beyond. He couldn't be doing this alone. It was too much for one tracer to handle. Yet, as the illusion took hold, she felt no other presence. And the man was gone. Gone with her father.

"Over there." Cidelyn's voice barely registered as he caught his breath after climbing the ladder.

She followed where he was pointing, to a space between the rooftops. But that was a little too vague for her. She reached down and put his arm around her shoulder to steady him as they rose. He nodded in thanks. It seemed she had made a decision to trust him somewhere along the way. He was all she had—the only way she might reach her father. But even if that hadn't been the case, something had shifted. She guided them both over to the area he had indicated.

The illusion was the same as before. The edge of a cliff beckoned them, threatening a fall to the ground too far to even see. The only difference was a dimmer sun. The illusion didn't scare her this time. Emilyn was prepared and willing and stepped off the cliff with no hesitation. He stopped her when they reached the edge of the roof.

"Wood," he said, gesturing to where something supposedly rested, connecting the two rooftops. "It's large, but it won't support us both."

"One at a time, then," Emilyn said, slowly climbing up, careful to feel where the edge was. Standing, she took slow steps across, narrowly reaching the other side without slipping. With a deep breath, she was able to climb down safely. "Your turn."

Cidelyn stood but was hesitant to climb on, looking drained. He was about to try anyway, and before she could advise him not to, his eyes locked onto something behind her. Across his face, she saw the purple light of the sky get brighter. Turning around, she saw something truly daunting.

The illusion drooped away around them, the light abandoning it and racing away to join its brethren at the city's edge. There, the light had coalesced in the sky above the city, becoming solid and ... spreading in all directions. Forming a dome. Its descent was slow as if it wanted the people inside to know they were about to be trapped.

"Please, tell me that's an illusion ..." Emilyn said as more of an afterthought than anything else, her heartbeat rising as the dome of light collided with the ground, entrapping the city and mountain within its borders.

"I don't think it is ..." There was fear in Cidelyn's voice. She felt that same fear. And on some level, she knew it wasn't an illusion. The barrier was real—as real as the man who had taken her father. Unity Falls was trapped.

Unable to process what she was seeing, she turned around to find Cidelyn had made his way across the plank, and she offered a hand to help him down when his lack of breath threatened to collapse him. He gratefully took her aid but nearly did collapse trying to get down onto the rooftop. Stabilizing him, their eyes settled on their surroundings. Neither of them said a word.

"I can't see him," Cidelyn said, searching for the cloaked man, shaking his head. "I don't know where he went. I'm sorry." He sounded so pained to say it. Nowhere as pained as she was to hear it, however.

She closed her eyes. It wasn't his fault. He had tried to help her. But she had failed. She couldn't stop that man. She couldn't save her father. She let go of Cidelyn, sinking down against the wall on the roof, and did her very best not to cry.

She didn't understand what was happening. Why had the architects come after her father? Why now, after all this time? How was this barrier around the city even possible? And what was its purpose?

It turned out she was exactly what she had wanted to be. She wasn't her father's daughter. She was just her. But unlike him, she was useless. He would have already had a plan. He would be out there, helping people, stopping those who would dare to threaten his city. What was she doing? Crying on a rooftop.

Never underestimate the value of tears. She heard her father's voice in her head. Tears are the only part of our souls we can touch. They tell a story that is only ours. So, never be ashamed to cry. Tears mean your soul is still intact. That isn't the case for everyone.

Tears weren't going to get him back, though. How had she let this happen? Just an hour ago, she had been getting ready for her gallery's opening. Her very own art gallery. A dream that had been waiting to be born—one that she had brought to reality all on her own. Gone like breath on a mirror, before it could even truly live. And her father, who'd been taken right in front of her.

"Emilyn," Cidelyn's voice called to her, and she latched onto it. It was something, and she needed something—anything—to reel herself out of her own head. That was the most dangerous place she'd ever been.

She turned around, following Cidelyn's eyes to no specific place, finding her home being plunged into complete anarchy. Smoke rose at various points around the city. Illusions were appearing and disappearing with a frequency she had never seen. They were trapped.

This was a siege. The buildings that were on fire, the places where the illusions seemed concentrated ... they weren't random. The riverside supply station, the militia headquarters, the food and water stores, the central plaza, hospitals, schools ... The architects were targeting them all at once. The city would be completely subjugated in a matter of minutes if it wasn't already—and completely cut off from the outside.

Her home was dying. And there was nothing she could do about that.

At that moment, some part of her decided she wanted to believe in a higher power, after all. Simply because she wanted something she could pray to for this to stop.

"I've been terrified my whole life," said Cidelyn, proceeding to swallow. "This is different. I don't know what to do," the words came out quietly, almost as a whisper. A tear escaped his eye, rolling down his face and dripping onto the roof below them.

Tears are the only parts of our souls we can touch.

Emilyn took Cidelyn's hand again, and this time, it was a different kind of lifeline. She didn't know him, and he didn't know her. Not really. But at that moment, they needed each other to paint a picture just a little less terrifying than what their eyes were seeing. Their own little illusion.

A light shone out of the corner of her eye—from below them. They both glanced down, finding the dim, minuscule light emanating from the pocket of her pants. Reaching inside, Emilyn's fingers found a folded piece of paper. She hadn't put it there. Quickly unfolding it, a single sentence displayed itself, words and letters denoted by tracer light.

My safe spot. You know the one. Knock five times. Kyshel.

Emilyn used to slip sheets of paper into Kyshel's pockets so she could use tracer light to send her friend notes. Long-distance tracing wasn't easy, but a specific person or object to reach toward helped. Kyshel would have to have a tracer with her in order to do that. More importantly, she was alive. That was the best news Emilyn could have received. She must have slipped the paper into her pocket when the power had gone out at the gallery.

Her safe spot. Emilyn knew where to go. Doing so wouldn't get her father back, but it was something. It was a little hope, and a little hope went a long way.

"What was that?" Cidelyn asked as Emilyn returned the paper to her pocket. The illusion would fade, but it would be there in case of another.

"A message from my favorite person. C'mon, I know where to go." She helped him stand up, looking in the direction Kyshel would be waiting for them—a safe spot, of which few now remained.

The Watchful Gaze of the Merciless Sky

Fire had always been the wrong color. It never appeared as something capable of as much destruction as it was. It never acted like something capable of snuffing out life in the way it did. It came across as fleeting, burning bright only to fade away soon after. The way in which it existed unsettled Emilyn. It was simply the wrong color for what it was.

Fire danced across the city, sparks left in its wake, each a force of nature all its own. Each tearing down a tiny piece of her home. Each brought to life by the people who had taken her father. Were the fires illusions? Meant to scare the city into submission? Or were they real, for the same purpose?

"They're real," Cidelyn's voice snatched her from her darkness and back into the darkness around her. His voice was somber, echoing that same darkness. "I think I can walk on my own now," he added, gently removing his arm from her shoulders and taking a deep breath as they emerged from the building and out onto a scarily empty street.

"What made you collapse like that?" Emilyn asked, though it was a distant question far from what her mind was focusing on.

"I have to share," Cidelyn said, gesturing to the moon on the other side of his head. "Damn thing feeds off me ... or something. I don't really know. I never have much energy."

"We've got a bit of a walk ahead of us," Emilyn said as her eyes flittered toward her pocket, hoping to find a glow again. "Are you up for it?" The ability to see through tracer illusions had very quickly become an incredibly valuable skill, and she was fully aware of how fortunate she was that he was there. But that aside, she wasn't about to just leave him behind.

Nodding, he said nothing else and examined their surroundings. It was a street Emilyn walked down every day, and yet it was foreign to her. Fires bellowed behind the broken windows of a cafeteria she often ate in. A scorched copy of one of her pieces they had hung up to promote her gallery lay beneath one of the shattered windows. On the other side of the street was a merchant stand for fresh fruit, spilled out and charred. Kymelyn, the owner, had always smiled and said hello. Emilyn hoped she was okay. To that end, there were no souls to be found at all, alive or dead. No screams for help. No cries under the purple sky. It was like a twister of fire had burned through and carried them all away, leaving a scorched city in its wake. And yet a barrier surrounded the city. The people couldn't have simply left, could they? The silence that accompanied that question quickly became eerie, promoting an empty city to somehow feel that much emptier.

"Under the watchful gaze of the merciless sky, chaos is birthed from emptiness in plain sight, building until it blankets all things as if it were the sky. By the time you know it's there, it's too late." Cidelyn spoke the words almost reverently, and Emilyn knew them well. It was the signature quote from The Merciless Sky, a book whose author had been lost to time as it remained the oldest known book on Seranno detailing stories from well before the renaissance when tracers were prosecuted. Cidelyn shrugged. "Feels appropriate. Do you think the architects took everyone?"

"That's the only explanation that makes sense," Emilyn replied, except it didn't make any sense at all. Why take everyone? They got her father, who they clearly were after. They could have their revenge on him, so why even bother with the city? What did they gain from lighting it on fire or from taking all the people in it? "We need more information," he said. That was an understatement.

"We need to reach Kyshel. She made it somewhere safe, and has at least one tracer with her," Emilyn gripped the paper in her pocket. "Maybe more. And maybe they know something."

"Maybe." Cidelyn seemed skeptical. "Where are they?"

"Kyshel is a former tracer. She goes through splits occasionally. So, she found a place she could go through that where she wouldn't endanger anyone around her. She calls it a safehouse," Emilyn explained. "It's close to the mountain, just south of the watermill."

"If it's meant to isolate her," Cidelyn began, "then why do you know where it is?" It was a fair question. She knew because Kyshel, like her, wasn't someone who easily trusted others. She had spent a lot of time and effort burying her past as a tracer and hiding her splits from those she called peers, so as to not let that taint her work or her image. But there was only so much she could do on her own.

"Because splitting is a nightmare." Emilyn recalled the first time she had seen Kyshel split. "When your soul splits in two, it becomes a battlefield of everything you are—and what you see can vary. At least, that's how she described it. And those are the nicer ones," Emilyn paused. "Some splits are worse, with actual illusions coming out. Active tracers can enter that battlefield and act as a guide to help the split resolve, putting things back into place. But that kind of connection, with your entire soul on display for the tracer to see ... it's difficult. Because it's intimate, in a way."

"And intimacy requires trust." Cidelyn finished, and she nodded. Kyshel was her best friend—practically her sister—and somehow despite both of their difficulties in being their authentic selves around others, they had grown to trust each other. Enough that Kyshel trusted her to be the only one who knew how to guide her through a split. As far as she knew, she was the only one who knew where Kyshel's safe house was. Emilyn wondered what her friend would feel about this changing. Whoever the tracer was that had helped her knew, and Cidelyn would soon know too. Maybe more. Glancing around at the barren city, it seemed somewhat irrelevant in the face of the merciless sky. Even so, it was a struggle not to worry. For more than just that reason. It had been some time since she had split, at least that Emilyn knew of. And traumatic or emotional events, like a home or a city set ablaze, were well known to trigger splits.

"I've never known what that's like." Cidelyn's voice became almost a whisper. "That kind of ... unconditional trust. No one wants to trust someone like me."

Seranno had supposedly long ago moved past letting prejudices and fear dictate life, but when you looked close enough, you could still find it. Fear of what one didn't understand was built into the human template. It could be buried, but it was always there. And oftentimes it was ugly and cruel. Cidelyn had felt that cruelty. She could see it in his eyes, which barely held their color in place, drained either by the moon or by the ugliest parts of society.

"I trust you," Emilyn affirmed. It wasn't in the way he was describing it, but she did. She felt he had earned it in trying to save her—in trying to help her save her father. If he was playing her, he wasn't doing it terribly well. He had pretty much agreed to follow her lead. And despite the weakness he seemed to be burdened with, he shouldered the weight of cruelty with strength. It was something she recognized, in her own way. No one had ever been cruel to her in that sense, but cruelty took many forms. The weight of expectations could often be just as burdensome.

"You didn't have much choice," he replied and was quick to continue. "But ... thank you," he said, quietly, as if uncertain how exactly it was meant to be said. She smiled, and then he stopped, his eyes darting to his left. "Tracer nearby," he whispered, and Emilyn looked around. They were in the middle of the pathway. No time to find somewhere to hide. Facing the direction opposite Cidelyn, she formed a mental image of their background. Turning back around, she let her eyes turn purple and extended her hand. Purple light slipped from her fingers, draining away and projecting the image in front of them. An illusion of their background, hiding them from sight. A little trick she wouldn't have thought of if not for the cloaked man. She wasn't sure she could even do it. It was a delicate illusion, but if the cloaked man could do it, then she would need to as well. It would come in handy, so long as whoever was approaching couldn't see through it. She conveyed to Cidelyn in her thoughts to stay still and silent, and he seemed to understand as he watched the illusion complete itself.

She thought about how the illusion before had concealed the ladder, as if it had reached out and blanketed it. She closed her eyes, envisioning her image doing the same. Instead of remaining static, it coated her and Cidelyn, wrapping around them and painting them as part of the corner behind them. When she opened her eyes, she found it had done just that. She could see the purple light, but to anyone else, they would be practically invisible. Theoretically, at least. She had only ever projected illusions in front of her. This was something new. It was ... exciting. Despite the circumstances.

A cloaked figure emerged from the direction Cidelyn had indicated. Not the same one that took her father. This one was shorter—less defined—and didn't hold the same presence she had felt from the other man. That cold, lack of anything at all he had tried to drown her in. No, this man was just another tracer. Were all the architects tracers? A small army might explain how they were doing this to the city and how the illusions at her gallery had even been possible. She wished her father had told her more about them.

The man paid them no mind, only glancing around before moving on. Looking for people to round up? Looking for them? She doubted it. As much as it scared her to think about it, the man who had taken her father had let them go intentionally. She didn't know why. But if he had wanted her or Cidelyn, he would have taken them. Still, that didn't mean all the architects would be as generous, and she wasn't about to take any chances.

Once the man was gone, she let the illusion fade while she fell to her knees, letting out a breath she hadn't realized she was holding. She stared at the ground beneath her, at the dirt, and at a little sliver of grass growing in a place where there was none. How had she done that? She had let her instincts take over in a way she hadn't before.

"What's wrong?" Cidelyn asked, leaning down next to her and speaking quietly in case the man was still nearby. She nodded as her breath caught up with her, indicating she was all right. "You know," he said, eyeing the same single blade of grass she was. "I think I trust you, too." He smiled. She wasn't certain if she had seen him smile yet. "It's ... nice."

She pulled herself together and sat on the street next to him, pulling her hair back over her shoulders and letting her focus dissolve for a moment. Just for a moment. Because it was nice to trust.

"You've really never had ... anyone?" Emilyn asked, looking back and forth between his eyes. He pulled his bangs out from blocking them, shoving them to the side. Which didn't seem out of place with his messy, unkempt hair.

"I thought I did, once," he confessed. "But he didn't really care. He had ulterior motives. And if I'm being honest, I don't know if I ever trusted him. But he was the closest thing I've had to a friend."

Suddenly, Emilyn felt guilty. Was she just using him because he could help her find her father?

"Even if you are," he said, shooting her an apologetic glance for hearing her thoughts, "it's okay. For so long, I refused to use my abilities to do anything but hide. But today, I decided to help someone in a way only I could. And that felt good. So, I'm holding onto that. Use me all you want. I'll let you until it stops feeling right."

"And then?" she asked.

He shrugged. "And then I go back to places where people can pretend they don't see me, and I can pretend they do," he said and looked up toward the merciless sky.

Peering around the lifeless city closing in on them, Emilyn wondered if it was all that different to Cidelyn than what he was accustomed to. The buildings and paths were lifeless in their own way to him. The sky was sealed away from her the way a normal life had been taken away from him.

That left her feeling conflicted and uncertain. Deciphering her own feelings had never been her strong suit. Even as a child, when things were simpler—clearer—it had been her father who had helped her sift through all the noise inside, all her contradicting emotions and desires and lack of certainty in why she was feeling what she was feeling. She had gotten better at managing the noise in his absence, but there were times when she was left questioning whether she had managed it or just convinced herself she had. She sympathized with

Cidelyn, and she found she did trust him, but was that just because she needed him to find her father? She chose to believe it was not.

Emilyn stood up and offered her hand to Cidelyn again. This time, she did it without thinking about what he could do for her or what he wanted to hear or what she needed. She just did it, because it felt right. He took her hand and stood up.

"I can't promise I'm not using you. And I can't promise I'm not a little bit scared of you," she said, glancing at the moon. "But I can take you somewhere you don't have to pretend." She owed him at least that. And while she didn't know who else was with Kyshel or how they might react, she knew Kyshel would be accepting. Or at the very least, blunt about how she felt. And Emilyn ... she would do her best. "Whatever's going on right now, neither of us is better off alone. And using you or not, I meant what I said. I do trust you. And that's not something that comes easy to me. So, how about a deal? Say I'm using you to find my father. Then in exchange, you can use me too. To know what it's like to have a friend."

He gazed at her for a long moment—the look on his face a mixture of intrigue, sadness, and hope. It eventually settled into one of acceptance. "I like that sound of that," he said and looked to the path ahead of them. "All right, friend, lead the way."

A Trembling Storm

Silence had always appealed to Emilyn. There was a serenity to finding a spring of quiet amidst a desert of noise—like the eye of a hurricane. Thoughts came and went with more clarity, and truths were clearer. She would give anything to not have been subjected to the truth brought about the silence she and Cidelyn were drowning in. Like a voice stripped of speech.

The artistic capital of Seranno, normally filled with so much life, was barren. Devoid of anything beyond those who had conquered it. They hoped to avoid more of them, carefully peering around every corner for more architects as Emilyn led them down a less direct path toward Kyshel's safehouse. They spent the majority of the trek in relative silence as well, and Emilyn tried to focus her thoughts by listening for each of Cidelyn's footsteps behind her. If he was listening to her, he would find little more than worry about her father or what they were doing to do once they found Kyshel. Or missing the jacket she would normally have been wearing. She felt as wrong without it as she felt wrong sneaking through her own home.

They didn't run into any more architects, and the voice of her father inside her found that suspicious. What were they were doing? Where were they? A horrifying thought gave her pause. What if there were people all around her, hidden behind illusion? Screaming, burning, begging for help as she walked right past them? She shook her head. No. Cidelyn would be able to see through any illusion like them. Beyond that, everything around her had a gravity to it that illusions often lacked. Her instincts told her that the destruction and emptiness around were real, as much as she might wish otherwise.

"You're thinking very loudly," Cidelyn commented, derailing the spiral her mind had started down. Probably for the best.

"Sorry," she said, wondering if he'd listened in on every terrifying thought she'd just blasted through. "It should be right around the corner."

Nearly at the base of the mountain that bordered the city, Emilyn brought them to a stop. Unity Falls' towering watermill was just down the path, though it had ceased turning, and beyond it, the water calmly rose up the mountain as if the world beneath it hadn't irrevocably changed. The area was a mixture of storage caches for the city and tourist attractions for the mountain and its legendary view of the city and surrounding landscape. To the side of one of the farthest-back storage buildings would be a hidden cellar entrance to the safehouse Kyshel had claimed after stumbling upon it while exploring as a kid. Its hidden nature and markings within suggested it had been a supply depot of its own for the tracer network centuries prior—back during the times when tracers weren't understood or accepted. The rooms inside were set up in a way only tracers would benefit from for practice. Empty and spacious with few distractions so as to promote focus. That and the place just had an aura to it that felt ... right.

Carefully making their way through the buildings, Emilyn found the entrance with ease but kept a distance from it, worried they may be watched. While Cidelyn listened for tracers, she retrieved the paper in her pocket. No new note, and no indication if she could reach Kyshel the same way she'd reached her. Cidelyn nodded that he heard no tracers in the vicinity, though of course, that didn't rule out non-tracers. There was no way to know. All Emilyn could do was hope she hadn't just led them right to her best friend.

Moments of agonizing silence and indecisiveness later, she nodded to Cidelyn, and they quickly and quietly made their way over to the cellar entrance, burrowed into the ground, and locked the door from the inside. Emilyn knocked five times, over the course of five heartbeats. The time it typically took for an illusion to completely take form. After a moment, the door slowly opened, and Emilyn and Cidelyn each took a side to help pull it up. Beyond it, Emilyn found someone she didn't know, purple light dancing around her clenched fists.

The woman immediately let her guard down when she saw they weren't architects. "It's okay," she quickly stressed, and Emilyn realized she had taken her own defensive posture.

She had been expecting Kyshel. The woman likely came to the same conclusion. She'd whispered the words in a northern accent and had dark skin. Not from Unity Falls, Emilyn guessed. She looked vaguely familiar—enough so for Emilyn to believe she had been at the gallery. "Kyshel is here. She asked me to reach out to you," she let the light fade away, stepping back so they could step inside and close the doors.

"Where is she?" Emilyn demanded, her voice coming across more forceful than she'd intended. Yet, she had to make sure Kyshel was okay.

The woman held up her hands. "I can take you to her, but she's ... what is the term you use for it ..." The woman paused, but there was concern in her voice. Emilyn had a singular guess as to what she was trying to say.

"Splitting?"

"Yes!" the woman nodded. "She is—"

"I can help her. Take me to her."

"Of course. I ..." the woman stopped when she saw Cidelyn backing several steps down the stairs and almost tripping. She was terrified instantly. This was what he had meant. This was the reaction most people gave him.

"He won't hurt you," Emilyn promised, bluntly. She didn't have time for that. "Where is she?" she asked, but the woman seemed to have lost all focus. Her eyes were wide, trained on Cidelyn. Emilyn grabbed her arms and forced the woman to look at her. Her green eyes transitioned from wide to startled, snapping out of her gaze. "Where is she?"

"I ..." She paused, seeming to gather herself. "Room four."

Emilyn let her go, left Cidelyn behind, and darted down the stairs into the main gathering room. There were other people there—several of them. But she paid them no mind, rushing past them. Room four. There were only six rooms. If Kyshel had already been in one, isolating herself, she must have felt it coming in time to get away.

Room four. Emilyn shoved the door open and found her friend thrashing on the floor, illusions spilling out of her and back in as if in sync with her heartbeat, coloring the room in her pain behind a purple hue. Emilyn tucked her hair back behind her ears and quickly sat down next to Kyshel, reaching out toward her soul.

String the stars.

She was in the space between minds—hers and Kyshel's. The infinite darkness and light surrounded her, welcoming her on one side and looming over her on the other. A bridge rested between their souls. Across it was a trembling storm, thundering with purple flashes as memories clashed for control or escape.

She ran across the bridge. Into the storm.

Inside were many images Emilyn herself had seen. The city on fire. The lack of life. This was what she had been worried about—that the trauma or emotional distress of the siege would trigger a split.

Focusing on the images floating around her, she found recent memories of the gallery opening intermixed with ones of people in the city getting dragged away by the architects. She saw herself talking with Diselyn in the gallery. A sense of pride dripped from that memory, and Emilyn traced it into her own. Another of the two of them talking just before venturing into the gallery. She captured that one as well, committing it to her soul. There was one of the gallery members Kyshel had been charged with leading to safety getting brutally murdered. One of them was the girl outside. So that memory couldn't be real—just a fear manifested. It resonated with an aura that affirmed as much. And it gave way to others of the same kind, leaving guilt, horror, and terror in their wake, thus fueling the fire of the storm around her. Projecting one of the images she'd captured, Emilyn replaced one of those with that one, and the storm shook. Let it tremble. This fight was far from done. An image of one of Kyshel's own galleries on fire flew past Emilyn, but she caught it with her own light and tried to replace it. That one was real and fought back, worming away from her and fleeing into the storm. Emilyn cursed and pushed back, daring that particular memory to resurface. It had to be the trigger of the storm, the source of the split. That would have enough of an impact to cause all this. She snatched an image from the night they had met when Kyshel had called out a teenage Emilyn for sneaking into her gallery. She took another memory of the first award Kyshel had won for her work. And another of how much she had loved being a tracer, projecting a beautiful illusion of a sunrise for a little girl who had been denied seeing one by people that belonged to the Trace Away Movement.

The image of Kyshel's gallery ablaze returned, and Emilyn threw everything she could at it—as many of Kyshel's happiest memories as she could find. She couldn't replace or overwrite any memory, but she could push away the worst ones and allow her soul to stitch itself back together. And that was exactly what began. The fear and horror retreated, allowing the storm to begin to dissipate. Kyshel's soul began to stabilize and calm itself. As the clouds of the storm cleared away, Emilyn found Kyshel herself at the center of her soul, blurred as the two conflicting sides reached both in and out at the same time, trying to escape and remain. She was crying softly, her usually perfect golden hair a blurred mess.

"Kyshel?" she asked, her voice breaking. Seeing her like this was always the hardest part. Splits like Diselyn's were easier to deal with. She didn't know him, had no connection, and it was minor enough that all she had to do was project a happier memory to help him stabilize. Kyshel's were often like this, leaving her trapped inside herself while her soul tore itself apart. The best thing Emilyn could do besides identifying and replacing the memories responsible was to give strength to the part of her friend's soul trying desperately to hold on. She leaned down behind her and wrapped her arms around Kyshel. "I'm here."

Emilyn closed her eyes, thinking about her father and Cidelyn and her Gallery and how awful all of this was but how she couldn't face it without Kyshel, the one person who got her. In a world full of illusions, wrong colors, and subtle prejudices, their friendship was something real and true, and Emilyn would brave any storm to find her.

"I'm here," she whispered again and opened her eyes. She was back in room four, holding Kyshel in the same position as inside their minds. She wasn't thrashing anymore. She was still. Calm. But breathing. Her heart was beating steadily. Emilyn focused on their happy memories together, letting them flow into Kyshel's mind, letting them join the illusions still projecting around them.

There was a time when Emilyn had looked at all the artists and galleries around Unity Falls and wondered if there would even be room for her. It was Kyshel who had made room for her. Encouraged her. That was who she was. The one who always made room, even when there was none. She was blunt and stubborn and sometimes insensitive, but she was also radiant, filled with heart, and the best friend anyone could ask for. And Emilyn would do this a hundred thousand times just to silence whatever doubts filled Kyshel's mind. That was what Emilyn projected, and slowly the illusions began to fade away. The split was resolving.

Emilyn sat back, letting Kyshel rest against her, and she felt Kyshel's grip on her arm tighten. She again let out a breath she hadn't realized she was holding. This terrified her every single time, but this was not the split that would take Kyshel.

An accented voice came from the door—the woman who had greeted her. "Is she okay?"

She had long black hair pulled into a long pony tail and wore a glimmering blue dress and heels Emilyn hadn't even noticed before. Past her were several others looking in on the situation, worried or curious. Had they seen all of that? Kyshel and Emilyn's reputations would be different from then on if they had. But that was a moot point with the city literally on fire.

"She will be," Emilyn said, gently removing some of Kyshel's hair from her face and again checking that she was breathing. "She just needs rest." Looking back at them, Emilyn met each of their faces. These all were the people from her gallery. Kyshel had gotten them all there to safety. She spotted Diselyn and Crysalyn and even Forest in the very back of the group, and she smiled, looking back to Kyshel.

Thanks to her, part of her gallery had survived after all.

***

Gavelyn watched over the city in flames from the massive window adorning the governor's office at the city's center. Peering over buildings burning, illusions flaring and fading, the watermill grinding to a halt, and chaos claiming the area of the city that used to be his home once upon a time, he acknowledged every aspect of Unity Falls as it was snuffed out.

And he felt nothing.

That was simply the way of things. The city was small, irrelevant, and insignificant. Like this office, which was meant to signify power and authority, it didn't matter. Zarlyn did matter.

The man lay comatose on the bed behind Gavelyn. He had been a hero once. A force to be reckoned with. And he had been the source of his own descent. He had split. The splinter that became a fatal wound for the hero of Unity Falls: his own soul. A daughter left behind.

Gavelyn felt nothing. No sympathy. No pity. No remorse. He knew what he had to do.

He closed his eyes and let the silence of the defeated city focus him as he reached toward Zarlyn's mind. The other side was surprisingly easy to reach. He had expected the man to put up a fight. Instead, he found the bridge between them and followed it into the hero's soul. A chaotic flurry of memories snapped away, exploding into colors that became a forest lesser creatures would describe as beautiful.

Zarlyn himself rested on his knees in the center of a clearing, a garden of flowers surrounding him in a circular pattern. He looked to be in a meditative position, though Gavelyn approached from behind and couldn't see his face.

"Hello, old friend," Zarlyn said, though he didn't move. His words spoke of friendship, but his tone was one of pure neutrality. Gavelyn said nothing, stopping at the edge of the garden and waiting. Finally, Zarlyn stood, purposefully taking his time in doing so. When he turned to face Gavelyn, his face displayed the same neutrality as his voice. "I know why you're here. My answer is the same as it was a decade ago."

"You speak as if you have a choice in the matter," Gavelyn said, matching the neutrality in his own tone. "Past events should have taught you otherwise."

"Past events," Zarlyn mused, remaining stationary. "They taught me a great many things. None of which you're privy to. Not so long as you cling to this person you think you are."

"I already have what I need from you, old friend. But she would still like your loyalty. She can save you, you know? Free you from this place," Gavelyn enticed. "Give you back all you've lost. Let you see your daughter again." Zarlyn displayed no sense of enticement or interest, maintaining a blank expression.

"I rather like it here. It's quiet." He gestured with one hand, and every flower in the garden rose sharply, transitioning via purple light into a shard of a memory. "You are not welcome here." The memories flew at Gavelyn like knives, stabbing into him, assaulting him with the associated emotion. Joy, grief, love, pain, laughter, misery, and an overwhelming sense of protection that could only come from a parent. They pierced Gavelyn like his soul was made of paper, dissolving him into nothing.

He jerked backward, nearly stumbling onto the floor. He was back in the governor's office, the burning city before him. He was breathing heavily. He turned around, glaring at Zarlyn's comatose body on the bed. He had severed the connection. That took an extraordinary level of focus and practice, certainly against another of competent focus.

Gavelyn scoffed. Of course, Zarlyn had made it look simple. He was nothing if not an overachiever. And for the briefest instance, that made Gavelyn angry. Angry enough he could destroy his old friend's body—let his soul wrangle with itself for all eternity and have no place to go if a victor was ever decided.

All that was gone in just as brief of an instant, snapped out of his mind. And he felt nothing once more. Very well. He had what he needed from Zarlyn, but she still wanted more. He would deliver. There was one way to make Zarlyn cooperate.

All he had to do was acquire Emilyn.

Bonds That Cannot Be Broken

Fifteen Years Ago

Zarlyn felt too much. Emotions cascaded through him like blood, their flow giving him life alongside the threat of crippling him at any moment. It was his gift and his curse—what enabled him to be the person he was but at the same time what prevented him from being the person he wanted to be. They called him a hero. He never agreed with that word. He did some good because it felt good. It brought him a quiet he had never been able to find otherwise. And in that calm, he felt the things he wanted to feel. Love and pride in his daughter.

From a distance he watched her practicing projecting illusions in front of her. Simple things. Her favorite toys, her favorite foods, an image of one of her teachers or classmates, and everything else that dominated the mind of an eleven-year-old. Jade, her pet carbuncle, jumped at each one, surprised each time to find it wasn't tangible but landing gracefully on all four paws. The little creature held the same determination Emilyn did, and that was a stubbornness Zarlyn recognized. The way she held herself implied a desire to be the best she could be. It filled him with pride and also reminded him why he was so angry.

"To think you have any right to speak to her," Zarlyn began, his eyes focused on Emilyn and Jade farther off in the clearing, but his words directed toward the taller figure next to him. Gavelyn. A man

Zarlyn now only knew by name, his once-friend contorted behind the guise of a callous creature so far separated from his soul that he was unrecognizable despite his features remaining unchanged. A complete lack of soul he wanted nowhere near his daughter. "How very arrogant of you," Zarlyn snarled. "That wasn't our deal. And if you do it again, I make no assurances as to what I will or won't do to you."

Gavelyn scoffed beside him but displayed little else. His features remained blank as always, an impenetrable wall of stone with not even so much as a crack to peer through.

"Arrogance is no longer something I'm capable of," Gavelyn said flatly. "But I see it's something you have embraced. Your emotions will be the death of you, Zarlyn."

"Perhaps," Zarlyn responded, calming himself as best he could. Gavelyn was likely correct, with one amendment. Zarlyn's inability to control his emotions would likely be the death of him—not the emotions themselves. "But I'd rather die because of them than become what you have."

"I am free of burden," Gavelyn stated firmly. "If I were to die now, I would die in peace." Was such a thing possible in a world where souls tore themselves from bodies?

"Peace and nothingness are not the same thing," Zarlyn responded.

"They're more alike than you realize."

Zarlyn scoffed at that but decided it would be best to reaffirm his original point rather than continue to argue with whatever it was that remained of his old friend.

"Part of our deal was to leave her out of it," Zarlyn stressed. "I help you and your architects, and in exchange, Emilyn gets her mother back. That's it."

To Zarlyn's surprise, Gavelyn curtly nodded beside him, acknowledging the statement. Zarlyn narrowed his eyes at him, but the face behind the cloak did nothing in response.

"As it is," Gavelyn stated. "I will not violate it again." Zarlyn didn't believe that. Once a deal was broken, it spoke to the ability to do so again. Perhaps that was why Gavelyn had done it—simply to show that he could. A demonstration of where the power lay. What game was he playing? Why even talk to Emilyn at all? Zarlyn felt a fire rising inside him, an inferno he longed to drown Gavelyn in. It would be child's play to manifest it, to bring an end to whatever Gavelyn was doing right then and there. Watch him burn. But something stopped him. Several things, actually. Emilyn, for one. Her mother, a prisoner. Gavelyn himself. There was once a time Zarlyn would have died for the soul beside him. He would have directed that inferno at anyone who dared threaten Gavelyn ... instead of at the man himself. He closed his eyes. Emilyn. He felt his emotions calming—felt the fire and rage retreat inside him. And he opened his eyes to a clarity he hadn't felt a moment ago.

"So, what is it this time?" Zarlyn asked, wishing he didn't need to know the answer. Some time ago, Gavelyn had reached out to him to let him know he had found Emilyn's mother and to leverage the woman he loved against him. He still didn't know why. Out of nowhere, his friend had become the founder and leader of a group of tracers supposedly "like them" that had ideas to bring Seranno into a golden age. Self-appointed heroes. Bringers of chaos, to the cities they had terrorized. Architects, to Gavelyn and whoever he reported to. He denied such a person existed, but Zarlyn hadn't bought that for one second. Changes like this didn't just happen. Old friends didn't turn on each other for no reason, forcing compliance through leverage in the way Gavelyn was. All Zarlyn knew was that he didn't have much choice. But he would be damned if Emilyn got involved, or knew how involved he was. The things he was being asked to do. He could step back into the darkness, but he would shield her from it no matter what. Thus far, the deeds had been limited to simple shifts in little details of the city, creating illusions here and diving into a soul there. Ripples in the water. Things that seemingly had no consequence and were unconnected, though Zarlyn was sure that wasn't the case. Gavelyn was a strategist—always had been. Zarlyn just hadn't determined what the game was yet ... what pieces he had been shifting around the board.

"Assassination," Gavelyn replied promptly. "Unity Falls governor, Waylyn."

Zarlyn glared fire at Gavelyn but only received that infuriating nothing in retort. "You assured me I wouldn't have to take a life," Zarlyn said, suppressing the memories that thought brought to his mind's forefront. The act of taking a life left a soul tainted—haunted. Vulnerable. Zarlyn had done it before, long ago. When Emilyn was born, he had vowed never to again snuff out a soul. Gavelyn, more than any other soul, knew what that meant to Zarlyn. Yet, he was the one asking him to let that particular shade of damnation embrace him again.

"Variables change. Assurances repent. This is what must be done," Gavelyn replied and said nothing else.

Zarlyn shook his head, closing his eyes to keep his emotions in check. "I won't," Zarlyn affirmed. "I can't." His tone shifted to one of a quiet pleading. "You know I can't. Better than anyone."

"The past is irrelevant," Gavelyn said in that infuriating neutral tone. "I suggest you let it fade away as I have."

Zarlyn provided his friend with a horrified look. "How can you say that?"

"Because neither of us has a choice," Gavelyn said, his voice on the cusp of betraying some minuscule sign of care. Almost. But almost was anything but. He turned away from Zarlyn, beginning to walk toward the trees.

"What does that mean?" Zarlyn demanded, his fingers forming into a fist, purple light dripping from his knuckles. Gavelyn stopped, perhaps sensing what Zarlyn was preparing to do. He remained silent for a long moment. Zarlyn could feel the distance between them—a seeming canyon. Gavelyn was something insurmountable and yet right in front of him. That distance was like the bridge in the space between; only, this bridge Zarlyn was unable to cross. Still, he tried. He reached. Searched for whatever remained of his old friend.

Across the bridge, he saw nothing. Gavelyn's soul was somewhere far away, buried beneath an image of a man without one.

"If it's any consolation," Gavelyn stated in the space between, from the space across the bridge Zarlyn could not reach. His voice was hollower there than in reality. "I will accompany you. The task will take the both of us. One to distract with an illusion. The other to carry out the deed."

The deed. The erasure of a soul. The implication was there—a strike of lightning in the black of the space between. That job would fall to Zarlyn. That was the point. Not the death of the governor. Not whatever that would accomplish. Zarlyn was to be the one to take a soul. Gavelyn, or whoever he worked for, wanted that version of Zarlyn. The version he had tried so hard to bury so far beneath the identity as a hero his town had created around him. Perhaps in that nature, he was not so different from Gavelyn.

"It will be done in one week's time," Gavelyn added. "You will know when." There truly was nothing behind his words. No sign of any kind of soul.

"What happened to my friend?" Zarlyn asked quietly, his voice carried by the echo of the space between them—across the bridge.

"There are certain bonds that cannot be broken," Gavelyn replied, and suddenly Zarlyn could hear and see him more clearly. As if he'd ... allowed Zarlyn to see him more clearly. Like a blurred image coming into focus. "Such as that between a father and daughter," he continued, and suddenly Emilyn was running around him in the space between, chasing Jade. Smiling. Laughing. She was his entire soul. He would do anything to keep that smile on her face. "Ours ... was no such bond." Emilyn shattered. The space between tore itself apart, glass falling to give way to reality. And as reality resurfaced around them, Gavelyn's back was still to Zarlyn. He resumed striding away, his cloak spreading behind him in the gentle wind. Zarlyn wanted to say more—continue trying to reach his lost friend—but something stopped him. He let Gavelyn go, let the light go, and lamented what had become of their bond. Perhaps Gavelyn was correct. Maybe their's was a bond that could be broken. But that didn't mean it had been broken. Not yet. His friend was there. Buried. Zarlyn had felt him in the space between, for that briefest of moments. The question remained of how he had reached that state of nothingness. He had to learn more. And the only way to do that ... was to continue working with the architects.

A Raindrop In A Flood

Fifteen Years Ago

Zarlyn was in awe of how strong Emilyn was despite growing up without her mother. The chains that bound him didn't bind her, and he would do whatever it took to make sure that never changed. Once he was certain Gavelyn had gone, he had returned to Emilyn but waited a moment before joining her. Watching her successfully project illusions, even if she was unable to maintain them for more than a few seconds, brought a smile to his soul. Gavelyn was right about one thing. He had no choice. If this was the only way to give Emilyn the opportunity to know her mother, he would do it. And if that meant embracing the darkness inside him one final time ... so be it. This time, it would be his tool, not the other way around. It would protect the things he loved. From anything and everything. Including himself.

He still hadn't wrapped his mind around Emilyn's mother even being alive. Jiselyn had died when Emilyn was born, and yet Gavelyn had allowed him a glimpse of her inside his memories ... alive. Captive but alive. Who was he trying to fool? His choice had been made the moment he'd seen her. He would do anything to get her back—to give Emilyn what she deserved. A parent who could be everything she needed.

"Is your friend gone?" Emilyn asked as the purple light faded from her eyes and hands. What a question that was, and she didn't even know it. Zarlyn nodded, sitting down in the grass in front of her and putting on the bravest smile he could.

"Yeah," he lamented. "He's gone. But I'll see him again." He had to believe he would.

"Then why are you crying?" she asked, her face forming the purest look of worry—one that only a child could manage. People lost that when they grew up. At a certain point, looks of worry became more than just worry. Fear. Judgment. So many other things people would be better off without. That purity died at some point, in everyone. He wished he could have it back. It would make things ... simpler. He hadn't realized he was crying, and felt his face, finding just a few tears there. He was quick to wipe them away.

"I have to do something ... something I thought I wouldn't have to. And it's ... sad," he said, and even that was probably too much. But Emilyn's was a curious soul. She would want to know—want to help. So, he had to tell her something, to keep her away from it all as best he could. "But I'll be okay; don't you worry," he added, gently touching the side of her face. She didn't seem convinced, but she didn't seem to want to pry either. Instead, she rushed into him, hugging him and burying the side of her face in his chest. Radiating support and belief.

That had been unexpected, but he wasn't going to argue with it or ask why. He would simply accept that she was the best thing to ever happen to him. He wrapped his arms around her in return, leaning his head against the top of hers. Jade, the little monster who rarely ever showed Zarlyn a tenth of the affection she did Emilyn, climbed onto his leg and nestled into his lap, squirming her way between the two of them and purring. It was strangely nice. Another thing he wouldn't argue with.

"I love you," Emilyn said into his chest, and his smile became far more genuine, taking in her warmth.

"I love you, too," he said and loosened his grip around her. She stepped back and sat down, pushing her auburn hair behind her ears and petting Jade as she, to his surprise, remained curled up in his lap.

It was said that carbuncles could touch the space between. Not in the same way that tracers could, but they could feel what was there. And they often reacted to it. It accounted for certain strange behaviors they displayed. Zarlyn found it hard to believe. But he had never been around Jade when traveling to the space between until today. Perhaps she could feel an echo of it lingering on him—feel the loss he was feeling for Gavelyn. Or the hope he was feeling for Jiselyn. Reluctantly, he gently placed a few fingers on the carbuncle's head, stroking the crimson fur between her three ears. The last time he had tried, the little beast had attacked him. Emilyn had found that hilarious. He had found it annoying. Now, though, Jade seemed to accept his touch. He wondered how long that would last.

"Whatever you're doing is good," Emilyn said, very matter-of-fact like in her own special way. "Because you're good. You're a hero. Everyone says so." He could only hope that would be true someday, even though he knew it wouldn't be. In that moment, he didn't feel like a hero. Emilyn, like everyone else in Unity Falls, was a victim of his grand deception. He had helped people, and done so without reward. And that supposedly made him a hero. The other thing it did was give him a rush of feelings that quieted the fire inside—quelled the rage. He did things others perceived as heroic but only because they prevented him from doing things others would perceive as horrific.

Those ignorant souls were blind to how tainted he was. Things were better that way. Let them call him whatever they wanted. Let them bury him under this persona he had crafted. He had Emilyn. He was going to get her mother back. Those were the things that mattered.

"How's your practice going?" he asked, finally changing the subject. Emilyn shrugged, looking a little defeated. But still determined. From the first illusion she had created, stringing two stars together in the night sky, she had been so determined. So was frustrated with herself, but he could see it in the dark blue of her eyes that she wouldn't let that stop her. She was a fighter, like her mother.

"I can't make them stay," she lamented, continuing to pet Jade, who was more than happy to continue taking affection from both of them. "And I'm really sleepy," she said with a yawn.

Tracing was taxing—especially at first. The focus needed. The energy required. Zarlyn remembered more than one occasion when he had passed out from trying too hard. He didn't want that for Emilyn. There was no need for her to push herself so much and so quickly like he had to when he learned. Those were different times.

"That's enough for today, then," he said. "We'll practice more some other time."

Emilyn shook her head. "No, I want to keep going."

Zarlyn offered her a kind smile. "You will. But you're not going to get anything if you fall asleep. Trust me, a few dreams, and you'll be good to go."

Emilyn pouted a little but didn't argue with him when she was unable to hold back a yawn. "Okay," she relented and stood up. "But can we try again tomorrow?"

"I promise," Zarlyn said, also standing, letting an upset Jade leap back onto the grass. He took Emilyn's hand and started them on the walk through the forest and back home. It was late and it would be a long trek. He had a feeling he would end up carrying her part of the way, but at least for the moment, she seemed strong enough to walk, Jade trailing behind. Zarlyn was just waiting for the little Carbuncle to leap at him from her strategically advantageous position. Startling him seemed to have become her favorite pastime. He suspected Emilyn encouraged her.

"So, what was I doing wrong?" Emilyn asked. "I did what you said. I traced the images! And I saw them! But they didn't stay."

"I saw them, too," he said, trying to sound encouraging. "You didn't do anything wrong. It just takes practice. And focus. You'll get there."

"How do you focus?" she asked. "When you use tracer light, how do you make your mind quiet?"

Selfishly, he thought to himself. In no way he wanted her to repeat. He thought back to when he had learned. He had been much older than her. Focus and clarity had come more easily to him than it would to her. It had been Gavelyn who had shown him how to focus.

Calming the eternal race of your thoughts won't come easy, he had said. You need a grounding phrase. Something that won't necessarily quiet your mind but unite it. Give all those racing thoughts a single destination. Boats heading down different rivers that lead to the same ocean.

"Most tracers come up with a focus word or phrase," he said. "Something that pushes all your thoughts in the same direction. Like the water that goes up the mountain," he said, hoping a reminder of one of her favorite places—a place she associated with calmness—might help her understand. "Always going the same direction."

"I like the water there," she said, closing her eyes for a moment. "It's quiet."

"Exactly," he said. "One day, you'll be able to make your mind like the water. And you'll be able to create anything. I promise."

She smiled at that and looked up at him. "What's your focus word?" she asked. He had made several of them over the years, changing as his priorities shifted. tracer light was so heavily dependent on the tracer's state of mind.

"Something I care a lot about," he answered, and saw the gears turning in her head as she narrowed her eyes at him. "Don't try to figure it out. And don't try to come up with yours right now. You'll find it when you need it."

"Okay ... but ..." She trailed off into another yawn and Zarlyn accepted defeat, letting go of her hand, and reaching down to scoop her up. She was small for her age and still light enough to carry, so long as he didn't have to do so for too long. Despite the fact that, if she were more awake, she would insist on walking herself like a big girl. She was a little too wise and grown up in that way, but he was growing to accept it. She was still his little girl, and sometimes that meant carrying her home. It wouldn't be the first time. Besides, he had endured far worse for her and would do so again.

Jade looked upset that she wasn't the one who got to be carried—at least one of her three eyes giving Zarlyn a look of jealousy. Back to her usual disillusionment toward him, he supposed. Fine. The little beast could walk herself. He shot the look back at her and she backed away, following behind him, her little paws crinkling leaves in the path.

Emilyn was too sleepy to object to any of it. As soon as her head fell against his shoulder, her eyes closed, and she was off to the world of dreams. No turning back now. He was in this one for the long haul. That was all right. It would be a relatively short walk home. Nothing too unbearable. Even if Jade was his only company. If only to avoid speaking to the carbuncle, he let his mind wander back to Gavelyn and the words his friend had spoken in the space between.

There are certain bonds that cannot be broken, such as that between father and daughter. Ours was no such bond.

Those words had stung. They had pierced Zarlyn in ways he didn't know they could. They had prevented him from saying more. Not because he believed his and Gavelyn's friendship had not been one of those bonds but because he wasn't convinced his bond with Emilyn couldn't be broken. And that terrified him. If she knew the things he had done, the souls he had snuffed out, and the things he was now being forced to do, what would she think of him? Would that bond endure? He could only hope and pray that she would understand. She was wise—far wiser than any eleven-year-old had any right to be. He had no doubt she could understand, but would she? Those were two very different things.

His mind began to unravel, thoughts of failure dancing around like little sparks escaping their source. Emilyn seeing him differently, failing to rescue Jiselyn, Gavelyn being lost forever. Could he protect his daughter? Could he save her mother? Could he find his lost friend? He was little more than a raindrop in a flood, so what could he even do?

Emilyn. He focused his thoughts, letting them wash toward a single destination. He took a deep breath and concentrated on his steps, one after the other. And the fire faded once more. He decided to spend the rest of the trek home doing the only thing he could in the face of all this adversity.

He prayed.

The Girl That Said I Cannot

The space between had been known by many names. Some called it Journey's End. Others called it Perdition, and those vile enough to seek it were those who belonged within it. It was none of those things to Emilyn. It was her friend. A solace when she was afraid. A warmth when she needed it. Something so grand and so minuscule at the same time. People like the Trace Away Movement's followers would have others believe it was something that swallowed away all the good in the world. A lack of understanding denoted fear, and fear often became judgment. People like the architects seemed to work hard to incite fear. Emilyn hated them more for it with each passing second. And with each passing second, she better understood just how little she could do about them. So, she ignored them. Taking advantage of the silence, she projected a blank canvas in front of her. She always painted in silence. Most artists seemed to prefer an auditory source of inspiration, but she preferred to just let her mind guide her hand, no sound louder than that of the wind or the water. It was a nice distraction that would have worked at any other time. But Kyshel was next to her. She had not woken up.

This was far from the first time Kyshel had split, and Emilyn was well acquainted with her recovery time. Anywhere between a few hours to a day. Kyshel would be okay. But their home was not, and Emilyn just wanted to hear her voice. Or see her father. But all she could do was hide. And stubbornly refuse to leave Kyshel's side despite knowing a distraction would do her soul well. Finally convincing herself to acknowledge the other people in the bunker despite her guilt, she stood up just in time for the door to open.

The woman with the thick accent stood there, a bottle of water in her hand, an apologetic look on her face. She had changed out of her dress and heels and into a dark grey sweater and sweatpants, and she was barefoot. Comfort looked strange in a world on fire. She had let her long black down, and it was hanging almost the entire way down her back. Her change into more home-esque attire reminded Emilyn that she was still wearing the same shirt and pants from the gallery, minus the jacket she had left with Diselyn. She suddenly found herself longing for her usual leather jacket, but knew she would be unlikely to find one in the bunker in the stash of clothes Kyshel had stockpiled. Leather jackets weren't really her style.

"Thought you might be thirsty." The woman offered Emilyn the bottle. Slowly, she took it, realizing just how hungry and thirsty she was. She suddenly felt like she could drink the whole river, and eagerly opened the bottle to take a long drink. The woman seemed to find that amusing.

"Thanks," Emilyn said, wiping a bit of stray water from her lips. The woman's eyes shifted to Kyshel, and Emilyn glanced back, hoping she might be waking up. But she wasn't, and the woman offered another apologetic look.

"You two are close?" she asked, and Emilyn nodded. "She splits often?" Emilyn knew Kyshel wouldn't want her talking about that with anyone, but Emilyn found herself wanting to answer honestly. It felt nice to talk to someone right then.

"Every once in a while," Emilyn shrugged and revealed the piece of paper still in her pocket. "I'm just glad you managed to get me this before she did." Emilyn sighed. "Thank you for that."

The woman smiled. "I'm just happy I could help. I'm not very experienced," she confessed.

"Projecting an illusion that far away isn't easy," Emilyn said. "It took me a while to make it work."

"She said ... it's like looking for a single face in a crowd. Daunting, but all you need is a glimpse and you can make your way." Emilyn smiled, remembering Kyshel telling her those same words. "But, as it turns out, it's kinda easy to find someone when the crowd is ..." She paused. Gone. When the crowd is gone.

"What's your name?" Emilyn asked, and the woman seemed to lighten back up a little.

"Jacquelyn," she said, offering her hand. Emilyn shook it.

"Emilyn," she replied, and the woman smiled.

"I know," she said, and Emilyn cursed herself a little. It was her gallery.

"What's it like out there?" Emilyn asked, gesturing to the door.

"Everyone's scared," Jacquelyn explained, shrugging. "Crysalyn tried to rally them a bit, but then Kyshel collapsed and that left everyone even more freaked out. We took stock of the supplies in here, but that's about it. With the nine of us, we'd be fine for about a week down here as far as food and water go. But space is tight, and most of us don't know each other."

It was a fair concern. Stress, fear, a compact space, a ticking clock, and a city on fire were not a good combination by any stretch of the imagination.

"Where's Cidelyn?" Emilyn asked. "The boy that was the with me."

"The one with the ..." she paused and hung her head. "I'm sorry for how I reacted to him."

"Apologize to him, not me," Emilyn said, more bluntly than she had intended. They both offered apologetic looks. A lack of understanding denoted fear. But at the same time, Cidelyn may just be their one and only chance at survival. It would do no one any good to be afraid of him.

"He's in the next room over," Jacquelyn said, looking guilty. Emilyn nodded thankfully, walking past her and into the hallway. The dark grey of the walls seemed to stand out, their lack of color drawing attention. Another way to eliminate distractions for a practicing tracer. But her attention focused on the man in the hallway—a man she remembered if only for the simple reason that he had been ...

memorable. Forest looked identical to how he had at the gallery, as if nothing at all had changed.

"Forest?" Emilyn asked, and he bowed his head to her. Something about that was odd. Maybe bowing was an Est way of greeting?

"Emilyn," he said and smiled his same strange smile as before. She still couldn't identify what was strange about it, though. "It's a pleasure to see you again." He offered his hand, and she shook it. He was charming, if odd.

"I don't think there's much pleasure about what's going on," she said, and she could practically see the gears turning in his head, seeming to ponder if he had offended her in some way. "But it's nice to see you, too," she quickly clarified.

"Yes," he replied, gathering himself. "These ... architects seem to have taken everyone by surprise." Emilyn narrowed her eyes at him.

"You haven't heard of them?" she asked, wondering how that was even possible. The architects had struck all around Seranno for the past decade and a half since she was a little kid. They were infamous. Everyone knew about them because there was no one on Seranno they hadn't affected in some way.

"Should I have?" he asked innocently. He was being genuine. And that made it all the stranger.

"Where are you from?" Jacquelyn asked from behind Emilyn, echoing her own thoughts.

"The southern continent," he answered as if that should clarify it.

"The architects have been just as active there as anywhere," Jacquelyn said, distrust lining her voice. Though that may have been a stretch. They were all on edge.

"I see," Forest replied, though he did sound uncertain. "Have they done anything like this before?"

"No." Emilyn folded her arms, thinking back to what little she had learned from her father about the group. "They usually do things more subtly, pushing things in a certain direction."

"And what direction might that be?" he asked.

"Whatever might spark change," said someone, joining the group. Emilyn glanced past Jacquelyn to find Diselyn. "The architects believe they're the ones paving the way to a new Seranno." Emilyn was glad to see he had recovered from his split, at least physically. And she was glad to have helped. She offered him a kind smile, flashes of the memory he had relived dancing around the corners of her vision.

"I see," Forest said, seeming sad as he peered at Diselyn. Emilyn turned toward the door to room five, grabbing the knob. Forest's hand found her arm at that moment. "I believe he wished to be left alone." Emilyn gently removed her arm from his grasp.

"I'm just going to make sure he's all right," Emilyn said. "I never would have made it here without him." Forest stepped back apologetically.

"Forgive me," he said. "There was an altercation with a few of the others who were alarmed by him. I sought to provide assistance but he seemed to prefer isolation."

"You have a strange way of speaking," Jacquelyn said to him, and his eyes widened toward her in complete alarm.

"What is strange about it?" he asked, actual fear in his tone as he placed a hand on his chest. "Have I offended you?"

Room five's door opened before anyone could respond to that, and Cidelyn peered out at four of them, looking nervous.

"You're thinking very loudly," he said quietly, to either Emilyn or Jacquelyn.

"What?" Jacquelyn asked, confused.

"He can hear your thoughts because you're a tracer," Emilyn said bluntly and shrugged. "Explain later."

"I would really rather you have not shared that," Cidelyn said, and Jacquelyn looked petrified. Being the only other tracer present, she needed to know. She would have found out one way or another.

"Nobody's gotten much of what they want today," Emilyn replied, and Cidelyn couldn't argue with that. "Are you okay?" He seemed surprised by the question, and she remembered what he had shared with her. That no one had cared enough to ask him things like that before. Eventually, he nodded.

"My strength's coming back." He glanced to the moon to his left and then looked to the floor, not meeting Jacquelyn's eyes. Emilyn wondered if he was listening to her thoughts. If she was truly scared of him. "Kyshel's still asleep," he figured, and Emilyn nodded, sighing.

"She'll wake up," she said. She had to. Emilyn felt a chill at that moment, as if her body had delayed noticing that the cold of the night had set in. Power was still out across the city, and though the bunker had a generator for light, it had little heat. And Emilyn's arms were bare. She folded them together and tried to ignore it for the moment.

"So, do we have a plan?" Diselyn asked out of the blue, looking toward Emilyn. She met his gaze but wasn't quite certain why he was asking her. Jacquelyn's gaze fell on her as well, and Forest seemed to decide it best to join them. Emilyn suddenly felt very small.

"Plan?" she asked, quietly. "To do what?"

"I don't know," Diselyn shrugged. "Something. Anything. You're Zarlyn's daughter. He fought the architects before. Surely you must know something?" There was a desperation to his voice. Pleading. Emilyn looked back to Cidelyn but found no hope for assistance in his eyes. So, she panicked, stepping into the room past him and closing the door before anyone could object or ask another question.

"I'm no leader ..." Her voice broke a little. "They can't think ... just because I'm his daughter. What can I do?"

"It's not just that. They saw you with Diselyn at the gallery," Cidelyn explained. "You took charge, and saved his life," he went on, and Emilyn wanted to argue that was Kyshel as much as it was her. That Kyshel had led them out of the building, to this bunker, that they should be looking to her instead. But she couldn't say that because Kyshel wasn't awake. It was a poor argument anyway. "And they saw you force your way in and save Kyshel here. You didn't ask permission. You just did it—something none of them could do." Emilyn ran her hands through her hair, frustrated.

"Stop saying things that make sense," she begged, and he almost smiled.

"Sorry." He sat down on the bed. Its sheets were perfect and untouched. He hadn't sat down yet. How long had he been in there? How long had she been with Kyshel? "Watching people is kinda the only thing I know how to do."

"I can't help them," Emilyn said, quickly sitting down next to him. "I'm not my father."

"They don't believe that," he said calmly.

"Well, they should!" she silently screamed at him, and then closed her eyes, hoping he heard her apology in her thoughts. "He helped people because he could. Because he knew how to. I just ... get lucky, sometimes. And sometimes not. If they expect me to do something ..." Emilyn paused, sighing. "I'll get them all killed."

"No one's asking you to start a revolution," Cidelyn replied. Emilyn was afraid that was exactly what they were asking her to do. "They're terrified. So am I. They just want a voice of reason."

"So, why mine?"

"Because they saw you do something incredible. Twice. Who else would they look to?" Cidelyn asked, and she hated how logical his words were.

"Kyshel. She's a natural leader."

"Sure," he agreed. "But those people watched you save her. Never underestimate the value in what you see."

"I can't," she reaffirmed. "I mean, what am I even supposed to tell them? I don't have a plan. Not for them—not to get my father back. I have nothing." She missed him. She missed him so much. When had she gone from the girl he raised, so determined to be just like him, to the girl that said, "I cannot"?

"Maybe tell them ... a bunch of artists versus a bunch of terrorists?" Cidelyn asked. "I see absolutely no flaw in that plan." He smiled and chuckled.

She did as well, seeming to deflate a little. It shouldn't have been funny ... at all, in any way. But laughing felt good in that moment. So, she let herself. A bunch of artists against a bunch of terrorists ... that would be something to see.

"I'm scared, too," Emilyn confessed and looked Cidelyn in the eye. "I'm not him," she said, thinking about her father. Zarlyn would know exactly what to say and do. He would inspire people. That was what he did. He inspired her every day, even in a coma. By doing nothing other than being his selfless self. But that wasn't her.

"So, be you," he suggested. "You're smart and brave—"

"And impulsive and reckless," she interrupted.

"And strong," he finished. "They have your father, and you're doing your best to think about what everyone around you needs. I'm probably the least-qualified person to say so, but that sounds like a leader to me."

Emilyn watched him for a moment. He barely knew her at all, mind reading or not. And there he was somehow saying the things she needed to hear, even if she didn't want to hear them.

"Nobody's gotten much of what they want today," he retorted and she scoffed, bumping his shoulder lightly.

"I told you to stop saying things that make sense," she said quietly.

"I've got too much that doesn't make sense." He gestured toward the moon, which almost seemed to be eyeing them quizzically. "Have to take advantage of the things that do," he sighed. Emilyn stood up, gathering herself. Whether he was right or not, these people were looking toward her. She might not be able to help. She had no idea what to do. But if they wanted someone to speak, she could do that. She just had to channel her inner Kyshel. Bold. Confident. Blunt. Things she mostly wasn't. But if there was ever a time to step out of her comfort zone, it was now. Besides, this was her gallery – these people were because of her. With a renewed sense of focus, Emilyn took a deep breath and opened the door.

The Gallery

Seven rooms became the entire world. Three training rooms. One storage room. One wardrobe room. One relieving room. One gathering room. The entire world. And it was on the verge of collapse. The tension in the bunker could be felt from corner to corner, a string binding fear to isolation and looping in panic along the way. Emilyn couldn't believe she'd let Cidelyn talk her into doing something about that. But she had. And if she was going to try, she was going to need room seven. A change of clothes would do her confidence well.

Entering the room at the end of the hall, Emilyn found the others had already raided Kyshel's wardrobe. She wasn't surprised. The room was mostly barren save for three racks of clothes shoved against the right side wall. Disheveled from recent company but still enough to outfit a small army. Kyshel would spend countless hours examining the latest fashion trends, and something to represent every one of those trends could be found in that room.

Two leather jackets at the end of the rack caught her eye, and she lifted one from the hangar to find her name written on said hangar. Kyshel's handwriting. Examining the jacket, it was an exact copy of the jacket she always sported. Emilyn smiled, running her fingers along the jacket's edges and feeling grateful to have someone who thought of her when preparing for the end of the world.

Closing the door, she stripped out of the sweaty clothes she had been wearing since the gallery and picked out a dark undershirt that matched the black of the jacket and her pants. Sliding that over her head, she trudged over to the nearby mirror and pulled the jacket over her shoulders. Looking more like herself, she began to feel more like herself again. Unity Falls was dying, Kyshel was hurt, and her father had been taken, but this was a small victory regardless—one she would hold on to as long as she could. One thing was missing, though. She spotted a small drawer underneath the rack of clothes and opened it, finding several hair ties inside. Exactly what she needed. Pulling her hair back, she tied it into a pony tail that reached halfway down her back. Satisfied, she strode out of the room with a confidence she hadn't had when she'd entered.

The hallway fed into the larger gathering chamber at the other end, and it was there she rejoined Cidelyn, who had decided to emerge from his own isolation. The walls surrounding the gathering chamber had maps etched, carved, and painted onto them, of the city and the surrounding areas. Mostly forest aside from the mountain. Various safehouses were denoted on the maps by deeper carvings or stronger colors, and the safest routes between them were highlighted in a similar fashion. The city had changed in the centuries since the tracer Network had been active, but the detail was remarkable. Or perhaps, the dedication. The Network had helped so many tracers move around Seranno safely, to find these places where they would be free to practice their abilities without the threat of being hunted. Tracers had eventually become a foundation of society itself, but before then, places like the bunker they stood in were the only safe places in all Seranno for someone like her.

Crates of old supplies filled the room. They were perhaps centuries old and yet perfectly preserved as if left only hours prior. Tables, chairs, abandoned lanterns, and old board games and card games Emilyn didn't recognize gave life to the space. They were likely games meant to promote focus and clarity. Kyshel had guessed that, at least. The remaining guests from her gallery filled the rest of the room, and Emilyn's attention settled squarely on them. Nine.

There were nine survivors of the siege that she knew of. Hundreds of people in Unity Falls, and only nine accounted for.

She knew Diselyn and Jacquelyn standing by the entryway to her left. Forest lingered just past them, and of course, Cidelyn was by her side. Farther back was a tall woman still in her dress, her brown hair pinned up but beginning to show signs of coming undone. Crysalyn. She had been pining over a portion of the map when Emilyn had walked in. The remaining two Emilyn didn't know, though she remembered seeing them in the gallery. Both men, also still in their suits. Emilyn hadn't spotted any men's clothes in the wardrobe. One of the men was taller, bearded, and had slicked-back black hair that glistened even in the dim light. The other was shorter with a face full of stubble that fed into wavy brown hair and bangs carefully positioned to reach toward the left side of his head. With Kyshel back in room four, that accounted for all nine of them.

Crysalyn made her way over to Emilyn and Cidelyn, though she seemed careful to avoid making eye contact with him. She extended her hand to Emilyn, and Emilyn slowly reached out her own to take it. That was Crysalyn, curator of the United Illusions Gallery, and Emilyn still had trouble believing she had been at her little gallery.

"Emilyn," she said, her voice higher than Emilyn would have thought. "A pleasure." She was speaking to her. Crysalyn was speaking to her. Suddenly, all that confidence dissolved, likely coming off her body in sweat despite how cold it was. "I wish it were under better circumstances." Emilyn merely stared at her for several seconds before her brain decided to remind her that she should probably use words.

"Um, yes, me as well. It's very nice to meet you," she said, and Crysalyn acknowledged her with a slight head bow, disregarding any awkwardness. It had to be something she was accustomed to at this point. By the art in the sky, why wasn't she the one everyone was looking to for answers? She was the only person in the room that everyone knew, even if only by name. Emilyn remembered when the power had gone out at the gallery, it had been Crysalyn's voice initially trying to calm everyone. But she had failed. Why?

"Iridelyn," the taller, bearded man introduced himself from the far side of the room with his hand raised, but he didn't approach her. Nor did the shorter man, who spoke up next.

"Yomalyn," he said, nodding to her. "A pleasure."

"Emilyn," she replied, even if it was a bit redundant at that point. Regardless, Emilyn did a recount in her head, meeting everyone's eyes as she did so. Jacquelyn, Diselyn, Yomalyn, Iridelyn, Forest, Crysalyn, Cidelyn, and herself, with Kyshel still asleep. These were the people she may spend what remained of her time with. They would all likely die or be taken wherever all the other people had been taken. But no matter the outcome, these were likely the last faces she would see. The people who had come to her gallery, looked over the memories she had painted, and knew her intimately because of them, whether they understood it or not. These are the people she would have to walk through fire with. They were all looking at her.

"Did you see anything while you were out there?" Crysalyn asked. "Any indication of what's happening?"

"The architects have taken everyone. The streets were empty," Emilyn replied.

Iridelyn sighed. "So it is them?" he asked, but Yomalyn shook his head.

"We don't know that," he said, an air of condescension riddled between his words. "It could be anyone."

"Anyone?" Jacquelyn asked, her tone questioning his sanity. "What other group do you know of that uses illusions to terrorize cities?"

"They've never done anything to this scale before," Diselyn chimed in. "But I agree. It is likely them. And if Emilyn says so, I believe her," he stated firmly, placing a little too much trust in her for her liking. It would be smarter to question her—be certain. Then again, she had been in Diselyn's mind. She had saved him from splitting. He probably felt indebted to her, though she wished he wouldn't.

"That's a bit of a leap, friend," Yomalyn said, and while Emilyn didn't mind him questioning her, his tone was a bit on the condescending side. She let it go, chalking it up to nerves.

"What does it matter?" Jacquelyn asked. "Architects or someone else, they've taken the city, and we can't just stay down here."

"We can for a week," Crysalyn said. "That's enough time to let clearer heads prevail and determine how we move forward."

"That's only if we all share equally," Iridelyn said, stepping forward. "But we don't know each other. We're not friends. We have no reason to trust one another."

"We have one pretty good reason," Diselyn countered him, pointing at the door. "Our home is on fire. And we're trapped inside ... whatever by the skies that barrier is. No one is coming to help us."

"But what are we even going to do?" Jacquelyn asked. "The architects are tracers. Powerful ones. And we have one trained tracer and me. But we're socialites. What can we do against terrorists?"

"We can fight," Yomalyn was quick to say. "Like our ancestors. Find where they're keeping the people and set them free."

"Dial it back, hero man," Iridelyn said beside him, and Emilyn was surprised she didn't see an eye roll from him. "I'm not dying for any of you."

"You realize how selfish you're being, do you not?" Jacquelyn asked, the air between them filling with something seething like boiling water.

"Selfish?" Iridelyn demanded of her. "I'm not expecting any of you to die for me, either. I'm being practical. And besides that, I was agreeing with you, in case you missed that part. We can't just go out there and fight."

"We need a smarter plan," Crysalyn said, careful to keep her tone neutral.

"And what other plan is there?" Yomalyn asked her. "Stay in here for a week and hope we come up with some way to not starve to death?"

"I'm merely suggesting that we focus on surviving, perhaps trying to escape the city, rather than fighting the architects," Crysalyn explained.

"I do not believe we can escape," Jacquelyn said, wrapping her arms around herself as if chilled by more than just the cold. She was a tracer, and even if untrained, she could feel what Emilyn could. That barrier was something ... unnatural. She was likely correct. There wouldn't be a way past it. "That barrier is something more than an illusion. It's real."

Iridelyn waved his hand at that, scoffing. "It's not real. It's a trick. An elaborate illusion, sure. But a trick. We just need to get to it."

"And you think we're just going to stroll up to it?" Diselyn asked.

"Of course not," Iridelyn replied. "We need—"

"To stop fighting each other," Crysalyn interjected, her voice finally showing signs of cracking and letting her own frustration slip out. "That accomplishes nothing."

"Again," Yomalyn replied to her. "If you have a plan, by all means."

"We're not just going to come up with something right away," Jacquelyn retorted.

"We don't have all the time in the world," Diselyn added, and Iridelyn said something. And Crysalyn said something. And Yomalyn said something. And they all just became ... noise. Chaotic, unstable, and toxic words that dissolved into a void of nonsense that would lead nowhere. Emilyn closed her eyes. If there was one thing she was trained for, it was filtering out noise. Focusing.

String the stars.

Letting the tracer light emerge, it surrounded her before coalescing into her hands and eyes. Reaching her hand up, it danced onto the ceiling, spreading across the room and dripping into the empty space in the center of the room. The image that formed in the light was that of her father, the picture she had painted of him. It was a moment of purity. He had saved a life. And he had done it with the entire city watching. But that wasn't the point. He had just done it. Because it was right.

Silence enveloped the chamber as all eyes found something in that picture—something that meant something to them—their static voices and faltering words finally sinking into the floor below.

Emilyn sighed and let the image float there after her hand fell to her side. "My father was a hero," she began, looking to Cidelyn, who nodded. "But I'm not him. None of us are. We all hope that we will be when it comes down to it. In those moments that require a split-second decision; we all hope we'll just know what the right choice is. The one that will have an ending like this one, where no one is hurt and everyone is praising us. Because we're all selfish, and we're all selfless. And that's the truth. We don't know what the right decision is. We don't know what we'll do in those moments. We just have to trust ourselves and live with whatever ending we create. My father would have something more hopeful to say right now. But he's not here. We are. And we have to trust ourselves. I don't know what will happen if we go out those doors. And I don't know what will happen if we stay in here. What I do know is that we can survive. We can find a way. If we work together. We all have good ideas, and we all have bad ones. The key is to take the best parts of us all. Look at the map around us. The people who made it were just as scared as we are. I'm sure some of them wanted to fight. And I'm sure some of them wanted to hide. They did both. And they sparked a change that shaped society moving forward. Let's just ... follow their lead, okay? We can hide, and we can fight. There has to be a way." There had to be a way to get her father back.

Everyone was silent for a long few heartbeats. The truth was that Emilyn didn't know where any of that had come from. But if it had done what she needed it to—taken a step toward uniting everyone—then she wasn't going to argue. The illusion began to fade, and she let the light slip away from her, her eyes returning to their normal dark blue. And she took a deep breath, looking to Cidelyn, who offered a kind smile.

"I always knew you had a good speech in you, Ems," a weak voice came from behind her, and Emilyn turned around to find Kyshel leaning against the hallway wall. She looked gaunt without makeup ... and strange in a dress that was messy instead of her usual pristine look, but Emilyn didn't care about any of that. She flung herself toward her friend, wrapping her arms around her in the embrace she needed so badly. She buried her face in Kyshel's shoulder, planning to never let her go again. She was so happy to see her. Kyshel weakly wrapped her arms around Emilyn in return, and Emilyn swore she'd never been happier. "I'm so glad you made it."

"I'd never miss a chance to get inside your head," Emilyn joked, and it was a terrible joke, but they both laughed, though Kyshel's laugh was weak. "Sorry," added Emilyn, finally releasing her friend. "Are you okay?"

"Thanks to you," she said and looked over the jacket Emilyn was wearing. "Feeling like yourself?" she asked, and Emilyn nodded in thanks, sighing a massive sigh of relief. Kyshel looked around at everyone. "Look at all of you. Arguing over who would get to watch me sleep, I presume?" she joked, and someone scoffed, though Emilyn wasn't sure who. It didn't really matter. Kyshel looked to Jacquelyn and nodded. "You may have saved my life, getting my message to Emilyn. Thank you."

"Happy to help." Jacquelyn smiled and then looked at Diselyn, Yomalyn, and Iridelyn. "I'm sorry. I wasn't trying to be argumentative."

"Paint under the canvas," Diselyn said, shrugging. "We're all on edge."

"Right," Crysalyn said, silently apologizing as well. Iridelyn and Yomalyn didn't seem to do anything of the like, but they didn't continue to fight either. Baby steps. "So what now?"

"You all heard Emilyn," Kyshel said, and stepped forward with Emilyn's help, her arm draped around her shoulder. "We find a way."

Crowns of Rotted Wood

The world was made of strings.

They were all around her, twisted and contorted into something that resembled a corridor. Coalesced for her to stand on. What was beneath them? There was no way to tell. The strings were almost pristine in appearance, with absolutely no sign of unraveling and no indication they were worn in any way. Yet they felt ancient. As if time had passed and while they acknowledged its passing, they were unburdened by it in the same way she was.

She felt confined. Isolated. Standing in the middle of the passage, she could reach her arms to either side. While she couldn't see an end in either direction, her instincts seemed to tell her they would lead nowhere. And ... everywhere.

She took a step, and her body felt weightless. It was effortless to move and difficult to stop. As if gravity still surrounded her but she wasn't entirely bound to it. Not like she was back ... wherever she had come from. Where had she come from? She had images, but they were distorted. Faces formed in her mind, but she couldn't put names to them.

She couldn't remember her own name.

That should have terrified her. Instead, she felt at peace. There was a calmness dripping from the strings like water, melting into her.

Making her feel safe. Welcome. She didn't know who she was, but this place accepted her. It was as alive as she was. It seemed to pulse, aligned with the beat of her own heart. And something about that was comforting, like being wrapped in a warm blanket.

There was a light at either end of the corridor. Had it been there a moment ago? It was far enough away that it didn't illuminate her surroundings, yet she felt it was within reach. And she felt a powerful longing for it. Gazing toward it and taking a couple of steps in that direction, a figure slowly came into focus down the corridor, silhouetted by the light. The figure was completely still, intertwined with the strings themselves.

"Hello?" she asked and found that her voice didn't echo. It seemed to go nowhere, and yet it reached toward the silhouetted figure in the same way her hands would. A moment passed, and the figure's form was suddenly facing her despite not moving from the edge of the corridor. Its head seemed to tilt slightly. She couldn't see if the figure had eyes but it was clear she was being watched. In distorted movements, the figure made its way toward her.

"Emilyn?" Kyshel's voice coursed through her mind before her eyes found her, worry on the outskirts of it as she said her name. Her name. She knew who she was. Emilyn. She was Emilyn. She let her eyes slide open and found Kyshel looking down at her, looking relieved that she was awake. "Are you okay?"

Emilyn sat up, swatting her own hair aside and focusing on her friend. She nodded. "Yeah, I ..." She paused, seeing an assortment of illusions down the hallway. Strings. They were all strings. Had she done that? "What happened?" she asked and found purple light dripping from her fingers.

"You were trembling," Kyshel said and looked to the illusions, which thankfully began to fade. "And projecting in your sleep," she explained, looking back at her. "Nightmare?"

"I don't know," Emilyn said, willing her tracer light to leave her. It seemed hesitant to do so, but finally, the purple light faded and her eyes returned to normal. Was it a nightmare? Strings. That was all she remembered. "I guess so." She took a deep breath. "Sorry. Did anyone else ...?"

Kyshel shook her head. "Just me. Everyone else is asleep." That was good. Though Cidelyn and Jacquelyn may have felt something if she had been reaching out. "Are you sure you're okay?"

Emilyn knew it was more than just concern that was prompting her to ask that. Tracers trained to control their dreams—to prevent this very thing from happening. Emilyn had spent countless hours with her father, honing her control over her abilities and her body's natural use of them. Training it to not just ... happen. To only generate illusions at her conscious command. She had been a kid the last time this had happened. Her father. That had to be why. She was so worried about him. It was shaking her to her foundation, and her powers were reacting. She needed to focus.

String the stars.

She felt herself calming a little.

"I'm okay," she promised Kyshel, furnishing a weak, unconvincing smile. "I'm just worried about dad."

Kyshel gave her a sympathetic look and followed that with a hug. "We're gonna find him," she assured her, and pulled back from the hug, looking her in the eye. "We will. Promise."

"And if he's ... gone, when we do?" she asked, and Kyshel shook her head.

"Don't think like that. Don't you dare. Those thoughts won't do you any favors. Besides, you said they took him alive? Why would they if wanted to kill him?" she asked, and Emilyn knew she was right. Still, she couldn't help but worry. She stood up, letting the blanket fall to the floor. She had volunteered to sleep in the hall, without a bed, so some of the others could have beds. She supposed that had been a good decision considering what had happened.

Her thoughts were swiftly cut short by a banging on the door. Someone was trying to get in. Kyshel's eyes went wide and Emilyn ushered her behind her, stepping forward quietly. The banging continued. The others began to emerge from the rooms and Emilyn gestured at them to remain silent. Jacquelyn's were the first eyes she found, and hers looked terrified. Emilyn tried to give a reassuring look, but she had a sinking feeling that she was just as scared. She couldn't think about that. She found Cidelyn and gestured for him to join her. He awkwardly made his way through everyone and crouched by her side, now at the bottom of the stairs leading up to the door, where the banging slowed but didn't cease.

"Can you hear anything?" Emilyn whispered, barely audible. Cidelyn nodded.

"It's an architect," he confirmed. "But his thoughts are hazy. I don't know what that means. But he saw ... purple light coming from the door. He thinks a tracer is down here." That was what Emilyn was afraid of. This was her fault. An architect had caught wind of her accidental illusions and now they were going to get caught because of her. "He's thinking he should signal for more to come." So much for hoping he'd just leave.

"We have to stop him before he does!" Someone whispered loudly. Yomalyn, Emilyn thought, but she wasn't sure. What were they supposed to do? They had seconds to decide.

"He's about to send up an illusionary flare," Cidelyn said, and that would be it. They would have to fight or run, and both would end badly. Emilyn looked back at Kyshel, who didn't look as scared as everyone else, but Emilyn knew she was still recovering. And Jacquelyn was shaking, holding her hand to her mouth to stop herself from making a sound, and looking like she could cry. Crysalyn was trying to comfort her. Iridelyn was whispering with Yomalyn, and they looked combative. Diselyn's eyes were focused on her, pleading with her to make a decision. Forest seemed contemplative, unphased by what was happening. Finally, she met Cidelyn's eyes beside her. They were indecisive but thinking the same thing she was. That they only had a moment to decide. She thought about what her father would do. He wasn't a violent man, but he was a protective one. She honestly wasn't sure what he would do. But there was no time to decide. There was no choice. These people were looking to her. She had to act. Cidelyn's eyes shifted to pleading, asking her not to do what she was thinking. But he didn't speak the words.

String the stars.

Her eyes fell purple, and the light emerged from her skin, surrounding her hands and reaching for her fingertips, begging to be given form. Illuminating the area, the architect would know she was there. So, she quickly undid the latch on the door and shoved it open.

And she was too late.

The illusion of a flare raced into the sky, a purple comet that exploded into sparks well above the tallest buildings. High enough that anyone in the city could see it. The architect met her eyes, the same purple light covering them. Once again, there was no time. Emilyn let her instincts take control.

She threw her hands forward, the purple light dancing forward and manifesting into an illusion of herself throwing a punch toward her opponent, a move Emilyn was uncertain she could effectively do herself. The illusion of her landed her punch and it exploded around the man into a cloud, allowing Emilyn to run in and attempt an actual punch. Which she landed, her fist colliding with the man's jaw, but she wasn't certain which of them it had hurt more. She wasn't trained to fight. The man stumbled a single step back before recovering and thrusting his own arms forward, copying her idea and manifesting a false form of himself. Only he formed three of them, and suddenly she was surrounded. And she didn't know which one was real. Focus. She had to focus.

A kick hit her leg from the left, and she fell onto her right knee. Left. He was on the left. She threw a punch, hit nothing but air, and felt a kick to her backside, landing her face-first on the ground.

"Stay down," the man said in a raspy voice, the heel of his boot digging into her back. She grunted in pain and couldn't directly see what he was doing, but she saw the night illuminate from an illusion he projected that prompted a cry from a voice that sounded like Jacquelyn's.

Falling down is just an opportunity to get back up. Her father's words rung through her mind as she closed her eyes, trying to focus. But the trick is ... getting back up doesn't necessarily mean standing up. It means finding something you couldn't find before.

Emilyn reached out toward the man's mind and found herself in the space between, the wooden bridge suspended in the blackness. The man stood on the other side, and while his hood blocked his eyes, she could see him ... smiling.

"Thinking you could invade my soul?" he asked, stepping across the bridge. And she felt heavier with each step he took. "You're weak, little girl," he snarled. "We're trained to resist such attempts," he explained, and she remembered Cidelyn saying that his thoughts were hazy. His mind was guarded in some capacity. "We can create things you have no idea are possible. And you never will," he finished, stepping across the bridge to her side. He was inside her soul, and he was infecting her. She felt so weighed down that even there in the space between, she found herself immobile. "You ..." he said, looking around, examining her thoughts. "You're the one Gavelyn searches for. Hmph. Fortune smiles on you, hero's daughter," he said, and the weight began to lift as he backed up onto the bridge. She could breathe again. "That is disappointing. He fought back, even in a coma. Or so I'm told. You just ... whimper beneath my boot."

"Where"—she struggled, willing her mouth to speak but it responded dispassionately—"is he?" she demanded, even with her voice weak. The man stopped, looking down at her. But he said nothing. "Where ... is he?" she insisted, her voice growing stronger. She felt a surge of strength, a fire rising inside of her. And she felt ... angry. "WHERE IS HE?!" she screamed at the man, her voice breaking, and he fully turned back toward her, his expression falling. She plunged a fist into the space beneath her, using it to push herself up. Then she put the other one down, doing the same. The man stepped forward, and the weight pushed her back down. But she fought it. And she screamed.

The man stumbled backward, a memory of hers flying across the void and into him like a burst of wind from a hurricane. The weight lifted, just a little. Another memory hit him and forced him back to the bridge's halfway point. And she found herself able to rise—only onto her knees. That would be enough. She locked her eyes onto him, that anger flooding them. She embraced the chaos that was calling to her. A longing to let loose, to let go of the focus she had spent her entire life honing. She did. The space between became a storm of her own memories, all of them one by one darting toward the invader and pushing him across the bridge and out of her soul. He wasn't welcome there. And he wouldn't breach it again.

Finally, he was flung off the bridge and back onto his side. She was able to stand again, and she stepped onto the bridge, accessing his soul but just barely. She felt fear from him. He was afraid of her. Good. At the forefront of his thoughts was an image of what he was seeing in that moment, and it forced her to stop. She saw herself, filled with rage, and her eyes were crying out purple light. It was running down her face, dripping onto the bridge and fading away. It surrounded her hands in a way that it never had before, almost like ... armor. And she understood why he was afraid. Because she became afraid. Afraid of herself, of what she was about to do to him. She closed her eyes. She didn't want to see that. She willed it away, stepping back off the bridge and into her own soul. What had she been about to do? How had she done any of that? Opening her eyes, she found the storm of memories was still there. And it looked eerily similar to something she had witnessed just the night before, and several times before that.

She tried to return to reality but found herself unable to. The storm grew larger, and she turned back toward the bridge, but it and the man were gone. He had severed the connection. Because he saw what was happening before she did. And now it may be too late. This was how it began.

She was splitting.

A Feather Braving a Hurricane

An idea can never die.

A split was an idea that refused to compromise. It simply demanded it exist, and while it may be quelled for a time, it would always return. Once a tracer split, it was something they would have to live with. Or not. It was why tracers were taught from the beginning to focus, as a lack of focus in situations of extreme emotional distress was typically the cause of a soul splitting itself in two. Emotional distress had been forced upon her. A lack of focus she had allowed to infiltrate her soul. The combination shattered something inside her. Something she was uncertain could be rebuilt. Her soul tore itself apart, and she felt drawn to those stars she had strung together so long ago then more than ever before. That singular point in the sky. Half her soul wanted to rip itself from her flesh and fly toward it. The other half longed to remain, but it was weak. That was more her. Or at least, the side she still felt fully intertwined. The storm in the space between was the other half, and it was prepared to engulf her. No one was coming to help her. She would be lost, either dead or comatose like her father. Then, she wouldn't be able to find him. She closed her eyes and pleaded with her own soul to find a way together again.

String the stars. Nothing changed. She remained in the space between. She tried again. Nothing. That was supposed to be her grounding phrase. The storm overtook her, and she became lost in a haze of her own memories. There was the first time she'd seen Kyshel split. The day her father had fallen comatose. The day Jade died. The worst days of her life, swirling around her on display, thriving amidst her anguish. There was one she didn't recognize, though, and she latched on to it.

She was playing with Jade in the forest. Her father was speaking with someone. A hooded figure. An architect ... and she recognized him. Or rather, she recognized his feeling. Absolute nothingness surrounding him like armor. This was the man who had taken her father speaking to him fifteen years prior. She wanted to move closer, hear what they were saying, but that wasn't part of her memory. Nor was it the will of the storm.

"Emilyn."

Her name rung around her, echoing throughout the storm as she was forced out of the memory and into ... her loft. Everything became silent. The dim light of a nearly-set sun drowned the space, and she found herself sitting on her bed, staring at a blank canvas, brush in hand. She remembered this day. Her loft was a mess. She had decided to try her hand at painting but hadn't been able to figure out what to paint. She'd settled on a memory of Jade.

"Perhaps ... something different this time?" a voice filled the room, but there was no one present. Whose voice was that? It sounded confident, assured. And it wanted to help her. It wasn't part of the memory. "Something to tether you."

"Tether me?" Emilyn asked the voice. "To what?"

"Yourself."

Emilyn wasn't certain why, but she wanted to do what the voice said. And she had an idea. To draw the painting, she had wanted to draw back then but had been too scared to. The only memory she had of her mother. She had died giving birth to her, but Emilyn had met her once. In the space between. Just for an instant. She had been on the bridge, gazing out into the void. Then she was gone. Her father hadn't believed her, but she knew it was real. She'd been afraid to paint it. Not this time. She felt content as she painted, focus returning to her.

She let out a breath that she felt like she had been holding for years, finding herself back on the ground. Kyshel, Cidelyn, Forest, Jacquelyn, and others all surrounded her. She was alive.

She sat up and found a string reaching from her chest, heading past Kyshel and toward Forest. It was golden, glimmering in the night, and it connected to his chest as well. It was soothing and warm. The moment she connected her eyes with his, it was gone. As if it had never been there. No one else seemed to have noticed it. The voice in her loft. It was his voice. He had stabilized her soul. How?

"What ..." She began to speak to him, but her eyes settled on what rested at his feet. Past Kyshel and Cidelyn, who were eerily silent, was the man she had fought in the space between. The man who had shown her an image of herself she would never forget—an image that his own face now mirrored. Only instead of purple light crying from his eyes, it was blood. She didn't need to ask. He was dead. She had killed him. She didn't know how. She didn't know what she had done. But she had taken his life. That blood was on her hands as much as his face.

"You truly are his daughter." An emotionless voice came from behind her, and she stood up, finding the cloaked figure. The man who had taken her father.

"Gavelyn." That was what the architect had called him. His face showed just the slightest hint of surprise. She could see his eyes; his hood was down. They were green but faded. Losing their color. They were accompanied by black hair that was unkempt and wavy—uncared for—falling in a strange mixture of natural and unnatural.

"You know my name," he stated, remaining in place. A statue of nothingness. "And I know yours. So let's be blunt, shall we? You're coming with me. Resist, these creatures perish." He gestured to all of her companions. "Cooperate, and they join the others unharmed."

"There are more coming." Cidelyn's voice came from behind her, and Gavelyn's eyes narrowed on him, perhaps only just acknowledging his existence. He said nothing and looked back to Emilyn.

"You have no other options." Gavelyn remained a statue. "And if you squabble for long, I will remove the ones you do have."

“Why?” Emilyn asked, finding speaking strange. As if her voice were a distant thing. “You took my father. You could’ve taken me then. Why didn’t you?”

“He kept so much from you, child,” Gavelyn said, his voice betraying no single emotion. “I simply wish to illuminate you.” That was not an answer to her question. Gazing at his stone wall of a face, she figured she wouldn’t get any from him. She wanted to give up—let him take her to her father. But what would happen to everyone else? If they could escape, they would have a chance. If she gave up, all their chances died. And possibly so did they. She was her father’s daughter, as he had said. And she knew what he would do.

She turned around and met everyone’s eyes. They were terrified. Of Gavelyn and of her. She didn’t blame them. She wasn’t sure exactly what she had done, or what they had seen. Letting her eyes linger on the body of the man whose soul she had destroyed, she found something she hadn’t been able to find before. The willingness to make the hard choice. She locked eyes with Forest.

“Whatever you did to me,” she said, despite having no idea what that was exactly. “Undo it.”

He was silent, and there seemed a reluctance to his posture. In that moment, he didn’t look ridiculous or strange. He looked understanding. With their eyes locked, the golden string emerged once again, linking the two of them. Again, no one else seemed to notice. In the space between, the image of the picture she had painted in her loft shattered. The canvas was blank once again. The storm returned.

Only this time, she would control it.

In reality, she let the light overtake her, and now she could feel it crying from her eyes, enclosing her hands at the same time. And she focused on the storm inside her soul, capturing it in the light. Thrusting her arms forward, she conjured an illusion of it on top of Gavelyn. The twister formed from the purple light encompassed him. He remained unphased and unimpressed, simply watching her, his cloak billowing in the wind. Wind. There shouldn’t be wind from an illusion. He noticed it as well, finally displaying an emotion—curiosity.

"To conjure something very nearly real ..." he said, his voice calm and yet somehow carrying through the wind. "Your potential is matched by few," he said, and then he stepped forward, as if the storm wasn't even there. "But you have no idea what you're capable of—or even what you're doing right now. You cannot control it. You're but a feather braving a hurricane. Bold. But eventually, you will be consumed. Just as your father was."

Suddenly, she felt the weight she had felt before bearing down on her, shoving her onto her knees, growing stronger as Gavelyn approached. Without consent she found herself in the space between once more, Gavelyn standing in front of the bridge on her side, his eyes focused on the storm now behind her. They were glowing purple, a pure and absolute focus radiating from them. The light didn't dance freely around his hands as it did hers. It was still, prepared to obey him. His very gaze seemed to still the storm. She felt what she imagined Kyshel felt every time she had helped her through a split. Her soul stitching itself back together, her memories settling into place rather than trying to escape. Gavelyn was doing what she always did. He was finding the source of the split and overcoming it. She felt overwhelmed as her emotions became her own again.

"Why ..." she mumbled through bated breaths, "are you ... helping ... me?"

"You are needed," he put it simply. "A split soul will do us no good."

As focus and clarity washed over her soul, she felt weakened but back to herself. She had no idea what to make of any of what had just happened. Back in reality, she was still on her knees, and Gavelyn's hand was offered to her.

"Cease this," he stated firmly. "And they will not be harmed. Of this, you have my word."

Emilyn tried to respond. She wanted to take his hand. Give up. But her thoughts became hazy. She was ... so ... tired. She felt herself hit the ground beneath her, but she didn't fully register it. She was still conscious, and she felt feet assaulting the ground nearby, running to her. But a different pair of feet appeared directly in front of her eyes, dark shoes without laces. Forest. He had ... appeared ... in front of her. She couldn't see Gavelyn's face, but his hand had fallen. Other hands were grabbing at her from either side. She didn't know whose. Words were being spoken but she couldn't understand them. Everything was fading away. She was turned around, back toward the entrance to the bunker. Her eyes found the man she had killed. The shame she had avoided earlier hit her in those hazy moments.

She was in her loft once again, staring at that same blank canvas. And Forest's words came back to her. Something to tether you. She couldn't explain it, but she felt that she needed to do that again. Gavelyn had fixed her soul, but she was still missing a tether. Something to fall back on if it happened again. Her grounding phrase hadn't worked. That image of her mother had, but she couldn't be sure if that was her or whatever Forest had done to her. She needed something else. She needed ... herself. Like he had said. She began to draw, focusing on what she had seen of herself in the mirror of the gallery. She didn't like drawing herself. It felt strange. But that was the point. This was an image of herself in the moment when her dream was becoming a reality. It was the best she had ever felt. She could tether herself to that. She felt that sensation upon finishing the picture. The loft wasn't messy anymore. The sun had set and yet a different light filled the room. She felt just a little more whole than she had before.

Her eyes opened to Cidelyn sitting in a chair beside a bed. Back in the bunker. She had expected to wake up wherever Gavelyn had taken her. Had it all been a dream?

"Not quite," he said, helping her sit up. She had no energy. Moving felt like an impossible task. Was this how Kyshel felt every time?

"I have ... a lot of questions." The words fumbled out of her mouth, barely coherent. Cidelyn nodded.

"I think we all do," he replied and shrugged. "Ask away. I'll answer if I can."

"Why ... are we still here?" That's what she decided to start with, still half expecting an architect to kick open the door and drag Cidelyn away.

"Forest," Cidelyn stated, very matter-of-fact-like. "I don't know how he did what he did, but Gavelyn suddenly became a lot more interested in him than any of us. Forest leveraged himself, and Gavelyn let us all go. But there are architects outside. They know we're here."

"What did he do?" Emilyn asked, despite the fact that the answer scared her.

"I think teleportation would be the best way to describe it," he said, and she recalled him manifesting in front of her. Not an illusion, she gathered. "As for what he did to you, I have no idea."

"And ..." Emilyn paused, looking back and forth between his eyes. "What did I do?" she asked, her voice small. "To that man?" Cidelyn shook his head.

"All we saw was a wave of light, from you to him. Then, he was screaming and ... ended up as he did. If I had to guess, I'd say you somehow ... overloaded his soul. His thoughts were ... not anything either of us wants to hear," he explained. What did that even mean?

It meant she killed him. It meant she was a killer.

She half expected Cidelyn to hear her thinking that and tell her something different—that she did what she had to do—but he didn't say anything. She didn't see any judgment in his eyes, either. She wasn't sure what to make of that.

"Is everyone else okay?" she asked, and Cidelyn nodded. The door opened at that moment, and Kyshel stood in the doorway, looking relieved. She locked eyes with Emilyn, and without hesitation, she rushed over and wrapped her arms around her, which made Emilyn feel like collapsing. She let herself get buried in her friend and her warmth. And she found herself crying.

"I'm sorry," she said to Kyshel, pulling back. "I don't think I ever understood exactly what you went through each time you split. I do now. I'm so sorry." Kyshel gave her an appreciative smile and embraced her again.

"Don't be," she said, wiping away a few of her tears. "You always get me through them. I'm sorry I couldn't do the same."

"You did," Emilyn assured her. "More than you know."

"Glad to see you up," Jacquelyn said from the doorway, all the others behind her.

Emilyn offered them a smile as best she could. She wondered how terrified they all were of her. But they didn't seem terrified as they shuffled into the room. "What's going on?" Emilyn asked, and wasn't that the question of the day.

"We're not gonna pretend to understand any of this," Diselyn began. "But we know what we want to do."

"We're not gonna pretend we're completely okay with what we saw, either," Jacquelyn said, and Emilyn felt a spike of shame. "But we don't blame you. And we're all still here."

"Not all of us," Yomalyn added, and Kyshel directed Emilyn's attention to her.

"You did what you did for us, trying to save us. It was scary, but it was brave. It was dark, but it was light too," she began and sighed. "I told them all about your father being taken. And now with Forest taken too ..." She paused, reluctant to speak her next words. "We want to get them back. Make a stand. We can't hide now. We might be the only chance they and everyone else have."

"You ..." Emilyn paused, trying to sit up a bit more and struggling. "You want to fight?" she asked, and one by one, they nodded. She wasn't sure that was what she wanted to do. As scared as they might be of her, she was likely more scared of herself. But she had found something she hadn't been able to find before. People who were willing to stand with her.

"A bunch of artists versus a bunch of terrorists," Cidelyn said, managing a smile. "What could possibly go wrong?"

Emilyn laughed a little, and it hurt, but she let it. She needed it. Everything. That was the answer to his question, but she didn't say that out loud. Gavelyn's words rang through her thoughts, but they took on a different meaning. The eight of them would be feathers braving a hurricane. No idea what they were capable of or what they were even doing.

But maybe, just maybe, they would come out on the other side.

The Judgment of a Single Breath

Souls were said to be the purest form of a person, representing everything a person was. They could break as a heart might, but they could heal as a cut would. They could be lost, taken, shifted, and invaded. Beings who could reach inside souls were long thought the things of myth and legend, buried beneath stories of stars and heavens and titans who could rend the very land inert. That was until the Age of Memories, when these beings came together, united by a longing to reach a singular light in the sky. Others feared them, though they meant no harm, only seeking to belong. Forced to hide, the tracer network was born. A safe haven for those who could breach souls, it taught that souls were more sacred than ever believed and the act of touching one was a blessing—that they ought to use their gift to improve the world. And eventually, the world would recognize that. Eventually, it did. The renaissance built a new foundation for society on Seranno, allowing tracers to thrive. What the history books didn't mention was when a tracer invaded a soul as an act of war and tore it apart from the inside, using memories and emotions as weapons of mass destruction, leaving voids in their wake as they carved a path of endless suffering. It was all Emilyn could think about. That all the books she had read and everything her father had taught her painted tracers in a light that hid the horrific things they were capable of—

things the Trace Away Movement warned about. The very thing she had done to that architect.

She didn't remember it. Not truly. But pieces had come back to her. She had used her own memories as weapons, tearing apart everything that man was. That was something she was going to have to live with. The people around her somehow still trusted her in spite of what she had done, and they wanted to make a stand. But she wasn't certain she could put herself in that position again.

It was like a poison, taking a life. Not one that would kill her. Or even hurt her, really. One that would fester in the darker parts of her soul, waiting for the right moment to remind her of what she now was. A killer. Then there was what Gavelyn had said. She had no idea what she was capable of. A feather braving a hurricane. Doomed to be consumed by it just as her father was. At least that served to remind her why she was agreeing to any of this. She had to get him back.

"What are you thinking about?" asked Kyshel, sitting across from her in the empty room. She had gotten so accustomed to Cidelyn knowing what she was thinking that Kyshel having to ask seemed strange.

"What I did to that man, outside," Emilyn confessed. She would have dodged the question with anyone else. "What Gavelyn said." You truly are your father's daughter.

"You were defending yourself," she said, bluntly. "And us. You did what you had to."

"But not what I even meant to. It's all fuzzy," Emilyn said, pulling her jacket a little tighter around her, and she looked Kyshel in the eye. "Did you ever use your powers ... like that?"

"Did I ever kill anyone?" Kyshel asked, and Emilyn flinched a little at the directness. Kyshel nodded, slowly, taking a deep breath. "My powers showed up when I was little, and I was an ... unwell child, as you know. Mother and Father had hired someone to watch me since I couldn't return to school until I got a hang of my powers. And she was the nicest person you'd ever meet. She made every effort to understand me. But she wouldn't let me do what I wanted. The daughter of wealthy parents, I wasn't used to that. I lashed out and treated her horribly. And one day ... I shouted that I hated her. That she wasn't my mother. I didn't realize I was creating an illusion from her memories, making her relive her own mother's ... abusive tendencies. She had spent so much time trying to make sure other children didn't have to go through that. And I lost myself in the space between, in her soul. I couldn't get out. I was so scared. I clawed my way out, through her memories," she paused, letting her eyes settle on her fingers, which were trying to decide what to do with themselves. Finally, she looked at Emilyn again. "I got out. She didn't."

Emilyn tried to find words, but none fell out. Instead, she let her own fingers fall over Kyshel's and leaned forward, closing her eyes and letting their foreheads lightly connect.

"I guess the point I'm trying to make"—Kyshel's voice broke as she tried to recover her usual graceful demeanor—"is that I know it's horrible. I know it's horrible. But at least you did it to someone who was threatening you. Not someone who just wanted to help," she leaned back, managing a smile. "And I'm here for you. By the art in the sky, always."

"By the art in the sky," Emilyn repeated. It was an old saying, from the tracer network, for those seeking that particular light in the sky. Now, it was a universal grounding phrase. Only now was Emilyn beginning to understand why. "Always." She appreciated what Kyshel had just done more than she knew how to express. She wasn't alone. That had been what she'd needed to be reminded of.

"Sorry if I seemed judge-y," she said, and Emilyn couldn't recall a single instance of her coming across as judgmental. Though, admittedly, she hadn't quite been aware of her surroundings at the time. "It brought up all that, and I was hoping that was something you wouldn't have to go through."

Emilyn shook her head. "Nothing to apologize for," she said, and it was true. It made sense. She could take everyone else being a little afraid of her. But Kyshel? She was glad to not have to find out what she would do if Kyshel was scared of her. "Besides, you're always a little judge-y," Emilyn added, and Kyshel smacked her arm.

“There are two kinds of people,” Kyshel began. “Those who make the tough choices to wear colors that just don’t go together at all. And those who tell them they look like a carbuncle dressed them. I am a highly distinguished member of the latter.”

“As a member of the former,” Emilyn replied. “I can attest to that.” Kyshel smiled, and they both seemed to be in lighter spirits.

“I have offered for years to fix your wardrobe,” Kyshel stressed, giving a defeated look. “But you’re stubborn. You must be an artist.”

Emilyn chuckled. “Pretty sure both can be traced back to my father,” Emilyn replied. Stubborn could have been his region name. “Speaking of which,” Emilyn went on, thinking back to what Gavelyn had said. “I was wondering if you might have some tracer insight on grounding phrases?” Emilyn asked. “When I was splitting ... it didn’t seem to do anything. I thought that was the whole point?”

“If that was how it worked, no one would ever split,” Kyshel said, and that made sense. It was a kind of ridiculous question once she said it out loud. But Kyshel didn’t mock her for it. Zarlyn’s training had been … few and far between. He had taught her, but he had always subtly encouraged her to not rely on it. Only telling her what he felt she needed to know. He never said why, and there were some bits of knowledge he hadn’t shared that she had learned herself. She was as much self-taught as she had learned from him, and Kyshel knew this. Emilyn had never pushed her to share or to teach, afraid it might bring up memories better left buried. It had to have been an adjustment, living life without her abilities. To her credit, Kyshel did nothing short of thriving at any given moment. It was something Emilyn was envious of. “Grounding phrases are meant to prevent splits before they begin. They help focus. But what no one bothers to tell anyone is that they’re just for show. They don’t have any actual power. Hence why they can be changed. They just remind us how to focus—stay calm. There are other ways to do that. But a phrase seems to be a common choice.”

“Did you have a phrase?” Emilyn asked, and Kyshel shook her head.

"Breathing exercises," Kyshel explained and shrugged. "You might be surprised by how much the way you breathe can affect you," she went on. "But you have a phrase, and it works for you. I'd stick with it." Emilyn nodded and sighed. Kyshel tilted her head. "What are you not telling me?"

"Gavelyn," Emilyn began, accepting she wouldn't be able to hide anything from Kyshel. "He said I had generated an illusion that was very nearly real. I created that storm and the wind ..." Emilyn paused. It was ridiculous that she was even thinking it. "Is that even possible?"

"I would have said no, but ..." Kyshel sighed. "I was there. I felt that wind. It was—"

"Real," Emilyn interjected.

"It was something," Kyshel replied, and Emilyn recalled what had happened in the space between. How the light had become an armor of sorts.

"Do you think it's possible?" Emilyn asked again, and Kyshel shrugged.

"I think there's a lot we don't know about tracer light," she said. "And about Gavelyn and the architects. They could've caused that wind. Like the barrier around the city." Emilyn took a deep breath.

"We're in a bit over our heads, aren't we?"

"Oh, definitely," Kyshel replied, smirking. "But at this point, we've got precious little to lose."

"I want to save him," Emilyn said, thinking of Zarlyn. "Both of them. Everyone else, too. But what can we even do?"

"We can be smart about it," she said. "Yomalyn thinks we can just fight, but he's not actually thinking if he's capable of such a feat," she explained, and Emilyn chuckled. "Iridelyn just wants to be a hero. But at least he's smart enough to know we can't just charge in. Diselyn wants someone he can back, whether he really believes them or not. He's a representative. Kinda what he does."

"And Crysalyn?" Emilyn asked. "She seems like the natural choice to lead."

“I can’t figure her out. Probably because I haven’t spent as much time with her. Best guess is her façade of strength is crumbling and she’s doing her best to hold it together. Not thinking about much else. Then there’s Jacquelyn ...”

“She’s terrified,” Emilyn agreed. The girl was the youngest of the group. Not a child but certainly less experienced. Emilyn gathered she had been at her gallery for a source of inspiration, not as a prospective buyer or representative. “And she doesn’t know how to use her powers. But she could be a big help.”

“What about Cidelyn?” Kyshel asked. “How did you say you met him?”

“He saved me,” Emilyn explained. “And honestly, the fact that he can sense nearby tracers and see through illusions, might be our biggest edge.”

“And I’m the only one who finds that suspicious?” she asked, and Emilyn tilted her head.

“Hardly,” she admitted. “But he had several chances to betray me and he didn’t. I wouldn’t even be here without him.”

“So, you trust him?” Kyshel asked, bluntly.

Emilyn took a moment, but she nodded. “I think I do.” She braced herself for Kyshel chiding her over that.

“Good enough for me,” she said, taking Emilyn off-guard. “But if he is playing some game and he hurts you, I’ll throw that moon at his little moon.”

Emilyn laughed, and it felt wonderful to laugh. She had no doubt Kyshel would find a way to do just that.

“Any idea what’s up with that, anyway?” asked Kyshel, as if someone having a moon floating their head was only a little bit weird and not the strangest thing anyone had ever seen on all of Seranno.

Emilyn shook her head. “He said he can’t remember anything from before it just appeared one day,” she explained, remembering what he had said about how his life had been since that day. Lonely was an understatement. “I wish I could help him.”

"I think you already are," she replied. "You're probably the first pretty girl who hasn't run away screaming," she joked, but Emilyn didn't find that nearly as funny. "You're helping him by being a friend. And I would know; you're pretty good at it." That made her smile. She wished they could stay there a lot longer. Kyshel had really opened up, and it made her want to do the same. But it was all just ... too much. All she had were questions. And all she could do was avoid them until an opportunity to answer them presented itself. Even so, Kyshel had a way of calming her more than any grounding phrase. So it was with reluctance that she stood up, and helped Kyshel do the same. Her strength hadn't quite returned but there were more conversations that needed to be had. Kyshel seemed less focused on that and more on her hair, pulling it to one side and then the other, unable to decide which look she liked more. The difference was minimal to Emilyn. It would kind of glow no matter how she wore it. That was just the way of things. Kyshel seemed unsatisfied.

"Hair tie." She held out a hand, holding her hair with the other. "I know you took the whole stash. Who else?" she asked, but it was closer to an accusation than a question. Emilyn smiled and retrieved one from her jacket's inside pocket, placing it in her friend's hand. "Thank you," she said and tied her hair together into a messy bun in the back that somehow still looked like it had been intricately planned that way. "Cute?"

"As if it needs to be right now," Emilyn replied, and Kyshel folded her arms. Emilyn rolled her eyes, smiling. "Yes, cute. Satisfied?"

"Never," she replied and turned toward the door. "But your approval is enough for now. C'mon." With that, she took Emilyn's arm. "Might as well see what we can come up with to get everyone killed."

The Gallery Rises

Something powerful had happened in that room. Not a display of light or a show of force. Words. Hope. The birth of something that had saved lives. Maybe only a few. Maybe only one. But that had been enough. It could still be felt. The room had a gravitas to it that endured. The history of it all wasn't history at all. It was right there. Tangible. Like carvings. Emilyn ran her fingers along the wall, which showed an ancient map of her home. If those people, terrified, alone, and outnumbered, could stand up to their oppressors, then maybe so could they.

Everyone had gathered in the bunker's central chamber, eyes darting between each other and the door as if expecting the two architects outside to burst in at any moment. But they hadn't. Why let them remain in private? What had Forest been able to offer that had left Gavelyn completely unconcerned about them? Then again, maybe he had no reason to be. They were terrified, alone, and outnumbered.

"Feeling better?" Diselyn asked Emilyn as he entered the room, the last to join the group. Emilyn nodded.

"Getting there," she said, looking around. "Anyone else find it suspicious they're just letting us stay in here?"

"I think we're way past suspicious," said Yomalyn, shrugging. "But they know where we're at. Guess that's all that matters to them."

"Maybe," Jacquelyn said softly. "But letting us stay means Gavelyn is keeping his promise we wouldn't be harmed. That matters to us."

"Not sure what good it does us," Diselyn replied. "Other than not being harmed, I mean." It was a fair point, on both sides.

"Anyway," Iridelyn said, gesturing to Cidelyn. "This one's got an idea." He seemed ambivalent toward Cidelyn, which she supposed was better than afraid. At least everyone seemed to be growing okay with his presence. Cidelyn himself seemed the most uncomfortable, however.

"Right," Cidelyn said, awkwardly, and looked to Emilyn, who gave him what she hoped was an encouraging nod. "Those two outside, they're kind of loud. Not as guarded as the last one. They're thinking a lot about a supply boat that's supposed to arrive on the river soon."

"Will a boat be able to get through the barrier?" Crysalyn asked, and Cidelyn shrugged weakly.

"They seem to think so," he replied, and Kyshel spoke up.

"How does this help us?" she asked, probably because supplies were the one thing they weren't hurting for.

"Because it's an opportunity to make a stand," Iridelyn said and looked to Yomalyn. "Without doing something stupid." Yomalyn rolled his eyes.

"Fighting isn't stupid," he replied. "It's something we might have to do," he said, with a glance to Emilyn that didn't go unnoticed. It was something she already had to do. "Doesn't mean I'm against this plan. Go on," he prompted.

"I say we intercept the boat at the Utopia Center bridge," Iridelyn said with full confidence, pointing to the area on the map on the wall. "Sabotage it or something. Stand up to them. Send a message, without getting ourselves killed." He was smiling, as if he was very proud of himself and everyone else should be too.

"I've heard worse," Kyshel said, and folded her arms. "But I could hear a lot better. How do you propose we get past the two outside? How exactly are we supposed to sneak around the city? And sabotage it how? Send what message?" They were good questions.

Iridelyn donned a stumped expression, deflating slightly. "It's not perfect," he admitted, his voice sounding uncomfortably small. "Just a thought."

Cidelyn spoke up bravely, though his voice sounded even smaller. "Actually, I can think of a couple workarounds." He shifted his gaze to Emilyn. "Remember how I helped you through illusions?" he asked. "I think we could use that to get past the two outside. But it might require all of us to act. Overwhelm them," he explained.

Emilyn nodded. "If we have the advantage of illusions and they don't, we might be able to take them," she admitted. Jacquelyn looked mortified but said nothing. She was worried she was going to be useless.

"Same with getting through the city," Cidelyn added, and Emilyn nodded again. They had done it once already.

"That leaves a lot hinging on you," Crysalyn pointed out, locking eyes on Cidelyn. "I'm not convinced you can handle it." That translated to her not being convinced he was trustworthy. He didn't need to see her thoughts to know that.

"Neither am I," Cidelyn confessed. "But ... well I know it's just because we're desperate but I kind of like ... being able to help."

He liked having friends. An almost smile crossed Cidelyn's lips as he heard her think that.

"I trust him," Emilyn said, sighing. "It's not a bad start. But Kyshel brought up good questions. What are we hoping to achieve?"

Yomalyn shrugged. "Let them know we're not just gonna sit here. They think they can have our city, but they can't. People will always rise up," he said, firmly.

"Not bad," Diselyn said, and he took on a very representative-like tone. "But perhaps think of streamlining it? They think they can have our people, but they can't."

"A city's not a city without its people."

Crysalyn said, nodding. "I like that."

"But how do we get that message across?" Kyshel asked.

"I wish we knew where the people were," Emilyn said. "Stealing supplies for them or rescuing some would send a pretty clear message."

"Hmm," Diselyn concurred. "They must be somewhere. The whole population ... that'd take up quite a bit of space."

"Maybe poking around will help get us that answer? We're planning to take a walk across the city," Yomalyn suggested, and Emilyn nodded.

"Maybe, but we can't rely on that," she said. "Still, stealing supplies isn't a bad idea. Might still get the message started. And more supplies buy us more time."

"Which would be great if they didn't know we're here," Kyshel replied, a valid point.

"What if we steal the boat?" Jacquelyn asked, reminding everyone she was there. "If it can get in through the barrier, it can get out, right?"

"Run away?" Iridelyn asked as if the idea was monstrous. "Leave everyone behind?" Jacquelyn shrugged.

"I'm just throwing it out there," she said, backing away a bit. Crysalyn nodded.

"It's a good idea," she said. "The river leads to Dawn Falls. We could try and get help?"

"If there was anyone who could stand up to the architects in force," Diselyn said, grimly, "it would have happened a long time ago. We're on our own." He wasn't incorrect, and that suddenly made the governments of old sound like a halfway decent idea. As it stood, cities throughout Seranno governed themselves, with a certain understanding between them for resource sharing and trading. It was a good system that allowed for a diverse world not oppressed by powerful rulers, but it had its downsides too. None of the other cities would spare a soul to help Unity Falls.

"Unfortunately," Yomalyn grunted. "He's probably right."

"Hear me out," Kyshel said, with a conspiratorial tone. "We have the advantage of seeing through illusions. They don't. What if we create a false boat?"

"What are we doing with the real one?" Crysalyn asked, and Kyshel smiled, stepping over to the wall bearing the map of the city. She pointed to an area on the river that was close to the heart of the map, where they currently stood. "Bringing it here. River's close by and like we already said, a big problem is that they know we're here. What if we let them think we left? Took the boat out of town. And assuming we do get an idea where the people are being kept, we can think about trying to get supplies to them. If not, like Ems said, we'll have it for us."

"So," Emilyn began, recapping, joining Kyshel by the map, "Cidelyn helps us past the two architects outside and sneaking through the city; then, we create an illusionary boat to trick them, steal the real boat, bring it here, unload the supplies, and then let it sail up the mountain so they think we've run away?" Emilyn asked, and Kyshel nodded. "Devious. I like it."

"Smart," Diselyn said. "But it does kinda do away with the whole message thing."

"The message will come across when we free the people," Yomalyn replied, and looked to Kyshel. "Count me in."

"Appreciate the vote, but one step at a time. We all need to be on board with this," Kyshel said, and she was right.

"Cidelyn?" Emilyn asked. "How do you feel?"

He looked around at everyone, gulped, and then nodded at Emilyn. "I can do it."

"Do we know when the boat is arriving?" Crysalyn asked.

"Tomorrow morning," Cidelyn replied and shrugged. "Best guess, anyway. It's hard to get precise details from them."

"That leaves us one day," Emilyn said, looking to Jacquelyn. "That's enough time to show you a few things. If you want?" Emilyn wasn't quite certain she was ready to teach anyone anything, and Jacquelyn didn't look quite certain she was ready to learn. Neither might have a choice. The girl looked terrified but also intent to help, and she bravely nodded to Emilyn.

"I'd like that," she said, managing a smile.

"It's a good plan," Iridelyn added, his confidence returning. "And we have a day to iron out the details."

"Agreed," Diselyn said, and Crysalyn nodded reluctantly.

"I believe it's the best we can do under the circumstances," she said. "And I do like the idea of letting them think we've fled. It has a bit of ... artistic flare to it."

Kyshel beamed at that. "High praise," she said and took a bow. "Art might just be what keeps us alive."

"We all agree, then?" Emilyn asked, surprised anyone agreed at all, including herself. It was ridiculous to think they could even try this. Yet, everyone nodded, and Emilyn took a deep breath. Her gallery, standing against the architects. Maybe they did have a chance at getting her father and Forest back. Though that was a slim chance, it was a chance. It all hinged on how tomorrow went. By the art in the sky, it would be a miracle if they even made it past the two architects outside, let alone the rest.

Maybe she couldn't be the type of hero her father was. Especially then, she didn't feel she deserved the mantle of hero's daughter. But maybe, just maybe, she could help inspire others. Maybe she could start to atone for what she had done to that man. She had to try. And maybe this would give her the chance to start finding answers to all of her questions. She was just glad to know she wasn't searching for them all alone.

Songs For A Different Man

Fifteen Years Ago

Take to the sky and don't forget to smile wide
Only above the clouds will the sun always shine
You can always find your way back to your heart
While you are on your way to claim the stars
An emerald bridge is waiting for you there
To take you somewhere there is love to share

The words hung around Zarlyn, drenched in purple light and bringing him back to a time when things were simpler. When the fire inside didn't have a say in the choices he had to make. Choices that often determined the course of souls beyond his own. Choices that still weighed on him. Like the one he was trying to make. He was hoping Jiselyn's words might help. They had a way of reaching him. Jiselyn wasn't a tracer, but she could reach into his soul in a way that even the strongest tracer couldn't dream of. She was a guiding light, and without her, he feared he couldn't be the father Emilyn deserved. But at the same time, to do what he needed to in order to get her back, the same result may be unavoidable.

As he waved his hand, the words dissolved into the air beneath, and the purple light swirled as he sent it another command. Forming into a much larger image, it gave way to a small stage, a single microphone propped up in order to let an angel's light shine that much brighter. There she was, her voice pouring into the room like a gentle breeze, soothing and wonderful against the heat of the rest of the world. He didn't need the memory on display to remember how Jiselyn had captivated the entire bar that night, but now it felt nice just to see her eyes again—listen to her voice sing those words she had written.

She had Emilyn's dark blue eyes, the same wavy auburn hair, and the same lighthearted smile. It made Zarlyn wonder what she'd inherited from him. Part of him dreaded the answer. He chose not to linger on it. Instead, he watched Jiselyn perform, and while the illusion replicated her voice, he didn't need it to. The moment had been seared into his soul—perfectly preserved. He let it consume him, choosing to live there for a moment. After finishing the song, she had returned to their table and kissed him, beaming so brightly one wouldn't even know there were other lights in the room. She hadn't performed in a long time, and that one had been a particularly special performance.

"Do you think she heard?" Jiselyn asked, placing a hand over her stomach where Emilyn was waiting to be born.

"She?" Zarlyn had asked. They hadn't known if they were going to have a boy or a girl, but Jiselyn had sounded so certain. She smiled down at their little girl-to-be and nodded.

"She," she reaffirmed, meeting Zarlyn's eyes. "Our little girl."

Zarlyn smiled as well. He liked the sound of that. A girl meant less chance of their child turning out like him. "In that case"—he placed his hand gently over hers—"I'm sure she heard. In fact, she's probably practicing in there. Already wants to be just like her mother."

Jiselyn chuckled. "I wonder what song she's singing?" Jiselyn quietly looked down.

"Maybe something to do with that name of hers we haven't picked out yet," Zarlyn said before taking a drink. They had decided not to name their child after either of their parents—or themselves—but they hadn't proposed any alternate ideas.

"Maybe ..." Jiselyn started, then shook her head.

He had understood her hesitance. It was a big decision. But somehow, in that moment, he knew exactly what he wanted to name their little girl.

"Emi," he proposed, and she met his eyes again. "After the emerald bridge in your song. A place where there's love to share."

She was silent for a moment, thinking on it intensely. "Emilyn," she replied, smiling lightly. "I really like that."

"Yeah?" he asked, surprised, and she nodded.

"Yeah," she said, laughing a light, joyous laugh. They had decided on their daughter's name! Happiness was said to be something found, not forced. He had found it in that moment, and so many others with Jiselyn.

"Emilyn," she said again, looking down, her voice breaking as she tried and failed to hold back tears.

"Emilyn," he repeated, letting out that same light, joyous laugh. It was the purest emotion he had ever felt.

"That's a great name," came another voice, and Zarlyn frowned as he watched the memory. He hadn't let it play out this far in a long time. "Sorry," Gavelyn said as he joined them at the table. "Couldn't help but overhear." He shrugged and looked to Jiselyn. "And sorry I missed your show."

Zarlyn had smiled at his friend. "Your loss, Gav."

Gavelyn poured a little of his drink into Zarlyn's cup and slid an untouched glass of water over to Jiselyn. "How about I make up for it with a toast?" he said, raising his glass, and Zarlyn and Jiselyn both did the same. "To Emilyn. The luckiest little girl on all Seranno to have you both as parents. You're gonna be great at it, both of you."

"Thanks, Gavelyn." Jiselyn smiled at him, joining in the toast. "To Emilyn."

"To Emilyn," Zarlyn said, and they all drank.

"You know how I know she's gonna turn out all right?" Gavelyn said, setting his empty glass down. "Because her uncle Gav's gonna teach her his ways!" he exclaimed, laughing, and then looked to Zarlyn with a more serious expression. "I mean it, Zar. I'd never let anything happen to her. Promise on my life, by the art of the sky."

Zarlyn watched as the illusionary him took hold of his friend's arm, each squeezing and nodding to each other. Back then, he'd had no doubt Gavelyn had meant those words. But that Gavelyn was gone. All that remained was a husk—one that felt nothing for his old friends or for their daughter.

"Also," Gavelyn's voice said, as the illusion began to fall. "I'm gonna show her that her mom's not the only one who can sing! Ha!"

"Oh, are you?" Jiselyn laughed.

Zarlyn had been shaking his head. "No, no, no, please don't," he pleaded, but Gavelyn smiled and turned toward the stage. "Try and stop me, Zar!" he declared and headed off to ruin eardrums.

Zarlyn sighed, and Jiselyn was laughing, and they were all ... happy. Sometime later, that had changed. Zarlyn wished he knew when that had happened.

The illusion faded away, and the silence of the water rising up the mountain replaced it. Zarlyn closed his eyes, wishing away tears. And sometime between when he had let the illusion begin and before it had faded, he'd made a decision. He took a deep breath.

"Do you feel nothing for those times?"

Gavelyn had been behind him for several minutes, remaining silent. Perhaps he had been waiting for Zarlyn to finish, or perhaps he had been enthralled by the memory as well. More likely, he was simply waiting to speak to a man with a clear head. He wasn't going to get that.

"To be honest," Gavelyn began, his voice cold. "I don't even recall that day."

Zarlyn stood, turning toward his old friend, a coldness of his own forging behind his eyes. He imagined his look to be one of disgust. "You forgot?" he demanded, simply and bluntly.

"It's irrelevant," Gavelyn replied.

"Irrelevant?" There was venom spewing from the word. "You were sincere that day. You promised to protect my little girl with your life. And that's irrelevant?"

"I was a different man," he replied, indifference skirting around his words.

"You were you!" Zarlyn fought the fire inside him. Gavelyn had just discarded something that had been sacred.

"I'm assuming you didn't ask me here to speak of things lost," Gavelyn replied. "I suggest you get to the point of this meeting."

Zarlyn scoffed and noticed that Gavelyn was dressed in civilian garbs, as opposed to the ridiculous dark cloak he'd been sporting lately. He would have looked like his old self had there been any semblance of soul behind his eyes. "I want to see her," Zarlyn replied, looking back toward the water. Jiselyn. He needed to see her—to let her know he was working to save her. "If you expect me to take a life, I need proof she's alive beyond just your word."

"To the contrary," Gavelyn replied. "The only way to see her is to take a life. That is the arrangement. It is nonnegotiable."

"Why?" Zarlyn demanded. "I don't feel I'm making an unreasonable request."

"It is not in my control," said Gavelyn.

"Then who is in control?" Zarlyn asked, feeling he may be on the cusp of an answer to what had changed his friend.

Gavelyn didn't take that bait. "Your request is denied," he stated. "You will be permitted to see her once your commitment can be assured."

Zarlyn took another deep breath. It was as he had guessed it would be, and his choice was made. "I won't do it," he replied, an equal level of firmness in his tone. If he couldn't confirm that Emilyn could get her mother back, then he couldn't risk her father getting lost in the darkness trying. She needed a good parent, and right now that had to be him. As much as he wanted to risk everything to get Jiselyn back, he couldn't take the chance of her ending up without either of them. "Not without seeing her first. Our arrangement ends here."

Gavelyn showed no immediate response to this. He simply watched the water for a long moment and let the silence dance around them. Zarlyn turned to walk way, taking that as a sign there would be no more words. He was wrong.

"That is unfortunate for us both," Gavelyn said, his voice quieter than before. "I urge you to reconsider. You may be able to walk away from me, but she will not be as forgiving."

"She?" Zarlyn asked, stopping and turning his head toward Gavelyn but only slightly. Their backs remained to each other. Gavelyn said nothing further to elaborate. "I guess I'll take my chances," Zarlyn finished and continued to walk away. He had made up his mind. His soul was set. It was a difficult choice, but he had to prioritize Emilyn. Even over her mother. He loved Jiselyn as much as it was possible to love and more beyond that, but he knew she would do the same. Their daughter came first, before either of them. It was the choice he felt he had to make, even if it widened the already immeasurable distance between him and Gavelyn.

Zarlyn stopped and took yet another deep breath, trying his best to remain calm and focused. He turned back around to say one final thing to his friend, but Gavelyn was gone. Only the silence remained. Zarlyn hung his head but was satisfied with his decision, and continued back into town. He had garnered precious little information but it was information nonetheless. Gavelyn felt he had no choice. He was working for someone—a woman. It wasn't much, but it was a start. A world existed where he could save his wife and his best friend and they could all be a family again. It had to exist. By the art of the sky, it had to exist.

But for that moment, he had to let it go.

With all the strength he could muster to hold back the fire inside, he kept walking. And walking. And walking. One step after the other.

A Trick of Memory

Fifteen Years Ago

Home.

It wasn't much, but it was theirs. The one place in Unity Falls where the fire had no reason to emerge. Where Emilyn soon would be as the school day was close to letting out. Figuring she'd be hungry, he'd decided to get something for her while he was out, if only to distract himself from Gavelyn. Even though Emilyn would likely complain since she was fond of his cooking. Fond of or simply accustomed to. He cooked often, as it was an easy excuse to spend carefree time together. That day, however, she would have to accept some fruit from the market. Free fruit at that. He usually wore something with a hood to prevent people from recognizing him, though it rarely worked. He hadn't had anything with him that day. While it was nice to get free food or supplies, he didn't want anyone to feel obligated to do that for him. Moreover, he didn't wish to set that example for Emilyn. Kindness was a wonderful thing. Taking advantage of it, less so. Even in his darker, more selfish moments, he tried to temper that. Sometimes, though, he failed.

He'd settled on some of Emilyn's favorite fruits and hadn't managed to pay for any of them, despite his insistence. Arguing with anyone from Unity Falls was a losing game. Beyond that, there was the danger of overreacting. He didn't seek out situations where he would need to use his abilities, lest the fire, precarious and threatening as it could be, make the situation worse before he made it better. His soul was a constant balancing act, teetering on the edge of bliss and ruin simultaneously. He hoped Emilyn didn't inherit the fire.

Their home was a small one. It wasn't much, but it was the best he could afford. It was actually more than he could afford, but he hadn't wanted to compromise Emilyn getting the best experience growing up that he could give her just because what he did didn't pay well. He wanted her to have her own room, her own things, and her own ability to explore and discover what she loved and the kind of person she wanted to be. He let her have the single bedroom while he slept on the couch in the living space that was just an extension of the kitchen. He didn't need much for himself. Because he hadn't had as much chance to explore and discover what he loved and the kind of person he wanted to be. He had been forced into so many things, one after the other. The upside of that was that he was comfortable with less.

Stepping inside, he locked the door, pausing as he heard pacing in the kitchen. He peered around the corner and found Emilyn. She looked upset. She shouldn't have been home yet.

"Emi?" he set down the bag of fruit on the counter and reached down to give her a hug. "Did school let out early?" She shook her head, and then hung it shamefully. He got down on a knee and gently placed a few fingers beneath her chin and lifted her face to meet her eyes. Jiselyn's eyes. "What happened?"

"I ..." she paused, deflecting her eyes, then folding her arms. "I might have accidentally ... scared ... the other students ... with an illusion ..." she explained, refusing to meet his eyes. Did she think he would be upset? "Miss Lilalyn says I can't come back until you can tell them my tracing is under control."

That made sense, and he should have expected it. It was the way of things. There were too few tracers in Unity Falls to build a select school or training ground for them. Some cities with larger populations had them, but Unity Falls could never justify it. Instead, it was the responsibility of the family to help their children learn to control their abilities. They wouldn't be allowed back in school until the parents could prove to the school's board of directors that the child had it handled and wouldn't alarm the other students or teachers—or worse. Zarlyn pulled Emilyn in for a hug, and she buried her face in his shoulder.

"I'm sorry," she said in a muffled voice, and she sounded so genuinely upset about it. He caressed the back of her head and kept the embrace.

"You have nothing to apologize for," he said, trying to sound as reassuring as possible. "It's perfectly normal. It just means we can't wait any longer to practice."

That got her attention. She pulled back from the hug, her eyes wide. "You're going to teach me?" She lit up, and he recalled how enthralled she had been by her light the other night, despite being frustrated she couldn't do much yet. It was all perfectly normal like he had said.

He nodded, and before she could get excited, he interjected. Not because he didn't want her to get excited but because he saw a shadow pass by the window on the far side of the kitchen. Another briefly passed by the window in the living area. Someone was watching them.

"On one condition." He held up a finger and gave her a moment to settle. "I bet Miss Lilalyn gave you some extra classwork to do so you don't fall behind, right?" he asked, and she slowly nodded, far less enthused about that. "So how about you head into your room and get a head start on some of that? I'll bring you some food in a few minutes and see if I can help. You get a few assignments done, and we can spend the rest of the day practicing. Sound fair?" She lit up a little again and smiled, nodding, grabbing her backpack, and heading off toward the room. Zarlyn escorted her and inspected her room. No sign of disturbance, and her window was sealed and covered as usual. "I'll be back in a few minutes, all right?" he asked, and she nodded as she started to get out her schoolwork. He began to pull the door closed, but she spoke up again.

"Just to clarify," she said in her negotiator's voice. "I'm not in trouble?" she asked, and he smiled, wishing he had more time to indulge her favorite pastime of finding a workaround to get something she wanted out of him. She was getting too good at it, but he had a bad feeling and couldn't engage her right then. He didn't want to alarm her, either. He shook his head.

"No, you're not in trouble," he clarified. "But I bet you are hungry?" he asked, and she nodded. "Food coming up right up!" he said and stepped back, pulling the door shut. Once he heard it latch, he took another look around. No shadows from the windows. No sounds at all. No indication of anything.

He blinked, and without warning or consent, he was in the space between, the bridge in front of him. Except it was only ... half the bridge. It cut off part of the way across, eliminating access to whoever's soul lay on the other side. That was nothing he had ever seen before, impossible to his knowledge.

"She is quite lovely, your daughter." The voice came from behind him, and he quickly turned around to find a woman lurking on his side of the space between. Impossible. He felt the fire rising, and he was prepared to defend himself. "That will not be necessary," she stated and gestured for him to unclench his fists. The fire inside him died.

"Who are you?" he asked, finding fear he thought he had long left behind intertwining with the words. He had a singular guess. The woman Gavelyn had been referring to. His vision of her was distorted. Not quite blurred but not plainly visible either. Like he could only see her out of the corner of his eye despite the fact that he was looking right at her.

"I've worn many names," she replied, her voice distorted in the same kind of way, a mixture between Gavelyn's nothingness and a heart that carried far too heavy a burden. "You may call me Valel."

"Are you responsible for what happened to Gavelyn?" he asked, embers of the fire burning back to life. "Did you kill my friend?"

"He is needed," she said, both answering and not answering the question. "As are you, a natural amplifier," she continued, appearing on one side of him and then the other, again and again, her voice coming from all sides. Amplifier? "Your kind is rare. You can enhance the tracer light of those around you. Quite useful."

"I have no idea what you're talking about," he grunted, and truthfully, he didn't. He had never heard the term amplifier before. She shrugged. He wasn't quite sure how he knew she did that.

"I do not need you to know what you are," she explained. "Your presence is enough."

"I don't know what you're saying, and I don't know how you're doing any of this. But know this," he said through clenched teeth, a strange weight beginning to bear down on him. "I have no intention of killing for you or anyone ever again. I'm not afraid of you," he went on, though that last bit wasn't entirely true. "And if you do have Jiselyn and haven't killed her yet, I don't believe you will."

"Curious," Valel replied, completely unphased. "You claimed you wanted proof and were denied. What makes you believe we haven't already killed her?"

"Why should I believe you even had her in the first place?" he asked, and Valel flashed an approving smile. Again he was uncertain how he could tell in that strange state of both seeing and not seeing her. "And even if you do, I'll find another way. That I can assure you. Emilyn won't say the words, but she misses her mother. I know she does. If she is alive I will find a way to get her back. The right way."

"Emilyn doesn't even remember her mother," Valel stated blankly. "So, how could she miss her?" she asked, and Zarlyn didn't fight the fire inside as it fought to break the chains weighing him down.

"How do you know that?" Zarlyn demanded in a calm fury, pushing against the weight. Finally, he began to break through it. The fire broke through, consuming him, purple light dancing around him in an instant. He yelled at Valel, drenching his fist in the light and throwing it at where she had last been. But she was gone. So was the fire. It was just ... gone. He couldn't feel it. The purple light dissipated and he turned to find Valel interacting with ... his memories. She shouldn't have been able to. Not without subduing him first. It was like he wasn't even a presence in his own soul. He ran toward her, his fear returning. She held up a hand, manifesting an image from her purple light. It was even more distorted than Valel was. As if it were nothing, she slid the image into his memories and let it fall naturally as if it had always belonged there and he reached for it to pull it back out and—"Dad?" Emilyn's voice interrupted him from washing the fruit. She sounded concerned.

"Yeah?" he called back, grabbing a towel to dry his hands. "What's wrong?" Her door opened and she emerged, staring blankly at him.

"Who were you talking to?" she asked. "Who's Valel?" She stepped closer. "You said that name a couple times."

"Valel?" he asked, shaking his head. "I wasn't talking to anyone, Emi," he said. He had never known anyone named Valel. He hadn't known anyone with an El region name. They were few and far between in Unity Falls.

"Oh," Emilyn said, pouting to herself a little. "I thought I heard you say that name. You sounded scared."

Zarlyn leaned down and helped her up, sitting her on the counter. "Just me in here," he said, smiling reassuringly at her. "No one to be afraid of."

She nodded reluctantly and sighed. "Sorry," she said, but he was the one to give an apologetic look.

"No, don't feel bad, it's all right," he said, cupping her face with his hands. "You thought I was scared and you wanted to help. That's brave of you. Never let go of that, and never apologize for it."

"Okay. You promise?" she asked, and he nodded.

"I promise," he said, and she seemed convinced.

"Then I'll get back to work, but ..." She reached down and took a piece of fruit. "I'm taking this with me!" She slid off the counter and darted to her room. Zarlyn watched her and chuckled, catching her mischievous smile as she closed her door. That little girl was something else.

Looking back to the fruit, he let his thoughts linger on Jiselyn, still surprised Gavelyn had provided the proof he'd asked for. Gavelyn had opened up his soul in the space between and allowed Zarlyn a glimpse of a memory. Jiselyn, worn and dirtied in a cell, but alive.

She was alive. He wanted to see her, but that was more than he had expected to get from his old friend. It didn't help that he now had confirmation that Gavelyn's soul was still intact. Which still begged the question of what had happened to him. But that was a question for another day. Today he had achieved a minor victory and he would take it. Jiselyn was alive. He wasn't happy about what came next in his arrangement with his old friend, but he was happy about that. The fire inside seemed quelled, satisfied with this. For the moment. With a renewed sense of duty, he retrieved the bowl of fruit and headed off to Emilyn's room. He had a deal to keep with her too.

***

Gavelyn had lingered too long on the memory that Zarlyn was watching—of the two of them and Jiselyn. He had greater concerns than a history that was no longer his. It was irrelevant. What wasn't irrelevant was Zarlyn's decision—poor as it had been. Gavelyn had to make one his own in order to correct that.

"The amplifier is back on track." Valel's voice came from beside him, manifesting as she always did. He wondered if that had bothered him at some point? "You provided him with the proof he asked for in your earlier meeting." Gavelyn felt nothing, though there was a faraway echo of ... guilt ... bouncing around in his soul, merely a fragment of an emotion long burned out of him. It flickered away before he could truly notice it was even there, a candle in a twister.

"I assume he had no choice?" Gavelyn asked, though he wasn't entirely certain why he had. He knew the answer. Valel's eyes settled on his, but he left them on Zarlyn's home on the street below.

"You seem discontent with that," she stated, though there was no implication behind her words. "I merely did as you asked," she went on. "Though I maintain that taking the girl may have been a stronger motivator."

"People like him need something to fight for," Gavelyn replied. "Take the girl and he would do anything you ask to get her back. But you want him loyal. That would destroy any chance of that." Valel smiled her strangely approving smile but said nothing. "Besides, our plan only works if Emilyn grows up unaware of all this."

Valel's smile faded into obscurity. "My plan," she corrected, though there was little hostility to the words. She, like Gavelyn, was beyond such emotional entanglement. Certainly not over something so simple. "You're fortunate I value your input."

"Zarlyn may not see it that way," Gavelyn said and finally met her eyes. She narrowed hers as he did, and he felt her reaching inside his soul. He didn't fight her. He never did.

"I could remove what remains of your friendship with him," she suggested, though it was neither an insistence nor a question. Merely a proposition.

Gavelyn let his eyes linger again on his friend's home, and that flicker of pain emerged once more, only to be snuffed out in an instant. He shook his head. "No," he replied. "That flicker is all that reminds me I have a soul. Without it ... I fear I will be of little use to you."

"Souls are for those who seek connection," she replied, also gazing down at the house. "You are above such things."

"Of course," he stated. "But if I didn't still have one, I would seek it out, would I not? An unfortunate circumstance of human nature. Knowing I still have one allows me to remain fully dedicated." Valel smiled her approving smile once again, and then she was gone. Her distortion clung to a different string, somewhere on the other side. In her absence, he allowed himself a final look at Zarlyn's home.

"There was some part of me that was sorry, old friend," he said, as the flicker ignited one more time. "But that part"—it was snuffed out—"is gone."

Gavelyn walked away, feeling absolutely nothing besides a gentle stab from the shards of a promise he'd left fractured.

The Space Between

"Why do you think it's called tracing?"

The question came from Kyshel, posed to Jacquelyn, who hadn't taken more than two steps into room six, instead remaining sequestered by the door. Emilyn offered a reassuring smile in hopes of easing her nerves. Sliding her eyes toward the floor for a brief instead, the darker-skinned girl reluctantly stepped deeper into the chamber.

"Because ... you trace the images you see, in order to create them?" Jacquelyn replied, though she was clearly uncertain. Emilyn did not fail to notice her eyes, again focusing on the floor beneath her. She also did not fail to notice her use of 'you' instead of 'we'. She was scared, but what was scaring her? Emilyn could only guess the answer was her, and what Jacquelyn had witnessed her do the night before.

"A common misconception," Kyshel's voice descended into full teaching mode and Emilyn swore she saw a glimmer in her eyes. She took a certain pride in this. "We call it tracing because the images we project are outlines like they've been traced over a picture. Our souls, memories, fill in the space between."

"Not to be confused with the place we call the space between," Emilyn added, giving Kyshel an apologetic glance for interrupting her monologue. "But we'll get to that."

"I have to confess," Jacquelyn began, hesitantly, but with a little more confidence. She was trying. "I've never actually ... projected anything. That note I made for you was ... luck, I guess? I mean you did kinda walk me through it."

"I did," Kyshel agreed. "But that was no small feat, so don't discredit yourself. You still did that. Everyone needs a little help to start."

Jacquelyn seemed to be a little bolstered by that, standing a little straighter.

"So why don't you tell us what you do know?" Emilyn asked, and Jacquelyn nodded.

"Barely anything," she confessed. "My parents are part of the Trace Away Movement. I was always afraid to tell them. Afraid to even research it because of how ... judgmental they were. So, I hid it from them and from myself. But I still wanted to make art, so I just tried the old-fashioned way. I was at your gallery because I wondered if you were the same since your father was a tracer but you were making physical art. And then I saw what you did at the gallery and everything happened and ... well, I'm starting to think there are worse things to be afraid of."

Emilyn wondered if she was thinking that she could change her family's views? It was what Emilyn would think in her place. She was finding Jacquelyn and she weren't terribly different in some regards. She had always been afraid of the Trace Away Movement, too. They were political extremists who believed tracers and tracer light were unnatural and as such should be extinguished before they anger nature and force all to suffer the consequences. As far as anyone could prove, the group had never progressed past occasionally violent protests but more and more rumors had surfaced over the years of tracers going missing. It was largely believed the movement was responsible, but there was never any evidence.

"So, we start from the beginning." Kyshel nodded to Emilyn, who gestured to Jacquelyn to watch closely. Closing her eyes, Emilyn reached inward and found the purple light swimming on the outskirts of her soul, excited just to be there. A child waiting to get picked to do something fun. It danced upon seeing her, surging out to take her hand. Then it filled her, manifesting around her hands. Emilyn let it embrace her skin, waiting to create something. That was all it wanted. Opening her eyes, she knew everyone else would see a blazing purple around her pupils. Everyone always assumed that a tracer saw everything in a purple hue, but what it really did was heighten the entire spectrum of colors in her vision. Not as in making them brighter or more noticeable—simply more vibrant and alive. Reds were more crimson, yellows more golden, grays more silver, though it varied depending on the initial color. It was like looking at the world through the eyes of an artist who could see even the tiniest differences in the various colors she had to choose from when painting a portrait. The world became a canvas, begging to be added to.

Jacquelyn stepped closer to Emilyn, examining the purple light. She had seen this before, but Emilyn understood the curiosity. Without someone to teach her—to let her actually see it up close—it would have been hard to satiate, not having learned herself. Jacquelyn lifted up one of Emilyn's hands and looked surprised as traces of the light sparked at her touch, dancing onto Jacquelyn's fingers and fading into her skin. Emilyn hadn't seen that happen before. Jacquelyn smiled, seeming to enjoy the sensation. If it meant she was less nervous, Emilyn was happy to let her continue.

"So," Kyshel started, drawing Jacquelyn back a little. Not to limit her enjoyment, though. Kyshel knew how it felt in the beginning as well as anyone. "Basics first. tracers have about three options at any given time. First"—she raised a finger—"a tracer can reach into someone else's soul and interact with their memories. You get there from the space between." She paused. "Yeah, we'll get there."

"Can the other person stop you?" Jacquelyn asked, and it wasn't the first time the question had ever come up. The ethics of what tracers could do had been debated for centuries. Because the answer was complicated. Emilyn shook her head.

"Not if they're not a tracer themself," she clarified, recalling what she had done to the architect outside ... and what Kyshel had done to the woman her parents had hired. "At that point, it's not called reaching but ... invading. It's dangerous. Most tracers abide by the unspoken rule to never do that." Jacquelyn wrapped her arms around herself, looking chilled. Emilyn couldn't blame her. "Don't worry. One advantage of learning now as opposed to as a kid: you have a better focus. And focus is kinda what it's all about."

"Okay." Jacquelyn nodded, but her voice was small. "I hope the other two are less scary."

"Depends on your definition," Kyshel replied. "The second option is delving into your own soul, interacting with your own memories. Just as dangerous, but only really to yourself."

"Is that what causes splits?" Jacquelyn asked bluntly, and Kyshel uncharacteristically shied away. "Sorry!" Jacquelyn was quick to add. "I didn't mean ..." she let the thought fade away, scolding herself. "Sorry."

Kyshel shook her head. "Don't be! Just caught me by surprise is all. But that's good. It's the kind of thing I need to confront more directly—talk about more," Kyshel said, giving Emilyn an apologetic look. Emilyn smiled reassuringly. Kyshel was one to talk, but only when she was ready. Emilyn would never push her.

"In that case," Jacquelyn started, but her voice was still contorted by uncertainty. "Can I ask ... what causes a split?"

Kyshel shrugged. "No one really knows. Extreme emotional distress seems to be the common factor, but there are different kinds of splits of varying severity that have no pattern or discernible trigger. I've gone through several. Some caused by emotional distress like the other day. Some just ... happen. I wish I knew why." Kyshel paused. "They're unavoidable," she lamented. "But not unstoppable, if you've got tracer friends."

"Good to know," Jacquelyn said gratefully, taking a deep breath. "Okay, what's option number three? Please say something a little less grim."

Emilyn smiled. "Option three is the space between," she answered. "Think of it as an access point to your soul and to others. But if you don't go in either direction you won't be lost. You'll just be there. It can be peaceful. A kind of escape, or safe haven."

"A place for tracers, and only tracers," Kyshel said, a bit wistfully.

Emilyn imagined she missed the space between. There were few places she could go for peace and quiet. This bunker had been one, but she'd given that up. Jacquelyn looked intrigued.

"What does it look like?" she asked, her eyes lighting up a little. Emilyn let the light wash away, disappearing back into her soul through her skin. She sat down, crossed her legs, and focused, gesturing for Jacquelyn to do the same. Kyshel stepped back, positioning herself as far back as she could on the wall. Jacquelyn sat down a few feet in front of Emilyn, linking their eyes. Not something at all necessary for the transition, but it was long said to create a stronger link between the two interacting souls. "Do I need to do anything?" Jacquelyn asked, and Emilyn shook her head.

"Not this time," she replied. "It only takes one to create the link. Once I do, we'll both be in the space between," Emilyn paused. "Are you ready?" Jacquelyn nodded, taking another deep breath and centering herself.

"I think so," she replied, and Emilyn wasted no time reaching out, her soul extending beyond her body. Emilyn liked to imagine it as strings of light, reaching out to intertwine with strings of light from another's soul, forming a union in the physical space between them that allowed them to transition into what they called the space between. But in reality, there was nothing to be seen. No grand connection between the souls that their eyes could see. Simply a feeling. That you were more than just you. That just across the bridge was a whole new world—but not one treaded lightly, as it was something sacred.

They were in the space between. A bridge lay in the blackness between them, a whole life's worth of memories and experiences behind them both. In its normal state, a soul came across as an ocean of sorts, but instead of entering it from above, they walked in from the sides.

We're all an ocean of our own, side by side in the infinity. Sometimes, oceans touch. Out in the world, that's natural. Undistinguishable. Why should it be any different here? A union of any sort is a beautiful thing. I truly believe it's why we were put in this universe.

That was a quote her father had told her once when she was little and exploring the space between. They were her mother's words—words she had spoken to her father before she died. Emilyn wished she had known her. But she had little fragments like that to help her feel close to her. It was much easier to feel that in the space between. In the place where souls could touch, she had to believe more souls than just two could be present. Any soul that had ever touched those left a mark. Maybe something tiny and indistinguishable. But it was there. Some piece of her mother's soul lived on in her own. She believed she could sometimes feel it. Just barely, somewhere on the outskirts. But it was there. And it made her feel just a little happier.

Jacquelyn looked all around them in amazement, her mouth hung open and searching for words but finding none. Emilyn stepped onto the bridge but not too far. She didn't want to enter Jacquelyn's soul without her permission. Approaching the center, she leaned over the side railing and watched Jacquelyn, letting her take things at her own pace.

"This ... is ..." Jacquelyn started but shook her head. "I don't know the words. I ..."

"It's a lot," Emilyn agreed, looking around. By all accounts of their eyes, they were in a chamber. Their senses told them there were walls, but one could wander toward them and never find them. It was dark, but their souls were lit, and even if they weren't, they could just ... see. They knew where the bridge was. They knew which side was theirs. They felt everything on a deeper level in the space between. It felt like ... this was the core of what they were. Emilyn loved it there, and she dreaded the day she may no longer be able to reach it. That day was not today. Today, she could relish the serenity Jacquelyn was feeling because she could feel it too—or at least echoes of it, drifting away from her soul and across the bridge where Emilyn could touch them. Emotions were infectious things and far more so in the space between.

Jacquelyn made her way onto the bridge to join Emilyn but stopped briefly, likely feeling those same echoes from Emilyn's side. She was surprised, but then she smiled and continued forward. "That's incredible," she said, her voice both strained and longing to speak a hundred million words. "How have I had access to this place my whole life and not known about it?"

"You were afraid," Emilyn said. "No one can fault you for that. So don't fault yourself either." Jacquelyn joined her in leaning over the railing, looking into the infinity beyond.

"I know. It's just ... this place would have been ..."

"Exactly what you needed?" Emilyn asked, and Jacquelyn nodded, looking regretful. "Can I ask you a question?" Jacquelyn immediately shoved away her regretful look, meeting Emilyn's eyes and nodding again. "You've been nervous since we started. But that's not because of your parents, is it?" Emilyn asked, and Jacquelyn sighed, looking away again.

"Not exactly," she confessed. "But that is part of it! I mean ... it's complicated."

"This is the place where you can uncomplicate things if you want. You can see all your memories over there," Emilyn gestured to Jacquelyn's soul. "Sometimes, I find that looking back helps me look forward." Jacquelyn smiled a little, but she didn't try to recall a memory. Emilyn wasn't going to push her. It was something she would need to learn to be comfortable with on her own.

"I saw what you did," Jacquelyn said, though she was careful to keep her voice neutral. She was trying to convey that she wasn't trying to judge, but at the same time, it was something she wasn't entirely okay with. Emilyn understood the feeling all too well. "Outside, to that architect. I don't think anyone else could see it. But I could see his soul ... break. Because of whatever you did. It was like ... a cloud, but it erupted like a volcano. Shattered into a million pieces. I think I felt him ... die. Like he was reaching out in his final moments. I don't ever want to feel that again."

Emilyn felt a tear escape her eye, and she quickly wiped it away, taking a deep breath. She didn't know Jacquelyn had felt it. Had Kyshel felt it too? "I didn't mean to do that to him," Emilyn said, slowly, her voice breaking and her words tiny. A tattered feather braving a violent hurricane.

"I know!" Jacquelyn was quick to clarify, her hand finding Emilyn's arm. "I know," she assured her. "But that's what scares me. I've never been particularly good at focusing or being objective. I'm impulsive. Emotional. And I want so badly to help everyone, but I'm terrified of losing control of myself. With these powers, I could hurt someone or ..." she trailed off, and Emilyn placed her other hand over Jacquelyn's, still on her arm.

"Or do what I did," Emilyn finished for her, Kyshel's words from earlier coming back to her. She had to say it out loud. Confront it. If she was ever going to be able to live with it. Jacquelyn nodded but laced it with apologies. Emilyn managed a smile, doing her best to stay strong. "Lots of tracers have trouble focusing. And have that very same fear. It's why we create what we call a grounding phrase. A word or phrase that puts your mind in a particular place, focusing your thoughts on it alone. It's meant to help your soul stay calm."

"Does that really work?" Jacquelyn asked, and Emilyn shrugged.

"Most of the time," she replied. "But it has to be something strong. Positive or negative, whatever works for you. But if it doesn't force you to think about whatever it is, it won't work."

"Something strong," Jacquelyn echoed, looking into the infinity. Past her side of the bridge, her soul stirred and a memory came to the forefront, an image on full display. "Did ... I do that?" Jacquelyn asked, and Emilyn smiled.

"Yep. Don't worry. It never gets less weird. But you do get used to it." Jacquelyn didn't reply, instead trudging toward it but stopped when she let her hand fall from Emilyn's arm and noticed Emilyn wasn't moving. "What's wrong?" she asked, and Emilyn looked toward the memory.

"It's your memory," she said. "I won't go over there unless you want me to." That and she hadn't entered another soul since she'd destroyed the last one. Jacquelyn seemed to pick up on that and offered her hand.

"We have to trust each other, right?" she asked. "I already feel more myself than I ever have, even though I'm scared. And that's thanks to you. You've defended us so far. I trust you," she said, firmly. "I can feel you in here. I can't explain it. But you're a good person. I can tell. So, I trust you. And to be honest ... I've never really trusted anyone. Certainly not with something like that." She glanced back at her soul on display behind her. "But I feel safe here, with you. So, you have my permission," Jacquelyn said, smiling.

And Emilyn found herself smiling in return. She understood the feeling. She had trusted so few people, but Jacquelyn was genuine. She had been honest with her about what she was afraid of. The least Emilyn could do was take her hand. So, she slid her fingers into Jacquelyn's and together they crossed the bridge, fully into her soul.

"Whoa," Jacquelyn said, stopping, her grip on Emilyn's hand tightening. "Does it always feel like ... that?" she asked, referring to the initial warmth present when another soul fully entered one's own.

Emilyn nodded. It was a connection that words couldn't describe. "Never really goes away," she confirmed, and Jacquelyn seemed to like that answer. Approaching the memory on display, Emilyn saw a little girl she could only assume was Jacquelyn covering her eyes and rocking back and forth in place. Distant echoes seemed to be the voices of her parents, though they were muffled. Since they were from Jacquelyn's perspective. She looked so scared. She couldn't have been more than seven or eight years old.

"They were ... entertaining guests with an anti-tracer rant," she said, her eyes looking like they wanted to disappear inside her head. "This was one of their worst. Talking about a little boy in my school who had accidentally brought out the light and got sent home to learn to control his abilities," she explained, and Emilyn recalled her own similar experience. She had terrified the other students, though her teacher had been forgiving. "They wanted to hang him," Jacquelyn said, her voice breaking. "Use him to set some kind of horrible example. A little boy. That was when I decided I would pretend I wasn't one. Because I was so afraid of what they would do."

Emilyn listened to the muffles getting louder, though they were still too distorted to understand. She suspected Jacquelyn could understand the words but had chosen to forget them. Emilyn couldn't blame her. She watched little Jacquelyn stand up, tears streaming down from her eyes as they darted toward her window. With her ears freed, the muffles became screams but they were still discernable.

She shoved open the window, climbing out and standing barefoot on the roof. Climbing down in a way that signified it wasn't the first time, she landed in the grass and let her legs take her into the forest behind her home. She ran and ran and ran until her parents were too far away to be heard, though their voices still haunted her. Words seemed to hang around her, taunting her.

Blight on the world. Bringers of the apocalypse. Scourges on the natural way. Need to exterminate ...

One.

Little Jacquelyn's eyes pointed to something above her: a sparker planted high up on one of trees. Its light growing brighter as she acknowledged its presence, the little insect fluttered its wings. A light in the dark. Little Jacquelyn pointed to another.

Two.

The horrible words from her parents seemed to fade away, replaced by numbers, and Emilyn understood what she was doing. And why this memory, in particular, had come forward.

Three. Four. Five. Six. Seven. Eight.

"I would count sparkers until I forgot about them. Until I felt okay," Jacquelyn explained. "They helped me push my parents and the things they were saying out of my mind, so maybe they can help me focus now? As my grounding phrase. Counting sparkers," she suggested, and Emilyn looked at her, a new sense of respect for the younger girl filling her. How brave she had been, having to live like that. With parents that despised the very thing she was—to the point that she erased that person almost completely. Until now. Even to send Kyshel's message to her the other night ... it must've been one of the hardest things she'd ever done.

"I think that'll work well," Emilyn said, finding her own voice was still tiny and distant. Jacquelyn nodded, and Emilyn took a deep breath. "I think you're ready."

"Ready?" Jacquelyn asked.

"I think you've been ready for a long time," Emilyn added.

"Ready for what?" she asked, and Emilyn smiled.

"Everything."

They had a lot of work to do. But there was a whole world of possibilities to do it in. In the space between, anything was possible. Including forgiving herself for what she had done. If Jacquelyn could count sparkers in the face of true cruelty, Emilyn could string the stars in the face of her guilt.

Their path was filled with obstacles. It was time to start overcoming them.

The Stepping Stones

The stepping stones on your journey are rarely what you expect them to be. They may consist of overcoming obstacles you didn't even know existed or experiencing emotions you didn't even know were possible. But just as often, the stepping stones on your journey are literal stones in your path, a guide across a river that could carry you away. The point isn't what but how. A guiding light is only a light if you light it up, but there is more than one way to do so. Your path is yours. Make certain it remains as such.

Crysalyn had written the quote, claiming it was from her mentor when she was just beginning her journey into the business side of Seranno's art scene. It sounded more like something the tracers of old would say. Something that could be found in the manuscripts that once filled bunkers like these. Emilyn would have liked to have read some of those, garnering some insight into a different era. Things were never easy or simple for tracers, but they were much more so in the current world than back when tracers were hunted. When people like Jacquelyn's parents were the majority. Emilyn would almost rather fight architects.

"We're sure this is a good idea?" Jacquelyn asked, concern running parallel with her words.

"For the last time," Iridelyn said, exasperated and rolling his eyes, "it's this, or wait until they decide what to do with us." Yomalyn seemed to concur.

"I, for one, do not trust this Gavelyn to keep his word for long." He stood his ground. "Any soul that leads a group capable of holding a city hostage doesn't exactly scream trustworthy."

"I get that," Jacquelyn replied, "but what are we thinking long term?" she asked. "What happens after today?"

"Ideally," Kyshel said, "if they think we've escaped, we'll be free to look around the city and find what they've done with everyone."

"And we're still certain we don't want to actually escape?" Crysalyn asked.

"You're welcome too," Emilyn said, and she meant it. "No one would blame you."

"I would," Iridelyn said, folding his arms, daring Crysalyn to debate him.

Kyshel rolled her eyes. "No one smart enough to matter," she retorted. Emilyn spoke up before Iridelyn could debate that, no matter how futile it might be. "Seriously," she said, meeting everyone's eyes. "If we actually get that boat, anyone who wants to get out should be on it. No judgment. No shame. It might be the only chance."

The biggest issue is that they weren't 100 percent certain it was truly a chance. They theorized that if the boat could enter the barrier, it could also exit it, but for all they knew, the architects had to do something for that to happen.

"You're staying," Cidelyn said to Emilyn firmly. "I'm staying with you. No way I'm abandoning the only friend I have," he concluded, and Emilyn was grateful. Not just because he was their one and only hope for this plan or anything after it succeeded but because he was her friend too. His presence had a way of boosting her confidence. Maybe it was the fact that she knew she couldn't hide anything from him, so she didn't even try. Something about this was ... refreshing.

"Same logic," Kyshel agreed. "Though you have to admit, you'd be lost without me." She was joking, but she wasn't wrong, either.

"I'd be saner without you," Iridelyn chimed in, and Kyshel shrugged.

"Sanity's overrated," she affirmed.

"Speak for yourself," Diselyn replied. "I'd rather keep mine. Which ... is why I'm staying, too. I think I'd lose mine in guilt if I went. And I don't think ..." he paused, meeting Emilyn's eyes. "... that's what my daughter would want. These architects took her from me. You saved me from splitting. I'd like to help you get your father back. I think that's what she would want."

Emilyn put her hand on his shoulder, thanking him, and he nodded.

"They killed your daughter?" Jacquelyn asked, horrified.

"Them or someone who looked like one of them. It was a long time ago," he explained. "I can't deny that the possibility of finding out what happened to her is weighing on me."

"Understandable," Crysalyn said, and everyone's eyes settled on her. She seemed to get the implication. She was the only one whose decision was uncertain. "I still think someone should try to reach another city to ask for help. Or at least ... I don't know, let them know what's happening. The architects could do this to any city, at any time. Maybe if they prepared—"

"They could what?" Iridelyn asked, angrily. "You think there's any preparing for something like this?"

"I don't know!" Crysalyn replied, uncharacteristically upset. No, not upset. She was scared. She probably had been the entire time and, like Kyshel, hadn't said anything before but couldn't contain it any longer. "There has to be something, someone, somewhere, that can help. I have to believe that."

"There is," Yomalyn said and gestured around the room. "Right here."

Crysalyn shook her head. "Your idealism is commendable, but misplaced on a foundation of too little information," she retorted. "We have no idea what's out there—what they're capable of."

"Same could be said for what's outside the city. Who knows how far they're spread," Kyshel added, though her voice wasn't confrontational like Iridelyn's.

"I'm scared, okay?" Crysalyn finally admitted. "Is that what you want me to say? I'm terrified. And yes, I want to run away. Think whatever you want of me from that."

"I think you're a selfish—"

"Stop." Emilyn cut Iridelyn off with more authority than she knew she had, and all eyes fell on her. She sighed. "There's nothing wrong with what she's saying. She's not a coward for wanting to leave, and you're not a hero for wanting to stay. We're all just trying to do what we can. We all can make a decision here and the rest will just need to accept that. Okay?" Emilyn asked, speaking to everyone. Finally, there were nods around the group.

"Sorry," Iridelyn said, to everyone's surprise, his eyes on Crysalyn. He looked uncomfortable saying it but this was a day for stepping out of one's comfort zone. Crysalyn offered him a look of acceptance.

"We're all on edge," she said. "I understand."

Emilyn hoped that was the end of that. "So, I take it that means you two are staying?" Emilyn asked Yomalyn and Iridelyn, who exchanged glances.

"We're with you," Yomalyn said and sighed. "And not because of some idealistic crusade," he finally admitted, letting his bravado sink a little. "My family's out there somewhere. I could never live with myself if I left them behind." Diselyn gave him a sympathetic look, which Yomalyn seemed to appreciate.

"Do you have children, Yomalyn?" Jacquelyn asked, and he shook his head.

"Nieces and nephews, though. Sad that it takes a thing like this to realize how absent I've been in their lives. I would very much like the chance to remedy that."

"I don't have a family to get back or some grand reason to stay," Iridelyn confessed. "But I've done nothing my whole life except judge things other people have done ... with authority I pretend to have. I'd like to ... actually do something. Believe in something, you know?"

As good a reason as any, Emilyn supposed. It was better than him pretending he was some kind of hero. Heroes weren't the goal. She had little interest in becoming one. Her father was a good man, who did extraordinary things. But she had lived every day seeing the toll it had taken on him. If he hadn't been a hero, he might still be with her. Not just because of his condition but because of whatever he had done in the past to earn Gavelyn's ire. It wasn't the life she wanted. She just wanted to get him back and ... whatever came after that.

"And you?" Kyshel asked Jacquelyn, who seemed surprised to be addressed.

"I'm not convinced this is a good idea ..." she confessed.

"It's a terrible one," Kyshel agreed. "But it's what we've got."

"I know," Jacquelyn replied and nodded. "Color me in. I've got a family to get back, too, even if they won't want me when I do."

"They'd be fools not to," Diselyn said, with a hand on her shoulder, and he didn't ask her to elaborate, nor did she seem like she intended to. Maybe she had shared her past with him? She was about the age his daughter would have been. Maybe they had bonded a little.

"All right," Emilyn said, no profound words to say. "Ready?" she asked, though the word seemed almost too small for the occasion.

"By the art of the sky," Kyshel said, and everyone repeated the sentiment. By the art of the sky.

"Remember the plan," Emilyn said, stepping toward the main doorway. "Jacquelyn, Cidelyn, and I go out. The rest of you stay put until one of us tells you it's safe." No one replied verbally, but they all knew the plan. They'd gone through it enough times.

The others weren't to interfere unless Cidelyn instructed, as it was up to him to see through illusions and be the decision-maker. He wasn't entirely comfortable with that, but it had been his idea.

"I'm ready," he said, standing behind her, likely having heard her thoughts. "As long as you are," he added, focusing more on Jacquelyn than Emilyn. The girl had trouble even keeping eye contact with Cidelyn but had insisted it wouldn't be an issue.

"I'm ready," she confirmed, making a point to look Cidelyn in the eye. "I will not be a problem. Emilyn trusts you, so I do too."

Cidelyn nodded, grateful for her trust. It meant more to him than he would admit.

"Good," Emilyn said. "Because your life might just be in his hands."

Jacquelyn gulped and looked to Cidelyn again. "I know." she returned his nod. "Tell us when." Cidelyn closed his eyes, reaching out to the two architects outside, listening to their thoughts. They stood there in silence for a long few minutes while he listened to them. Emilyn tried to keep her own thoughts quiet so as to not distract him, but she found that a difficult prospect. Instead, she focused on trying to reassure Jacquelyn. She hadn't had much time to teach her, and she didn't see herself as much of a teacher, but she did the best she could. They had focused on getting Jacquelyn comfortable with her grounding phrase and learning one illusionary trick. The same one Emilyn had used on the other architect. Creating an illusion of herself to distract while the real her went in for the attack. It was a simple trick. All Jacquelyn had to do was perform the move she wanted her duplicate to do in reality, then call upon the memory of doing so to generate the illusion. So together they had practiced several fighting moves, but admittedly neither of them was a fighter. All they could do was their best.

"They're getting some kind of instructions from Gavelyn," Cidelyn muttered, then paused. "They're ..." He paused again, his expression sinking. "Now, go now!" he whispered fiercely. Emilyn wasted no time, her eyes briefly meeting Jacquelyn's as they both refocused on the door, purple light emerging from them both. As her feet took her up the steps, she shoved the door open and focused her energy forward, letting her illusion make the transition from her memory into reality, forming from the purple light dancing off her fingertips. The illusion of her was just as efficient, leaping from the top step, out of the door, and smashing her fist into one of the two architects. Rushing through the purple light, Emilyn clenched her real fist and felt it collide with the man's jaw. It hurt her less that time, and she considered that a small victory for herself. Jacquelyn had managed to execute the same tactic to her right, but unfortunately, neither of their opponents were knocked out as they'd hoped. But they'd prepared for that. Emilyn nodded to Jacquelyn and they both were quick to generate more illusions of themselves in various postures, making certain to move around in an effort to confuse their opponents.

When did things ever go to plan?

The architect facing Jacquelyn saw through her illusions, as they faded away fast, and he was quick to project an illusion of a snarling four-legged creature that ferociously leaped at Jacquelyn. The girl screamed, falling down and holding her arm over her face as the creature descended on her. It faded into mist as it hit her, and her own light had retreated back inside her.

Emilyn's attacker simply mirrored her technique, generating an equal number of illusions of himself that instigated a large battle of illusions. A fake architect swung at her, but this time she managed to dodge under and hurl her light-infused fist into the illusion, forcing it to fade away. An illusion of herself landed beside her, fading away, and Emilyn spotted its killer, who hadn't spotted her, given the fact that he was conjuring another illusion at one of her illusions. She took advantage of his distraction, letting more light flow into her right fist, forming a much larger illusionary fist around it. And she ran at the man from behind. He heard her footsteps and turned around just in time for her illusionary fist to slam into him alongside her real one, a much stronger hit than her previous one. The man nearly flew away from her hit, and her expression fell alongside her light.

To conjure something very nearly real ...

Gavelyn's voice, plaguing her thoughts. The wind from that night. She shook her head. No, it wasn't possible. But her punch hadn't been strong enough to throw the man that far away. To physically knock him off his feet. She stared at her fist, wide-eyed, and suddenly felt very alien in her own skin. She felt trapped inside her own body. Her heartbeat was a fast but distant thing, loud and yet so far away. Reverberating around her, almost painfully. She felt small, so small. What was she? That man ... had she killed him? Just like the other one? Was she—

String the stars. The words echoed throughout her mind, in her father's voice. String the stars. Her mind went to that first night when everything was an adventure and she couldn't wait to learn. And she felt her heart calming, her senses returning to normal. The panic fading. She was herself. And she ... needed to help Jacquelyn.

The moment she could, she swung around and found Cidelyn by Jacquelyn's side, the light back on her eyes and hands. The four-legged creature had multiplied, joined by copies of the architect. One swung at Jacquelyn.

"Illusion," Cidelyn told her, and she bravely didn't dodge, letting her instincts carry her through the false attacker, and another swung at her while the creatures swarmed Cidelyn. He paid them no mind, as if they weren't there at all, completely focused on helping Jacquelyn. "Illusion," he said again, and Jacquelyn again took the hit, letting the illusion evaporate around her. The final two manifested to either side of her, and Emilyn ran her way.

"Left!" Cidelyn declared, and Jacquelyn was quick to dodge a punch from the left attacker, copying Emilyn's move and dodging under in order to land her own attack, this time on the man's stomach. He cried out, his own light vanishing and all his illusions with it. He fell over, and while Jacquelyn was in position to knock him out, she hesitated, seeing him squirm on the ground, her own expression contorting.

"Counting sparkers," she muttered, and Emilyn shoved the heel of her boot against the man's face, watching his hands fall limp, signifying that he'd lost consciousness. Emilyn took a deep breath and then approached Jacquelyn, taking her hands. They were shaking, almost violently. "Counting sparkers ..." she said again, more frantically, closing her eyes. Her fingers connected with Emilyn's wrists, and the grip on something real and tangible seemed to help her. "Counting sparkers," she said, much calmer, her breaths slowing. Finally, she opened her eyes, meeting Emilyn's.

"Are you okay?" Emilyn asked quietly, and she nodded, letting go of Emilyn's arm.

"Are you?" Cidelyn asked, though there was no judgment in his voice. Emilyn glanced back at the architect she had defeated. He was alive. That was ... all she could ask for at this point. She would be fine. Just like Jacquelyn, she had her own journey of learning control ahead of her.

“Yeah,” Emilyn said, and Cidelyn seemed to understand. She wasn’t okay, but she was better than she might’ve been.

That was enough. He pursed his lips together to show that he understood, then turned toward the door.

“It’s safe,” he called to everyone, and slowly they emerged, looking over the two unconscious architects littering the grass. All things considered, that had gone almost shockingly well. It was a beginning, and with every beginning, there would come an end.

A Leap of Light

"Hey," came Kyshel's voice, her form manifesting in front of Emilyn. She offered a kind smile. She knew Emilyn well enough to know she wasn't fully okay with what had just happened but was well enough to recognize the achievement. "You did it," she reassured, putting her hand on her friend's arm. "That's no small thing." Emilyn did her best to return the smile, centering herself as best she could.

"Yeah," she nodded. "But it's just the start. We need to get going," she said as Yomalyn, Iridelyn, and Diselyn began to drag the two architects over to the nearby support beam for a balcony jutting out of one of the buildings. With some heavy-duty rope Jacquelyn had found in the bunker's supplies, they tied the two hooded figures to the beam, satisfied with themselves.

"Good to go," said Yomalyn, testing the ropes. Tight enough around the architect's waists that they weren't going to move. The three of them rejoined the group, and Emilyn looked to Cidelyn, who already seemed to be showing signs of his overexertion. The moon seemed to leave him in a rather constant state of low energy, and if he pushed himself a little, like he just had to, he felt drained. The two of them had agreed to not mention his exhaustion to the group when formulating the plan. There was enough to worry about, and hope they could do any of it was in short enough supply.

"Cidelyn?" Emilyn asked, trying to honor his wishes to keep it between them despite the fact that he was clearly struggling.

He shook his head. "None nearby that I can hear," he confirmed through a bated breath.

Diselyn gave him a worried glare. "Are you hurt?" he asked, and Cidelyn was quick to shake his head.

He didn't want the attention on him. "Fine," he said, very matter-of-factly.

Emilyn walked over and took his arm, helping to steady him. "One of them got a hit in," she lied, and she didn't like that. But the last thing she wanted to do was upset him. So, she would do what she had to do, like it or not.

Jacquelyn immediately looked guilty, her eyes going wide. "Was that when I got knocked down?" she asked, panicked.

Cidelyn managed a reassuring smile. "I'm fine," he assured her. "Just ... got the wind knocked out of me. That's all," he explained. That wasn't technically a lie.

"All right," said Kyshel, rallying everyone to focus on her. She had a way of doing that Emilyn never understood. "If we're good, then we head this way." She pointed to their right, more on the outskirts of the city than through it. But that was kind of the idea. Don't take the obvious route. It was one advantage they had over Gavelyn and his architects. Unity Falls was their home. They knew it better than their enemies. Now, it was time they fought for it.

Everyone fell in line behind Kyshel as she led the way, Jacquelyn right behind her, and Emilyn and Cidelyn took up the rear of the group. Once they were behind everyone, Cidelyn mouthed a silent "thank you" to her. She nodded. She didn't fully understand why he was so intent on keeping it a secret, but she would respect it as best she could. For the moment, that meant helping him walk as long as it seemed reasonable to do so. He was their guide, after all.

I'm sorry you had to step in, Emilyn said to him in her thoughts. I should have helped her. But I froze. I did it again. What Gavelyn said. An illusion that seemed more real than it should have. It scared me.

The moon seemed to move just a little closer into her vision on the other side of his head, as if peeking around to look at her. Cidelyn looked up at her, back and forth between her eyes, and he did it again. She felt reassured. Understood, not judged. She appreciated that feeling and tightened her grip on him just a little. He leaned a little closer, letting her support him. The moon retreated back behind the other side of his head where she could only see a sliver, as if it had heard all it needed to.

"Freakishly alive, isn't it?" Cidelyn asked quietly, glancing cautiously at the moon. Emilyn nodded.

"That's probably the nicest way to put it," she replied, and he chuckled a little. She was glad to see it. A little brevity was welcome.

"Anyone forget the part where we're supposed to be quiet?" Yomalyn asked the two of them. "Besides," he whispered. "You can't do jokes without me."

"Is that cause you're a joke?" Kyshel asked from the front of the group.

"Since when are you funny?" Emilyn asked Yomalyn, and he looked offended.

"Since ... yesterday," he confessed. "Look, I'm trying. We've all been so serious ..." He paused. "Understandably. I got tired of Kyshel making fun of us," he said with a shrug. "Hoped I could lighten the mood a little," he finished with a smile Emilyn found more disturbing than amusing. She pursed her lips and shook her head.

"Maybe your nieces and nephews will find you funny," Iridelyn suggested. "Little ones are easier to dupe, friend."

"You'd be surprised," Diselyn commented. "And don't you try to be funny, either," he ordered. "It's just strange."

"You all should probably get used to Kyshel making fun of you," Emilyn suggested. "I have it on years of authority, it's kind of her thing."

Kyshel shrugged.

"Quiet," Cidelyn said sharply, and everyone fell deadly silent, standing completely still. They were huddled against the edge of a building on the edge of town. The barrier's edge was only a few blocks away. Emilyn kept a close eye on their surroundings. Though she was certain Cidelyn would be able to provide adequate warning of their presence being detected, it made her feel better to be extra cautious. Yomalyn was right, regardless; they should have been quiet to begin with.

"We're safe," Cidelyn said, several of them letting out the breaths they had been holding in. Cidelyn had let go of Emilyn, his eyes settled on the barrier. The moon seemed drawn to it as well. "False alarm ... Sorry ..." he muttered but only barely, his thoughts elsewhere. Emilyn followed his gaze but found nothing.

"What is it?" she asked, concerned, and he seemed to snap out of his daze.

"Something ... else ..." he whispered as if it wasn't the most ominous thing he could have said. He shook his head, refocusing. "Later," he said, and turned to rejoin the group, but Emilyn lightly grabbed his arm. He sighed. "Later. I promise," he said, and she let go.

Does it have to do with whatever you heard from those two earlier, when you gave us the go-ahead to attack? You said they had gotten instructions from Gavelyn? She asked inside her thoughts, hoping he was still listening. There had been an alarming urgency to his tone that she hadn't been able to ask about then because of ... well, urgency. Now there was this. What are you not telling me?

He looked over to her and mouthed "I don't know yet," with an unspoken addendum of "I'll tell you when I do." Emilyn wanted to know more, but she decided it might be a good time to embrace patience. She trusted him. If it was something she needed to know, he would tell her.

The group continued, and Emilyn found herself missing the sun. It was there, past the barrier. It would be in the middle of the sky right then. But instead, they were drenched in the purple-pink hue the barrier left in its wake. Not that that wasn't a color she was accustomed to, but she missed the warmth sunlight provided.

They encountered no resistance in the city. It was the same eerie quiet it had been before, lifeless and depraved of anything at all. No wind to howl through the streets, no small waves crashing against the edges of the rivers, no carbuncles chasing critters into spaces too small for humans or them to fit through and no sparkers waiting for night to fall so they could shine. It all felt so empty.

The only upside was they were able to arrive at the river quicker than intended. And again, to their surprise, they found no architects waiting for them. She'd figured they'd be waiting to greet the automated supply boat right at the city's edge. Then again, it would sail right to its destination at the primary dock at the city's center, so maybe they didn't feel the additional effort was worth it. It didn't matter. They would get to it first.

They positioned themselves about a block away from the nearest bridge, a small arched wooden one that rose well above the river to not block access to the boats. It was one of the older bridges in the city, back before the city had expanded to cover both rivers that converged at the mountain's base. Newer bridges were flat and sturdier, and able to be drawn back to allow boats through. Emilyn liked the wooden ones better. They felt more connected to the city's past and had been rebuilt or repaired enough times that she could see the different styles of wood that made them up. As a kid, she had liked figuring out how many times a bridge had been modified by counting the different types of wood that made it up.

Across the river was the outer market district. It stretched in a crescent shape around until meeting the river again, as the water itself was a crescent in the opposite direction. The inner market district continued on their side of the river. Beyond it on the other side were abandoned houses, waiting for their families to come home. They currently stood on the edge of the old factory district, which bled into the farms outside the city. The rivers were the deciding factor in how everything ran in the city. Everything arrived via boat. Supplies of all kinds, food and water stores, tourists, and travelers from other cities. It made sense to a point that the architects had left a way for boats to enter, though gazing at the barrier's edge, Emilyn couldn't figure out what that was. It stretched down onto the water itself, which seemed unbothered by its presence. Must have been nice.

"I think I see it," Jacquelyn said as everyone except Cidelyn leaned over the river. He was behind them, keeping his thoughts open for architects. None yet. Jacquelyn pointed down the river, and

Emilyn squinted to where she had indicated. Sure enough, she could make out an approaching boat downstream headed their way.

"You're up."

Diselyn had once worked for a company that had helped design the boats and how they functioned and had pointed out that they were designed to stop if an obstruction was detected in their path. Emilyn would have assumed that tracer illusions wouldn't be able to fool them, but he had said that extensive tests had proven otherwise. Emilyn hoped he was correct. They had one shot at this. They had no way of knowing when the next boat would arrive.

Reaching out, Emilyn let the light overtake her, and she directed her fingers toward the wooden bridge. She had witnessed one of them collapse when she was a child, and she called on that memory, letting the purple light surround the bridge and simultaneously blend it in with the city background behind as well as project a collapsed bridge in the water beneath it.

While she did, the boat just passed through the barrier. As if it weren't even there. But it was, and it reacted. The edges of it that touched the boat seemed to shimmer, darken, and thicken as if pushed up and bunched together. It was real, but it had somehow allowed the boat to pass through.

"I've got someone," Cidelyn said, his voice trailing off as his eyes turned toward the source of the thoughts he was hearing. He looked to Emilyn. "On the boat."

"On the boat?" Crysalyn asked. "I thought they were automated?"

"They are," Diselyn said and shrugged. "Doesn't mean people can't be there, too. They just usually aren't."

"Well, they are now," Kyshel said. "We've got to do something. Is it an architect?"

"I can't tell," Cidelyn said, more surprised than anyone else. "I can hear the thoughts, but they're unclear. Like there's some kind of interference. But they're definitely coming from the boat."

"The boat that's speeding up," Jacquelyn pointed out. "Not slowing down."

"Whoever's on board must have seen us cast the illusion. Taken manual control," Diselyn said.

"All right, what do we do?" Crysalyn asked.

"Nothing we can do," Iridelyn chimed in. "Not if it doesn't stop!"

"Is there another way we can make it stop?" Yomalyn asked.

"No time," Kyshel said, sighing and watching the boat approach. Jacquelyn was right. It was speeding up. There was no time. And they only had one option left that Emilyn could think of.

"Don't—" Cidelyn started, but he was too late. Emilyn let the illusion fall and took off toward the real bridge. The light surged around her, and she could swear she was running faster than she knew she could. There was no time to find out and no time to think. One step after the other, as quick as she could manage. Her friends yelled after her, but she chose not to hear them. She wasn't quite certain what had come over her—what even made her think she could do this—but she was doing it. That she was certain of. Reaching the bridge quicker than she should have been able to, she felt the light surge around her again.

She wasn't certain if she jumped or if the light propelled her somehow, but her feet left the ground and her eyes watched the bridge leave her behind. And if she had timed it right ...

She collided with the boat.

The Truest Lie Ever Told

It was the cold she should have noticed. It was more of an afterthought. She had noticed it, but she hadn't registered it. Not because she was otherwise occupied but because it seemed beyond her, in a sense. The light had pushed her senses past things as little as warm and cold and toward things she couldn't understand. Things she couldn't think about in that moment—like how she had even made it into the boat. It didn't matter how. Not at the moment. She'd made it. And she wasn't alone.

Emilyn let her body slide back, swinging off the top of the boat and onto the crates of supplies. She should have felt some pain from that landing, but it was ... distant. The light seemed to mitigate it, shifting itself toward the parts of her body that would have hit directly and creating a shield between her and the crates. Still, she crashed and was fully aware of how inelegant it had been. Furthermore, the noise got the attention of the other soul on board, who came rushing out the door of the navigator's cabin.

A woman with long black hair emerged, her eyes and fists glowing purple. A stark white traveler's cloak contrasted her hair, tucked inside a waistband reaching around her midsection and expanding again in layers around her legs. A single carrying pouch adorned one of her shoulders and hung out over her opposite side. Her expression was initially fierce but fell upon seeing Emilyn. Her fists fell and the light evaporated from them and from her eyes, revealing black ones that matched her hair transitioning into an awestruck expression. Finally, standing up on her own and actually feeling the purple light around her, Emilyn was struck by just how much of it there was. Not only had it taken on the thicker guise it had before and in the space between, but it coursed around her arms in spirals, more solid than it had ever been before, linking into pools covering her fists. Her own jaw hung open as she examined herself, letting her fists fall open and watching the light drip off only to be instantly replaced by more. It was there and it was warm, but it was also as if it wasn't there at all. Like it was just ... her. She didn't know what to make of that.

And then it was gone, flickering away as a gust of wind crossed their path, washing off of her like dust. Immediately, she found herself longing for it to come back.

"Well, that was ... dramatic," the woman said, adopting a more relaxed stance. There was no hostility in her voice, so Emilyn let her own stance relax as well. Whoever this woman was, she was no architect. "Props for the glow-up, though. How'd you manage that?"

"You first," Emilyn replied, not at all because she didn't have an answer to that question. "Who are you?"

"You attacked my boat!" the woman responded. "You first."

Emilyn folded her arms. "This isn't gonna work until one of us answers, and I'm willing to bet I'm more stubborn than you," Emilyn said. "So, how about you stop the boat and we'll both be honest? It's not safe here."

"Gathering that ..." the woman said, and sighed. "That's fair, I suppose. But outnumbering me isn't. Your friends stay off until I get some answers from you," she stipulated, gesturing to the city side where the group was trying and failing to catch up. Emilyn nodded. The woman retreated into the cabin. After a moment, the boat's engine calmed down and she could feel it slowing down. "All right," the stranger said as she re-emerged. "Coming to a stop."

"That traveler's cloak," Emilyn said, looking over the woman. "It's Unity Falls design," she knew that from Kyshel once ranting about that exact design being too "bulky". Traveler's cloaks were typically meant for travel by land between cities, out in Seranno's wilderness. They were designed to be practical, not eye-catching. But this one seemed customized to a degree, removing some of the layers from the top and re-applying them to the bottom half. Like a practical dress, of sorts. It was old but not tattered. Worn but cared for. "Are you from here?" Emilyn asked.

The woman shook her head. "No, but I got it last time I was here. My turn. Your name?" she asked, and Emilyn let herself relax a little more.

"Emilyn. Yours?"

"Adalyn," she answered.

"Lyn. I thought you weren't from here?" Emilyn asked, and Adalyn narrowed her eyes.

"You clearly haven't ventured far," she replied. "Unity Falls isn't the only city with Lyns."

"Emilyn!" Cidelyn called from the riverside as the boat slowed to a complete halt. He looked like he was about to pass out, breathing heavily. "Are you okay?"

"Ems, how did you," Kyshel started but trailed off on seeing the newcomer. "Who's this?"

"Just figuring that out," Emilyn called back. "And I'm all right. Stay there for now."

"Like we have a choice," Yomalyn muttered. "You're the only one here who can make impossible jumps. Apparently."

Emilyn ignored that and held up her hands. "All right, they'll stay over there," she promised. "Are you delivering supplies to the architects?"

"Architects?" Adalyn asked and shook her head. "Are they who did ... whatever that is?" she gestured to the barrier. "I thought it was just an illusion, but I could feel it when I passed through it. Weird stuff." She shook herself a little. "And no, to answer your question. I just hitched a ride on a supply boat. Into the worst place I could be, apparently. What on Seranno is going on here?"

"That is the question," Emilyn replied, a bit defeated. She was getting tired of questions. "The Architects seized the city. The population's ... well, we have no idea. Gone. And we're trying to stand up to them. Kinda," she explained, and it sounded far more ridiculous than it was. Though it was pretty ridiculous.

"A little rebellion," Adalyn said, approving. "I can get behind that. So, what are you, what's left of the city's militia?"

Emilyn sighed. "Artists."

Adalyn laughed and then caught wind of Emilyn's unamused expression as she looked down. She forced herself to stop laughing. "Oh."

"Yeah," Emilyn replied. "That's us. More or less." Mostly less. There was a lot she wasn't just going to tell this woman. "What brings you here?" Emilyn asked. "Besides really bad luck."

"That," Adalyn replied. "And I'm looking for someone." Emilyn got the distinct sense she wasn't going to elaborate on that. "Why'd you attack my boat?" Adalyn asked, and Emilyn tugged on her jacket a little, pursing her lips.

"That whole thing about standing up to them," Emilyn said. "Really bad plans are kinda coming with the territory. Like stealing a boat."

"Those are the fun kind." Adalyn smirked and then stepped aside. "In which case, it's all yours." She gestured toward the small cabin.

Emilyn squinted her eyes. "Just like that?" she asked, and Adalyn shrugged.

"Why not? It's not mine."

"I tell you that you've just floated into a city that's literally on fire and being held hostage by terrorists, and you're going to just give up the vehicle that brought you here knowing if it passed through the barrier it could probably pass out of it?" Emilyn asked, and Adalyn tilted her head.

"You think too hard and too much. Besides ..." She paused, if only for dramatic effect, and smiled. "Who said I had any plan of leaving?"

"Me," Emilyn replied, disbelief backing her words. "I did. I am. You should leave, while you can."

"Nah," Adalyn said. "Anarchy's just a game. I'm good at games. I'll stay. Maybe I can help and find who I came here to find."

"And that is?"

"Not that it's any business of yours," Adalyn replied. "But I'm looking for my father." She looked pained at the thought. "Name's—"

"Adalyn?" Diselyn asked from the ground, reminding Emilyn everyone was there. He was on his knees, helping Yomalyn and Jacquelyn reach a ladder across the gap between the ground and the boat now that it had stopped and drifted closer to the side. His eyes were wide, and Emilyn put the pieces together. But there was no way. "You said your name was Adalyn?" he asked, almost reverently. She nodded.

"Yeah," she replied, her voice hesitant, as if recognizing something in his.

"And your father?" he asked, desperately, barely breathing. "What was his name?"

"Diselyn," she replied, and he let out whatever breath he had been holding in, gasping.

"I ..." he started, his eyes watering, emotions pleading to be released from them. "I ... thought ..." he started, but he had no words. "I ... thought I'd never see you again. I searched for so long ..."

"Dad," she said, her own eyes widening as she finally connected his voice with her memories. He nodded, tears now plummeting from his eyes. He climbed onto the ladder without care and quickly made his way across, father and daughter racing toward one another after so long apart. Emilyn was quick to step aside lest she be pummeled. There seemed to be no doubt in either of their minds as their arms wrapped around one another. "I can't believe ..."

"Neither can I," Kyshel muttered beside Emilyn as she boarded the boat, folding her arms. "I'm an optimist, but—"

"You are not," Cidelyn interjected, climbing off the ladder, and Kyshel smacked his arm, and he let out a barely audible ow.

"If I were," Kyshel continued. "This would be a bit much, even for me." Emilyn didn't say anything. She watched Diselyn and Adalyn embrace, happiness radiating from them. Coincidence or not, despite the world being a dark place at the moment, they had found one bright spot.

"You're crying," Cidelyn pointed out, and Emilyn suddenly felt the tear trying to escape her cheek. She was quick to wipe it away but found Kyshel's hand taking hers just as quickly.

"You'll see him again," she said, and Emilyn managed a weak smile. It was difficult to look at and not imagine how long she would refuse to let go of him if her father ever woke up. She was happy that at least one family got to be reunited. Even if Kyshel was right.

"She's not an illusion," Cidelyn pointed out.

"But is she who she says she is?" Kyshel asked.

"Guys," Jacquelyn stressed, appearing beside Kyshel. "Stop! Can't you see how happy they are?" Emilyn could. For her, it was like looking in the mirror through a broken window. The mirror was perfect. Her window was broken, shattered by a single-minded desire to get back what the mirror was showing. She could stomach that feeling all she wanted, but it would always come back.

"Wh ..." Diselyn's voice cut through the cracks, the sheer disbelief in it resonating with Emilyn as he cupped his daughter's face, shaking his head and smiling the most real smile she had ever seen. "Where have you been? All these years?"

"Everywhere!" Adalyn replied, her voice breaking. "It's a long story."

"C'mon," Emilyn said to Kyshel, Cidelyn, and Jacquelyn. "Let's give them some privacy, and with that, they made their way toward the cabin."

"We can't just stay here," Yomalyn said, and Crysalyn nodded.

"I agree," she said. "Father-daughter reunion or not, the architects could arrive at any moment. They could already be wondering where the boat is."

"We need to head back," Iridelyn concurred, and Emilyn glanced back at Adalyn and Diselyn—and then at Crysalyn.

"If you're still planning on leaving, you might get some company," she said, and Crysalyn nodded.

"I'd welcome it," she said, looking to Kyshel. "I agree it looks too good to be true—too coincidental—but that ... that's genuine."

"Some coincidence I can accept," Kyshel replied, "but the timing is too weird. No architects have tried to stop us. Then, the boat that's supposed to be unoccupied has Diselyn's long-lost daughter on it?"

"A daughter he last saw during an architect attack," Emilyn added, sighing. She had been young during that attack, Emilyn remembered from Diselyn's memories. One thing she had learned about the architects from her father, a reason he had cited for keeping her as far away from his war with them as possible, was that they liked to recruit young. Indoctrinate children into their beliefs. Train them while they were more susceptible to conditioning. "We need a new plan."

"Right," Yomalyn said. "We can't bring her back to the bunker."

"Why not?" Iridelyn asked. "It's a place they already know about. Bringing her there won't change anything." A fair point.

"She's a tracer," Emilyn reminded them, but Cidelyn shook his head.

"I can't tell what she's thinking."

"All architects are tracers, right?" Jacquelyn asked, and Kyshel shrugged.

"That we know of," she replied. "But we don't know much about them." Another fair point.

"So, what do we do?" Cidelyn asked, and Emilyn could feel eyes on her. She sighed, cursing her lack of leadership skills. She had always been more of a follower.

"We keep going with the plan," she said, though her voice was even less certain than her words. "If she's the lead-in to some kind of trap, it's not a great one considering they already had us trapped." They were missing something; they had to be. Well, something else. They were missing a lot.

"Let's get going, then," Kyshel said and gestured toward the chair to Crysalyn, the only one besides Diselyn who knew how to direct these kinds of boats.

"Hey," said Diselyn, speaking up himself, as if on cue, gesturing them back to where he and Adalyn stood. "I think you guys should hear this." Everyone made their way onto the back, open side of the boat again.

"So, this boat," Adalyn started, her voice going very conspiratorial. "You thought it was headed to the docks, right?" she asked, and Emilyn nodded.

"The supply docks, yeah. Where else would it be going?" she asked. It was a standard operation—supply boats arrived every few days, and the docks had been set up for ease of access to the food stores. Emilyn used to sit on the roof of their old house to watch the boats come in.

"The City Center Complex," Adalyn replied, firmly. Instinctively, Emilyn glanced down the river toward the massive building. It spiraled above the others, though not too much higher. Unity Falls was no metropolis, but it wasn't a small city either. The spire in the center reached for the stars just as tracers felt drawn to do so, standing above the rest of the city. It was built above the spot where the rivers met, allowing them to travel under it. The city's political leadership was based out of the building, and it was seen as a symbol of unity. Why would a supply boat be going there?

"Of course." Kyshel recoiled as if it were obvious. "The Center Complex is massive! Above and below ground! Where else in the city could the architects have taken everyone? Why didn't we think of that?"

" 'Cause I've never been there?" Emilyn guessed. She'd only ever seen the building from the outside.

"Same here," Cidelyn said, and Jacquelyn nodded.

"Only once," she said and shrugged.

"Too many politicians there." Iridelyn rolled his eyes, and Yomalyn concurred.

"Never had a reason."

Kyshel blinked a few times. "No one's been to our city's only cultural landmark?" she asked, unscrupulously.

"It might be a landmark, but they don't just let anyone in, you know?" Diselyn said. "You've got to be a little on the important side, socially or politically speaking."

"I've been there," Crysalyn said, sighing. Diselyn gestured to her.

"Case in point."

"Kyshel's right. It's the only place that might be able to hold the population," she explained.

"So why don't we scope it out?" Adalyn suggested. "If the people are there, maybe we can do something?"

"Doubtful," Crysalyn replied. "That building is a fortress when it wants to be. The reason it's culturally significant? Not because it represents unity. That's just a way to cover up a dark history. It was used to hold tracers."

"Hold?" Kyshel asked, narrowing her eyes at the taller woman. "How?"

Crysalyn shook her head. "Lost to history," she replied.

"Maybe for the better," said Emilyn, jumping in. "It doesn't matter right now, anyway. There's nothing we can do for anyone there. We stick to our plan for today."

"I agree," Diselyn said, with a glance at Adalyn. "Tomorrow is certainly not promised. But today, we can do what we came here to do and live to see that tomorrow." Emilyn knew what that translated to. He didn't want to take any further risks today. The sooner they returned to the bunker, the sooner he could sit down and talk with the daughter whose life he missed. Emilyn full-well understood the desire to make up for lost time. "Do you need me?" Diselyn asked Crysalyn, referring to piloting the boat, but she offered him a smile, shaking her head.

"I believe I can manage." He nodded thankfully. Crysalyn turned away, heading toward the cabin. Her smile fell in an instant. She likely thought no one was looking. She entered the cabin, shutting the door behind her. Emilyn watched her for a moment and then walked toward the cabin door.

"We're doing it," said Yomalyn from behind her. He sounded prideful—just a little happy. "We're actually doing it. Taking a stand!"

"For all the good it'll do the people in there." Iridelyn gestured toward the City Center Complex.

"It's a start," Jacquelyn said, echoing Yomalyn's enthusiasm. "Oftentimes, getting started is the hardest part."

"That," Kyshel chimed in, "is the truest lie ever told."

The Choices We Make

The sentiment of victory wasn't something Emilyn was feeling. A weighted feeling was eating away at her. It was like a whisper—only, she had no idea where it was coming from. It was more than Adalyn's convenient arrival or the ease with which their plan was going. It was something inside her.

Cidelyn was watching her walk away, and she met his eyes. She left words unspoken between them, simply nodding to let him know she didn't need him right then. Her instincts were pointing her elsewhere in that moment. He returned the nod, and, as he reluctantly joined the conversation, Adalyn's eyes went wide as she suddenly noticed the moon next to his head. Their voices became echoes to Emilyn—flickers in the wind. She opened the cabin door. Crysalyn had no reaction to her presence. She sat in the chair, focused on urging the boat forward. Emilyn wasn't quite sure what she wanted to say. So, she started with the obvious, taking the seat next to Crysalyn's.

"So," she said, tilting her head. "This is it? We drop off the supplies and then you're off?"

Crysalyn sighed but kept her eyes focused forward. "If you would like to judge me as the others have, please just be blunt about it," she said with an edge of resentment. Emilyn shook her head.

"No judgment here," she said, and she meant it. "I wish I could leave. I wish I could make my friends leave." She glanced back at Cidelyn and Kyshel fondly. "But Gavelyn has my father."

"I'm sure he'd want you to go as soon as you got the chance," Crysalyn said more sincerely.

"A better daughter might." She glanced at Adalyn and Diselyn, then back to Crysalyn. "But I've never been a good daughter. I'm selfish and stubborn and I have a bad habit of not stopping even when I know should. I guess that comes from my mother. But I didn't get to know her. I do know him. I need him, even if he can't talk to me. I'm never gonna stop until I get him back."

"And they are never going to let you do it alone," said Crysalyn, also sparing a glance back at Cidelyn and Kyshel. Regret filled the spaces between her words like a drink spilling out a glass, unwilling to be contained.

Emilyn sighed. "Who did you lose?" Crysalyn's eyes became pained. She chose to say nothing. "You know, the first time I used tracer light was creating an illusion of strings linking two stars together," Emilyn said with a smile, pulling her legs up on the chair, holding them together with her arms, resting her chin on her knees. "Everyone I've told that to likes to ask me why strings?" She shrugged. "I was a kid. To a kid, strings tie things together. To a kid, that concept can be a wild thing. But you come to realize as an adult that strings ... well, they tie things together. And when they're untied, things aren't the same. I grew up watching my father with strings untied from my mother, so I know what it looks like."

"Do you remember what you said about not being like your father?" Crysalyn asked. Emilyn nodded. "I respect that. I never put much stock in heroes. No intended offense; I believe your father is a good man. But as good as he is, he couldn't save everyone. Sure, he can help a tracer through a split or help people see what is real, but what about the people those tracers hurt before he shows up? He can't help them." She paused, sighing. "My sister was one of those people. A tracer lost control in a split. Illusions were everywhere. Kisilyn stepped onto a floor that wasn't actually a floor and it was the last step she ever took. I found her at the bottom of a staircase.

I'm not some radical like a member of the Trace Away Movement, but I'm not fond of tracers. Too much power that can't be contained at all times. You at least try. I respect that. It's partly why I became involved in traditional artwork. My own little stand against tracers, even if I know it won't accomplish much. But I have learned that this world can be a cruel place for those of us left in the wake of those like you."

Emilyn understood. It was partly why she never delved too deeply into her abilities once her father became comatose. She was afraid of being the type of tracer Crysalyn was describing. Someone like Gavelyn and his architects. "Is that why you want to leave?" Emilyn asked, her tone neutral.

Crysalyn looked down and sighed. "I never did say I was leaving." She looked away, and Emilyn frowned, letting her legs fall back down. Then, she understood what had been bothering her—why her instincts had led her to talk with Crysalyn. She thought it was because Crysalyn needed someone to talk to. No. It was because she had noticed something but hadn't actually seen it. Guilt. That fallen smile Crysalyn had worn. Then, there was the obvious clue—the one her eyes had seen the entire time but she had been so focused on getting through to the woman that she had failed to see what was right in front of her.

Crysalyn wasn't piloting the boat. And looking around, they were heading away from the bunker. Emilyn gulped.

"Where are we going?" she asked, even though she fairly certain she knew the answer. Crysalyn now held a more noticeable look of guilt but kept her tone neutral. Businesslike.

"I simply let the boat resume its course," she admitted and looked Emilyn in the eye. "I'm taking you to your father."

Emilyn didn't move. She kept her eyes locked on Crysalyn. "Why?" she asked, her voice backing away into itself as she spoke.

"We were never going to succeed," she lamented. "What did you expect we could actually do?"

"So, you turn us in instead? You could've left! Let us at least try!"

"This way, you might all get to live," Crysalyn said calmly. "I saw an opportunity for that and I took it. This crusade of yours would have ended very differently. You said it yourself. You will never stop until you get your father back. And when that gets you killed, everyone out there will die with you."

"This isn't the way," Emilyn said, panicking. What could they do? She could see it now. They were minutes away from the city center. Even if they jumped off the ship, architects were likely all around them. They'd never make it back.

"There's no way," Crysalyn said. "There are only the choices we make. Choose to live, Emilyn. Don't be like the rest of your kind and bring others down with you. Surrender gracefully and live. Please."

"Emilyn ..." The door opened to Cidelyn, whose eyes went wide as he heard her thoughts and then looked to Crysalyn.

"We need to get off this boat," Emilyn said, ushering Cidelyn out and speaking loud enough for the others to hear.

"There's no point," Crysalyn said behind her, but Emilyn ignored her.

"Crysalyn's turning us in! We need to ..." She trailed off as her eyes took in their surroundings. Architects were on the rooftops, on the ground, and they were watching them. They had entered the City Center Complex District. The boat was slowing down. Yomalyn and Iridelyn were yelling, but Emilyn didn't hear their words. Jacquelyn was panicking, but Emilyn didn't hear her words. Diselyn was speaking things that had been left unspoken for so long to Adalyn, but Emilyn didn't hear his words.

"What do we do?" Cidelyn's voice. The only one she was hearing. He was surprisingly calm, but it was a front. Terror filled his eyes, and it was spreading to her. What was going to happen to him? To all of them?

"I don't think there's anything we can do," Kyshel said as the boat passed under the spire, slowing to a stop at the long dock underneath. She glared at Crysalyn but didn't say anything. Instead, she looked to Emilyn and wrapped her arms around her. "In case I don't get to say it again," she began, her voice breaking a little. Emilyn wasn't certain she'd ever heard that kind of vulnerability from Kyshel. "Thank you for trying."

"I love you, too," Emilyn said, closing her eyes and burying her face in her friend's shoulder. "Whatever happens next, we face it together." Her words were laced with a bravery she wasn't feeling.

"Together," said Kyshel, echoing the false bravery. Emilyn offered her hand to Cidelyn, and he looked so afraid, but he took it. For once, she could tell what he was thinking. About the last time he had been captured. He had been studied, tortured, and treated as less than a human. She wasn't certain she could stop that from happening again, but if she could, she would.

"Thank you," she said, giving him the best smile she could, "for saving me."

"Thank you for being my friend," he replied, tightening his grip on her hand. She nodded and hoped her thoughts conveyed everything she needed to say.

As the boat stopped, Emilyn expected the gathering of hooded architects to board and wrestle them apart from one another—drag them away kicking and screaming and fighting for as long as they could. At this point, she wanted them to try. But she knew she wouldn't succeed. Or even if she did, she couldn't save everyone. Not her friends and not her father. Their choices were gone. But the architects merely stood there on the dock, waiting. Surrounding the boat on both sides but immobile. Statues. Predators, waiting for their prey to make the first move.

"What are they waiting for?" Yomalyn asked, breaking the silence.

"Whoever's in charge?" Adalyn guessed.

"Gavelyn," Diselyn concurred, holding Adalyn close. As if on cue, the far door to the spire's interior opened, and Gavelyn strode out. He looked the same as all the others, his hood up and eyes darkened by it. But just like before, Emilyn knew it was him. That cold nothingness wrapped around him like light wrapped around shadows, marking his presence wherever he went.

Crysalyn strode past Emilyn and confidently positioned herself in front of the group, poised to trade their freedom for her own. Emilyn wanted to hate her. And she very nearly did. But she also understood why she had made her choice. She just wished she had allowed the others to do the same.

Gavelyn stopped at the dock's edge, matching Crysalyn's poise. They were both effortless in their own ways.

"May I introduce myself as Crysalyn, Curator of the—"

"I do not care," Gavelyn intruded, and it was clear from his tone he did not. "Your friend negotiated your safety. And yet, here you all are. Though as it appears ..." his eyes settled back on Crysalyn. "Not by choice."

"Our resistance was futile," Crysalyn replied, not backing down beneath his lack of emotion. "This is our best course of action."

"Your friends do not agree," he stated firmly.

"They don't have to," she said, glancing at everyone behind her. "They will understand one day. That is the whole point."

"You deceived them," Gavelyn stated, and she faced him once again. Without a movement of his body, his eyes shifted purple beneath the hood. Crysalyn suddenly gasped for air, her fingers rushing to the side of her head. She fell to her knees and let out a horrified scream that echoed throughout the dock beneath the entire spire. "There is no place for those whose allegiances shift so ... easily."

Crysalyn's scream died, and her body collapsed onto the boat in front of everyone—her eyes and mouth wide open, silenced in her final expression. Emilyn stifled her own scream, bringing a hand to her mouth. There was a scream behind her that sounded distantly like Jacquelyn. Cidelyn's hand, still in Emilyn's, flinched, and he was silent. Completely silent. Kyshel was breathing heavily, her eyes locked on Crysalyn.

The purple light faded from Gavelyn's eyes and he looked across the boat, locking eyes with every single one of them until his gaze settled on Cidelyn. Nothing. He felt nothing for the life he had just taken. Emilyn could almost hear the tear that fell from her cheek hit the floor.

"Take them."

The order was Gavelyn's, and architects surrounded them in moments.

Emilyn wanted to fight them, but she couldn't. All she could do was look into Crysalyn's lifeless, still-open eyes.

And cry.

The Smaller Picture

Tracers were taught from the start that the eyes are the keys to everything they can do. That the light concentrates around the eyes because without them—without sight—illusions would be chaotic. Unpredictable and dangerous. And when a tracer looks into the soul of another, they do so with their eyes through the other's eyes. It was rumored that a tracer could look into the eyes of a person who had died and glimpse whatever fragments of their soul hadn't yet faded away. It was something tracers tried to avoid. It was why closing the eyes of those passed was expected as much as respectful. Invading the remains of a dying soul was said to prevent that soul from moving on to whatever came next. That felt like a violation of something sacred. And that was why Crysalyn's open, terrified but lifeless eyes would haunt Emilyn for the rest of her life. Because her soul might be trapped, unable to find whatever peace waited for them in the art of the sky.

Emilyn missed the sky. She missed the calm it carried when there were no clouds. The serenity it bathed her in when she lay on her back and gazed upward. She felt no serenity from her current surroundings.

She existed in a windowless room, with only a bed, desk, chair, and dim lamp for company. It was a comfortable prison—one she hadn't expected to wake up in it after she had lost consciousness. But it was a prison nonetheless. Worse than that, she felt a void inside her when she called on the light and it didn't answer. It was there, deep inside her, but it was afraid, hiding from something. She could feel its presence but it was distant and unwilling. That left her feeling cold—cold like she wouldn't be able to feel warmth even if the air around her began to boil. She remembered what Crysalyn had said about the spire. It had been used to hold tracers. So, theoretically, there must be something in place that stopped them from accessing the light ... that made them ... ordinary. That sat strangely with her. But it was drowned out by the only sound she could hear—that of Crysalyn's scream before she had died.

She lay back on the bed, closed her eyes, and begged that sound to vacate her soul. To hear or think about anything else. Anything at all. But all she could think about was if there was something she could have said or done. How had she failed to see what was right in front of her and gotten everyone captured. How she may never see her friends or father again.

Click.

The lock on the door was unlatched from the outside, and the door opened with a creak that was a blessing to her ears despite the face it gave way to. Gavelyn. His hood was down, yet seeing his eyes again only amplified his aura of nothingness. He said no words as he closed the door and the lock latched again, trapping him with her. Or more accurately, trapping her with him.

"Why can't I trace?" Emilyn asked, finding her voice strained, like speaking took more effort than it should. Gavelyn casually retrieved the chair from the desk and positioned it in the exact center of the room. "What did you do with my friends?" she asked as he calmly sat himself down and placed his hands, palms down, onto his legs, locking eyes on her. He was a statue, and she knew she would get no information from him. But she had to try. It was all she had left. "What did you do with my father?" she demanded, her voice the edge of a storm, calm but threatening. For all the good it would do her.

"You have left me in something of a predicament," he stated, his voice a narrow line. A string with no embellishments, perfectly formed. "I have made assurances that no harm would come to you. Yet, you continue to place yourself in situations that dictate that very response. So, tell me, what am I to do with you?"

"Seems you've already found your answer," Emilyn replied, looking around the room she was slowing growing to hate. How long had it even been? Days? A week? Food, water, and changes of clothes she had left untouched had been left for her, but those deliveries came at random times. She had no basis of what time of day it was aside from her instincts.

"This?" Gavelyn asked. "Merely temporary accommodations. Which may change depending on your cooperation."

"With what?" she snarled, though she hadn't quite intended to. Seeing his face made it easier to hate him. And she wanted to hate him.

"Your father," he said simply, and her hatred shifted to desperation. Gavelyn knew it, too. He was in complete control. "He is needed. But he is ... resisting. You would make an excellent motivator. But as stated, I assured that no harm would befall you. As such, any threats involving you would be null. My predicament, as you can see."

Emilyn narrowed her eyes. "Why bother keeping your word?" she asked. "You have everything you want. What difference does a promise to Forest make? Who is he to you?" she asked, and Gavelyn's mouth very nearly twisted into a smile. Nearly.

"I see Zarlyn's influence in you," he said, fondness reaching for his words but falling just short of grasping them. "He liked to ask questions, too. That insatiable curiosity is what left him in his current state. You best not follow in his footsteps."

"Explain to me what that means, and I'll consider it," Emilyn replied, asking a question without asking a question. Gavelyn seemed almost amused by her attempts at being clever.

"Convince your father to complete the mission he was tasked with fifteen years ago," Gavelyn said. "And I'll consider ensuring your friends live."

"What do you mean convince him?" Emilyn asked, a glint of hope shining through. Had he woken up? "He's in a coma." Gavelyn tilted his head, surprised. Or almost surprised.

"Did he teach you nothing?" Gavelyn asked. "His soul can be reached, child. I have spoken with him. But he is, understandably, somewhat hostile toward my presence."

"You've spoken with him?" Emilyn asked, desperation filling every crack in her voice. Gavelyn had spoken with him. Did that mean ... she could have been speaking to him all this time? No. She had tried reaching him. So many times. His soul had been too split—too torn. She had been denied every time. But if Gavelyn had reached him, that could only mean ... her father had locked her out. Why? Why would he do that?

"It's a simple task," Gavelyn replied. "One I will show you if you attempt to convince him of the error of his ways." Emilyn thought on it. It should have been a simple decision. The possibility to hear her father's voice after over a decade seemed too good to be true, but it was true. If Gavelyn had proven one thing, it was that he wasn't a liar. He hadn't lied yet. He was honoring a promise he'd made, even if she didn't understand why. But it was like walking a tightrope over a volcano. It was real, but it came with high risk.

"What do you need him to do?" she asked, and he was silent for a moment, deciding what to tell her.

Finally, he sighed. "Zarlyn is a natural amplifier," he explained, and he knew full well she had no idea what he was talking about. "Very rare. In fact, another hasn't been found since. Tracing is amplified around him. The power is stronger, more ethereal, closer to reality than otherwise. We need him to provide that talent in order to achieve our ends."

"Which are?"

"Beyond your limited scope of reasoning."

"You've attacked my home. Hurt and killed my friends. Whatever your ends are, I'm pretty sure my father wouldn't want me to help you achieve them."

"In that you are correct," Gavelyn agreed. "So, the question then lingers: what do you want?"

Emilyn felt a tear escape her eye. "I want him back," she said, breaking. "More than anything."

Gavelyn slowly stood, and then offered his hand to her. "Allow me to give him to you," he offered. It felt so genuine. He wanted to reunite her with her father, on some level. "A deal where we both get what we need." Her eyes settled on his hand. Gloved. Foreboding. But tempting, calling to her. If he hadn't killed Crysalyn, she might have taken it.

"I think I'll find another way," she replied calmly and watched his hand retract. He showed no sign of disappointment. That almost disappointed her. It was a difficult thing to say. She wanted so badly to speak to her father. But now that she knew she could, or at least might be able to, there had to be a better way.

"Perhaps I was wrong," he said flatly. "That response is more like your mother than father. He is a selfish creature, a slave to his emotions, and I thought much the same of you. My apologies."

"Selfish?" Emilyn asked. "Did you even know him?" Gavelyn smiled. A genuine smile. The only emotion she had seen from him. It was startling.

"Far better than you, it seems," he returned the chair to its place tucked under the desk and retreated to the door, bestowing a knock to signal its latch to be undone. He looked back at her one final time. "I suppose I will leave you here with your thoughts, where you will be safe," he said hauntingly. "Should you change your mind ... I'll be watching."

The door opened, and two hooded architects were positioned outside. What stood out wasn't their contrast with Gavelyn but the weapons held in their hands. Staffs of some kind. Since when did they use weapons? Unless ...

Whatever was blocking her tracing wasn't specific to her. It was suppressing all tracer light.

"Wait," Emilyn prompted, and Gavelyn turned back toward her. "Before, you said I didn't know what I was capable of," she said, recalling the conversation. A feather braving a hurricane. "What exactly did you mean by that?"

He looked at her with his great nothingness, giving no hint of an answer. "Ponder that while you sit with your thoughts," he suggested. "You may be surprised what you see when you find the smaller picture."

She gave him a look of confusion, and he merely closed the door, the click of the lock the last thing she heard before being consumed, yet again, by the loudest silence she'd ever known.

The smaller picture ... what had he meant by that?

Perhaps ... he had said his ends were beyond her scope. Maybe he meant that instead of trying to figure out that—that being the bigger picture—she needed to look elsewhere? It sounded like something her father would say. Something profound about seeing the steps and not just the goal. No, she had little doubt Gavelyn knew her father. It was in the way he talked, even if this wasn't the version of him her father had known. The words he chose—the way he looked at the world, his desire to keep his promises—it was very ... Zarlyn. She could see why they were friends at one point. And then there was her mother. It hadn't slipped past her that Gavelyn mentioned knowing her too. He had said ... she reacted more like her mother would have. She cursed. She didn't have enough information. Sighing, she lay back on the bed again and let her eyes close.

String the stars.

Gavelyn had been there that night when she'd performed her first illusion. Her father hadn't wanted him there. That much had been clear. Whatever he was trying to achieve, it had begun back then. That left her at a distinct disadvantage. The architects' first attack on Unity Falls had occurred not long after that night. But her father had stopped them. It was what he was best known for. Something had happened to the governor, and a massive illusion had appeared over the city. But Zarlyn had found whoever was leading the attack and stopped them, breaking the illusion. At least ... that was what everyone said. But had she ever actually heard it from him?

No, no, no. She couldn't start doubting him now. Yet, Gavelyn's words were rooting themselves in her soul, instigating that very doubt. He is a selfish creature, a slave to his emotions.

Another few tears dared to break out of her closed eyes, and she was quick to wipe them away. By the art of the sky.

"Dad," she whispered in the dim light, opening her eyes. "What did you do?" she asked no one and found more tears emerging. Tears she had been holding back for some time now. They stung. Emotions she wished she didn't have. She knew where they had come from. "Why?" she asked, demanding her father hear her. Now that she knew he could. "Why wouldn't you talk to me?"

She tried to retreat inside herself—to the space between. But like her father, it denied her. All she could do was drown.

The Man Called His Name

Jacquelyn huddled into her legs, pulled up against her chest. It was so cold. She had never done well with the cold. She had felt nothing but cold since the architects took the city. It reminded her of when she was little. Her parents had "tested" whether she was a tracer or not. It had been before her abilities had manifested, or at least before she discovered them. They had locked her in the basement, in the freezing cold, for a whole day, with only a little food and water. They had taken everything else out, leaving her in a barren room. They wanted to see what she would do. At the time, she had little concept of why, and if she had been able to discern as much, she likely would have conjured an illusion if only to keep her company. She couldn't help but think that if she had, something akin to her current accommodations would have been the result. If her parents had their way, this or worse would be the fate of all tracers.

She and several hundred other people were in a large stadium-like chamber beneath the City Center Complex, the large space Kyshel had mentioned. There was space to move around but only a little. It wasn't terribly crowded yet, but she suspected that could change at any moment. The outskirts of the chamber were lined with bars keeping them locked in. She couldn't reach the space between for solace. She found it strange to be missing something she had only just discovered, but she did. She wanted so badly to run and hide in there because she was scared. She was so scared.

This was everything she had spent her entire life fearing. The whole reason she had hid her powers from her parents, from everyone. It had found her anyway. Her nightmares seemed to have a way of doing that.

It had felt so good training with Emilyn and Kyshel—to finally be who she was. To have people accept that person. It had left her with a warmth that still lingered, the only trace of heat she had. Even Yomalyn, huddled beside her breathing warm air onto his fingers, had made her feel that. He was a bit trigger-happy, perhaps, but he hadn't judged her. None of them had. She was stuck in this place made of a somehow worse version of the worst nightmares she'd ever had, but she was thankful she was stuck in it with people she could call friends.

Yomalyn reached his arm around her and rubbed hers, trying to help her stay warm. It wasn't helping, but she appreciated his efforts. He was oddly protective when he wanted to be. She wished he would show that side of himself more often. He at least tried to be brave. She just whimpered every opportunity she seemed to get. And those had been plentiful.

It was just the two of them for the moment. Iridelyn had struggled—badly—screaming and shouting curses she had never even heard and had been separated from them before they were even tossed in the cage. Diselyn and Adalyn had vanished into the crowd. Emilyn, Cidelyn, and Kyshel all had been taken in different directions, away from the cage. Jacquelyn had no idea why. So, she was stuck with Yomalyn. But strangely enough, she was okay with that. There could be far worse company to have ... like her parents. She wondered if they were safe—or alive—and then wondered why she cared. They wouldn't. It was her curse. Doomed to care for the two people who would refuse to care for her, once they knew she was the thing they hated most. It wouldn't matter at that point that she was their daughter. She would be a heretic first and foremost, and they would treat her as such.

"Hey," Yomalyn said, and she looked at him. "I told you, no sad faces. We're gonna get out of here. You'll see." She admired his optimism and wished some of it would spread to her. But she was shielded against things like optimism. That shield was only reinforced by the image of Crysalyn's body on the boat. Jacquelyn managed a weak smile to Yomalyn, and then laid her head on his shoulder, which seemed to surprise him. Maybe her, too.

"Okay," he stuttered. "Right. Good idea. Stay close to stay warm," he said and scooted just a little closer to her.

She liked that. Not because it was him but because it was something she'd never had. Closeness. She'd never been able to get close with anyone—afraid she'd show her true self. Afraid of her parents. They had broken her, in a way. But Yomalyn and Emilyn and the others—they already knew. And what was happening wasn't their fault. She was glad they knew. "Yomalyn?" she asked.

"Hmm?" he replied, and she took a deep breath.

"What were your parents like?"

"My parents ..." He paused. "They were ... um ... not great," he said, though the words came out awkwardly.

"How so?"

"They ... wouldn't let me sleep over at my friend's house," he said, and Jacquelyn lifted her head, narrowing her eyes at him.

"That's it?" she asked, and he smirked a little. Somehow, that did spread to her. He shrugged.

"I was hoping you wouldn't ask," he confessed. "They were actually pretty great. But I didn't think that's what you'd want to hear about." She leaned back on his shoulder, the smile fading.

"Maybe I do," she said.

"Okay," he replied and shifted his gaze to the ceiling, letting his thoughts take the wheel. "When I was a kid, I had this crazy idea that I could only know so many people. Like, there wasn't enough room in my brain for more than my family and a friend or two. My grandparents were ... forgetful, and I think it made me afraid I would forget my parents or something, if I got to know too many people." He chuckled, and Jacquelyn did too. "When my mother got wind of that, she didn't tell me how ridiculous that was or try to right me.

Instead, she sat with me after class and wouldn't take us home until I could give her the name of one of the other students waiting for their parents and something significant about him or her. Not gonna lie, I kinda hated it at first. You know how it is after class; you just wanna go home. But she was helping me make friends. Prompting me to talk to people. Just one person, not even every day. A couple times a week. All I had to do was say hello. And it worked. I made a lot of friends." He smiled. "She wouldn't have really kept us there, I know that. But I'm grateful for what she did. Crazy thing is ..." He paused for emphasis. "I still remember her." Jacquelyn laughed a little, and he did too. It felt nice. "My father. He's ... Kyshel?"

"What?" Jacquelyn looked up, and followed his line of site toward the gate nearest them. Sure enough, it was being closed and locked after a girl with long blonde hair had been tossed in. She was on the cold floor, not moving. Several people had gathered around her. Jacquelyn was quick to stand up, pushing through people and rushing to Kyshel's side, Yomalyn right behind her. She reached under Kyshel, helping her up, and Yomalyn sat down, allowing her to lean against him. Her eyes were barely open. She was weak, and barely conscious. But she was alive. What had they done to her?

"Kyshel, you're ..." Jacquelyn trailed off, gulping when she saw a bruise across the side of her arm exposed arm, the sleeve torn off. "What did they do to you?" Kyshel managed to shake her head.

"Don't know," she muttered, barely audible. "Testing ... light ..." She managed a tiny bit of focus. "Saw Cidelyn ... and Forest ..." she tried to sit up more but failed, falling into Yomalyn. "... have to ... get out ..." she trailed off, her eyes closing as she slipped into the land of dreams. Jacquelyn looked at Yomalyn, who shook his head. What had she meant? More importantly, could they keep her alive in their cage? She looked around, but no one seemed to be volunteering to help. So, together she and Yomalyn lifted her up, putting either of her arms around them, and they took her over to the corner they had claimed. Gently lying her down, Jacquelyn let Kyshel's head rest on her legs, and she could feel her breathing. In and out, in and out. She was right about one thing.

They had to get out.

Gavelyn watched the man who called himself Forest, his eyes closed as he sat in a meditative stance in the exact center of the meeting hall. The rectangular room was adorned with his architects lining the walls, ready to act if need be. Gavelyn suspected they wouldn't be necessary, but he wasn't about to take chances with a man as important as this. When Gavelyn had stumbled upon him at the bunker, he hadn't realized who he was. But there had been a dissonance to him Gavelyn recognized. There was no mistaking. He was the same as her. He now wore all black, a form-fitting traveler's cloak, perfectly trimmed to lose the hood and layered bottom sections that made it a cloak. The change of clothes hadn't caught Gavelyn's eyes. His previous outfit molding into his new one had. If he hadn't been certain prior, he was after that. That left only two other problems to address.

Emilyn had rejected his proposal, but she would come around. Weeks alone in a windowless room would drive anyone to a certain type of insanity. The type filled with desperation—a longing to be anywhere else. He knew it all too well. All he had to do was wait. He was nothing if not patient. He had waited sixteen years for all this to come to pass. He could wait a few more days. Besides, he had the other problematic individual to occupy his time.

The door behind him opened to reveal the boy with a moon orbiting his head, dragged in by two architects. He wasn't struggling. He looked drained and gaunt, but that wouldn't have been from anything his people had done. He suspected the boy was trying to reach his friends. He would soon learn that such emotional entanglements would do nothing but burden him, no matter how much he longed for them. The boy's eyes came to life just a little when he saw Forest, and he tried to rush toward him, but Gavelyn merely held out an arm, and the boy stopped in his tracks. He was so young to be burdened with what he was. Gavelyn suspected he would collapse if he tried to run to Forest.

"Why is he here?" Cidelyn asked, looking around the room for the first time, his voice barely even alive. "He doesn't look like a prisoner."

"He's not," Gavelyn replied. "He could leave anytime he wishes. But he knows if he does, I will be unable to keep my promise to keep you and your friends safe."

"Okay. Why am I here?" Cidelyn amended. "You clearly won't let me talk to him."

"He can hear you," Gavelyn said, and nodded to one of the guards that had brought the boy in. He manifested a knife, grabbing Cidelyn from behind and holding it to his neck. The boy tried to struggle, but he was too weak.

Forest's eyes opened.

And they glowed gold.

A glorious glow that encapsulated the entire world around them as if they were something greater than it.

Gavelyn nodded again, and the guard released Cidelyn, who struggled to gaze at his friend in the immense light.

"You just have to get his attention," Gavelyn clarified, and Forest's gaze shifted to him. He felt a pressure bearing down on him, and he grunted. Forest's eyes returned to normal, the golden hue fading away, and Gavelyn let out a breath he hadn't realized he was holding. Cidelyn watched Gavelyn and then looked to Forest.

"How do you have power in here?" Cidelyn asked, and that informed Gavelyn that the dampeners had some kind of effect on him as well. Or at least, he noticed something was different. That was useful information.

"Surely you have a more intuitive question than that," Gavelyn suggested. He would have been disappointed if he was capable of such a thing. "Can you not sense you are in the presence of a greater power?" Cidelyn looked at him, baffled.

"Greater power?" he asked, and Gavelyn gestured toward Forest. "Forest?" he asked, and Forest's eyes settled on Cidelyn. He said nothing. Cidelyn met his gaze. "Who are you?"

"A better question may be what are you," Gavelyn suggested. "I present to you our namesake, a creature everyone on this formerly insignificant planet should refer to as nothing less than a god. Forest is not his name. He is called the Architect. And he will be our salvation."

All the architects lining the room bent to one knee on Gavelyn's command. Forest ignored this, returning to his meditative stance. Gavelyn watched Cidelyn's response carefully as the boy approached Forest. His steps were slow, and his hand was outstretched.

"I ... can," Cidelyn said, his words coming between bated breaths. "... hear ... you ..." Forest's eyes settled on Cidelyn's, and he looked sorrowful.

"Forgive me, friend," Forest said, the first words to pass into the air since he had arrived in that place. That was what Gavelyn had hoped for. "For you are now burdened with a weight you will not be able to bear. This will not be without pain. But it will pass. This I swear." Cidelyn stumbled backward, falling down, his hands clawing at his head as true agony embraced him.

He screamed.

Amplification

Fifteen Years Ago

The art of the illusion was the burden of the creative, a candle the size of a sun. Something that both grounded and allowed one to soar to heights never before known to those bound by gravity. A balancing act, walking a fine line between what one was creating and what another saw. Amplifying one threatened to obscure the other, and when it came to illusory technique, that was a dangerous game. It was also a game Zarlyn was being asked to control.

He stood at Gavelyn's side at the base of the City Central Complex, a spire of a tower that loomed over Unity Falls, daring to impose law over what it once considered the lawless. Tracers. And, as Zarlyn was learning, amplifiers. They were an incredibly rare sect of tracers who interacted differently with the light, wherever it came from, able to influence it to be more potent. More intrusive on the souls being touched, allowing for the illusions to at least feel more real and, most importantly, for larger amounts of tracers to interact with one another to generate a single, powerful illusion. A conduit of sorts. Zarlyn had never known that he was one of that group, but it made a certain sense. Accessing the light had always come naturally to him. There was an effortlessness to the way he would touch the souls around him. He supposed he never realized it required significantly more from everyone else. It explained why he had been so effective in preventing splits. It explained why he and Gavelyn had been so much more effective together than apart, in the past at least.

Five architect's flanked them on either side, faceless and soulless creatures as far as Zarlyn was concerned—every last one of them. They were on nearby rooftops and streets, spread around in a concerningly ritualistic fashion. To Zarlyn's knowledge, what they were about to do would not require any specific position, merely proximity to him, so what was the point?

"Are you prepared?" Gavelyn asked, not a single drop of care behind his words. Zarlyn was nothing more than a tool to his old friend.

"Would you be?" Zarlyn asked, taking a deep breath. He was about to become the focal point of a larger-scale illusion than he had ever seen, and he had no idea how that would feel to him. A hint of pride crept onto Gavelyn's face, and Zarlyn didn't know what to make of that.

"We have waited for this moment for some time," he stated, and then looked to Zarlyn with his soulless eyes. "We begin now." He nodded to the architects surrounding them, and Zarlyn braced himself. He had no desire to be a part of this, but he knew now Jiselyn was alive. Before, he had pondered a better way to get to free her but he had come up short on both an answer and time to come up with one. So, this was the choice had. He had suppressed his doubts, but he knew they still lingered. This was the only choice, wasn't it?

A spike of connections tore into him like a hundred knives, piercing every inch of him. It screamed like no pain he had every felt, but at the same time, it was strangely empowering. Because he could feel every single one of them, touch all of their souls at once. Things made more sense in that moment. Touching too many souls at once was another major cause of splitting, but a centralized point of interaction—an amplifier—mitigated the danger, shifting it to the individuals. Would it do the same for him?

A singular vision for an illusion coalesced through him and redistributed itself to every architect connected to him as the skies began to turn a distinct mix of purple and pink. Instead of the light reaching out from one of the tracers, it seemed powerful enough to simply manifest where the illusion was born, tearing itself into the sky. On the far edge of town, illusory clouds twisted together in the sky and shot toward the ground in the form of a howling funnel of rage that stood between the city and the sun. It wasn't real—Zarlyn knew this—but it looked real. Most illusions from any single tracer had that same purple pink hue around them, even if it wasn't obvious to everyone. Experienced tracers could hide it better, but this was different. It wasn't present at all. This was a true illusion, funneled through him and he knew at that moment it was true.

He was an amplifier.

And for a single instant, he did not care. It was glorious. So many souls unified through his own. A single consciousness spread amidst many, thinking and acting as one. It was a power unlike any other, and it satisfied a desire within him he had buried alongside every other soul he had destroyed. He basked in it, falling to his knees. Except he hadn't chosen to do that. A pressure had manifested, pushing him down. No, not him. One of the others. He pushed back against it, but the pressure became his instead, transferring from the others into him, those glorious connections now twisting and contorting his own soul. But he resisted. He could do it. He could hold it. He had to hold it at bay. For Emilyn and Jiselyn.

Emilyn. He focused, letting the clarity coast over the pain he was feeling and ease its intensity. And he breathed. Just ... breathed. As he did, he could feel distant connections forming without his consent, to people across the city. Their fear reaching out to him. What was that outside the city? The clouds have never done that before. It was screaming; why was it screaming? Are we going to die? Zarlyn tuned them out, but the anarchy and chaos settling in wasn't so easily vanquished from him.

Gavelyn's eyes weren't glowing, nor were his hands swimming in the light. He wasn't participating in the mass illusion as his minions were.

The large central doors to the spire burst open, and a squad of Unity Falls Militia soldiers ran out in a dispersal formation. These weren't the volunteer soldiers the Unity Falls Militia typically employed. No, they had an air of professionalism about them. These were the governor's guards. Exactly as Gavelyn had predicted, and why he had wanted to have the architects gather in a position where the governor could see them from his window up in the spire.

"Stop what you're doing!" one of the guards insisted, and they readied their staffs for a fight. None of the architects moved or even acknowledged the presence of the guards, but Gavelyn took a single step toward them before raising his hands in a faux surrender.

His eyes glowed, and Zarlyn felt another spike as Gavelyn used him to reach out into the souls of every single guard. All at once, Zarlyn knew who they were. He knew their names, their families, their passions, and their fears. He was helpless to watch as Gavelyn decimated their souls. All at once. Ripping out their own memories and using them to shred their souls in the space between. He did it with such horrifying efficiency that Zarlyn couldn't help but wonder if Gavelyn had always known what he was. As if a single entity, each of the guards screamed in unison and then collapsed, and Zarlyn could have sworn their collisions with the ground were synchronized.

He felt them die. All at the same time, in the worst way. For all the power he felt, he was completely powerless.

Zarlyn was no stranger to taking lives. Nor to invading and desiccating souls in such a manner. But this was something worse—something far more callous. Echoes of each of them ricocheted in the space between. Gavelyn didn't seem to care, but it nearly crippled Zarlyn.

"Stand," Gavelyn said, his back to Zarlyn. "Our job is not yet complete, and as your distance to them increases, our time decreases." As in, the farther he got, the more difficult to maintain the mass illusion it became. Once the city realized the danger wasn't real, order would return. And the architects needed to be finished by then. They wanted the governor to be dead by that point.

With difficulty, Zarlyn pushed his body upward, bearing the weight of a small army of souls. He managed to follow Gavelyn. Placing some distance between himself and the architects also made it slightly more bearable, step by step. Though passing by the corpses Gavelyn had left in their wake brought it right back.

Stepping through the entryway left open by the guards, they found the hallways barren. The only sound came from the howling of the storm outside, a haunting echo that Zarlyn could feel as if it came from the palm of his hand. For all intents and purposes, that was exactly where it was coming from.

Death.

Zarlyn felt the end of a soul distantly, followed by another and another. And from the glimpses of those souls that passed through him, he was able to piece together part of the plan that Gavelyn hadn't mentioned.

"It's not just the governor, is it?" Zarlyn forced out, his voice fighting him along the way. "It's the government. All the high-up positions in the city. The militia leaders, the dock officials, the Tracer Management Council, all of them ... you're using the chaos to take them all out." Zarlyn wasn't sure which scared him more between the implications of what he was involved in or the fact that he didn't sound terribly alarmed by it. Despite the sting of the deaths as he felt them, there was a distant part of him that was impressed. No. That was his old self. He was someone else now. He was a father.

Emilyn.

"Is that a problem?" Gavelyn asked as he strode down the corridors, Zarlyn struggling to keep up with him.

"A problem?" Zarlyn demanded. "You'll leave the city in complete anarchy!" The government would collapse in a matter of moments. Those leaders were part of a carefully constructed infrastructure, and without them, the foundations that kept the city in a state of unity would fall. But Gavelyn knew that full well.

"Your concern is wasted," he stated. "We have no intention of letting the city fall. We are simply allowing the next in line their due chance at leadership." Zarlyn stopped, and Gavelyn did as well.

"Your people," Zarlyn stated, confidently horrified. "Am I right? Those next in line are your people?" he demanded, and his thoughts ran wild. "How long have you been planning this?"

"Long enough." Gavelyn began up a stairwell. "You were the missing piece." Begrudgingly, Zarlyn followed, though each step seemed a struggle in his weakened state. Zarlyn wanted to ask more—know more—but he suspected Gavelyn was done answering questions, so he didn't bother trying.

Why was the building abandoned? Surely those guards and the governor hadn't been the only occupants. The spire housed a large majority of the city's officials, and while it was clear that many of them were spread out across the city as the architects culled them, it didn't add up. Not a single one in the spire? The only explanation was there was some indication of the assassination attempt on the governor, but why had he remained then?

Zarlyn would get his answer shortly, as the governor stood at the end of the corridor that the top of the stairs fed into, the door to his office open behind him and revealing the large window overlooking the city. Through it, Zarlyn could see the sky outside. The funnel was over the city. That meant soon enough, someone would realize it wasn't actually doing anything. With the lights dimmed, the governor stood silhouetted with that as his background. Purple light filled his eyes and covered his hands.

Gavelyn did the same, allowing the light to dance across his fingers. Both their lights seemed brighter than usual, even if the light was dim. Zarlyn suspected it was his range of connections. He was amplifying them. While he himself slumped against the wall, his strength faltering. Gavelyn didn't care.

"Gavelyn," the governor said flatly, with an air of familiarity. His voice was raspy. He wasn't surprised in the slightest. "I see you found your amplifier."

"He serves his purpose," Gavelyn replied, and Zarlyn grunted but was unable to further comment. The implications hung in the air, however. The governor was, on some level, aware of the architects' plans.

"The purpose of the sky is not the purpose of man," the governor replied. "Has Valel truly twisted you so?"

Valel? The name echoed in Zarlyn's thoughts, opening a door he hadn't realized was even a door. But where did it lead? Where had he heard that name before?

Emilyn. She said she had heard him saying that name, days ago when Gavelyn had shown him proof of Jiselyn's captivity. He hadn't known what she was talking about. She had said ... he sounded scared. He searched his mind and his soul for Valel ... it was like ... an imprint. He could see ... something out of the corner of his eye. But nothing was there when he turned to look. This was no coincidence. He had to make a choice, right then.

He chose to place his trust in his daughter.

On instinct alone, he focused all his strength on Gavelyn. In the space between, Gavelyn's back was to him. He summoned his own memories and formed them into shards, hurling them at Gavelyn's back. The force of a lifetime of memories striking him all at once, Gavelyn collapsed. Both in the space between and in reality. Zarlyn let out a breath, breathing fiercely to catch up. He wasn't quite sure how he had done it. But Gavelyn was unconscious. For how long, he did not know. Hopefully long enough to get answers. Shoving his hand against the wall and willing his knees to push, he insisted his body prop itself up. It refused, and Zarlyn collapsed alongside his friend.

That was when the fire started.

Paintings of Soul & Memory

Fifteen Years Ago

The fire rejuvenated him, burning through his weakened soul and empowering him. But only with just enough strength to sit up. It provided more clarity than it did any physical strength, but he would take it. He had fought the fire for so long. It had no reason to assist him. He found himself grateful it had.

"I will admit," the governor said, approaching, the light dissipating from his hands and eyes, leaving them only in the purple light from the window, "I am surprised."

"Valel," Zarlyn spit out. "Who is she?"

"That I cannot answer," he said, sounding remorseful. "But one meeting made it clear she is not from here ..."

"Unity ... Falls?" Zarlyn asked, and the governor shook his head as he examined Gavelyn's unconscious form.

"Seranno," he clarified. "The power she possesses is something far beyond you or I. She can access the space between as we can, but whereas we feel as if we are a part of that place she does not. She feels ... beyond it."

Zarlyn scoffed. None of that was possible. Beyond Seranno? Beyond the space between? He was saying she was some kind of god or from another world. Those may be the same thing for all he was concerned. The fact of the matter was that he wouldn't believe she was either.

Except ... that imprint he felt in his soul ... it felt unnatural. Unnerving. Beyond, like he was saying. Zarlyn shook his head.

"She's the leader of the architects, isn't she?" he asked, and the governor shrugged.

"Unclear." He glanced at Gavelyn. "But he does what she wants."

"Which is?"

"She's after someone," he explained. "Someone like her. She calls him the Architect. Like the group but singular. Maybe he's who they were named after," he stepped over Gavelyn and toward Zarlyn. "Look, as happy as I am to tell you everything I know, you are in no shape to move, and I would like very much to be anywhere other than here." He glanced back at Gavelyn and then turned toward the stairs. Zarlyn grabbed his arm and yanked him back, delving into the space between. A place where he had his strength. In fact, in there, he'd had everyone's strength.

"He's not the only one you need to be afraid of," Zarlyn replied, and the governor gulped. He could feel the power Zarlyn held in that place. "Now, tell me how in all the sky you even know any of what you're saying."

The governor sighed. "She told me," he answered, bluntly, and Zarlyn narrowed his eyes. "I was part of the plan, making sure all the other officials were out of the building. She wants the Architect, and she needs the city to ..." He paused, trailing off as confusion lined his features. "She needs ... I ... I can't remember," he said, and his expression shifted to horror as he came to a realization, pleading with Zarlyn's eyes. "We need to go. We need to run!" he cried, panicking. "We need—" he was ripped from the space between.

Zarlyn turned around to see Gavelyn, his eyes locked on where the governor had been. He then vanished, transitioning back into reality. Zarlyn quickly did the same. Back in his weakened form, he remained against the wall for support. In front of him, Gavelyn had risen, his eyes and hands glowing. The governor had done the same. Zarlyn felt them both pulling from him, amplifying their abilities. He tried to stand, but his body simply fell back down.

"What did she do to ME?" The governor demanded of Gavelyn, horrified panic dripping from his words. Gavelyn said nothing.

"TELL ME!" he screamed and launched a blast of light at Gavelyn, illuminating the corridor. He merely stepped to the side to avoid it. How had he been able to do that? "Why bring me in on the plan only to kill me?" he asked, and again Gavelyn was silent. "Why let me remember anything?"

The governor was filled with so much pain. He was terrified. Not of Gavelyn, but of Valel—of what she had done to him. Zarlyn could feel all of it.

"ANSWER ME!" The governor threw a fist at Gavelyn, who merely held up a palm and allowed their light to clash instead of their fists. The governor struggled while Gavelyn remained a statue, a barrier of light stopping the governor's fist from reaching him. With his other hand, Gavelyn wrapped his light-infused fingers around the governor's neck and shoved him against the wall. The governor grunted as he struggled to breathe, but he wasn't gone yet. "I suppose you would be the wrong person to ask? Do you even have goals of your own? Or is there nothing left but her puppet?"

Gavelyn tilted his head in indifference, and Zarlyn could see it through their connection that he was about to snap the governor's neck with his bare hand, and Zarlyn reached out to try and stop him, but it proved unnecessary. With his own free hand, the governor reached past Gavelyn and let the light race from his fingers, climbing up the opposite wall. Tearing out an illusion of that wall, he flung it toward Gavelyn, who had just enough of a reaction for the governor to shove his hand from his neck and slip away, back in the fight. Gavelyn seemed unbothered by this.

Bracing himself, the governor raised his fists, sweat dripping from his temples. Gavelyn projected an illusion of his own, a stampede of monstrous carbuncles charging down the corridor toward the governor. Despite knowing they weren't real, the governor still stepped to the side to avoid them, just in time for Gavelyn's fist to collide with his face. Stumbling backward, he quickly recovered and again threw his own fist at Gavelyn, which he dodged with elegance. The governor took a few quick steps back, and Gavelyn halted in place.

Letting his hands stretch out in either direction, Gavelyn closed his eyes and let the light flow from his palms, down his fingers, and onto the floor, either side wall, and the ceiling. An illusion of Gavelyn himself formed on all surfaces, aligned with the direction of each as if gravity were no longer a factor. At the same time, Gavelyn breached the governor's soul and attacked something. The governor's own sense of gravity. Zarlyn could see it on the governor's face. For a brief moment, the governor didn't know which of the approaching Gavelyns was the real one. It was an attack that would only be effective for a brief instance—the body would quickly recover any lost senses that way. But a brief instance was all Gavelyn needed. The real Gavelyn regained his grip on the governor's neck and wasted no time.

"Wait!" Zarlyn called out, unable to act in his current state. Infused by the power of the light, Gavelyn snapped the governor's neck in an instant. As if the act meant nothing, he released him, and the body fell limp at his feet. Zarlyn gazed at Gavelyn at that moment, observing his friend feel absolutely nothing for the life he had taken.

And he retreated into the space between.

He found Gavelyn there, his back turned to him.

"Was what he said true?" Zarlyn asked quietly. "Valel is who changed you? She made you forget? All those memories I threw at you a moment ago. You don't actually remember any of them, do you?"

Gavelyn said nothing.

"Everything we did ..." Zarlyn's voice grew, a tear rolling down his cheek as he approached his friend. "The good and the bad, you don't remember any of it? You taught me how to use the light," Zarlyn said, pulling forward an image from his memory of when he had projected his own illusion. "You gave me a home when my parents died." He showed an image of Gavelyn embracing him a long time ago. "You were my brother, Gavelyn. For all the skies, you promised to protect MY CHILD! Simply because she was mine," Zarlyn cried. "Does that mean nothing to you?"

His back still turned to him, Gavelyn sighed. A sigh that had weight to it. "Your words are as pointless as resisting Valel," he replied, his voice smaller than before. "She is as the governor said. Beyond us. Beyond this place. I surrendered to her a long, long time ago."

Zarlyn shook his head. "I don't believe you did," he said firmly. "You were the one who taught me that you don't give up. That there is no such thing as going too far. You fight. You fight and you fight and you fight, and when you can't fight anymore, you keep fighting anyway. If you can't stand the picture you've painted of yourself, you paint a new one."

They were flowery words—words Gavelyn had once himself said to Zarlyn when he had been at his lowest. But he realized as he spoke them that they were exactly what had happened. A new picture had been painted. Only Gavelyn wasn't the one holding the brush.

"That's what she did, isn't it?" Zarlyn asked. "To you and to him." Only, the governor had realized it too late. "And to me." She had done something to him. He didn't know what, but she had altered something inside him.

"It's not like what we do," Gavelyn inferred. "Invading souls. What she does is ... deeper than that. The governor remembered precisely what she wanted him to remember."

"Why?" Zarlyn asked, recalling the governor's own confusion over it. Finally, Gavelyn turned around.

"You. All of this was for you. I don't believe you understand how vital you are, old friend. She will ensure your loyalty. Crippling your city, while it has other meanings, was to show you how far she is willing to go."

Zarlyn wasn't a man who frightened easily, but that did carry a very specific implication. Valel didn't seem like the type who would just let Emilyn remember her name. It was the same tactic. Show how far she would go. He tried and failed to take a deep breath.

"It's your city, too," Zarlyn pleaded, making certain to look his friend in the eye no matter how callous they had become. "It's the home my daughter will inherit one day. We can make it better than this, you and I. Valel isn't a god. I don't care where she came from. She can be stopped. You and I ..." He placed his hands on Gavelyn's shoulders. "We can stop her."

"No," Gavelyn said firmly. "We cannot."

"You don't know that! You haven't tried!"

"I have to assume that I did," he said, bluntly. "And I have to assume that I failed. I will play the role assigned to me, and I will play it well. I suggest you do the same."

Zarlyn sighed. "And what role is that, exactly?" he asked, though it was light. Fleeting. He wasn't sure he wanted to know.

"She has a very particular mass illusion in mind," Gavelyn answered, surprising him. "It will not be possible without you."

"If I do ... what she wants me to do," Zarlyn began, again pleading with whatever remained of his friend. "Then what good am I to Emilyn? As a father? If I become the man Valel wants me to be—the man I used to be—then I wouldn't be the father she deserves."

"She may regain her mother," Gavelyn said, but again Zarlyn worried about the cost of that. "One parent is better than none," he added, stepping back, seeming to wage an internal debate. "That parent could be you. The you right now. You could take her and run."

Zarlyn narrowed his eyes at Gavelyn's. He couldn't believe he was suggesting that. But in his eyes, he saw something he hadn't a moment ago. It was there, just a little bit, on the fringes of his friend's soul. Pain.

Did that mean he was being serious? Or was this a test?

Gavelyn said nothing further, and the moment passed as quickly as it had begun. And that was it. Zarlyn had no more words to grab at his friend with—no more willpower to cling to. Gavelyn looked down, to his right, and then back at Zarlyn.

"She's arrived," he said and vanished from the space between. Zarlyn was quick to do the same. Upon returning to his body, he found that some of his strength had returned. The mass illusion had faded, the links severed. The sky outside confirmed that, returned to its usual daylight. And standing in the governor's office was a woman who seemed ... distorted to his vision. It almost hurt to look directly at her, even from behind. Valel, he guessed.

He and Gavelyn approached her, Gavelyn far more casually than Zarlyn. They both stopped several feet behind her, just after entering the office. She was overlooking a city reeling from a catastrophe he had helped cause. She had an air of satisfaction about her. It was the most he could tell, as looking at her became increasingly difficult and her form itself further distorted.

"The two of you did excellent work," she said, her voice a strange mixture of coldness and warmth. Welcoming, but dispelling. "Continue to perform, and one day, your Emilyn may be reunited with her mother."

It did not escape Zarlyn that statement very intentionally claimed Emilyn may be reunited with Jiselyn but said nothing of him. And how far down the path would that elusive "one day" be? What type of man might Zarlyn be by then?

He spared a look at Gavelyn, considering his suggestion. He could take Emilyn and run. But against a being like Valel? Could they escape her? It was clear then, standing before her, that yes, she was the one who had taken his friend from him. She had taken the woman he loved from him. She would not take his daughter.

She had taken something else from him—something he might not recover as he had no recollection of it—but he was certain of it. The imprint on his soul felt like her presence did then. So, Zarlyn did what he knew to be best in that moment.

He turned around and walked away.

A Work of Art

It began with a spark. A single ember that held within it ... a universe. It lingered inside his soul, refusing to be extinguished, and seeking ... a connection. As it found one, Cidelyn felt it expand from an ember into a flame. A flame that latched onto him as if he were all it would ever need to survive. It spread, blazing into every corner of his soul and bridging him with something far beyond him. It hurt. In a way, he couldn't describe. Like heartache given physical form, both everywhere and without a singular origin point. An agonizing and excruciating pain that tore open every wound he didn't even know he had. Then, it sewed them back together. The pain was gone. As if it had never been there. An instant of agony in exchange for ... a warmth he couldn't quite explain.

Yet, he was alone. He was no stranger to isolation, be it self-inflicted or thrust upon him. He felt as though it should bother him, being a singular entity in a space of pure emptiness and blackness. He didn't feel alone. It was unlike reading thoughts of tracers or seeing through their illusions. Those things made him different. This felt welcoming.

This was the space between. He wasn't quite sure how he knew. Or how he had been able to access it.

"Take care in this place," a voice came from behind him, and he quickly swung himself around to find Forest, eyes locked on him. "Like most things, it is far more than it appears." Cidelyn remembered then. Gavelyn had brought him to Forest. And Forest had done ... what, exactly? Forest clasped his hands behind his back and took a moment to look around the void as if seeing things Cidelyn could not. Cidelyn followed Forest's eyes, and pockets of strings became visible to him. Though it was as if he was seeing them through Forest's eyes and not his own. It was a strange sensation. He closed his eyes, a weight seeming to push at them. An impossible weight that should have crippled him. "Breathe, friend," Forest commanded. "You are safe. What you are feeling will pass."

Cidelyn did as he instructed, taking a breath. Then another. The weight did pass, or rather faded. But it seemed to linger elsewhere in the space between, waiting for a chance to return. Opening his eyes, he met Forest's, who seemed both burdened and unconcerned.

"What are you?" Cidelyn's voice asked, though Forest hesitated to provide an answer. "Gavelyn called you a god."

"I am not a god," he was quick to retort. "Merely an architect," he added, and Cidelyn got the distinct impression he associated that word with its intended meaning as opposed to what first came to Cidelyn's mind.

"Of what?" Cidelyn asked.

"Strings," Forest replied as if that should answer all his questions.

"What did you do to me?"

"I tied our strings," he replied. "I do apologize. It was the only way to speak to you without Gavelyn present." Cidelyn began to ask another question, but Forest held up a hand. "Forgive me. My power is limited at the moment—as is our time. You must find Emilyn. I can contain Gavelyn and his followers long enough for you to escape. Beyond that, you will be on your own."

"Find her and do what? We're trapped here."

Forest smiled. "Trapped is merely a matter of perception," he replied. "There is much that can be done from within a cage. This particular cage dampens what you call tracer light. It does so without prejudice." Cidelyn understood.

"Meaning the architects don't have the light either," he said, and Forest nodded.

"They ..." He paused, seeming unwilling to refer to them by name. "They are as disabled here as your friends."

"But you're not."

"I am not a tracer. I am—"

"An architect," Cidelyn interjected. "What does that mean?"

"It means you need to trust me, Cidelyn," he replied, and there was something about the way he spoke. He left a certain gravitas behind each word. "You must find Emilyn."

"Why?" Cidelyn demanded. Not that he didn't intend to do just that, but there was a lot he needed to know before he did.

"She is without strings," he said. "And you are with far too many. The two of you are enigmas."

"Let's pretend for a moment I know what that means," Cidelyn began, and Forest again held up his hand.

"Let us not. Time is limited. When you return, flee. Take Gavelyn's key, and find your friend. And I will find you." Cidelyn felt himself getting angry. He couldn't remember the last time he even felt the sensation. But it was potent in that place. Heightened.

"You've got to give me more than that!" Cidelyn demanded. "None of this makes any sense! And I have no reason to trust you. The only thing I know about you is that you lied about who or what you are, and made some kind of deal with Gavelyn. You—"

Forest held his palm face up, and the moon next to Cidelyn raced away from him, darting straight at Forest and positioning itself above his palm as if trapped. Cidelyn released a breath as if he had been holding it his entire life. He was free. The moon was gone. He felt the burden torn away from him in an instant, and for the first time in every memory he had ever formed, he felt truly alive.

"Help Emilyn; help me," Forest decreed. "And I will do what I can to help you." He lowered his palm and released the moon, and it immediately darted back toward Cidelyn. No, no, no. The burden returned, blanketing him all over again and reducing him to little more than a shadow of a person. He had felt it. That thing other people felt every moment of their lives that they took for granted. The freedom to live. He had felt it for a wonderful moment, and then it was gone, and everything was so much worse. The moon floated around his lifeless frame as he became a slave to it once again.

"Do you know who did this to me?" Cidelyn asked, his voice the weakest it had ever been. And yet, it contained a fury he didn't know he had. He looked up, meeting Forest's eyes again. His voice transitioned to a calm that frightened him. "Do you know what I am?"

Forest walked over to him, his steps somehow reverberating across the nothing they stood in as if the void were made of water. He placed his hand on Cidelyn's shoulder opposite the moon, and Cidelyn felt calmer, somehow.

"You are a work of art," he said, offering a kind smile. "I seek the artist." He looked to his side as if something were there, but Cidelyn saw nothing. Forest let his smile fade, looking back to Cidelyn. "Our time is passed. Find Emilyn, and I will do what I can for you. I give you my word as the Architect."

Cidelyn was back in reality, staring at the carpeted floor beneath him, his hands and knees holding him up. To his left was Gavelyn, grunting in pain while on his knees. All around him, the other architects were in similar positions. And in front of him, hovering above the ground and wearing golden eyes, was Forest. Cidelyn looked up, meeting his eyes. Whatever connection they had shared had been severed. He looked to be struggling—in the same kind of pain Gavelyn and his followers were in. Cidelyn rose to his feet, and Forest kept his eyes locked on him. Key. He heard the word in his mind, the last ember of whatever connection they had shared. An image of exactly what he was looking for seemed to have been left in his thoughts, and he found the key in question linked to Gavelyn's belt. The older man managed a scoff as Cidelyn retrieved it from him, and then looked back to Forest.

"Run."

Cidelyn gulped, looking down at Gavelyn as he stepped back, and then at Forest again, and then he turned to run toward the door.

"We had ... a deal ..." Gavelyn grunted through clenched teeth.

"I am not bound by such things," Forest said, and that gave Cidelyn pause. He wasn't honoring whatever deal he had made with Gavelyn. Would he honor the one he had just made with Cidelyn?

"She ... will ... find ... you," Gavelyn forced out, and Forest's eyes locked on the man, a gaze that Cidelyn couldn't blame Gavelyn for describing as godlike.

"That is an inevitability," Forest replied. "The question is whether or not she will find you." His gaze rose to Cidelyn, who took a step back. "Run."

Cidelyn stumbled back as if an invisible force had shoved him out of the door, which then sealed of its own accord as his back found the opposite wall. He closed his eyes, trying to calm his racing heart as he took in everything that just happened. He found that he couldn't. That wasn't something one just took in. So, he focused on what he could. Emilyn. He had to find Emilyn.

He could hear thoughts again. He hadn't been able to before. Whatever was dampening tracer light had prevented it. But now he could hear Gavelyn and the others in the room beyond, their thoughts a mixture of fear and anger and everything in between—a storm of words Cidelyn didn't have time to sift through. Behind him and below him and above him, he could hear more thoughts. So many. Architects. Tracers trapped below. There were so many. More than he had ever heard before. They were an oncoming wave threatening to carry him away—drown him. At the same time, they were fading fast in a way he had never experienced before. They were distant and becoming more distant. The only explanation he could come up with was that whatever Forest had done had returned his abilities, but now that the connection to him was severed, they were fading once more. If that were the case, he had precious few moments to get any kind of clue where Emilyn was.

It was that moment he found himself longing for a grounding phrase like tracers had. He simply needed to focus. Dig through all the noise of voices and thoughts and fears, and find Emilyn. He was familiar with her thoughts. Her thoughts were nice. She didn't judge him. She wasn't afraid of him. She even thought of him fondly. He liked hearing that, even though he knew he shouldn't listen to her thoughts without her permission. He tried not to. But he had found himself wanting to. Selfish or not, an invasion of privacy or not, that familiarity would help him narrow her down amidst the wave.

There was a large ensemble of voices beneath him. Architects. Surrounding some kind of cage. He suspected that was where the population of the city was being held. Focusing on that, he found only a few voices within that area. Jacquelyn. She was alive. Scared but alive. Yomalyn was with her; he could tell from her thoughts. And ... Kyshel. He could hear her thoughts. He shouldn't have been able to. Her voice was erratic—unstable. That meant she was either panicked, unconscious, sleeping, or splitting. Only one of those was a scenario he was willing to be okay with. He searched around her. No sign of Emilyn. He sighed, drawing his focus away from that place, searching closer to him. All around him, he found architects, their thoughts plain and relatively unconcerned. Guarded, to an extent. He did his best ignore to them and shifted upwards. There were quite a few on the levels above him as well. Most mundane. Some of them architects, some of them the people who had worked in this place. Dormant tracers. He shouldn't be able to hear them either. And was that ... Diselyn? No, but it felt like him. Like Kyshel, that person's thoughts were all over the place. Cidelyn looked past him, scanning as far as he could. Nothing and nothing and nothing, and then ...

That familiarity he was looking for. That warmth that tugged at him, drawing him closer. Emilyn. She was three floors above him. She was alone. Isolated. He could tell from her thoughts. Gavelyn had been her only visitor. She was thinking about what he'd said. She missed Kyshel and ... and him. She didn't want to be alone. He understood that. He latched onto it like a tether between the two of them. He could feel his abilities fading, but that tether remained strong. He could use it to reach her. Just like that, he found himself in the same moment had been in when all this had started. When he had heard her name in an architect's thoughts and knew she was in danger and where she was. That was all the information he had to go off of then, and he had made a choice to help her. To find her, warn her, and help her. He made that same choice again.

He opened his eyes, and he knew where to go. He had minutes before his abilities were gone, but while they were present, he could use them to avoid architects. Stealth was not a strong suit of his due to his constant companion, but in exchange for that, he had an advantage no one else had. Forest's words lingered in his mind.

A work of art.

He didn't know what that meant. But he intended to find out. This was the closest he'd ever been to answers, and just like the tether between himself and Emilyn, he had no intention of letting that slip away.

Thoughts. Hallway.

He slid around a corner, hiding from view while two architects that looked to be on some kind of patrol passed by. Glancing into their thoughts a little longer, he uncovered their route. Once they rounded a different corner, he carefully walked through the hallway and turned to where they had come from. A staircase presented itself, and he quickly made his way up. Up one floor, then the next, and then to where he needed to be. At its end was a corridor split three ways. Two that led to either left or right and traversed the outskirts of the building, twisting around and meeting again at the other end of the singular corridor directly in front of him. Two groups of architects were on either side but none down the middle. He could hear from their thoughts that they would periodically check the middle but mostly stuck to the edges where they had windows that looked upon the city. Confident that both groups would remain stationary for at least a few moments, Cidelyn followed his tether toward a door about halfway down the center corridor. A lock clung to it, and Cidelyn retrieved the key he had taken from Gavelyn. Twisting the lock, it unlatched, and he cursed the sound it made. But he got no indication the architects had heard. Quietly, he removed the locked and placed it gently on the floor. Slowly to hopefully avoid any sound, he opened the door. And there she was.

Lying on the bed in a dimly lit and nearly empty room, her head turned toward him. Her eyes lit up alongside his. He crossed into the room, and she ran toward him, wrapping her arms around him in the most wonderful embrace he'd ever had. He didn't need to hear her thoughts in that moment. Her pure joy at seeing him was plenty for him.

In that moment, the burden of the moon he had recently felt all over again seemed negligible. Irrelevant, even. He let that feeling consume him, and he didn't want to let go of her. But he knew he had to. They had a chance—and a slim window to take advantage of it. Because he found he could barely hear her thoughts.

Lifelines

Emilyn had never been happier to see anyone in her entire life. She clung to Cidelyn like a lifeline. She had no idea how long she'd been trapped in that room with nothing but her thoughts and Gavelyn's words. She wasn't one to ever long for company, but the loneliness had begun to eat away at her. The feeling she would never see anyone again. She had tried so hard to be brave—to declare she would find another way out. But her bravery had been little more than bravado. Eventually, she would have taken Gavelyn's deal. That thought frightened her. But there was Cidelyn. He had saved her again. She felt she didn't deserve that, but she selfishly chose to accept it anyway. Accept him.

"How did you—" she started, finally letting go of him, but he held a finger to his lips, and she let the words go. Quietly, he turned around and gently closed the door. Then, he hugged her again. And it felt so nice, so she smiled and returned it. He had come back for her. Only two people had ever done that.

"Forest set me free," he whispered, though she got the feeling there was a lot more to that story than he was saying. "Explain later." Fair enough, she lamented, assuming he'd read her thoughts. So, he still had his abilities. That was something. "Everyone's being held on the bottom floor."

"Do you know what's stopping us from using the light?" she asked, and he shook his head.

"All I know is mine will be gone in seconds," he explained. "We need to go now," he said and took her hand with a confidence she hadn't seen from him prior to that moment, turning back toward the door and quietly opening it. "Should be safe." Emilyn stole a glance at the lock on the floor, a key inserted into it. How had he gotten that? She followed behind as he led them down the corridor, stopped at the intersection between two side corridors, and then led them into the staircase and down.

"We'll only have a few minutes before they notice you're gone," he said, and Emilyn couldn't quite figure out what was different about his voice, but something was. "And my powers are gone. We'll have to sneak around the old-fashioned way."

"Best let me take the lead, then," she said and smiled. "Been sneaking around my whole life. Mostly into art galleries. Sometimes out of class," she added. It had been an occupational hazard of being her father's daughter. He nodded, and let go of her hand so she could move in front of him as they neared the bottom of the staircase. But before they reached it, she turned back around to face him, cutting him off. "But before that, tell me whatever it is you're not telling me."

"There's a lot I'm not telling you," he replied honestly, and she narrowed her eyes at him. "All of which I have every intention to. But not here."

She sighed. "Fine. But tell me something," she stressed. "Kinda freaking out a little."

"Forest called himself the Architect," he said, and she looked taken aback. "Not an Architect. The Architect. Whatever that means. But he's definitely not on their side."

"Is he on ours?" Emilyn asked, and he shrugged.

"He's on his own side, but ..." He paused and shook his head, letting the thought trail off.

"What?" she insisted, and he sighed.

"He took it away," he said, gesturing to the moon beside him. "And then gave it back. I was free. For a moment. I think he can help me." Emilyn looked back and forth between his eyes, her own widened. And she let out a huff, alongside a slight smile.

"You could have led with that," she said, and he shrugged, returning the smile.

"Still working on believing it," he confessed. "He showed me the space between."

Emilyn let her smile fade. Okay, so he did have a lot to say. And he was right. Not the time. "Where is he?" she asked, and he shook his head.

"He said he'd find us," he explained. "Last I saw, he was with Gavelyn. But he ... um ... he can hold his own." Add that to the list of mysteries. Emilyn had trouble imagining Forest staying focused long enough to do much of anything.

"Okay," she said. "Well, then, we'll see what we can do about the others until he does. You said they're on the bottom floor?" He nodded.

"It's a big, open space—like an arena. They have everyone fenced in," he explained. Nothing ominous or horrifying about that whatsoever. Emilyn missed the days when her problems consisted of which shade of red to use for painting a picture of Jade. Actually, she just missed Jade. The little carbuncle had a way of calming her nerves.

"All right, we'll start there," Emilyn said and started to head forward, then stopped and turned back to Cidelyn, who looked confused. She pursed her lips. "I don't suppose you know how to get there?" she asked, and he was silent for a moment, searching his thoughts.

"I think ... there was another staircase ... opposite side?" He sounded very uncertain, but they really didn't have another choice. The opposite side would mean traversing a few corridors, likely crawling with cloaked menaces.

"Do they have the light?" Emilyn asked, though she was relatively certain she knew the answer since she had seen those two architects armed with pikes outside her cell.

"No!" he exclaimed, in a whisper. "Sorry. Forgot to mention that. Whatever is dampening tracers is universal." That was both good and bad. Good in the sense that it was an even playing field as far as the light was concerned. Bad that light was the only way she really had to fight them. If they got caught again there would be very little they could do. That just meant they had to be careful. Because choice was not a factor. Kyshel and Jacquelyn and all the others were trapped. And as Emilyn had reminded people time and time again, she was stubborn. She wasn't going to stop. And she certainly wasn't going back to that cell.

Peering around both corners at the edge of the staircase, she found the corridor ahead free of architects. So, they proceeded forward, Cidelyn keeping an eye out behind them while she scouted out their options. Approaching another intersection of corridors, she quickly pulled back when she found several architects around the corner. Opposite the way she guessed they needed to go but they would see her. Their footsteps indicated they were heading in their direction, and she raised her hand to cast an illusion to conceal them, cursing when she remembered she couldn't. So, they huddled against the wall as tightly as they could and held their breaths.

The nice thing about them wearing hoods, Emilyn realized as they passed by, was that their vision to either side was limited. And she and Cidelyn managed to stay just out of their vision as they strode by. Waiting until they were out of earshot, Emilyn let out her breath and then nodded to Cidelyn. And surprisingly, she smiled, just a little. Even with their lives on the line, she found that exhilarating. Given the look on his face, she was glad that he couldn't read her thoughts in that moment. Instead, she took his hand and took them down the same path those architects were on. Careful to stay a good distance behind their enemies and careful to keep an eye out behind them, the pair followed in their footsteps, Emilyn figuring that meant they were less likely to encounter other architects. That, and they seemed headed in the right direction. Her instincts were good. They followed the group to a staircase that headed toward the lower floors. They waited for a few moments before trudging, quietly as they could, down the stairs, though Emilyn's boots weren't exactly the quietest when stepping off the carpeted floors and onto hard-floor stairs. Fortunately, the architects seemed to be out of both sight and earshot.

The stairs twisted and reversed several times, and they proceeded down several floors as quickly as they could once they were certain it was safe. Finally reaching the end, the stairs trailed off into the arena like space Cidelyn had described. A massive underground chamber that had audience sections and what Emilyn could only describe as a massive combat ring, though it was currently filled with several hundred people that made up the population of her home. She knew there were places where tracers were made to fight for entertainment, centuries ago. Given this place also had some kind of dampeners available, she assumed this was one of those places. Underground as if to hide the unethical nature of forcing innocents to fight one another.

She and Cidelyn emerged on an upper level that connected to the audience seating, the staircase giving way to a path in either direction that lined the course of the arena, overlooking the caged residents of Unity Falls. She led them down the right path that the staircase faced away from, in case anyone else appeared through it. That way the chances of them being spotted were mitigated.

"What do you think they're doing?" Cidelyn asked as they knelt down behind the rail and carefully looked over the massive cage.

Emilyn shook her head. "No idea. And that's certainly not the whole city. Unity Falls has thousands of people." She paused, sighing. "Where are the rest?"

"Question number three," Cidelyn commented. "How in all the skies of Seranno are we supposed to free them?"

Examining the area, Emilyn found that there were three gates leading into the fenced area. One large gate was close to where she and Cidelyn were, and two smaller gates formed a triangle coordination across the arena. And there were too many architects to count standing watch around the fences. Some giving food and water to the residents within through little shelves in the fence that only extended out one side at a time. And she had no idea what to do.

“I don’t know,” she confessed, frustrated, leaning back against the rail and sinking to the floor. She looked over at him as he did the same. “But we have to try something.” He chuckled. “What?”

“Yomalyn was right,” he said, and that sentence alone was more than enough to instigate confusion. “We are terrible revolutionaries.” She chucked as well, and was more surprised that he had begun to develop a sense of humor than what he said. She liked it, though. Whatever Forest had shown him, however, he had proven he could help, it had given him a little hope, and a little hope had boosted his spirits. If she could, she would take some of that right then.

“First of all,” she replied. “Yomalyn is never right. About anything,” she said flatly, only partially in jest. “Second, no one said we’re revolutionaries. Just trying to survive.” By revolting. She cursed to herself. “Third ...” she trailed off as she followed Cidelyn’s eyes to a faint purple glow coming from her jacket pocket. That should not have been possible.

Quickly reaching inside she retrieved a small piece of paper with words glowing purple on it. A tracer note, just like Kyshel and Jacquelyn had done before. But neither of them should have tracer light. With a quick glance to ensure they hadn’t been spotted, she and Cidelyn eagerly read the note.

We’re below you. Have plan. Head to main gate. Trust me. –K

Emilyn looked at Cidelyn, but they didn’t dare peer over the rail to try and find Kyshel, though she had clearly spotted them. Heading to the main gate was dangerous. Whatever Kyshel was planning would have to be timed with their arrival, meaning they needed to head there right away. Luckily it would only take them a few moments to get there. She looked at Cidelyn and took a deep breath.

“I trust her,” Emilyn said, confidently.

“I trust you,” he said with the same confidence. She offered her hand and he took it. “Let’s go.”

She nodded, and they stood. She meant it. She trusted Kyshel with her life. Though how she’d managed to send the note was a mystery, neither she nor Cidelyn seemed to doubt its authenticity. So, they latched onto some of that hope and headed toward the main gate.

A Tapestry Unclaimed

The scale of time was not something one was meant to understand. A drop of water or a hurricane—to time, it was all the same. To a person, they were radically different. One was something barely noticed, the other threatening to bring life to a sudden and violent end. But on the scale of time, they balanced the same. Like people, they were irrelevant, meaningless things. Because of that, it felt odd to understand that she had missed time. Not because there were empty pieces of her memory but because she understood that something should be there.

Kyshel was no stranger to missing time. When she experienced a split, she often only remembered fragments of time. Faces. Or feelings. Either of which may or may not have been real. But because there was something, she could piece the puzzle together, or someone like Emilyn could fill in the blanks. And all was right. Things were balanced. This time, things were different. She hadn't split—at least not that she could recall. But there had been time between the boat and the cage that occupied a void within her mind. She remembered Crysalyn and what Gavelyn had done to her. She remembered being taken away. Then the cold floor. Jacquelyn and Yomalyn helping her. Her eyes flittering open and closed as she tried to remain conscious. Jacquelyn had said she had claimed she had seen Cidelyn and Forest, but she had no recollection of that. All she knew was that something was different.

She could feel the light inside her again. It had vanished years ago with her first split, and it had left a void inside her. An emptiness she had tried to fill with physical artwork, and while that helped to some extent, it wasn't the same. Nothing would be the same. A connection to the light—to the space between—was something irreplaceable in every conceivable way. It was like being linked to something bigger than you, something that bound every soul together. Being severed from that was traumatic. She had never quite recovered. Yet, there it was. Something had changed. Jacquelyn had said that her light was gone, yet Kyshel's were returning. She wished Diselyn were with them. He was a former tracer like her. Was he experiencing this as well?

"You're sure?" Yomalyn asked, and Kyshel glared at him.

"No, I'm making it up," she said, rolling her eyes. "Of course I'm sure!" She looked to Jacquelyn. "It's not a feeling you forget."

"And you don't remember what they did to you?" Jacquelyn asked, even though Kyshel had already answered that. "Anything at all?" She shook her head.

"Nothing." She looked to her hands, wishing she was somewhere she could call on the light. "But it's back. I don't know how, but it is."

"So, you might be able to get us out of here?" Yomalyn asked, and Kyshel punched his arm.

"Illusions," Kyshel stressed. "Nothing real. I can create whatever you want, but I can't make them unlock the gate."

"I know that!" Yomalyn angrily whispered. "I'm just saying there might be something you could do." Kyshel shrugged.

"Maybe? But there'd have to be someone on the outside to actually open the gate. And we'd only have one shot to give said person a chance. There are a lot of architects around."

"And said person isn't exactly ... said person," Jacquelyn lamented, and Kyshel conceded that to her with a gesture.

"Can you see into my memories?" Yomalyn asked, and Kyshel shrugged.

"Probably." She gave a disgusted look. "But I don't particularly want to."

Jacquelyn chuckled, and Yomalyn mocked her laugh. "Hilarious," he retorted. "I was just thinking—"

"Stop that," Kyshel chimed in, and he sighed.

"I was just thinking," he stressed, ignoring her. "I have a pretty vivid memory of a rockslide. What if you could use that to make it look like the ceiling was collapsing? They'd probably run, and if we could get someone on the outside they'd have their chance to open the gate?"

Kyshel gazed at him for a long moment, her head tilted.

"What?" he asked, and she shook her head.

"That's actually not a terrible plan," she confessed, and Yomalyn beamed a little. "But don't let it go to your head. We still need someone outside for it to work." It was something. Kyshel wished she knew where Emilyn was. They had all been separated when Gavelyn took the boat. Whatever his interest in Emilyn was, she was probably far away. Same for Cidelyn. She wondered if the architects had done something to restore her abilities. This place was, at one point, a sort of testing ground for tracers. There were likely things present—like whatever was dampening tracer light—that had been outlawed. But why make her a tracer again just to throw her in with the other prisoners where she could help them? Unless they hadn't realized? She cursed that hole in her memories and let it eat away at her. Worse than that ... was she even upset about it? She felt whole for the first time in years. She didn't want that to disappear. "All we can do for now is wait," she said, begrudgingly. She was not a patient person. She was used to getting what she wanted. But even she had to admit their situation was precarious, and waiting was the only thing they could do. She tugged at her hair. It was a habit of hers when she was nervous, and she hadn't even realized she was doing it. Nervousness. That wasn't something she hadn't felt in a while either. Having her power back was wonderful, but it was scary. She hadn't been that person in a long time, and she didn't know how she would handle it. She closed her eyes, and for the first time in a long time, she delved into the space between.

It felt like going home, and it calmed her. She just sat there and took it all in, feeling strong, protected, unbreakable, and ... vulnerable. The makings of a portrait finally coming together. And she felt happy. Happier than she had in a long time.

She wasn't certain how much time had passed while she was in there. Hours. Days. It didn't matter. She would stay there as long as she could, as long as the light continued to welcome her instead of turning her away.

Eventually, she heard Jacquelyn's voice calling to her. Distant, far away, and she contemplated letting it stay that way. Reality was so dull by comparison. Colorless. A tapestry unclaimed. Ironic that in the void between souls things were so much more vibrant. She would have just continued to ignore Jacquelyn had it not been for a single name.

Emilyn.

***

Gazing at the piece of paper in her hand, Emilyn felt an overwhelming trust in her best friend. She didn't know how it was possible. She didn't need to. Kyshel was relying on them.

"I trust her," Emilyn said, meeting Cidelyn's eyes, and he nodded.

"I trust you," he replied, and their fingers slid together. "Let's go."

The main gate was to their right, down one level, so they searched for another staircase down. They found one down the upper-level pathway. Careful to avoid any architects above, they noted that they would have trouble doing so below. Emilyn was actually rather certain it was unavoidable they'd be noticed right away, as they'd be right in front of the gate. Whatever Kyshel was planning, she had to make it happen pretty quick.

As they neared the bottom of the stairs, she gathered from the look on Cidelyn's face that he had figured much the same. But also like her, he understood that it was this or it was nothing. With their friends in danger, so many unanswered questions, and their own inability to stay hidden forever, the choice was simple. Emilyn was never one to be religious, but in that moment, she offered a silent prayer to whatever deity might have been so kind as to care.

Together, she and Cidelyn exited the staircase, and the sound of Emilyn's steps immediately caught the attention of several architects, who turned around and rose the pikes they carried, hurrying into the small corridor between the stairs and the gate. They may not have their light, but those would hurt a lot.

"How did you escape?" one of them asked. Emilyn shrugged.

"Your boss is a little distracted," she said, remembering what Cidelyn said. "Just kinda walked away. You might wanna go give him a hand?" There were at least seven of them at a quick count—more of them likely close by on the path around the cage. They had surrounded her and Cidelyn. She gulped, ready for a fight. As short-lived as that fight may be. "Yeah," she confessed. "Didn't think that would work."

"What now?" Cidelyn asked as they stood back-to-back, surrounded by cloaks and pikes.

"I was about to ask you that," Emilyn replied. "Guess you can still hear my thoughts."

"Not funny," Cidelyn replied, and Emilyn shrugged. It was a little funny.

"Take them," one of the architects ordered, and then a cracking sound filled the air above their heads. Emilyn looked up to see the ceiling tearing itself open—and quickly at that. The tear expanded in seconds, racing from one corner of the ceiling to the other, little bits of rock and dust crying out of it.

Then, it collapsed.

The architects ran one direction or another, but she and Cidelyn were right in the epicenter of the collapse, pieces of the ceiling plummeting onto them. Instinctively, Emilyn covered her head as best she could while she fell to the ground and braced for impact. Noise became voided, though Emilyn was fairly certain she had screamed as she hit the floor and the dust of shattered rock filled her lungs and eyes.

It took her longer than it should have for her to realize she was reacting but not feeling any of it. Nothing hit her. The air she was breathing in was normal. And upon her senses understanding this, she found she was inside a piece of the fallen rubble and debris. It was an illusion.

Cidelyn stood above her, slightly silhouetted by the dust cloud but appearing unscathed and unphased, his hand outstretched toward her. As her senses recovered, she managed to reach for him, though her arm seemed to struggle with cooperating with her eyes as to where his hand was. He understood, though, and gently took her hand, helping her stand. She embraced him to regain her balance and footing and nodded to affirm she was okay. He returned the nod and slowly let go of her to let her senses fully recover before rushing toward the gate.

Right. Plan. She understood then. An illusion of the ceiling collapsing was meant to cause chaos and give time for them to unlock the gate. Cidelyn proceeded to do exactly that. Removing the keyless latch, he dropped it to the floor and grabbed the edge of the gate, sliding it to his left and all the way open. Just as surrounding architects reached them.

But it was too late. There were hundreds of people inside the cage, and they became a storm as they rushed out, charging right past Cidelyn and into their would-be captors. The entire group of architects, both the initial ones guarding the gate and their reinforcements, were slammed into by the residents of Unity Falls before they could even think to swing their pikes into position. Their cloaks were lost in the crowd. As was Emilyn. In seconds, she couldn't even see the gate and lost what direction it was from where she stood. Fighting against the tide, she managed to find the wall of the corridor now that the illusion had faded, and she clung to it, letting people rush past her and into the stairwell. Distantly, she heard yelling from other architects, but the roar of the crowd overtook them. Despite her momentary disorientation, she couldn't help but smile.

It was time for Unity Falls to fight back and show Gavelyn and his architects that they chose the wrong city to subdue.

As the crowd passed by, Emilyn found herself able to move again—and found Cidelyn clinging to the cage wall behind the gate, perhaps not having expected the stampede. He looked relieved as well. He had done that. She wouldn't have made it to the gate in time, but he had. He had freed them, and she felt bad that he probably wouldn't get an ounce of gratitude for that. Still, the air of freedom blanketing the chamber swept them up. It felt good.

"Emilyn!" It was Kyshel's voice, followed by arms wrapping around her face getting enveloped in golden hair. But she didn't care, it was wonderful. She wrapped her arms around her best friend and smiled. After getting separated and being trapped in that room and losing her light ... seeing Kyshel was about the best thing that could've happened. "I can't believe that worked!" she exclaimed as she pulled back.

"So, that was you?" Emilyn asked, surprised. "And the note, that was you too?" she asked, and Kyshel smiled, nodding quickly. Emilyn had never seen her so ... excited. "How do you-oh," Emilyn was interrupted by another embrace, this one from Jacquelyn. That surprised Emilyn, but she welcomed it and returned the hug.

"I'm so glad you're okay!" Jacquelyn exclaimed, pulling back. "When Gavelyn took you, I …" she paused, composing herself. "Thank you," she managed, calmly, and looked at Cidelyn, who remained a few feet away. "Thank you," she repeated, and he looked surprised. His face turned red a little, but he managed a nod. Emilyn smiled and pulled Jacquelyn and Kyshel into another hug. She didn't want to ever let go of them.

An architect rounded the corner, pike in hand, looking like he had been run over. He likely had. He looked panicked and prepared to strike at them, but another pike smacked into the back of his head. As he collapsed, Yomalyn stepped out of the cage, looking satisfied with himself. His clothes were worn and his hair a distinct mess, yet he somehow looked more alive than the last time Emilyn had seen him.

"That felt good," he sighed, a smile on his face, and then looked at everyone. "And skies, it's good to see you guys." He retrieved the pike from the fallen architect and passed it to Emilyn. "Call that a thank-you?"

Emilyn took the pike from him, and with her free hand gave him a hug as well, which seemed to surprise him. But she couldn't help herself. Because it was good to see even him.

"Right," he said, flustered after she released him, and straightened his shirt a little, standing a little taller. "Yeah, good to see you guys." He nodded to Cidelyn.

Kyshel shook her head, and punched his arm. "Screw your head back on, hero boy," she said after Yomalyn flinched away from her and she stole the pike from him. "We're not done yet."

Cidelyn was kind enough to retrieve another pike from the ground and toss it to Yomalyn. "Understood," he replied. "So, what's the plan now?"

That was a good question. It was likely a riot upstairs, and a horrifying thought crossed Emilyn's mind. The residents of Unity Falls had no idea tracer light was dampened, or rather had no idea that might not be the case as soon as they reached the outside. Out there, the architects would have the advantage again. At this point, it would be a slaughter. They had to do something.

"We need to keep everyone from going outside," Emilyn stated, and Yomalyn donned a look of confusion.

"Wasn't the whole point so everyone could go outside?" he asked, but Kyshel followed Emilyn's line of thought.

"The light might not be dampened outside. We don't know. Once the architects realize what's going on, that's where they'll go to get the edge again."

"Exactly. We need to keep everyone inside."

"Won't we just be trapped again?" Jacquelyn asked, and Cidelyn chimed in.

"It'll be a stalemate," he said. "They won't be able to come in; we won't be able to go out. We would be trapped, but ... less so."

"Better than being in a cage," Yomalyn agreed, and Emilyn nodded, recalling her windowless room. Better than that.

"All right," Jacquelyn reluctantly agreed. "So, how do we do it?"

"I think you're forgetting something important," Kyshel replied, and Emilyn gave her a confused look. "Your father is probably here." Emilyn's eyes went wide, cursing herself for that not even occurring to her. If the architects were retreating, Gavelyn would probably try to take Zarlyn with him. She cursed again. “You should go. We’ll figure out something here,” Kyshel promised, and put her hand on her friend’s arm. “Go find him.”

“Don’t worry,” Yomalyn said, confidently. “I’ve got a plan.” Kyshel sighed.

“You really wanna stick around to see whatever trainwreck that is?” she asked, and Emilyn didn’t respond. “Go!”

Emilyn looked to Cidelyn. “Come with me?” she asked, and he seemed surprised. “None of us should be alone, and we make a good team. Besides,” she looked to Kyshel. “You’ve gotta stay to keep him in check.” She gestured to Yomalyn, who sighed.

“I do enjoy putting him in his place,” she replied. “Now, seriously, go!” Emilyn glanced to Cidelyn, who nodded and joined her, and the five of them headed up the stairs, ready to split off at the top. Once there, they found that chaos ruled supreme. It was less of a brawl and more of a race to reach the outside first that became a brawl. There were few architects amidst the crowd, however. At least, few conscious ones. Souls were everywhere, fighting any way they could.

“There you are!” Iridelyn’s voice came from their left, and he was quick to embrace Yomalyn. He had a bloodied lip and a broken pike in one hand. No trace of Diselyn or Adalyn with him. “Whatever you guys did, a bunch of people showed up and let us go. Guess you were being kept in a separate cage?” he asked, and that was a daunting thought. More than one cage ... how many people had they just unleashed?

“Must’ve been,” Yomalyn confirmed, clasping his friend’s shoulder. “We’ve got a plan.”

“You still haven’t said what that plan this,” Kyshel chimed in, and Cidelyn got Emilyn’s attention, gesturing down a corridor to a staircase they hadn’t ventured up yet. He was thinking her father may be kept in a similar situation to where she was kept. Higher up and isolated. He was probably correct. She nodded, and they headed off in that direction.

As they approached the staircase, she dared a look back at the group they had left behind. Yomalyn said something, and Kyshel's eyes lit up purple, the light entrancing her hands. Emilyn smiled. She really did seem more alive.

She had found her friends. Now, it was time to find her father.

The Makings of a Portrait

Yomalyn got a grip on the pike, tightening as he, Jacquelyn, Kyshel, and Iridelyn worked their way through the complex. Kyshel's tracer light seemed to dissuade any ideas of attacking them, and it allowed them a relatively quick journey to the main entrance. The large double doors were fully open, and people were pouring out into the sunlight. He couldn't blame them, but Emilyn was right. Inside was ultimately going to be safer. Climbing up a little on a support beam with a widened bottom just large enough for his foot to stand on, he peered out the doors. More cloaks were outside, and they were regaining their light. He could see their purple eyes from there. It wasn't stopping the people of the city, though. They were ready to be brave and take a chance, regardless of the risk. They weren't about to be caged again.

Traditionally, Yomalyn had found himself more of the risk-taker type, and the person he'd been back when his father had died would have been at the front of that crowd. And probably the first to die. He had been filled with so much anger, and it had never really subsided despite finding ways to manage it. And when this had all had begun, he'd been the most eager to take the fight to the architects. But his new friends had shown him a better way, and while he hadn't agreed with it at first, he was coming around. Beyond that, for the first time in years, the anger had truly let him be. Just a little bit. He found the person he'd been before all that—the one who was just a little more hopeful. That little boy who'd been afraid he'd forget his parents took control, and he was happy to let him.

"Get everyone's attention?" Yomalyn asked Kyshel. "And maybe project me as far out as you can?"

Kyshel scoffed. "Do you think I'm a miracle worker?" she asked, and he shrugged.

"Kinda, yeah," he confessed, and she smiled.

"You're right." She positioned her hands toward the floor. Yomalyn would have sworn by the skies that her eyes became even brighter, and liquid light began to pour from her hands onto the floor, spreading in every direction, down every corridor in sight, up every support beam, and across the entire ceiling until seemingly everywhere was flooded. At a glance, it would have seemed out of control, but she was aware of every movement the light made with a precision even Yomalyn understood was rare for tracers. Out of the light sprung illusions of him, in the same position he was currently in standing on the support beam. Some of the copies appeared out of the ceiling, upside down, or sideways out of the walls, and intermixed with people across the room. And as they appeared, the chaos began to subside. People lowered their fists and seemed to come to their senses. The remaining architects didn't hesitate to take advantage of the situation and dart toward the exits to join their companions outside. Yomalyn's eyes widened, and his jaw dropped, and all the copies of himself he could see echoed the expression, which caused him to immediately cease it and look to Kyshel, who didn't even seem phased by what was legitimately the most impressive tracer illusion he'd ever seen. Her eyes were locked on him, though, and that was a little terrifying until he understood what she was doing. She was both capturing a memory and projecting an illusion of it at the same time. That was something he'd only heard of incredibly advanced tracers being able to manage. "Consider me impressed," he said, and his copies all spoke the words at the same time, startling him.

"I'm glad," Kyshel said, annoyed. "Be impressed faster. Can't keep this up forever."

"Right," all of him said, and he gulped. "So, here's the deal everyone," he tried his best to sound authoritative, but there was an edge of nervousness to his tone. "With one obvious exception, tracer light is blocked while we're in here. Outside?" He pointed to the door. "Not the case. You go out there, you're either dead or a prisoner again." He paused, letting that sink in, expecting someone to yell at him. "Now, I know what you're thinking. If you stay in here, you stay a prisoner, too, right?" He shook his head. "Not so. If you stay in here and they stay out there, that's a stalemate. They can't come in because we outnumber them a thousand to one, and we can't go out there because they have tracer light. I know that it's not ideal. I know that's not what you want to hear, but I am begging you, do not throw away this chance. This whole thing is far from over, but for now, this place is a fortress. There are resources in here, and we're safe." He sighed. "Believe me. I want to go home too. It is so tempting to charge out those doors and take the chance that maybe, just maybe, I could get past them and go home. But what then? They still have our city. A week ago, I wouldn't have cared. I would've done exactly that. Because a week ago, I didn't care about my life. I didn't think I had anything to fight for. Now, I know I do, and so do you. Look around you. This city is our home, but all of you are what make it that. Stay here. Protect each other. There have already been deaths today. Your neighbors. People you knew. Don't add to that list. Don't let your anger guide you. I can't stop you from going out that door, but maybe your neighbor that's still alive can. Maybe your friend can or your colleagues or the person who held a door for you or the person who asked if you were okay on the worst day of your life. Stay for them. Please. By the art of the sky."

"You said it yourself," a voice from the crowd thundered. "We outnumber them! What if we all just go out?"

Jacquelyn stood up next to Yomalyn and put her hand on his shoulder, and an illusion of her joined in with his all around.

"You're seeing for yourself what a single tracer can do," she pointed out. "Numbers won't matter out there. They do in here.

Please. Listen to him." She glanced at Yomalyn, her voice small. "My whole life, I've been afraid of tracers. Because my parents ranted about the things they can do. But the thing is, I am one. And while it's ... the most wonderful thing I've ever felt, I get why they're afraid. If you go out those doors, you face the kind of tracers they fear."

Yomalyn nodded to her. Saying what she just had couldn't have been easy for her. No one else spoke up. Everyone remained eerily still as if expecting more. But Yomalyn had no more. He wasn't even sure where his words had come from, but that place had forsaken him. Now, all he could do was hope. They wouldn't stop everyone. He knew that. But if they could reach more than not, he could live with that. And hopefully, anyone that did venture out would be captured and not killed. He found himself taking Jacquelyn's hand, and he found she didn't stop him.

All the copies of them began to fade, the light retreating back toward Kyshel and leaving the citizens of Unity Falls to make their choice. Yomalyn and Jacquelyn climbed down and met with Kyshel and Iridelyn as her purple eyes melted away. Iridelyn whistled, folding his arms.

"I'll be honest," he began. "I never expected anything so—"

"Ridiculous," Kyshel finished. "You are not good at speeches."

Jacquelyn shrugged. "I don't know." She glanced at Yomalyn. "I thought it was rather inspiring," she said, and Yomalyn beamed. "Even if you obviously made it all up."

"Excuse me," he stressed. "I had the minute it took us to get up here to come up with that. I challenge you to do better."

"She did," Kyshel replied, smiling. "Just now."

Jacquelyn blushed, and Iridelyn spoke up. "Either way," he said, lightly hitting his friend's arm. That thing was going to fall off if it got hit again. "I think it's working," he pointed out, looking around. Several people had gathered at the door. Some had gone out, but after a moment, it became clear no one else was going to, several began to push them shut. Yomalyn thought about stopping them, suggesting they stay open so as to not take away anyone's choice, but he decided not to. There were other ways out if anyone so desired, and this sent a clear message to their oppressors.

They may be trapped for the moment, but they would find a way to take their city back. Yomalyn found his ever-present anger being replaced by hope. And that that felt good. He hoped his father would be proud of him.

***

Gavelyn's eyes settled on Zarlyn, and he pondered delving into his friend's soul once more. But it was fruitless. Zarlyn would simply banish him again. Besides, he had little to worry about. Emilyn would find her father shortly. The false man called Forest would find her soon thereafter. And events would proceed accordingly. He followed a plan, but it was not one that was set. Things shifted. Choices were made. And he adjusted as needed. This was only a minor alteration. The end result would be much the same. The destination was an inevitability. Let the journey be what it may.

Five pillars of metal surrounded the bed Zarlyn lay on, purple light swirling around them, caged like the people below had been mere moments prior. Sealing off tracer light from all who did not know how to look past them. All they had needed was an amplifier. The one left on the whole of Seranno would work, even if he was in a coma. Even if it wasn't his greater purpose. Emilyn would figure out how the dampeners worked, but she wouldn't be able to keep them active for long. She was ruled by her emotions and would, of course, try to reach her father. He welcomed her to try and welcomed the chain reaction that would ensue. And on the off chance it didn't, little would change. He knew his role, and he would play it well.

"We have all the makings of a portrait, old friend," he said, his voice hollow but also ... satisfied, he found. "Coming together after all these years," he continued, letting the light overtake his eyes, stepping back toward the massive window of the former governor's office. Turning around, he set his palms to the window and let the light flow into it. With Zarlyn's amplification, it had just enough power to ...

Shatter the glass.

A thousand shards hit the floor below Gavelyn or fell from the spire. Down below, his architects waited. Letting the light flow from his hands into the open air of the city sky, he stepped out of the window.

Onto the next step.

A Perception of Trust

It was said that the eyes of the universe could see the things that those who walk finite paths were not meant to. It was said that tracers could catch glimpses of those things. That was, in part, what had initially pushed the world against them. That it was not the place of those with souls to be able to see into others with such burdens.

Emilyn had never bought into that. It was such a spiritual concept, and she believed that tainted it, in the sense that the philosophical words were just an easy disguise for fear. Recent events had both helped her understand where that fear had originated from and why some may have turned to a spiritual explanation. Those things let her own beliefs linger in a state of uncertainty. It wasn't that she didn't believe—more that she simply hadn't decided to. And to her, it seemed that so many people were quick to underestimate the power of making the choice. Because that's all it was. It was a choice, and she hadn't leaned in either direction too far.

Cidelyn said Forest had called himself the Architect. Something about that hadn't sat well with Emilyn. It reminded her of that feeling when she first met him. That dissonance she hadn't been quite able to explain. Whatever he was, he wasn't like her. Whatever he had done to her the night she had nearly split was the one thing she had encountered in her life that challenged her to make a choice.

She and Cidelyn were gazing down a single corridor that led to a single door. Beyond it was the governor's office. Former governor. There was no telling what Gavelyn had done to her when he'd taken the city. All Emilyn knew was that if her father was in the spire, he would be beyond those doors. Cidelyn nodded to her, and together they approached the doors. Wrapping her fingers around one handle while Cidelyn took hold of the other, she took a deep breath. Together they pulled them open.

And there he was.

She ran to her father, darting across the office to the bed where he lay, comatose but alive. He was still there. It felt too easy, but she didn't care. He was right there in front of her. She knelt beside his bed and took his hand in both of hers, holding it up to her face and finally letting herself cry. She had him back, and nothing else mattered.

The light was back. She could feel the space between again. It was like it had never been gone—just buried—and it had finally found its way back to her soul. It only added to the swell of warmth wrapping around her heart.

"Emilyn ..." Cidelyn said, but she didn't look at him. She just left her eyes closed, sitting with her father. It was all she needed to feel whole again. Over a decade of taking care of him. She wouldn't let Gavelyn or anyone else take him away again. "Sorry," Cidelyn's voice again. "But I'm gonna assume you didn't notice these ..." He sounded concerned, and she knew she should look, but she didn't want to. She was selfishly happy and wanted to stay that way. No more problems. "I think your father is the dampener ..." he said regardless. "Or at least ... powering them somehow."

That got her attention, and though it was the toughest thing she'd ever done, she gently returned his hand to his side and stood up, wiping away her tears and looking to Cidelyn, who was peering over a monolithic pillar of metal between them, tracer light swirling around it as if trapped. She wanted to curse herself for not even noticing this thing, which was so obviously out of place, but in her defense, she had been distracted. There were four more of the pillars positioned around her father's bed in a pentagonal pattern. And feeling her link to the space between them back, she understood Cidelyn's theory to be correct, at least on some level. "Gavelyn," Emilyn started, examining the closest pillar. "He said my father is an amplifier. That tracer light is heightened around him. That very few exist anymore."

"Hmm," Cidelyn grunted, clearly deep in thought. "In that case, I wonder if these pillars are essentially ... reverse amplifiers?" he guessed, and it made a certain sense. Whatever they were doing, they made it so he nullified the tracer light instead of bolstering it. "Maybe that's why they're rare?" Cidelyn continued. "If something like this exists, they were probably exploited." Emilyn nodded, and then stepped past the pillars to join him, and felt her connection to the space between fade. Not sever entirely, but there was no denying it was buried again.

"Can you figure out how to turn them off?" Emilyn asked, looking to her father. Now that she was looking more objectively, he seemed ... strained. "I think they're hurting him."

"That," a familiar voice came from behind her, "would be ill-advised." Forest. He was not the same as Emilyn last saw him. He donned a black traveler's cloak, though it contained no hood and the layered sections of the lower half were trimmed. She supposed it was less of a cloak and more of a form-fitted single piece. His hair was about the only thing that remained the same, looking as perfectly placed and pristine as it had before. His demeanor of a bumbling man lacking a basic understanding of social cues was gone. There was a gravitas about him now. The feeling of dissonance lingered. "Though it is, of course, your choice," he added after a moment. "I would caution that doing so may jeopardize the tenuous peace your friends have managed to instigate below."

Emilyn knew on a logical level that he was correct. Tracer light being nullified inside the spire was the only thing preventing the architects from retaking the building. But her father was clearly in pain. She hated that choice.

She found Cidelyn's hand on her shoulder and looked back and forth between his eyes and she knew what the right choice was. She sighed, closing her eyes and asking her father to forgive her. She put her hand over Cidelyn's, and he managed an encouraging smile. She shifted her eyes back to Forest, who stood with his hands clasped behind his back. He met her gaze with a relentless fearlessness that was somehow also a force of calm. He meant them no harm. But that didn't mean he was harmless.

"Who are you?" she asked, and Forest looked to Cidelyn.

"What have you told her?" Forest asked in a very neutral tone.

Emilyn narrowed her eyes at him. "Just that you call yourself the Architect," Emilyn answered for Cidelyn. Forest simply inclined his head at her words to confirm their validity. "A name that's not the least bit suspicious." She folded her arms.

Forest smiled a strangely welcoming smile. "I assure you any link between myself and the group entrapping your city is in name only." He inclined his head again. "But I do not fault you for believing otherwise. I would be suspicious as well. I wish to prove to you who I am."

"Why?" Emilyn was quick to ask, her voice filled with frustration she hadn't realized she was feeling.

"Put simply," Forest replied, unphased by her vicious tone, "I need your help. Both of your help."

"With what?" Cidelyn chimed in, though his tone was decidedly more open-minded. "You didn't get the chance to say earlier."

"Our time was limited then," Forest replied, pausing. "Allow me to properly introduce myself. I am the Architect." He bowed, briefly. "And I ask for your help in restoring balance to the strings of your world."

Emilyn immediately found herself back in the dream she'd had only days prior, of a corridor made entirely of strings. To the line of light that had connected her and Forest when he'd helped her through her split, like a string. But more than that, to the very first illusion she'd ever brought to life.

String the stars.

"What does that mean?" Emilyn asked, her voice losing its integrity and becoming small. Like she was somewhere she didn't belong. Forest, the Architect, sighed. "I do not believe you will believe me," he stated.

"Then why say it?" Emilyn demanded, stepping closer to him, doing her best to challenge him. "Try us."

"This universe is not what you perceive it to be," he said bluntly, meeting her challenge. "Everything you see around you—every person, object, animal, and particle of dust—is tied together by the strings of creation crafted at the Culmination. They are the building blocks of what you call reality. Everything is tied together ..." He paused. "It has to be, or else it wouldn't be able to exist. Which is what drew me here. Something here is unbound to the strings."

"Here as in Unity Falls?" Emilyn asked, though it felt like the most ridiculous question she could ask, given the words he had just spoken. Strangely enough, however, she found herself following him. Not believing, necessarily, but understanding. Universe made of strings. Something not tied to them. That something bad.

"Seranno," he clarified, unsurprised by her question. "I came here seeking that which is untied but found a far more concerning situation. This world feels wrong to me. Not as it once was, long ago. What you call tracer light ..." He paused, looking to them both. "It wasn't something ever intended to exist. Something has shifted the strings here in ways that should not be possible," he stepped over to the swirls of light dancing around the pillars dampening that wonderful thing he claimed should not exist. It almost seemed to shy away from him, and he seemed to lament this, though he continued to be fixated by it. "I can fix it. But I fear that in doing so, I might lose the opportunity to understand precisely what happened. And that is what I need your help to determine," he finished, looking back to them.

Emilyn gazed at him for a long moment, uncertain exactly what words should pass by her lips next, if any. That had ... taken a turn. She tried to speak, but nothing came out, so she looked to Cidelyn. He held a look of consideration but was at a similar loss for words. The fascinated look in his eyes indicated a very specific word, however. Belief. He believed it all. She looked back to Forest. "I ..." she started, and shook her head, unable to believe what she herself was about to say. "Okay," she said, raising her eyebrows and trying to keep an open mind. "Hypothetically, say we believe you. So you're ... what, the ... guardian of these strings?" she asked, and then closed her eyes at how ridiculous she sounded. And cursed her own forgetfulness. Architect. He had said he was the Architect. And she knew what that word meant. Forest was claiming he was the one who had designed their universe. As bold claims went, that one was up there.

Forest, to his credit, simply smiled. "As stated, I do not expect you to take me at my word," he said, striding back to the opposite side of the room where he had initially been, allowing the purple-pink hue of sunlight passing through the barrier around the city to pierce the large shattered window and illuminate one side of his face. "I intend to provide evidence and clarity. To do so, however, may require one thing from you," he explained, locking eyes on Emilyn. "Trust."

Emilyn looked back and forth between his eyes, and suddenly everything seemed slightly less ... hypothetical. That dissonance became a physical entity, occupying the void between them. But it no longer alarmed her. Instead, she found it to be ... alluring. Not in a way that sought to take away her choice in the matter. It was a question, waiting for her to provide an answer.

"Will you trust me? Do you recall our experience inside your soul several days ago?" he asked, and she did. His words had remained with her. Something to tether you. "I can help you find what you are missing, Emilyn. I seek only to understand. Not harm. This I vow to you."

There was such a gravity behind his words. A force she couldn't explain. They both seemed as though they weren't meant for her and connected to her at the same time. This was real. All of it was real. He was inviting her into something larger than herself, and she didn't know what to make of that. She found her breathing intensifying, her heart beating just a little faster. She wanted to. She felt like she needed to. But at the same time, he wasn't influencing her, and a significant part of her doubted him too. He couldn't be who he claimed to be. He just couldn't be. She knew her world. It wasn't made of strings and it wasn't broken or altered. It was her home. There was understanding in his eyes. If she chose to not trust him, he would understand. And she cursed him for that.

"He did save us before," Cidelyn reminded her, stepping up beside her to meet her eyes. With reluctance, she met his. She hated that they made her feel stronger. "He saved me just earlier today, in ways I can't explain," he confessed, and she remembered what he had said about Forest offering to help him with the moon, which seemed oddly drawn into itself, orbiting opposite Forest around Cidelyn's head. "Given what he did to Gavelyn," Cidelyn added, seeming to recall something. "He's at least not on their side," he sighed. "I know you don't need my opinion, but if you want it ... I think we can trust him."

"Of course I want it," she replied, offering Cidelyn what she hoped was the same strength he had offered her, though she was surprised he would think she wouldn't value what he had to say. "What did happen to Gavelyn?" Emilyn asked Forest, and he inclined his head again.

"He retreated," Forest explained. "Joining his followers outside." That didn't exactly answer the question she'd asked, but did clarify Gavelyn's status. Good to know. It was suspicious he hadn't taken her father with him. Maybe whatever Forest had done had taken away the chance? Forest looked like he wanted to say more—try and gain her trust—but to his credit, he did not. He had said his piece and left the choice in her hands. So many people had seemed to underestimate the power of being given a choice. Forest didn't appear to be one of those people. She looked to Cidelyn, sighed, looked back to Forest, and held her head high. "I trust you." They were such small words yet some of the most meaningful she had ever spoken.

Forest understood this, conveying a look of pure gratitude. "Thank you, Emilyn," he said, inclining his head, which strangely compelled her to do the same, though she resisted the urge. He held out a hand to her, palm up. "If I may?"

With a reassuring nod from Cidelyn, she settled her eyes on his hand and then slowly slid her own fingers over his. She wasn't certain what she had been expecting. But his skin felt normal. That was both reassuring and anticlimactic. Weirdly, it made her smile. Forest returned the look, and she trusted him. For reasons she wasn't sure she understood yet, he seemed to trust her in return. Their hands linked. She nodded.

"I'm ready," she affirmed, and Forest looked to Cidelyn.

"We shall return shortly," he promised, and then everything changed.

In an instant, the office raced away, leaving them behind. Cidelyn was gone. Her father was gone. The spire was gone. Unity Falls was gone. Though they hadn't moved in the slightest, they were somewhere far, far away from anywhere she knew.

The Architect's Eyes

It was a small eternity before Emilyn's senses caught up with her body, lost behind in the race toward realization. For the briefest moment, she had been something else entirely. Just a soul in a vast and incomprehensible universe—so small and so insignificant and yet tied to something so large and vital to absolutely everything. Then came breathing. The beating of her tethered heart. She was alive. And she was among the stars.

As her senses poured back into her all at once, she screamed and clung to Forest, shoving her head into his chest and crushing his feet under her own. Her arms flung around him for all the life she had in her because there was nothing else she could take hold of and no ground beneath her and she was in space. They were in space.

He held on to her gently. He sought not to overwhelm her, but it was all for naught, as he had already failed spectacularly. She closed her eyes, failing just as miserably to calm herself. Her heart beat faster than she could ever remember it beating, and her breaths became a level of rapid that would have been comical in any moment that there was a planet beneath her feet.

Except there was a planet beneath her feet. Just much further away than she was used to.

"It's okay," Forest soothed, his voice commanding a strangely perfect amount of reassurance. "You're okay."

Taking a long moment, letting his warmth conceal her until it steadied her, she did the bravest thing she had ever done. Slowly, Emilyn opened her eyes. It was real. Space. She was in space. "How ..." she started through bated breaths. "What ..." she tried again. It was absurd. This was absolutely absurd. Until it became surreal. The stars she had strung together as a child ... she was closer to them than she ever thought possible. More than that, she was among them. It suddenly became ... wonderful. "You took us to space!" she exclaimed, not a single clue what else to say or do.

Forest smiled. "It may be more accurate to say that I moved space to us," he clarified, and she looked up at him, suddenly realizing how close to him she was. Not that there was any other option.

"Meaning what exactly?" she asked, confused in the best and worst ways imaginable.

"Meaning the strings I told you about—I can interact with them. On the other side. Doing so, I simply shifted Seranno's location in space. We didn't move at all."

"You nudged a planet?" she asked, and he adopted a confused expression.

"I am uncertain as to the meaning of nudged," he replied. "But if it allows you to better understand what has transpired, then yes, I nudged a planet."

She laughed. This was absurd. This was so absurd. Letting her eyes drift downward, she took in the most astonishing sight she had ever seen. That was her home beneath her. Everyone and everything she had ever known and ever loved was down there somewhere, so far away and yet seemingly close enough that she could touch if she just reached for it. A lush green sphere amidst a dark void of stars.

"There are ..." she shook her head. "No words for that," she turned toward him, nodding ferociously. "I believe you! I believe you," she said, and then her eyes went wide. "No air in space!" She covered her mouth, wide-eyed, and he chuckled. She felt ridiculous.

"Air bubble," he clarified, though there was no visual evidence of any such bubble. Clearly, she was breathing, though. "And I'm glad you believe me. Though I admit there are several reasons I chose to bring you here."

"You mean other than to be dramatic?" she asked, only half joking. Surely there were less terrifyingly brilliant methods by which to prove he was who he said. The Architect. "I'm not understanding why you feel the need to prove anything to me at all? I'm no one. You're ... you."

"You are certainly not no one, Emilyn," he replied, and suddenly, coming from him, that felt like the best compliment she'd ever received. "You are my friend. And I trust you. You are here because I need to verify for myself that the one I seek, the one untied to the strings, is who I believe it to be. I received a glimpse before, when we connected, but I must be certain." Emilyn gave him a confused look, narrowing her eyes at him until she finally understood.

"You think it's me?" she blurted out. "I'm the one who you're looking for?" she asked, alarmed. "But I'm not different; there's nothing special about me," she rambled, but even she knew it wasn't true. Things had happened to her in the past week she hadn't been able to explain, and it didn't do her or Forest any good to deny them. She looked down, took a deep breath, and then looked back at him. "What do you need?" she asked, finding her fear so loud in a place so silent. She felt cold, despite his warmth. She was scared.

"Nothing that will bring harm to you," he vowed. "I wish to connect, as we did before."

"Okay…" she replied, and he attempted to clarify.

"I wish to generate a string linking you to me," he began. "What you would call my soul is not quite as yours is but it may help you to think of it as a temporary union between your soul and mine. For a moment, we will be one being. We will be able to see through one another's eyes, externally and internally," he explained, and she gulped. "I understand if that may sound frightening."

"Absolutely terrifying," she clarified, and chuckled a little, if only for her own benefit. He looked back and forth between her eyes.

"I only ask," he amended. "I will not force you to do anything. I will return us the moment you wish it." Emilyn looked past him, toward the two stars she had strung together as a child. She always found them, and even from their home instead of hers they were easy for her to pick out.

"My very first illusion was a string," she said, thinking fondly of that time when things had been simpler. "Linking those two stars," she looked back at him. "Was that actually an illusion?"

"I do not know," he answered honestly. "But if you can see the other side … that would confirm what I believe." She lamented, adopting a somber expression.

"I've dreamt of a world made of strings …" she confessed. "Someone was there, watching me. And I've been able to do things tracers shouldn't be able to. If we … connect, will you see all of that?" He nodded.

"If you allow me to, yes."

"Will it help you?" she asked. Would it help her?

"I believe it will." She gulped, and took a deep breath, readying herself.

"Do it," she braved. "On one condition. I want to know everything. Whatever answers you find might be ones I'm searching for too." She wasn't sure where she had found the confidence to make demands of someone like him, but there it was. It would be partners, or it would be nothing. He inclined his head. "But I do have a question first."

"Of course," he replied, kindly. "What is your question?"

"I know why I'm trusting you," she began. "Why are you trusting me? You said it yourself this ... connection goes both ways. I'll be able to see through your eyes, too. Right?"

"That is correct."

"So why?" she asked, and he seemed to struggle to find an answer. She wasn't sure if she found that comforting or terrifying.

"Your gallery," he replied. "I quite enjoyed it." She narrowed her eyes, though couldn't help but smirk a little at the compliment.

"That's not an answer."

"Is it not?" he asked. "You are genuine. Your artwork suggests as much. And when Diselyn collapsed, you did not hesitate to help him. I learned all I needed to you of that night, long before I suspected you of being the one I am in search of." Emilyn couldn't help but smile.

"Speaking of," she had a realization. "We were linked before, why couldn't you find what you needed then?"

"Your soul was in tatters," he explained. "A battlefield. Splitting, I believe you call it. Not an ideal situation in which to search for something specific."

"And what is this specific thing, specifically?" she asked, and he moved a hand to the space in between their hearts. His palm up, a golden string burned into existence. He calmly wrapped his fingers around it.

"Evidence of one of these," he explained. "Are you prepared?" he asked, and she nodded, surprised at her own confidence. But there was a familiarity to the string. She felt drawn to it. Forest released the string, it simultaneously latched onto both of them. She jumped, but it seemed to ignore her skin, delving somewhere inside her. At first, she felt nothing, as if it weren't even there. And then all at once, every single aspect of her soul ignited, a fire dancing across everything she had ever been and stretching so far beyond her. She understood. Everything he had said she understood because he was right there. A part of her, and her a part of him. One being. Though she retained her own thoughts and awareness, his thoughts and awareness were hers as well, and it was unlike anything she had ever experienced. An empire lay before her, inviting her in, and it was so much and so little all at once.

"You are safe," he said, though it was as if she heard the words from his mind before his mouth. She appreciated them nonetheless. All around her vision began to alter itself. Colors became more vibrant. The silence of space became less of a void and more a state of serenity, a single beat of her heart so much more of a wonderful thing than before. She looked to Seranno beneath her and it became a swirl of colors, like paint waiting to meet a brush that would reshape its form and give it new life. And she saw them. The strings. They bridged the gap between every planet and every star, a hundred thousand of them shooting out of all of them in all directions. Everything was linked, just as Forest had said. Space was no longer a void of darkness populated by distant lights. It was strings and colors and life and … the space between. Between everything. Except there were more betweens and more everythings than she could ever hope to understand. An infinity, strings inside of strings inside of strings inside of strings. Even Seranno. She could pick a string and follow it from space down to a single blade of grass, and deeper into the planet, all the way to the core and beyond and she could see all of it. It was wonderful and it was too much. It was too much. It began to hurt, her entire soul feeling the fire of what Forest saw every moment of every day and she couldn't take it.

String the stars.

The words came from him, not her, and she looked into his eyes, finding tears escaping her own.

"You are safe," he repeated, and she closed her eyes, willing a calmness upon herself. You are safe. You are safe. She said the words to herself in unison with him.

"I apologize," he said, sorrowfully. "The Architect's eyes are not meant for you. But-"

"It was the only way," she finished, and she could see them. The answers he had been searching for in her. He'd found them. It was painfully obvious as she saw things through his eyes. Strings tied all things together.

But there were no strings on her.

"What does that mean?" she asked, and she more saw the answer than heard it.

"It means that you have been touched by someone of my kind," he stated, and the words carried a gravity to them. As if they were ones even he shuddered to say.

"Perdition?" she asked, though the word hadn't come from her. It was what the place he had been created was called. He nodded.

"Yes," he replied. "There are only two other beings whose creation stem from there. At least, only two capable of this."

A man flashed across her memories. No, not her memories. He had Forest's eyes, but his face was different. Bearded. His brother.

"He is dead," Forest clarified, and he refused to allow her to experience an elaboration of that. "Which leaves one option. The one I feared. If she has interacted with your soul, she is likely responsible for the alterations to your world as well. There is a larger plan at work. I must uncover it. Her involvement changes things."

"How?" she asked, and he allowed her another glimpse into his memory. A woman dressed in white appeared. Smiling. Laughing. Alongside Forest and his brother. "Your sister."

Forest nodded in confirmation, though he looked grim. "The Artist," he stated, and let his eyes linger over Seranno. "I am afraid your world has become her canvas."

That sent a shiver down Emilyn's spine, though she had no idea why. In a swift motion, Forest gripped and disintegrated the string linking them, and she felt as if a part of her had just died. It left her feeling hollow. She felt very little as the embers of the string faded away into the nothingness of space. She wanted it back.

"It is time we returned," he spoke, and she barely registered the planet rushing back to them, leaving them back in the office where she immediately collapsed. Arms caught her, though she wasn't sure whose. Her senses became hazy, and the image of The Artist flashed across her eyes. Only she wasn't smiling any longer. She wore a far more dangerous expression. One that lacked care. Her purple eyes were the last thing Emilyn saw before she drifted away.

Unbound

The strings were not bound by time. They were without beginning and without end. They simply were. They simply would always be. But they weren't without weakness. As with all things, the strings could be incapacitated. Erased, if only temporarily. They would reform anew, carrying the burden of creation just as The Three had for so long. The Architect knew what must be done. A universal method of cleansing that which must be forgotten.

Fire.

The fire of his own being, forged in The Culmination where he now planted his feet, where all strings coalesced. The birthplace of what lesser beings would come to know as creation.

All around him were the children of the strings, universes that carried the spark needed to birth life. An infinity of them swirled around him, spheres linked together by strings that inside diverged into an infinity more to become galaxies and planets and continents and life, down to the tiniest fragments of a single wisp of air. He could reach out and touch them if he so desired, follow the paths, and observe all facets of the worlds he had helped shape.

Such an endeavor would be fruitless. Only one of them bore significance. Only one had shown the capabilities to stand on its own, to be what they needed it to be. Moments ago they had become aware of its existence. The colors blanketing the long corridor of universes swirled red, their anger screaming across all Perdition over what he and his sibling had done. He felt them inside him, demanding that he walk the path forward. Demanding that his grasp on the chain in his hand be so strong that it tore into his flesh.

Emilyn felt the pain he felt. She saw what he saw. She was a passenger in his eyes, unable to exist yet fully aware of everything. These weren't her memories. These weren't things she knew. The more she saw, the more she believed these weren't things she was meant to know or understand. But she did understand them. They terrified her but left her unable to even scream.

A door of white manifested down the corridor as the Architect approached, searing itself into existence as if on command of his very presence. He pushed open the doors, the chain dragging against the ground beneath him. Emilyn realized he was crying. That he was as much a passenger in his own body as she was. Someone else was in control.

"Crafter," he stated, his voice a finality, shattering Emilyn's limited perceptions of what a voice could be. "Forgive me." The Crafter turned to face the Architect.

He wore a neatly-trimmed beard, his hair perfectly combed and positioned. Not unlike Forest. He smiled, forgiveness and understanding radiating from him. "There is nothing to forgive, Brother," he stated, glancing at a universe to his left that was not contained within a sphere. Instead, it was a swirling, shapeless form of yellow and white that sparked and pulsed and breathed of its own accord. It seemed to grow larger and then smaller as if exhaling. As if alive. "This was a foreseen eventuality."

The architect stepped forward but then stopped, grunting and falling to his knees, the chain clanking against the floor and even a sound that small echoed around all of them with an air of relevance.

"I ... cannot ... fight them," he said, his voice the purest pain she had ever experienced. Tears tore themselves from his eyes. "But ... what am ... I ... to be ... without you?"

"Two do not require the third," the Crafter stated calmly.

"But I ... need you ... Brother," he cried, and the Crafter placed a hand on his shoulder, smiling.

"And I you, Brother," he replied, and then the smile faded. "But such bonds are reserved for lesser beings. They shall need them far more than we," he sighed. "I am envious of them. But do not fear. What we have built together, you and I," he gestured to the unstable universe. "That will live on. They cannot take that from us."

"Do ... what must ... be done ..." the Architect struggled, and the Crafter nodded. Standing and approaching the universe, he wrapped his fingers around two strings that reached into it, binding it to the universes that came before. He tore open his own essence, letting it pour into them, a white light that filled the entire chamber. It was like a toxin, burning and searing the strings, lighting them afire with a flame of the same white hue. With a flare, they were severed, and the Crafter watched the fire spread to all previous universes but sparing the newest. They burned in complete silence.

The red swirls in the background ignited with a rage so pure and so strong that Emilyn nearly felt her own heart stop beating. The Architect grabbed the chain, leaping forward and wrapping it around the Crafter's neck.

"You are too late." The Crafter smiled despite the pain, and his eyes watched a freed universe drift away. "My final creation is free."

"Crafter," the Architect's voice said, but it was not him. The anger. The rage. It consumed him. "You will fail. That universe has no more freedom than you do time remaining."

"You are incorrect." He continued to smile, though he struggled to speak against the chain. "That universe has something long denied to the Three." His voice became a whisper. "Hope."

The Architect tore the chain through the Crafter's neck in one swift motion, and his body fell to the floor alongside his head, both beginning to dissipate into white light. The rage was gone. The red swirls calmed, though lingering in the sky beyond. The Architect was released, and he fell back to his knees, free to bear witness to what his hands had been made to do. He closed his eyes, trying and failing to will the tears away. He could not. He cried—as much as a being made only to design could do so.

The Architect faded away. The universe faded away. Emilyn was alone, in her own body, lying down. In a place she had been once before. A corridor made entirely of strings. Only, this time it felt far less whole. There seemed to be fewer strings than before, though she wasn't sure how she could possibly tell. As far as her eyes were concerned, the place was built entirely of them. But the place felt ... lesser. Just as before, a figure lingered down the corridor, silhouetted and distorted. Watching her. The figure approached, and the distortion seemed to align as she got closer, folding into something her eyes could conceive. Perhaps because this time she had a frame of reference. She had seen this person in Forest's memory, while they were in space. His sister. The Artist.

The Artist approached, and Emilyn found she could only concentrate on her eyes. A deep purple, both light and dark. Alluring, calling to her. She reached out toward Emilyn.

Emilyn's eyes snapped open. Quickly sitting up, she found she was breathing heavily. She was sweating. But she was herself again. Back in her own body. Back in control. Her hands were shaking, and she felt the ... the chain ... in her fingers. Tearing through Forest's brother. No. That wasn't her. But it had been her. It had been her only days ago, ripping through that Architect in the space between.

"You're awake!" Kyshel's arms flung around her, hugging her before Emilyn even realized she wasn't alone in the room. "I thought you had ..." she trailed off, leaving the thought hanging.

"What?" Emilyn asked, her voice weak and fractured. She tried to compose herself. What had happened? She had been with her father and Cidelyn, and then ... space. Right. She had linked with Forest. That was his memory she'd just experienced.

"Emilyn," she said, her voice cautious. She sighed. "It's been three days," she said. "I thought you had fallen into a coma like your father."

"Three days?" Emilyn asked, her body forced into recovery from pure shock. Kyshel nodded.

"Forest brought you here," she explained. "Cidelyn and I have been taking turns staying with you," she said and hugged her again. "I'm so glad you're awake."

"Forest," Emilyn echoed. "Where is he?"

"Present," he stated, from the other side of the room. Kyshel jumped, startled, and glared at him.

"I told you not to do that!" she insisted. "You can't just pop into rooms."

"Apologies," he said. "Emilyn sounded distressed."

"I am," she said, trying to stand up, though Kyshel seemed to insist she at least remain sitting. "What in all the skies did I just dream?"

"As we are no longer linked," Forest began, approaching them. "You will need to be more specific than that."

"Wait, that actually happened?" Kyshel asked. "I thought he was joking. So, you actually ... went to space?"

"I do not know how to joke, Kyshel," he answered. "I did not fabricate any of what I told you and Cidelyn." He looked to Emilyn.

"I was you," Emilyn said. "I watched you ... kill your brother," she explained, and Forest's face fell. "But it wasn't you! It was someone else, I think. But that place ... I can't ... what was that?"

"Perdition," he answered, sighing. "What you experienced was a remnant of my memory, a fragment left behind from our link, I'm afraid. I tried to shield you from such things, but it appears I failed. I do hope that is the final memory you experience," he lamented. "And I apologize."

"So, that really happened?" Emilyn asked, and he nodded somberly.

"I am afraid it did," he replied. "My brother, the Crafter, perished at my hand. Though I was not in control, as you said, it feels as though it was me. It lingers on," he explained, his eyes falling to his hands. To the chain. Emilyn extended her hands and gently rested them atop his. He seemed uncertain what to do with this gesture of support, but he didn't remove his hands.

"You said Perdition?" Kyshel asked, unphased by any of this. "Is that where you're from?"

"It is," he confirmed, standing again. "My siblings and I were created to create." He smiled fondly. "Universes and all that live within them. The Crafter, the Architect, and the Artist. Perdition bore the Culmination, where the strings originate."

"But someone created you?" Emilyn asked, thinking about the red swirls of emotion that controlled him before. He nodded.

"They are not relevant to our current crisis, and I have perhaps shared far too much as it stands."

Emilyn had enough fragments of information to piece together at least part of the puzzle. Someone had created Forest and his siblings and tasked them to create universes. They created one those someones we're afraid of, and those someones made Forest kill his brother in response. Yet he seemed to have escaped them.

"Oh, come on," Kyshel stressed. "You've already overshared! May as well commit at this point."

"What is relevant to you is that I escaped Perdition, and evidently, the Artist did as well. It is imperative that I locate her. I suspect she is misinformed. I would wish to rectify that. Did you see anything further?" he asked Emilyn.

"I was in a corridor of strings," she explained. "I've dreamt of it before. She was there, looking for me ... I think."

"That did not come from me," he said, ominously. "If she seeks you on the other side and you can glimpse the other side ..." he paused.

"Then what?" Emilyn asked, a little forceful.

"Then it's of paramount importance I find her. And that she does not find you."

"What happens if she does?" Kyshel asked.

"I suggest avoiding learning the answer to that very question," he replied. "She is likely in search of me, working for our creators," he said reluctantly. "But in that case, why seek you?" he asked Emilyn. "Why instigate any of this chaos? There are pieces of this puzzle I am lacking."

“That’s an understatement,” Emilyn said, and Kyshel helped her stand, though she seemed hesitant to do so. “So, how about we go over what we do know and see if any of those pieces fit together. Where’s Cidelyn?”

“When he has not been watching over you, he has been studying the dampeners surrounding your father,” Forest explained.

“As good a place as any to start,” said Emilyn, taking charge, heading toward the door after assuring Kyshel she was okay to walk. “Let’s go. And you can fill me in on the past three days while we walk.”

Origins

Dreams were strange creatures. Whether they deemed themselves to be remembered directly or not, they clung to souls. They demanded to have meant something, and often got their way. It was how they were to manifest that was always the question.

The door was white. The Crafter awaited beyond it. The chain dragged across the floor. It was the worst sound Emilyn had ever heard.

"Not much to say." Kyshel passed through the door as Forest held it open for the both of them. Emilyn remained still, and with a simple blink, the door returned to its usual wooden brown. There was no chain.

"Emilyn?" Forest asked, and she snapped her eyes to him before quickly forcing control over herself.

"Sorry," she said, stepping through the door. "You were saying?" she looked to Kyshel, praying she would continue so Emilyn wouldn't have to explain what just happened or think further about it. The latter didn't turn out to be difficult, as the once barren hallways now had people scattered about, refugees in their own home. They watched them curiously. With a certain hope and desperation.

"Not sure how much you heard of Yomalyn's speech, but he's kinda taken charge. Iridelyn and Jacquelyn are helping keep everyone calm and manage the food and water stored here. Luckily, it's a big building, so it's got a big kitchen! Even so, with the majority of the city in here, our supply is gonna run low pretty quick, so they're working on a rationing system. I'm on standby to help out if things get out of hand. But surprisingly, Yomalyn's had some pretty good ideas. It'll probably raise his spirits to know you're up. Oh, and that's the other thing—lots of people are having to sleep down in the ... rooms with the cages. They're not happy about that, but there's just not enough room. There are lots of problems, but those are the two big ones. We've lost a few people to heading outside. They've promptly run into the barricades the architects have set up. They've got the whole place surrounded."

"So, we need to figure a way out of here yesterday," Emilyn said, nodding. "Got it. Anything else I need to know?"

Forest perked up. "Yomalyn has taken to referring to himself, Iridelyn, Jacquelyn, and the others who volunteered to help them as 'The Gallery', " Forest said, and Emilyn looked up at him. "He seemed to think you would approve." Emilyn didn't know what to think of that, but it warmed her a little to know the people who had attended her gallery had banded together. Artists versus terrorists, after all.

"Speaking of," she began. "Any sign of Diselyn and Adalyn?"

Kyshel shook her head. "Unaccounted for. Iridelyn spent a whole day searching for them. He wasn't ready to stop, either, but there have to be priorities right now," she explained, and Emilyn took a deep breath, worried about what might have happened to them.

"It is a difficult situation," Forest agreed. "The sooner we can determine the best course to gain the upper hand in the current crisis and hopefully locate the Artist, the sooner the people of your home will be safe. Perhaps Cidelyn's research on the dampeners may yield an advantage we have yet to realize."

"It would be nice to know how they work," Emilyn concurred. "Maybe use them against the Architects somehow. Has Cidelyn found anything?"

"Last I heard, the only thing he found was a strong desire to throw them out that obnoxiously large window." Kyshel shrugged. "But that was the morning."

"I fail to see what that would accomplish," Forest commented. "I said as much when he proposed the idea. He provided a strong emotional response consisting of several words I am unfamiliar with. The coordination between the two was surprisingly satisfying." Emilyn laughed, and Kyshel huffed.

"This guy's great," she commented, smiling.

"I find I am fond of you as well, Kyshel," he replied. "In fact, I am pleased to call all of you friends, despite the short length of time we have been in proximity."

"Things like this tend to bring people together," Emilyn said, and then smiled. "And we're happy to call you a friend, too."

"Do things like this happen often?" he asked, and Emilyn shook her head.

"Thankfully, no," she clarified. "But my father told a lot of stories."

"Speaking of," Kyshel interjected, pushing open the doors to the former governor's office. Emilyn had gotten lost enough in the conversation and her thoughts that she hadn't even noticed how close they were. Her father remained still on the bed, surrounded by distinctively not-thrown dampener pillars, and Cidelyn peered over one of them, a hand to his chin as he thought. As soon as she saw him, she smiled, and with strength she didn't quite have she jogged over to him and wrapped her arms around him from the side. He seemed to have not even noticed the door open, so a hug caught him completely by surprise. He did jump a little, but she didn't let that stop her.

"Sorry, hi," he said awkwardly, smiling back at her and embracing the strange side-hug as best he could. She wasn't quite sure why she'd been so happy to see him, but she was. "It's ... uh ... really good to see you," he said, and she released him.

"You too," she replied. "Apparently I needed a rest."

"Apparently," he agreed and then looked concerned. "But for three days? Are you okay?" he asked, and she nodded.

Forest chimed in. "Merely a mental reset. Our link may have been more strenuous than I anticipated."

"Ah," he replied, looking back at the dampeners. "Well, I hope it was more relaxing than staring at these." He looked frustrated. A side to him she hadn't seen. Kyshel hadn't been joking, after all.

"No luck?" she asked, and he shook his head.

"Not even a little."

"When in doubt," Kyshel chimed in, giving Emilyn a knowing look. "Get some help, and start from the beginning." Cidelyn gestured concession to her, and she smiled. She did like getting acknowledged for her ideas. "So what do we know?" she asked, looking around. "Tracers plus whatever in the skies Cidelyn is have lost access to the light," she said, and Cidelyn sighed, but didn't look bothered. Kyshel's bluntness seemed to be growing on him. "Former tracers—me—have regained access to it." Emilyn raised her hand, and Kyshel pointed at her.

"Just you?" Emilyn asked. "Have any other former tracers come forward?"

Cidelyn shook his head. "Diselyn was the only other one we knew of," he replied. "No one else so far."

"True. If it's just me, that's not necessarily reliable information," Kyshel conceded, shrugging, and looked to Forest. "Sound right, Mister Architect?" Forest did not answer. Instead, his eyes focused on Cidelyn.

Cidelyn narrowed his eyes at him. "What is it?" he asked. "You're seeing something. What is it?"

"A string. A narrow one, indicating a thin connection. But a connection nonetheless," he replied.

"Connecting what?" Emilyn asked, and Forest approached Cidelyn, examining the moon.

"I am surprised I did not see it before ..." he mumbled, and then his eyes seemed to follow something invisible over to the closest dampener. He continued to speak without looking at anyone. "Aside from the loss of your insight into the thoughts of tracers, have you noticed anything different since being within the dampeners' radius?" Cidelyn shook his head.

"No, I don't think so," he said, but Emilyn thought of something. She wished Cidelyn could hear her thoughts so she could ask if it was okay to talk about since he had been hesitant to do so before. But they had little time for sensitivity, and it might be important. She looked at Cidelyn, who seemed at a loss. "Your strength," she said, for lack of a better term. He didn't seem to follow, and she sighed. "Before, you lost a lot of energy really fast when using your abilities for more than a few minutes," she explained, and he looked around at Kyshel and Forest, neither of whom seemed to have a reaction, and then he reluctantly nodded. "I can't speak for the past few days but that didn't seem to happen at all when you were helping me before. Right?" she asked, and he turned his head, thinking on it.

"I hadn't noticed," he said and nodded. "But I think you're right. Odd. What could that mean?"

"To the best of your knowledge," Forest began. "Was the moon the cause of that lack of energy?" he asked, and Cidelyn nodded.

"As far as I know." Forest nodded, more to himself.

"That makes sense," he mumbled.

Kyshel squinted. "Does it, though?" she asked, and Forest looked to her as if suddenly remembering others were present.

"The moon is currently draining energy from the dampeners," he clarified. "A single string is connecting them. Cidelyn has his strength because the moon, while still attached to him, has found a more stable source of what it requires ..." He went on, adopting the look of a man with a theory.

Cidelyn's eyes lit up. "You know what it is?" he asked, desperation in his voice. "What it's doing?"

"I have a theory," Forest clarified. "I do not know for certain," he added, and Cidelyn gazed at him, waiting for him to continue. "But I believe the moon is a conduit for tracer light. Furthermore, I believe it may be able to siphon the remaining energy from the dampeners."

"Siphon?" Cidelyn asked, his eyes widening. He was scared. But he was also invested. He needed to know. "What does that mean, exactly?" Forest gently took Cidelyn by the arm and guided him into the space between the dampeners and Zarlyn—the small space where his abilities would return. He flinched a little, almost in pain, as the transition took place.

"Please," Forest prompted and gestured to Kyshel. "Tell me what she is currently thinking." Kyshel perked up as if it were a challenge, and Cidelyn seemed to be at a loss but did as instructed, and met Kyshel's eyes.

"Um ..." he began, narrowing his eyes. "... general confusion ... and ... oh, um ..." his cheeks turned red, and he gulped. "Nothing I'm repeating."

Kyshel rolled her eyes. "It's no fun if you don't say it," she complained. Cidelyn didn't respond to that, instead watching Forest follow something between Cidelyn and Kyshel.

"Fascinating," he claimed, getting closer to Kyshel who moved her head back a little, confused. "A string was formed between you two and ..." He paused. "Subsequently faded." He looked to Cidelyn. "I assume you ceased reading her thoughts?" he asked, and Cidelyn nodded aggressively. Kyshel smirked. Forest nodded in response, stepping to a middle ground between them. "As suspected, when you hear the thoughts of a tracer, and likely when you see through their illusions as well, you establish a link between yourself, the moon, and the tracer. That energy you lose is tracer light." Forest paused, almost marveling at the concept. "You are fueling them, Cidelyn. The moon is taking energy from you, transitioning it into tracer light, and giving it to them. Your abilities are what you may call a side effect."

Cidelyn was silent, though his mouth hung open slightly, suggesting he wanted to speak but didn't know the words. The mystery of his entire life had just been spilled out on the floor before him, and Emilyn couldn't blame him for not knowing what to do with it. He stepped out of the dampener pentagon and walked over toward the window, where he could see a vague reflection of himself in the remaining glass. His eyes settled on the moon. Emilyn wanted to go to him but wasn't sure he would want that.

"So, I'm ..." Cidelyn paused. "What? A battery for the light?" he asked, his voice somehow all of amazed, shocked, and bitter.

"You are far more than that," Forest said, and Emilyn expected him to say he was a person first, or some other more eloquent form of reassurance. She did not expect the words that next came out of his mouth. "I explained to you before," he said, looking briefly to Emilyn, "that tracer light was never supposed to exist. Yet, it does," he went on, focusing back to Cidelyn, who kept his back to the conversation though was clearly listening intently. "I believe you, or rather you and the moon, are the origin point of tracer light."

The Moments That Escape Us

Fifteen Years Ago

Moments lost weighed over Zarlyn, hanging from his arms and preventing him from moving forward. Moments with Jiselyn, Gavelyn, and Emilyn that he could never get back. Things he could never change. Memories that might never get made. He knew from those moments that the choices that defined a person were as much the ones many deemed insignificant as the ones that could make or break lives. He had a choice to make, and it somehow fell into both categories. To stay in Unity Falls or to take Emilyn and run?

Given the partially-packed bag lying open on his bed and his instructions to Emilyn to begin packing, one might assume his choice had been made. The city was still reeling from the horrific catastrophe he had enabled Gavelyn and Valel to enact, and he knew full well he didn't deserve any semblance of a happy ending. Emilyn did, though. She was innocent, and he would preserve that for as long as he could. Every choice he made was for her, and this was no different. The chaotic state of the city provided him with the excuse he had given her—that the city wasn't safe and they were leaving to go somewhere that would be. He hadn't told her everything. He couldn't. The burdens hanging from his arms were his to stand with, not hers.

Jiselyn had been born in a small farming village in the northern territories called Keled, and that was where he wanted to take Emilyn. It was a place of peace, where they could live a quiet life, away from all the things reaching toward them. The areas surrounding Keled held the largest sparker presence on all of Seranno, and Emilyn was fascinated by the little insects. While they were in the forests, the open farmland meant lots of space for Jade to run wild and for Emilyn to safely practice tracing. She would love it there, and maybe he would too. But going there would mean abandoning both Gavelyn and Jiselyn to Valel. While that was a heavy choice to make, he could not escape Gavelyn's words from the night he had killed the governor.

One parent is better than none, he had said. That parent could be you. You could take her and run. Zarlyn knew that if he stayed, Emilyn might be left without a family at all, or possibly with both parents. Neither was guaranteed. Leaving could guarantee she had at least one parent, even if he wasn't the one she deserved. Every choice he made was for her. This was no different.

Skies and both of you forgive me, someday. He closed his eyes and repeated that several times, thinking of both Jiselyn and Gavelyn. His best friend and the mother of his child, left at the mercy of a monster.

Was Valel the monster, or was he?

He sighed and resigned to keep packing. He had one responsibility above all others. He was all she had. He had to keep her safe, and he had to live with the guilt that would bring him. It would be immeasurable and unbearable, but he would have to welcome it into his soul.

Jiselyn, forgive me. Gavelyn, find your way. He couldn't abandon Emilyn. He couldn't risk her being left alone. He would save them both if he could, and all he could do was pray that they knew that. He knew that, and yet he hadn't continued packing. Letting his eyes linger on the bag for a moment, he sat down and closed his eyes, collecting himself.

He jumped, startled by Jade leaping onto his lap and purring with discontent like the little beast was unhappy with his choice. He sighed and looked to find Emilyn standing in the doorway. How long had she been there? Her eyes looked away, riddled with uncertainty.

"Are you okay?" he asked, and she trudged into the room, plopping down on the bed next to him.

"I know why you want us to leave," she started, a kind of bravery to her words. She was as conflicted as he was and trying to sort through her feelings, and that was a brave thing to do. "But I'm afraid," she confessed. "We've never lived anywhere else. And it's so sudden. I know you said we're going to where Mom grew up, but I don't know anyone there, and ... this doesn't feel right," she said, and finally looked up at him. "What aren't you telling me?" she asked, point-blank, and he would have been proud of how intuitive she was if he wasn't terrified to answer that question.

He sighed. She was brave, and she was smart and too wise for her age. She could handle at least part of the truth. "The people behind the attack," he began carefully. "They're called the architects. I knew in advance they were going to do something, but I didn't know what exactly," he confessed, and that part at least was true. He hadn't known what they were going to do—only what he had been asked to do. "And that's why I wasn't here when the attack happened," he went on, and hated that she had to endure it alone, but she had hidden and handled herself better than he could have ever expected.

"You tried to stop them?" she asked expectantly, and he both loved and hated that was her initial reaction.

He hated it mostly because it provided him the opportunity to manipulate the truth, and he took that chance. "In a way," he replied, nodding. "I tried. Too late." It was a lie born of truths. He hadn't tried to stop them, but he had been far, far too late once he'd decided he wanted to.

"But they stopped," she said. "And they're gone now, right?"

"For now," he said. Another lie. "But they might come after me for what I did. That's why we're leaving. I know it's not fair to you, leaving school and your friends and our lives here," he said regretfully and put his arm around her. "But where we're going, you'll be able to practice tracing to your heart's content—as much as you want! There are whole forests full of sparkers and more food than you can imagine," he promised, placing his hand over Jade's head, who begrudgingly let him pet her between her three ears. She didn't like him, but she liked the attention. He still wondered if the tension he felt from her came from the space between. Could she actually sense the conflict in him? Could she perceive the decision he had made? Did she know he was hiding things from Emilyn? Could carbuncles actually touch the space between?

Jade looked up at him as those thoughts crossed his mind as if reacting to them, and he removed his hand from her head. She gazed up at him for a moment, as if disappointed, and then resumed resting her head on his legs.

"Okay," Emilyn said and seemed to be in slightly lighter spirits, though he wondered if she was forcing them for his benefit. "I know you always do the right thing," she said, and he wished she hadn't. "We're packed and ready." She picked up Jade, who didn't object. "But there better be lots of sparkers!" She smiled, and he managed to do so as well. She carried Jade out of the room, and he took a deep breath. One day, he would explain everything to her and let her decide for herself what kind of man he was. Let her judge his decisions. He simply hoped the one he was making then was the right one for her. More determined about that possibility, he stood up and packed more clothes and belongings. A picture of himself, Jiselyn, and Gavelyn rested on the shelf by the door, and he let his eyes settle on it for a moment. They were smiling, laughing, and happy. It hadn't been any kind of special occasion. Just the three of them enjoying the limited time they'd had together. The picture had been a memory he'd captured from someone else who had been watching them, and he'd used a frame built to conserve illusions. They were hard to come by, and he only had the one. That memory had always felt an appropriate use of it. He left the memory where it rested. Allowing it to accompany him would only be yet another source of guilt, and his heart would plenty cover that.

Finishing packing, he sealed the bag and tossed the strap over one shoulder and the opposite side, securing it. He looked around, bidding his home thanks and farewell, and hoping whoever inherited it would treat it well for it deserved love and warmth for what it had been to him and Emilyn. Joining Emilyn and Jade by the main door, he pulled her close and kissed the top of her head.

"Are you sure you're okay?" he asked before opening the door for the last time, and she bravely nodded, though he wasn't convinced. He got down on a knee and turned her around, helping her get her hair into a ponytail. "It's okay if you're not," he assured her. "I don't expect you to be. This won't be easy for either of us. I appreciate how understanding you're being, but ..." he turned her around and looked her in the eye, smiling at her. "You don't have to be. If you're upset, be upset," he prompted. "You have every right to be." Emilyn met his gaze and provided a determined look.

"I'm okay," she promised and looked down at Jade. "I've got Jade ... and you." She looked back up at him. "And that's all I need."

Zarlyn put his hand to the side of her face and smiled. "You're just like her," he said, seeing Jiselyn all over her face. "Brave to a fault. I am so proud of you." Jade butted into his leg as if pushing him toward the door. Perhaps she wasn't as judging as he'd thought. Emilyn smiled, and picked Jade up, nuzzling her face for a moment. "Someone's ready." He stood up and opened the door.

"She's just excited to have more space to run around and cause trouble," Emilyn said, and Jade purred at that. Zarlyn had no difficulty believing that was precisely what she was excited about, though he still found a glint of awareness behind the little monster's eyes. Awareness but perhaps understanding as well.

"Let's go find her some, then," he said, and Emilyn carried Jade outside. Zarlyn took a final look around their home, nodded in thanks, and then stepped out, closing the door behind him. They had their essentials; they had a plan; and they had time. This would work. This had to work.

Starting through town, they headed to where the two rivers converged and from there toward the edge of the city that opened up toward the massive forest between Unity Falls and Dawn Falls.

That they would traverse on foot, to stay hidden in case any of the architects tried to follow. At Dawn Falls, they would find a boat. It would be far less likely anyone would pay them any mind there. It would take several days to make it there on foot, but they would move slowly. They had food, water, and everything they needed.

The walk through the city was uneventful. People walking around with traveling cloaks and bags were a relatively common occurrence in the city. Traveling between surrounding cities for resource and art trade was the standard. The cities themselves often temporarily employed citizens for such things rather than having their own staff take care of them. Anyone looking at them would likely assume they were simply on route for a delivery or pickup. Or, with Zarlyn's relative fame, that he had been asked to render services to someone in a nearby city. It wouldn't be the first time that had happened, and it also wouldn't be the first time he had used that as a cover to leave without suspicion. The people of the city who often found such things for him to do would be yet another group he was abandoning, though that guilt was somewhat less crippling. He had made peace with the deception he'd crafted as a hero to the people long ago. They had survived and thrived before he'd taken that mantle, and they would do so again long after he left them. The city would likely be better off without him. He had done good, but he had also enabled catastrophe more than once. He did not wish for them to suffer further.

Unity Falls had always been a trusting city. Dawn Falls and Victory Falls had walls around their borders. Actual militaries to speak of. Unity Falls preached a more idealistic, welcoming approach. Perhaps that was what made it so easy for a group like the architects to infiltrate it. Walls and security measures for entering would have made that task far more challenging. Instead, the edge of Unity Falls simply melded into the beginning of the forests beyond, which were in sight when Zarlyn felt a presence in the space between. Instead of stepping into it to meet the eyes that watched him, he stopped and turned around slowly. Atop a nearby building stood a cloaked figure, the mountain silhouetting him. Gavelyn's eyes locked on Zarlyn's.

For a long moment, he considered confronting his friend—explaining his decision. But what he was doing had been Gavelyn's idea. Whatever remained of his friend had reached out and told him to run. He intended to take that advice, and if the shell of his friend tried to stop him, he would run faster. He knew this was a possibility, and he was prepared to fight Gavelyn if it came to that.

Gavelyn's eyes held his usual nothingness, but he also saw a glint of the same thing he'd seen in Jade's eyes. Understanding. Approval? No. But understanding. Zarlyn felt a wash of certainty. Gavelyn was not going to stop him. So, Zarlyn reached out to him in the space between, sending a single message.

Farewell, old friend. May you find your way.

Gavelyn did not acknowledge this, nor did Zarlyn receive a message in return. It was better that way. If Gavelyn tried to convince him to stay, he wasn't certain he would be able to say no. Finally, Gavelyn turned around and walked away. Zarlyn watched even after his friend was out of sight, and he sighed, wishing him well, wishing things could be different. But also thanking him for this chance he was giving him. While his knowledge of their departure was concerning, it was also a hopeful exchange, and Zarlyn was thankful for a little hope.

The Moments That Make Us

Fifteen Years Ago

Zarlyn let the past die, consumed by the fire.

"Everything okay?" Emilyn asked, and Zarlyn turned back around to her. She displayed no indication she had noticed Gavelyn. He nodded, taking a deep breath.

"Just saying goodbye," he answered and took her hand. "C'mon. We've got a lot of walking ahead of us." Stepping out of the city and into the forest, they stuck to the main path until the city was out of sight and then diverged into the forest itself. Zarlyn had grown up traversing these trees. He knew his way around and knew how to get where he wanted to go. He had practiced for hours and hours out there with Gavelyn, and he had shared his first kiss with Jiselyn among those trees. Emilyn preferred it as well. She enjoyed how natural the trees felt compared to the city, though she was fond of their home as well. The forest was a calm place, and that was what she truly liked about it; he surmised as much based on how much time she spent near the mountain, where the rising water exuberated quiet and calm. He suspected she would miss that, but he hoped Keled as a whole could provide a similar experience. From his brief time there, he remembered it being a quiet place.

As they walked, Emilyn let Jade run out ahead. Carbuncles never really needed training due to their supposed connection to the space between. So long as they had formed an attachment to those whose care they were in, they tended to always come back. The fact that Emilyn was a tracer only strengthened their bond, making it easy for them to find one another. He supposed Jade had earned some space to run wild, even if she had quite a lot of it coming her way. Even if that meant she would quickly get tired and one of them would have to carry her.

Emilyn was quiet again, which wasn't necessarily unlike her, but Zarlyn couldn't help but feel like she was doing the same thing he was doing. Not saying everything that probably should have been said. He felt hypocritical in wishing she would open up to him what she was thinking. This massive change had been very sudden, and he almost wanted her to be more upset about it. To scream and shout and hate him. Maybe because that's what he expected children to do—or maybe because that's what he felt he deserved. But he had to remind himself she wasn't a child. She was nearly twelve years of age, and as smart as people twice her age. Whatever was on her mind, he wondered if he could help her otherwise occupy her thoughts.

"Let's stop here," he said after they'd been walking for a few hours. Emilyn had earned a break. It was later in the day, and perhaps they would stay there for the night. It was a very small clearing he had once slept in as a child. They both removed their bags from their backs and took a seat, Zarlyn breathing a little sigh of relief. He wasn't as young as he was last time he'd made a trek like this, and perhaps he'd overestimated his current ability to do so. Emilyn caught onto that and tried to hide the little smirk that crept onto her lips at his exhaustion.

"We'll see if you think it's funny in a day or two," he said, offering her a bar of Kimi. Though her smirk faded, she was quick to snatch it from him, and the crunch from her biting into it seemed louder in the silence between them. "You wanna practice?" he asked, and she shrugged but seemed ready to do so, leaning forward and positioning herself in a more meditative way—the same Gavelyn had used to teach him in the beginning. It had been better to be sitting down during his first attempts. Tracer light wasn't related to any specific part of the body, save maybe the eyes, but it seemed to help the body adjust to its presence bits at a time. Sitting down removed the need for the legs to decide what they should be doing when projecting an illusion. Once she became comfortable with the basics, he would let her stand while practicing. She seemed to understand this and didn't object. She took a deep breath, and the purple light poured over her eyes and swirled around her fingers. While she reached out in front of her to the space between them, the liquid light poured out and coalesced but seemed to have difficulty forming anything. After a moment, it dispersed and retreated back into her fingertips. Emilyn looked frustrated.

"It's okay," Zarlyn encouraged. Truthfully even getting it to try to form an illusion took a degree of skill. "Try again—whenever you're ready."

She sighed and remained silent. The light again danced into the space between the two of them, this time melding into an image that almost looked like a face. A heavily disfigured one. It was quick to tear apart and run back to her fingers, where she let the fight fade away fully. She pulled her legs close and wrapped her arms around them, letting her chin rest on her knees. "Sorry," she said and looked away, and he shook his head.

"Nothing to apologize for," he said and figured suggesting that may have been a mistake. He had wanted to help distract her, but distraction was exactly the issue. She had a lot on her mind and didn't seem as enthused about practicing as she normally had. He just wanted to help her, but he didn't know how. "In fact, I'm the one who should apologize," he said, realizing that the simple word sorry was the one word he hadn't used when he had explained all of this to her. She looked back at him, her frustration slowly being replaced by concern.

"For what?" she asked, and he scoffed at himself.

"Not apologizing," he said and shook his head. "You shouldn't have to be punished for my choices. I'm sorry," he finally said.

"I know."

"No," he replied, firmly. "You don't. And I don't want you to. That's really why we're leaving. So you never have to know. So that you can live a better life. That's all I want for you, I promise."

"I know," she echoed but didn't say anything else.

And somehow, that killed him. She was trusting him. She knew he was hiding things, and she was choosing to trust him. By all the skies, he didn't deserve that trust. "Be angry at me!" he begged. "Please." He found tears escaping his eyes. "Say you want to go back home! Say I'm a terrible father. Say you miss your mother. Say ... anything. Because I can't take this. I'm supposed to be the strong one. I'm supposed to take care of you, and I feel like I'm failing because I don't know what to do with how understanding you are." He paused, finding himself bursting into tears he hadn't known were just beyond the edge, waiting to be cried. He wanted to stop, but the gates had been opened. "I don't know what to do about anything! And I'm sorry. I'm so sorry. You deserve so much better. You are the single most precious treasure in this entire world to me, and you deserve so much better than me, to have to live with my choices," he finally breathed. To have to carry the burden of his legacy. He cried, looking away from her. He had just unloaded onto her—onto his eleven-year-old daughter—all his burdens of being a parent that she should never have had to hear, and yet he had said them. What was wrong with him? He had just preached how he felt like he was failing as a parent and proceeded to do exactly that tenfold. "I'm sorry, Emi. I'm sorry. I shouldn't have said all that," he quickly added. "I ..." He trailed off, no idea what to say. What did he say after that? "I'm sorry," he added, quietly. Where had all that even come from? What did he do now?

So caught up in his breakdown, he hadn't even noticed that she had stood up and walked over to him until she wrapped her arms around his head and pulled him close to her, resting her own on top of his. And he couldn't stop himself from crying into her embrace. Everything he had been holding in flooded out into the open to judge him. Gavelyn, Jiselyn, Emilyn herself, all the guilt he felt. The rage inside him. The lies he had told. The person he had been. No ... the person he still was. That was his greatest failing and greatest deception. He hadn't merely tricked his home and his daughter into believing he was a good person. He had tricked himself. He had never stopped being the person he was before. He had simply ... painted a new picture.

Just like Gavelyn. Only Zarlyn had done it to himself. And somehow that seemed more monstrous a thing.

"I do want to go back home," she finally said, quietly, not letting go of him, as if it were easier to say without looking him in the eye. "I do miss Mom, as much as I can miss someone I don't remember. But I don't have to remember her. I have you. You're not a terrible father. And you don't have to be an amazing one, either. You just have to be mine. And you are. I wouldn't choose another one."

Zarlyn closed his eyes, a pain both wonderful and horrible washing over them. And he leaned into her, eternally grateful for her words even if he felt he didn't deserve them. "I'm supposed to take care of you," he repeated, his voice breaking. "And here you are taking care of me." A chuckle escaped him. "When did you grow up?" he asked, more to himself than her, and then he finally released her. "My most precious treasure," he repeated, finally looking her in the eye, and she smiled. "I love you so much."

"I love you, too," she said and hugged him again, leaning into his shoulder. He held her as tight as he could, so grateful for her. "So, maybe we can take care of each other?" she asked, and he nodded. He wished it wasn't the case. She shouldn't need to be burdened by him or any of his choices, but she was too intuitive. She was going to notice, and she was going to want to help. Because she was her mother's daughter and had an innate desire to help him that she seemed to have inherited from her for better or for worse. He wanted to stop her, but he wasn't certain he could. Precious memories of her emerged across his soul, and he was happy to add this one to that group he hoped would never stop growing. He embraced every single one of them, letting reflections of the sweetest smile he had ever known fill him with a new warmth and determination.

"Deal," he said and released her, proceeding to look around. "I know it's not dark yet, but I say we rest here for the night if that's all right with you?" he asked, and she nodded, looking out into the forest. Reaching out to Jade, Zarlyn guessed. Even as the incandescence of the moment began to fade away, Zarlyn let himself be happy. Just for that moment, he let it in. And he let the stress and worry and ever-present guilt fade away for a single, wonderful moment. To remind himself what he was fighting for her. Why he had made the decision he had made, despite the people he was leaving behind. Because Emilyn was worth it. He would destroy the world if it meant she'd be safe.

And that, perhaps, was why working with Gavelyn had terrified him so much.

***

Zarlyn had always been an intrepid embracer of curiosity. It was one of the few things Gavelyn recalled of his friend. He knew, letting his eyes linger upon the picture of himself, Zarlyn, and Jiselyn, that he had once been as well. That he had once been capable of the emotion present on his own face in the memory. He knew that because there was a tiny part of him that felt pained at Zarlyn choosing to leave the memory behind. He also knew that part of him to be insignificant. Irrelevant. Yet, his eyes seemed unable to look away.

Zarlyn's words had hung over him, a strong something within a vast nothing. He had spoken poetic words about painting a new picture of oneself, and Gavelyn knew with complete certainty that he himself had spoken those words. Believed them. An imprint of them existed somewhere inside him. He had no recollection of them, however—no indication where they had come from or why he had said them. Much like the memory he held in his hand. It wasn't something he could find in his own memory, yet it radiated a familiarity he was uncertain what to do with. He could dig, he knew. But digging was dangerous. He was aware enough of what had been done to him to know that. Furthermore, he didn't wish to. Unearthing what fragments of his soul defied their end would lead only to pain. He had no place for pain. And that was perhaps why he had sent Zarlyn away. Some part of him wished to spare his friend from pain. The pain he would relive all over again upon the inevitable discovery that Jiselyn had never once been in his custody.

"You lament his betrayal," Valel stated, manifesting across the room from him. Her presence didn't surprise him, nor did he feel the need to acknowledge it. "Tell me, do you feel pain once more?"

"No," Gavelyn said, blankly. "Merely echoes."

"Echoes have an origin," she said, appearing next to him. "Yours is meant to be gone." He tried to look at her, but he could not. The distortion tore into his eyes, and he looked away. "Perhaps that origin is connected to the choice you made today." She knew.

He wasn't surprised that she knew. It was merely a confirmation of what he suspected came next. "Perhaps," he confessed. "It was a moment of weakness."

"The moments that make us are often labeled as such," she replied, her voice not expressing disappointment or approval. "I do not fault you for your choice."

"But you cannot let me make it again," he stated, sitting down on the bed. "I understand."

"I know you do," she said, almost fondly. "Are you prepared?" she asked, and he nodded, though what was about to happen was not something one need prepare for. It simply was. He accepted that. Accepted her and the role he had to play. He didn't resist when she delved into his soul. He found himself in the space between, sitting on his knees in the nothingness. Submitted. Valel was ahead, amidst his memories. Further inside his soul than he was. He watched, but it would do him no good to know what she was changing or removing. He would only remember what she wanted him to remember. So, instead, he embraced the space between, letting the calm consume him fully while Valel worked. While she painted yet another picture of him, layered over the hundreds and hundreds that had come before. Somewhere, the original picture remained, faded beyond recognition. He had no need of it. He was what she needed him to be. He had accepted that long ago.

He found himself back in Zarlyn's home, the memory of the two of them and Jiselyn still in his hands. He rose, and let the frame slip from his fingertips. It shattered as it hit the floor, and the tracer light sealed within escaped, slithering into the air and fading away after so long in captivity. The memory faded, and Gavelyn watched the shattered, empty frame.

Once more, he felt nothing.

Through The Cracks of a Severed Soul

When the ideals that form the foundation upon which a person is made are shifted, the soul becomes an indecisive battleground as that foundation struggles to remain in place. Tracers call the sensation a split. Everyone else simply calls it shattering.

Emilyn struggled to imagine the shift happening inside Cidelyn as his soul wrestled with the idea that he was simply a victim, chosen to be the vessel of a power he couldn't even touch. She would have felt meaningless. Breath on a mirror, slowly fading away to give way to something else. Her heart broke for him. She could see that his own had sunk. All his life, he had wanted to know what he was, thinking maybe there was a purpose. That he could do something. Like he had done when he had saved her. But Emilyn could only guess he was feeling irrelevant instead. There was anger in his eyes. She understood that. Someone had done this to him. Taken away his life and his choice and his happiness and for what? The anger threatened to shatter him into pieces, and she wanted to help hold him together, but she found herself afraid she might get burned if she tried.

"Fascinating," Forest muttered, completely indifferent to or unaware of Cidelyn's cracked foundation. "Sister ... how did you manage this on your own?" he asked himself, his eyes locked on the moon. "To grant your power to the people of this world? And to what end? What do you stand to gain from this?" His voice was cold and calculating, intermixed with morbid fascination. They were good questions. Emilyn just wished he'd kept them to himself. Cidelyn remained silent, and no one seemed sure what to do with that. Finally, he closed his eyes and let out a long breath.

"Your sister did this to me?" Cidelyn asked calmly. The anger he'd seemed to be drowning in a moment ago wasn't present. He'd been angry before. Likely many times. He was probably decent at managing it. Forest nodded.

"She is the only one capable," he mused. "The power of illusions, the very nature of what tracer light is ... it stems from her. She is the Artist. Her role in creation was that of giving life to what I had designed, what my brother had crafted. Transitioning something dull into something vivid. The power you all have access to is merely an extension of her own."

"So, she creates tracer light," Kyshel began. "Then, she presumably creates the architects, whose name cannot be a coincidence," she went on, gesturing to Forest. "No offense. Then, she lures you into Unity Falls and traps everyone inside?" She had left out something Emilyn didn't feel brave enough to add to the conversation. It was her that had brought Forest into the city. Her lack of a connection to the strings. Information she still wasn't sure what to do with. Perhaps she understood what Cidelyn was feeling more than she knew. The anger and frustration would come in waves, giving way to an intense need to know more. To rebuild the foundation before it collapsed completely. "We're assuming she's responsible for the barrier, right?" Kyshel asked, and Cidelyn perked up at that.

"That barrier ..." His voice drifted as he recalled something. "When we were close to it, before you jumped on the boat," he said, looking to Emilyn. "I felt drawn to it. Connected, almost. As if ..."

"As if you stemmed from the same source," said Forest, finishing the thought. "Yes. If the Artist is responsible for the moon and the barrier, that would make sense. It's the same as when you connect to tracers, though the barrier being a more direct creation is likely what provided that connection you felt. You are aspects of the same origin."

"Are we sure the barrier is meant to trap us?" Emilyn asked, and Kyshel narrowed her eyes.

"What else could it be for?" she asked, and Emilyn shrugged.

"That's the question," she replied. "Because if it's meant to trap us, it failed." She looked to Forest. "We got out already." They had been to space. Well beyond the barrier's radius.

"Correct," Forest stated and adopted a reflective expression as he approached the window and let his eyes settle on the barrier blanketing the city. "If not a trap, then what could it be?"

It was an ominous question, and one no one had any idea where to begin to find the answer. There were so many pieces to the puzzle, and no two of them seemed to fit together at all.

"We need more information," Cidelyn said, and everyone seemed to concur. "The only way to get it may just be to play her game—see what happens next."

"I fear what that may be," Forest stated, and Kyshel scoffed.

"You and us all," she sighed, and then a knock on the door drew all their attention. Yomalyn's face manifested as the door slowly creaked open.

"We come bearing sustenance," he said, holding up a few bags of rations and bottles of water while gesturing to Jacquelyn, who held much the same. "You guys have been in here for a while. Unraveled the mysteries of the universe yet?" he asked as he distributed the water. Emilyn hadn't realized how thirsty she was, and the moment that bottle was in her hands, she was quick to down the whole thing. Yomalyn raised his eyebrows. "I'll take that as a no."

"Distract us," Kyshel said, opening a bag of rations as everyone sat down on the floor. "How are things out there?"

"Deteriorating," Jacquelyn said. "Everyone's staying calm, but it's tense." Emilyn sent her and Yomalyn both what she hoped was a reassuring smile.

"You guys have done an incredible job keeping the peace," she said, and Jacquelyn seemed to appreciate that.

"Not well enough," Yomalyn said spitefully, though it was directed primarily at himself. "We've lost too many. But we can't stop them from trying to go outside."

"You take away their choice, you lose them all," Kyshel said through her food. "You're doing the best you can."

"Gavelyn seems to be employing a siege tactic," Forest chimed in. "It is unfortunate, but all he needs do is wait."

Yomalyn sighed, nodding. "We'll run out of supplies eventually," he agreed and looked around at everyone. "Please tell me we'll be able to do something before then?"

"If it comes to that," Emilyn replied, glancing back at the dampeners and her father. She wished on every star in the sky that she could talk to him. "All we can do is turn off the dampeners and hope for the best."

"Let's hope a battle isn't the only choice," Cidelyn chimed in, and Emilyn agreed, happy to hear a little optimism in his voice. They both needed it.

"It won't be a battle," Yomalyn replied. "It'll be a massacre."

"What?" Kyshel asked, in jest. "The Gallery can't handle the Architects?"

"Hey," Yomalyn replied. "I thought that name was rather inspired."

"I like it," Jacquelyn said, smiling. "I think the people need something to rally behind. Unity goes a long way."

"The name of your city would seem to suggest the opposite," Forest replied, and Kyshel sighed.

"We're trying to be positive here."

"I meant no offense. The Gallery is a rather fitting name. The citizens below rallying together under its banner is a sight to behold, I am certain. I fail to see, however, how unity will prevent the massacre Yomalyn referred to a moment ago."

"It might not," Yomalyn agreed. "But a little connection can make us all just a little braver, don't you think?"

"Isn't connection your whole thing?" Kyshel asked Forest.

"Strings are ... my whole thing," Forest replied, though the words seemed to stumble past his lips, and Kyshel chuckled. "I fail to see what was humorous. We are discussing a precarious subject."

"Sure," Yomalyn replied. "But levity keeps us breathing a little easier," he said, and Jacquelyn nodded, smiling.

"It's nice to have friends in dark times," she said, meeting everyone's eyes. "That makes breathing a little easier."

"Are you all struggling to breathe?" Forest asked, and Yomalyn raised his bottle of water, ignoring him.

"To the Gallery," he toasted, shrugging. "May not have had the greatest start but it brought us all together." Kyshel and Jacquelyn raised their bottles, and after a moment, Cidelyn did as well.

Forest didn't have a bottle, so all eyes fell on Emilyn. She didn't think what had begun at her gallery warranted any kind of celebration, but looking around at all of them, she found understanding. Prior to that night, she'd had one friend. Now she had several. And despite the darkness closing in on them, that felt good. So, she raised her bottle. "To friends," she amended, and everyone seemed to accept that. Kyshel then began questioning when Yomalyn and Jacquelyn were going to acknowledge that they worked well together because they liked each other, so Emilyn decided to try and talk to Cidelyn instead. He seemed distant from even himself. When he saw her looking at him, he seemed afraid. He stood up and headed toward a corner of the room away from everyone else. He was used to isolation. Maybe that familiarity would help. She stood up to join him regardless, but Forest manifested next to her.

"Might you have a moment to speak?" he inquired, and she looked toward Cidelyn. She wanted to help. But he wasn't the only one that was afraid. Maybe her desire to help was more selfish than altruistic. Because she was failing to cope, herself. Acknowledging that, she sighed and nodded to Forest.

"Sure. Lead the way."

He headed toward what was once the wall-encompassing window and clasped his hands behind his back. Looking out into the sky, he found that night had set in. It was difficult to tell inside the barrier, but the light beyond it seemed dimmer. It came through in cracks that weren't actually cracks, just parts of the barrier where the purple-pink color was less vibrant. It seemed to almost flow along the barrier, brightening different parts of it at different times. Almost like it were alive. Gazing at it, she could almost feel what Cidelyn had described earlier. A connection. The Artist had done something to her as well. They were of the same origin, the three of them. She wanted to explain that to Cidelyn, but she lacked the words to try.

"I find myself struggling with something of an unusual sensation," Forest admitted, and she followed his gaze down to the architects gathered in force outside the spire's entrance. "Their name should not bother me. Yet, I find that it does, and I am uncertain as to why."

"Because it's your name," she replied, understanding. "Your sister gave it to them. And you don't know why," she guessed. "That hurts." Someone he cared for associating him with people he viewed as malicious. That sent a very clear message, and it seemed one he didn't know what to do with it. "When was the last time you saw her?"

"The day I killed our brother," he lamented. "She arrived shortly after. I can only assume that is why she associates my name with the likes of murderers." He paused. "Perhaps I do as well. Perhaps that is what burns inside me."

"Maybe you need a new name, then?" Emilyn suggested. There was power in names—in titles. Meanings and belongings and pathways that led to the foundation of a person, even the one who built the foundations of the universe. Those were the things one would find when peering through the cracks of a severed soul. She knew it from how many times she helped Kyshel through a split ... knew it from when she had very nearly split herself. "And I'm not sure Forest will cut it."

He narrowed his eyes at her. "I do not see any fault in it," he replied. "It eliminates the confusion that may stem from referring to me as the Architect."

"True, but the point isn't to help others see you more clearly. You need a name that is yours. That tells you everything you need to know about who you are and you want to be." His creators had deemed him the Architect, and he associated fear and anguish with them. She had felt that in his memories. As long as he used the name they'd given him, he would associate those things with himself as well.

"I see," he replied, and he seemed to actually understand what she was going for. "A name that is mine ... what would you suggest?" It didn't escape Emilyn that in asking her to provide a name, he was associating her with trust.

"Hmm ..." She thought on it and then smiled. "Arc." It was simple and encompassed who he wanted to be without disregarding who he had been prior to that moment. It seemed fitting.

"Arc ..." He let the name linger in the air for a moment and then returned her smile. "That ... feels correct."

"But do you like it?" she asked, and he seemed uncertain why that would need to be a deciding factor.

Even so, he tilted his head toward her in agreement. "I ... believe I do," he replied, and she smiled. "Thank you, Emilyn."

"You're welcome, Arc." He seemed to embrace it fully in that moment, and she was happy for him. She wished she could alter her own identity so easily.

"Let this be a new beginning," he stated, offering his hand to her. "I shall endeavor to do better from this moment on, so as to earn the name you have provided me."

She took his hand and nodded. A new beginning. "In the spirit of new beginnings," she said, releasing him. "Can I make another suggestion?"

His curiosity seemed to pique. "Of course."

"Earlier, when you figured out what Cidelyn is," she began, for lack of more fitting words. "You came across as kinda ... excited."

He nodded. "It is fascinating. I wish to understand how the Artist brought that into creation. In understanding, I may be able to keep my word and help separate him from the moon."

"Fair," Emilyn replied. "And noble. Well-intentioned, we know. But maybe scale back the joy a little, at least externally? For him, I doubt it's such a fascinating thing."

Understanding seemed to dawn on his face, and he looked regretful. “I have offended him,” he resolved. “I should apologize.”

“Yeah,” she replied quickly. “But before you do that, maybe give him a little space? Let his thoughts settle,” she advised and realized she had very nearly not followed her own suggestion. Not that it would have hurt him, per se, but something like that ... it wasn’t her place to tell him how he should feel about it. She simply wanted to make sure he knew she was there if he needed someone. She was pretty certain he knew that. It was a fine line to walk, and it was one she had always struggled with. Knowing not just the right things to say to people but the right time to say them.

“I see,” Arc replied. “I suppose I can take this moment to apologize to you, then, for the same insensitivity regarding your father.” She hadn’t expected that but pursed her lips together and nodded in thanks.

“I came to terms with his condition a long time ago,” she said, glancing at Zarlyn in the center of the room. “My choice to let go or hold on to him was taken away. But even if it hadn’t been, I’m not certain anything would be different,” she confessed. He was the only family she had. They had promised a long time ago to take care of each other. She intended to do that. Letting go of him was something that was simply not in her power.

“I wish to help him as well,” Arc stated, and she looked back at him. “If it is within my power. I cannot simply stitch his soul back together as I did yours. The Artist is close, and both our powers are limited when in proximity. Even if she were not, I fear he has stagnated in his condition for too long to recover any way other than naturally.”

“So I’ve been told,” Emilyn lamented, and then thought on his words, narrowing her eyes. “How close is the Artist?”

“Not what you are thinking,” he clarified. “For us, opposite ends of your world would be considered proximity. Though I am confident she is within the city, she would not orchestrate all of this only to not be present for whatever outcome she is seeking.”

"Have you thought about what you're going to do if we find her?" she asked, and uncertainty seemed to blanket him.

"It may very well depend on what that outcome she seeks is and her intentions behind it. My intent at the moment is simply to uncover precisely what that entails."

"And me?" Emilyn asked, looking between his eyes. His words still haunted her. She was disconnected from the very things that tied the universe together. And that was terrifying. "Any idea where I fall into that?"

Arc shook his head. "None, I am afraid. Whatever it is my sister has done to you, it has rendered you one of a kind, a severed soul in a universe forever bound together by billions of souls. Alive despite lacking the very thing needed to be. I must admit that I do find the possibilities of that intriguing." Emilyn didn't respond to that. She simply gazed out the window, and let his words sink in. She knew what he was saying, but the more she thought on them, the lonelier she felt. "You are quiet. Have I been insensitive again?" he asked, and she managed a weak smile, shaking her head.

"No, just thinking," she assured him. "I'm glad you're curious. Curiosity might just get us answers. It's a quality I've been lacking lately. I was always curious as a kid—even as an adult. But something's changed. I've never been scared to learn about the world around me or the one inside of me. Until the last few days. I want to know. But my drive to find out isn't there," she explained, fearing something had broken inside her. That a part of her foundation had already collapsed. "From the moment I made my first illusion, I always wanted to know more. There's a longing, always there, in the back of my mind. Pointing me toward a certain point in the sky," she said and pointed toward the sky. Even through the barrier, she knew exactly where it was. Where it had always been. "Right there. Or at least, in that direction. I don't know what's there. But the sky is the most unknown thing on all of Seranno. There's so much out there we don't know, but we can. I know we can. My first illusion was a string linking two stars together, because if they can connect with each other, then we can connect with them," she explained, thinking about her father and smiling at the memory. String the stars. "I still feel that longing. But it's about all I seem to feel." She looked to Arc, who had stepped back, his eyes throwing daggers of concern in her direction. "What?" asked Emilyn.

"Do all tracers feel that?" he asked flatly, intensity weaving itself between every syllable in his voice.

"As far as I know, yeah," she replied, and he grabbed either of her arms, looking into her eyes with deathly alarm. "It is important that you are certain," he stated, and she became afraid. He seemed to shift into someone else entirely. Gone was the socially lacking entity who was trying to help. He was the Architect again.

"I don't know! Yes, I'm certain," she exclaimed, freeing herself from his tightening grip, and getting the attention of everyone in the room. "Why?"

"What's going on?" Kyshel asked, quick to join them and keeping her eyes on Arc. "Was he hurting you?"

"Do you feel that as well?" he asked her. "Now that your abilities are present, do you feel drawn toward a certain point in the sky?" Kyshel looked toward Emilyn, who just shook her head in confusion. And then Kyshel looked out the window and pointed to the exact same spot Emilyn had just a moment ago. Arc looked taken aback. His eyes widened, and he seemed to scramble toward Jacquelyn, who whimpered a little. "And you?" he demanded of her, dragging her toward the window.

"Hey!" Yomalyn grabbed Arc's arm, stopping them. "What's your problem?"

"Answer the question," Arc demanded, and Jacquelyn didn't say anything, but her eyes spoke volumes as she looked upon the exact same location in the sky. Arc released her and ran his hands through his hair, something unsettling swirling in the air around him. That feeling of dissonance blanketed him again.

Yomalyn held Jacquelyn, who looked at Emilyn and Kyshel. "What's wrong with him?"

Emilyn shook her head. "I have no idea."

"You've figured something out," Cidelyn said, approaching Arc directly, the only one not keeping their distance. "What is it?"

Arc looked up, seeming to regain his focus and clarity when he looked at Cidelyn. Cidelyn, to his credit, didn't seem afraid.

"Forgive me," Arc said, though Emilyn got the distinct impression that apology was not the one she had discussed with him moments prior. And then Cidelyn fell to his knees, reaching his hands to his head as pure agony spread across his face and he let out the most vulnerable scream Emilyn had ever heard.

From Nothing To Something

The space between.

He was in the space between.

He could breathe again.

He was heaving air in and out. He was on his hands and knees despite the space between not having any discernible surface on which to brace himself. He had been on fire. Every corner of his soul set ablaze all at once.

"I am sorry," came Forest's voice. "If what Emilyn said is true, then the situation is far direr than I realized. I did fully intend to keep my promise to you, but I fear the ability to safely separate you from your burden may come too late. I truly do not know what will happen, but I must try. The Artist cannot be allowed to find what she is looking for."

A crippling weight forced Cidelyn down onto his stomach as if a single ember had suddenly and completely expanded into an entire universe of fire and been given form. Gravity. It was crushing him. It was the most excruciating thing he had ever felt. A hand was reaching into his very soul, taking hold of something, and pulling. Was this what it felt like to split? Like his very soul was being torn from him?

He had spent his entire life living in fear. Isolation, loneliness, and fear. And yet he had never felt a greater terror than he did in that moment. Something primal that wasn't supposed to even be acknowledged, let alone touched or removed, was being torn out of him. All he could do was scream. Except he couldn't even do that. He had no control, no power, and no body. Nothing. He was nothing. Completely and utterly nothing.

The space between was gone. Forest was gone. He was gone. There was nothing and everything and nothing. All that remained were his thoughts, but where were they even coming from? He had no form. He had no identity. No memory. No personality. He was just ... words. Floating in an ocean of absolute nothingness.

He could feel his memories dying. He tried to reach out before they were gone. To Emilyn. She had been so easy to connect with. She was a warm presence. The safest he had ever felt had been with her and he needed that more than anything, more than anything. He would have cried her name if he could. But he was nothing.

Until he was something.

Light. Purple light. It found him in the dark, a hand offering him salvation. He did not hesitate to take it. It brought everything back. His name, his memories, his entire life. He lived every moment again in that single moment.

"Hello brother," a female voice manifested in his ears as his body acknowledged the space between once again. He slowly managed to look up, finding a distorted figure ahead of him. He couldn't tell if the distortion was his own blurred vision or the figure herself. She stood opposite where Forest had been, last he knew. "Forgive my interference, but this is a murder I cannot allow you to commit." She did not seem to acknowledge Cidelyn, merely referencing him.

"Where are you?" Forest demanded, desperation tinging his voice.

"Somewhere I can see you flare and fade as you stumble around in the dark." She sounded amused. "Watching through the cracks of a severed soul."

"What is all this about?" Forest asked, and she sighed.

"Did you not piece that together a moment ago?" she replied and finally glanced down at Cidelyn. "Unfortunate you chose to immediately betray those you have grown to call friends. Fortunate, however, that they will serve as an adequate distraction until the final piece falls into place."

The governor's office swirled into form around him, and Emilyn's eyes were opposite his, filling the air above him. There were tears at their edges, and relief seemed to overcome her as his eyes opened. Had she thought he was dead? Had he been dead? He didn't have either answer. Emilyn, Kyshel, and the others were all speaking but he couldn't hear them. His senses were faded. Their words were as distorted as the Artist had been in the space between, but things were slowly returning.

Forest. Where was Forest?

He tried to sit up, but the others didn't seem to let him. His head was propped up on Emilyn's legs, and Kyshel was on one side while Yomalyn and Jacquelyn were on the other.

"You're okay," Emilyn said through tears that fell from her eyes onto his face, her voice breaking, and despite everything else, he couldn't help but smile, happy that hers was the first voice he heard upon his senses returning.

"I'm okay," he promised, though he wasn't actually certain about that. It didn't matter in that moment, though. She had worried about him. No one had ever worried about him. Just like when he had found her before, she was happy to see him. And that was something indescribably wonderful to him.

She looked toward Kyshel, her smile fading back into worry again, and he managed to sit up. Kyshel had fallen backward, shaking her head and looking torn. No, split. She was splitting.

Emilyn rushed over to her, panicking. She shouldn't be splitting. So long as her powers had returned, she shouldn't be. Actually, he wasn't sure about that all. But it wasn't normal, even for her. That he was certain of. The Artist's words hung in his mind as he watched Kyshel.

An adequate distraction.

Cidelyn looked behind him. Forest, on the floor, understanding the gravity of his mistake. Apparently, even the architect of the universe was prone to panic.

"Kyshel! Kyshel!" Emilyn cried, holding her friend, and Cidelyn realized she couldn't dive in to help Kyshel like she normally did. She was afraid. She was so afraid. Forest was frozen. Yomalyn and Jacquelyn didn't know what to do. But he did. An image of everyone raising the bottles in toast flashed across his mind, and it gave him the strength to rise. They had lost Crysalyn and Diselyn and Adalyn and the city and so many people belonging to it. He became resolute in a singular desire.

Not one more.

The Consequences of a Heartless Heart

The human heart was a mystery to Cidelyn. The ability to form relationships had been denied to him until recently, and while he still wrestled with the idea that that was, in part, his own doing, he maintained a similar struggle with the idea of doing that which had been denied him. He longed for the level of care present in those around him, for the heart that practically poured out of Emilyn, even if he wouldn't know what to do with it. He had touched only the surface of what others knew intimately, and in that moment, as Emilyn held Kyshel in her arms, begging for her to open her eyes, he understood how close he was to the other end of the spectrum. He was witnessing the consequences of a heartless heart as Valel punished Forest. He didn't want to reach that point of causing others pain, intentional or otherwise. So, in that moment, he understood one crucial point: he could help. Since he could, he would. Because the anguish playing havoc with Emilyn's heart was, for reasons his own heart couldn't explain, something he couldn't bear to see. She had lost her father. They had lost Crysalyn, Diselyn, Adalyn, and more. Now, her best friend, and someone he had grown to care for as well. He was not going to sit by.

He approached Emilyn and put a hand on her shoulder. He had been cold to her only moments ago, stepping away to isolate himself because that was all he'd known. It was the most uncomfortable comfort zone he had, and he'd clung to it despite longing for anything but that. No more.

"I can't reach her," Emilyn cried, her voice breaking as Kyshel sat lifeless in her arms. She wasn't dead. She was breathing. Her heart was beating. But Emilyn had always been the one to help her through a split. Not being able to do so was splitting her own soul. "I can't reach her."

"Get her inside the dampener circle with your father," Cidelyn suggested, though his words came out more forcefully than intended. "You'll have your powers back and hers will be gone, just like things were every time she split. Maybe you'll be able to reach her?" He had no idea if that would work. But it was the only idea he had. Emilyn seemed to follow his logic, not wasting a moment. She stood and hoisted Kyshel up in her arms, unintentionally ignoring Yomalyn's attempt to help, and carried her in between the dampeners. Gently propping her on the floor against Zarlyn's bed, Jacquelyn rushed in, likely thinking she may be able to help. Perhaps she could.

"What the hell happened?" Yomalyn asked, and Cidelyn looked over at him, and then let his eyes drift past his friend over to Forest, wide-eyed and frozen on the floor. He looked horrified. But he wasn't looking at Kyshel, Emilyn, or Cidelyn. His eyes settled on nothing, and Cidelyn knew he was thinking of The Artist, and what had transpired in the space between. Not on what he had just done, or the consequences. Yomalyn followed his gaze, and then looked back to Cidelyn. "What did he do? Talk to me!"

Realizing he was being just as vague and silent, Cidelyn looked to Yomalyn. "He tried to sever me from the moon." He gestured to the little spherical rock floating beside his head opposite Yomalyn. "The Artist wouldn't let him." He looked to Kyshel. "She fought back. Said Forest needed a distraction." Yomalyn gulped, uncertain what to do with that information.

"Okay," he mumbled in disbelief or confusion or both. "But we can save her, right?" he asked, desperation creaking in the cracks between his words.

Cidelyn shrugged. "I have no idea," he lamented. "But we're going to try." He stepped into the space between the dampeners to join the others and immediately felt heavier. He was back to normal within the pentagon as well, and that meant his fatigued state would start to settle back in.

Emilyn had her eyes closed, attempting to dive into Kyshel's soul. Yomalyn sat next to Jacquelyn and gave her arm a reassuring squeeze while Jacquelyn herself looked as though she was struggling to keep her composure. After a moment, Emilyn opened her eyes and met Cidelyn's. A single expression had never conveyed so much heartache.

"You still can't reach her?" Yomalyn asked, and Emilyn slowly shook her head.

"Something's blocking me!" she said, defeated. "I can't cross the bridge."

"Bridge?" Yomalyn asked, but Cidelyn knew what she meant. In the space between, something was stopping her from accessing Kyshel's soul. She couldn't save her. She was alive, but she was lost. Just like Zarlyn. Jacquelyn hurried to Emilyn's side and wrapped her arms around her, burying her face in her shoulder, her hands meeting at Emilyn's other shoulder. Yomalyn came to Emilyn's other side, and silently took one of her hands while resting his eyes on Kyshel, allowing a tear to escape. Cidelyn felt like his place should be with them. That had never been his role, as much as he wanted it to be. Instead, he kept with the promise he'd made to himself moments ago to help, and looked back to Forest, still silently staring into an empty void. He had caused this. His sister had done this. He could undo it. With a fierce determination to his step fueled by a fire he'd never known, Cidelyn quickly approached Forest.

"I know you can hear me," Cidelyn said, his voice cold. "So whatever you're thinking, forget it. Stand up, and fix this!" he demanded, but Forest didn't move or acknowledge his presence. Cidelyn sat down in front of him, meeting his eyes directly. And yet, somehow, it still felt as though Forest wasn't looking at him. "Whatever she did, she did because of you. I don't care about what you tried to do to me," Cidelyn said, surprised to find that was the truth. That if Forest had succeeded in tearing the moon from him and if that had killed him ... he didn't care. His sentence would be complete. His friends would be safe. "I care that you keep your promise. You promised you'd help me, and my friends are hurting. So, get up and do something about it. You're the only one who can."

Forest's eyes seemed to move and meet Cidelyn's, despite not moving in the slightest. He seemed indifferent to Cidelyn's words. All but one, at least.

"Promise?" he asked, and Cidelyn nodded.

"The promise you made. Does that mean nothing to you?" he asked, and Forest looked away.

"It was so obvious," he mumbled. "All this time ... how could I have missed it?"

"Missed what?" Cidelyn asked, and Forest looked to him again.

"What she is searching for," he replied as if that explained anything whatsoever.

"Think about that later," Cidelyn insisted, gesturing to Kyshel. "Help her," he instructed, but Forest remained in place. "Now!" The ferocity of his voice seemed to finally get Forest's attention, who provided a puzzled expression.

"You are angry," he stated. "Yet, you claim a lack of care for what I attempted to do to you."

"I'm angry that you, the supposed crafter of the universe, didn't think through the consequences of your actions," Cidelyn stated, and wondered if he was angry that Forest had failed.

"Architect," Forest stressed. "The Crafter was my brother, who I ..." He trailed off, his eyes, finally finding Kyshel. "It is happening again. Once again, I am a bringer of death. Only this time, it truly was by my own hand."

"She's not dead," Cidelyn replied. "She's splitting. And you can help her like you did Emilyn before. You don't need to be the Architect or a bringer of death. You just need to be—"

"Arc," he cut in. "My name is Arc."

Cidelyn returned his earlier puzzled expression, but he had no time to delve into it. "Okay, Arc," he calmed his voice. "Please. Will you help Kyshel?" Something seemed to change in Arc's eyes.

An understanding, perhaps, that he had opportunities to address the guilt he felt instead of wallowing in it. He stood up and approached Emilyn, Kyshel, Yomalyn, and Jacquelyn.

Upon seeing him, Emilyn adopted a protective posture over Kyshel, but Cidelyn stepped forward and nodded to her. Trusting him, she kept her eyes on Arc but didn't try to stop him.

"I'm linking myself with her," Arc explained. "Just as I did with you," he said to Emilyn. "I will attempt to stitch her back together in much the same ..." he drifted off, a worried expression settling on his face. "I cannot reach her. She is blocking me."

"I couldn't reach her either," Emilyn said, her voice the smallest Cidelyn had ever heard her.

"Not Kyshel," Arc clarified. "The Artist. She is preventing our strings from intertwining."

"The Artist?" Emilyn asked and looked to Cidelyn. "She's here?"

"She was in the space between," Cidelyn began, but Arc held up a hand.

"Please." He gave Cidelyn a look of both gratitude and pleading. "You were correct. What has transpired is because of my actions. Allow me to explain." Cidelyn nodded, and took a step away from him, closer to Emilyn, who stood up, leaving Kyshel with Jacquelyn and Yomalyn. She folded her arms and focused on Arc. "I attempted to sever Cidelyn from the moon, as doing so would allow me to destroy it and as such rid Seranno of tracer light. It is clearly a necessity of the Artist's plan, a claim which she proved when she interfered, preventing me from completing the act. At which point she enacted retribution for my actions," he finished, with a look to Kyshel. "I made a rash decision," he lamented. "This is the consequence."

"So, she did this to Kyshel?" Emilyn asked, glaring at him. "Because of you?" she asked and shook her head. "I don't get it. Why did you suddenly decide to try to kill Cidelyn?" She laced the words with venom, and Cidelyn couldn't blame her. Truly, he supported her, but he also hoped she would realize that her anger would accomplish little.

"When you informed me of your longing for a certain point in the stars—that all tracers feel this desire, even subtly—I understood what the Artist hopes to gain from this. It is something she must not be allowed to achieve," Arc explained, and Emilyn watched him, waiting for him to elaborate. He did not.

"Are you gonna tell us what that this?" Yomalyn asked from behind Emilyn, breaking the tense silence.

Arc kept his eyes on Emilyn. "I cannot. It is not something that can simply be told."

Emilyn, keeping her arms folded and her expression uncharacteristically cold, stepped closer to Arc. While looking up at him, she looked taller as a fire seemed to burn around her.

"I don't care what you are," she said, her voice a ferocious calm. She was not afraid of him, intimidated by him, or challenged by him. Quite the opposite. She was challenging him. "I don't care what you did," she went on. "The two people I love the most in this whole screwed up world are behind me in comas because of you and your sister. And I can't reach them," she stressed, tears forming in her eyes. "DON'T YOU UNDERSTAND THAT?" she screamed at him. "I can't reach them!" she cried. "So, I swear on all the strings and all the stars in all the skies, if you don't start telling us everything, your sister will be the least of your problems."

"Emilyn," Cidelyn said, trying to take her hand, but she stepped closer to Forest, who remained calm.

"You said it yourself," she continued. "I am not bound to your strings. I'm part of her plan. Gavelyn said my father is, too. She needs us both, whereas you seem perfectly content to take away another person I care about just to stop her from doing something supposedly bad that you won't even tell us." She paused, and it took Cidelyn longer than it perhaps should have to realize she was referring to him. "So, you tell me, Architect, why I should continue to trust you at all?"

Arc watched her for a long moment, and Cidelyn wished he could sense either of their thoughts. He stood in between them, and yet he found himself unable to act as the bridge they needed.

"I opened myself to you in a way I have not with anyone prior, nor am I likely to ever do so again," Arc replied, and Cidelyn guessed he was referring to their time in space. "You saw me, whatever me there is to be seen. And you chose to trust me then. Please understand that while the Artist very well may require you and your father to achieve her goals, she will ultimately sacrifice you both, alongside your world, to achieve her ends. That is the scale of what we face. And while I may not be able to elaborate further at this time, I vow to do so when I fully understand myself. There are pieces missing, but now that I know her end goal, I can begin to uncover them." Emilyn shook her head, and Cidelyn could see she wanted to trust him, but couldn't bring herself to.

"And we're just supposed to believe you?" she asked.

"Believe what you have witnessed," Arc replied, meeting her challenge. "The Artist does not care for you."

"And you do?" she asked, and he did not reply for a long moment. He seemed taken aback by the words, simple as they were. In Cidelyn's experience, it was often the simplicity of something that could carry the most complex of implications.

"I thought I had proven as much," he replied, his voice getting smaller.

"So did I," she said, the hostility fading from her voice, making way for grief. "I guess we were both wrong." She turned away, returning to her place next to Kyshel. Arc's eyes shifted to Cidelyn, who didn't know how to feel. He understood them both. He had stood by them both. Saved and been saved by them both. It was a position he thought he'd never find himself in. Ultimately, however, he found himself reiterating what end of the spectrum of hearts he wanted to make his way toward. He didn't want to find himself in the position Arc had been in. Not because he cared more for Emilyn, but because her words had helped him answer a question he had posed to himself mere moments ago. Had he been angry that Forest had failed? No, he had been angry that Forest had tried.

For the first time in his entire life, he truly wanted to live.

He had told Arc he didn't care that he had tried, but that had been a lie. To Arc and to himself. He did care. He cared more than he was even capable of realizing. That was the consequence of his heartless heart.

Meeting Arc's gaze, Cidelyn sent him as understanding of a look as he could muster and then turned to join Emilyn and the others next to Kyshel. Arc remained where he stood, watching them all. Sitting down next to Emilyn, Cidelyn took her hand in both of his, and she extended him a grateful smile covered by tears before she broke and couldn't hold them back any longer. No one said anything to her, just let her cry.

"She's just like him," Emilyn finally said, and Cidelyn's eyes fell to Zarlyn. "I can't feel her. I can't help her. And I need her. I need them both. They're my family."

"We are, too," Jacquelyn said, leaning on Emilyn's other side and hugging her arm. "We're here for you."

"We're gonna find a way to get them back," Yomalyn said, his voice saddened but determined. "Promise."

"I'm about done with promises," Emilyn said, her voice broken. "All they ever seem to do is hurt."

"How about a deal, then?" Cidelyn proposed, and Emilyn looked to him, as did Yomalyn and Jacquelyn. "We take care of each other," he stated, firmly. "No matter what happens. We take care of each other."

Jacquelyn managed a smile. "I like the sound of that," she said and looked to Yomalyn, who nodded.

"I'm in," he said, sounding more vulnerable than Cidelyn had heard from him prior. Finally, he looked to Emilyn, who was staring blankly at him. He frowned. In her eyes, it looked as if something had broken. Or as if she had realized something.

"Emilyn?" he asked, and her eyes suddenly focused on his. She seemed to be asking for understanding. But she also seemed different. Resolute. What had changed?

***

We take care of each other.

The same words Emilyn had once said to her father, in what felt like a lifetime long past. The words rippled through her soul, tearing open things she didn't even know were there. She'd been a little girl when she'd said them to her father, in a moment where he'd seemed to be at his lowest. Now, here she was at hers, those same words being spoken to her. She wondered if the decision they had sparked her to make was the same he had chosen to make back then?

She stood up, wiping tears from her face, and pulled her hands from Cidelyn and Jacquelyn. The two of them and Yomalyn stood as well, likely looking confused, but she didn't look back at them. She marched toward the door.

"Emilyn?" Cidelyn asked again. "Where are you going?"

"Outside," she put simply, her voice a shell of its former self. Striding past Arc, who remained where she had left him, she realized she may have been harsh with him, but she didn't regret what she had said. It had taken her far longer than it should have to understand exactly who he was. She had been too enamored by him—too caught up in what he could do and his interest in her—to grasp the larger picture. His sister's intentions may not be pure, but she doubted that his were either. And she couldn't help but wonder if she had stopped and realized that sooner, Kyshel might still be with her.

"Whoa," Yomalyn said, rushing past her and putting his hand on the door handles. "You of all people should not be going out there."

"Don't worry," she said, her voice calm and neutral. "I'm just going to talk to Gavelyn."

"I'm not sure he's the type you just go talk to," Yomalyn replied. "He kinda locked us up last time."

"He won't this time."

"What's going to stop him?" Jacquelyn asked, and Emilyn turned her head to face her.

"Me," she said simply and looked to Cidelyn, who bore a concerned look. "I have every intention of coming back."

"That's not what concerns me," Cidelyn replied, stepping closer to her. He cared, and she loved that he cared, but she knew that wouldn't do her any good where she was about to go. "What are you going to talk to him about?"

"My father," she said bluntly, and Cidelyn narrowed his eyes.

"Are you sure that's a good idea?"

"No," she replied, honestly. "But it's the only one I have." She didn't say anything else. She would let him decide for himself what his course of action would be. He gazed at her for a long moment of silence, and for once, she was glad she couldn't hear what he was thinking. She had a feeling his thoughts more than anyone else's might be able to change her mind. She wasn't about to let anyone do that.

"Okay," he said, sighing. "I trust you." He smiled, and she wanted to return the smile but found herself too broken to even try. So, she nodded and turned back toward the door, from which Yomalyn hadn't removed his hand. Looking to her and then to Cidelyn, then back to her, he reluctantly stepped out of her way. Walking briskly out of the room and into the corridor beyond, she left the only people she had behind. She didn't like deceiving them—any of them—but she knew they would never go along with what she was about to do.

The spire barely registered to her as she walked through it, down staircases, and past the starving and scared people who shared Unity Falls with her. Her mind and soul had never felt as focused before—far more focused than her grounding phrase had ever done. She had a singular purpose, and she would carry it out. She had to.

Cidelyn's words hadn't just reminded her of a moment with her father; they'd reminded her of a moment with his supposed friend as well. Gavelyn had said he could reach her father or that he knew how to, but Zarlyn had denied him. But the very fact that he could be denied meant that more of her father remained than she'd thought. It had been heartbreaking to turn down Gavelyn's proposal, but it had been the right thing to do. Still, he had the knowledge she needed and she knew how to get it.

Once in the large entry chamber where Kyshel had helped Yomalyn give his speech, she paid no mind to any of the people around her and strode straight toward the doors. Opening them, she didn't hesitate to walk outside. No single soul dared to stand in her way.

The architects were around the area in force, having occupied any possible escape route. They seemed to have determined precisely where the dampeners' range ended as they had formed a rather perfect line down the street and beyond. Gavelyn was where she expected him to be, at the head of the group, waiting to greet any stragglers who decided to take their chances outside rather than stay with Yomalyn and the Gallery. That was likely what they assumed her to be at first, but as she approached, she noticed Gavelyn instruct several of them to back away, though he himself remained. Correctly guessing they had positioned themselves a fair distance back from the edge of the dampeners' influence, she noticed she crossed the line, as she felt the light swirl inside her once again.

Gavelyn watched her as she approached and stopped just a few feet away from him. He said nothing. He displayed no curiosity, surprise, or interest of any kind. He merely watched her, his hands clasped to his front. He was often one to get straight to the point, so she decided to do the same. Turning down his proposal had been the right thing to do at the time. This was a different time. He was the only one who could reach the people she cared about, and there was only one way he would show her how to do that. She extended her hand to him.

"I'm ready to accept your deal."

Acknowledgement

In writing this book, I was given the opportunity to explore my passion of telling stories. For that alone, I am eternally grateful. To find the words to tell this story, I channeled my own wanderings of what lies within, and without, what we call souls. Now I am fortunate enough to not share the kinds of burdens that Emilyn and her friends do, but that does not mean that I, and perhaps you, cannot relate to the struggle of searching for identity. Ultimately that is what I sought to do with this story. For all those out there that aren't sure who you are at your core, I hope these words help you on your journey, and I know you'll find your stars to string.

Just as Emilyn found companions both before and during her journey, so have I. I am beyond blessed to be surrounded by a wonderful group of family, friends, and colleagues.

Susmita Dutta is the wonderful soul that not only granted me this amazing opportunity but guided me every step of the way with wisdom I will cherish for the rest of my days. I am completely and constantly instilled with awe at the care and grace with which her and her incredibly talented **team** at **Global Book Publishing** encourage their authors and help their visions come to life. I will smile every time for the rest of my life when I see the gorgeous cover they made for this book, bringing Emilyn to life. And never will a day come that I am not grateful for every editor that poured over the words I wrote with immaculate accuracy and delicacy to make certain you all never saw the typos that plagued the initial drafts.

To my fellow authors at GBP and to every person on social media and otherwise that gave me any kind of feedback on this story, especially in its early stages, I owe you a debt that can never fully be repaid.

I would never have found my voice without my wonderful **mother** and **father**, and my equally wonderful group of friends. You know who you are, and you know I love each of you with all the space between my soul and yours. Thank you for encouraging me to share the stories that live in mine.

There are and always will be a hundred thousand more souls I could list and thank here. A massive thank you to each and every one of them. These are people I would happily brave purple skies with, people who have been supporting my writing for weeks, months, years, and decades. So if you ever need pointed in the direction of a good soul, I know a wonderful few.

Thank you.

About The Author

Jeffrey Lee was born in 1994 in Indianapolis, Indiana. His love for stories like Star Wars, Harry Potter, and the Percy Jackson series ignited his kinship with the fantastical world and his passion for storytelling.

He often found comfort in those fantastical characters, and soon developed a passion for creating his own at a very young age, though it would be a long while before any of these saw the light of day. As he began to discover the kind of person he wanted to be, he grew a passion for these ideas and how they could help others in the way stories helped him.

With encouragement from friends and family and his long path of self-discovery and identity, he found his passion and this led to his debut novel Empire of Strings: The Space Between Souls, where he explores the themes of identity and self-discovery and their ever-changing nature and perception. If he isn't working or writing, he can often be found gaming or drawing.

Follow Author @

authorjeffreylee

author_jeffreylee

jeffreyleewriter@gmail.com

Made in United States
North Haven, CT
08 July 2023

38714077R00165